~ THE ~

PIONEERS

The Heroic Story of the Settlers
Who Brought the American Ideal West

David McCullough

Simon & Schuster

NEW YORK   LONDON   TORONTO   SYDNEY   NEW DELHI

SIMON & SCHUSTER
1230 Avenue of the Americas
New York, NY 10020

First Simon & Schuster hardcover edition May 2019

SIMON & SCHUSTER and colophon are registered trademarks of
Simon & Schuster, Inc.

For information about special discounts for bulk purchases, please contact
Simon & Schuster Special Sales at 1-866-506-1949 or
business@simonandschuster.com.

The Simon & Schuster Speakers Bureau can bring authors to your live event.
For more information or to book an event contact the Simon & Schuster Speakers Bureau
at 1-866-248-3049 or visit our website at www.simonspeakers.com.

Interior design by Joy O'Meara

Manufactured in the United States of America

3   5   7   9   10   8   6   4   2

Library of Congress Cataloging-in-Publication Data
Names: McCullough, David G., author.
Title: The pioneers: the heroic story of the settlers who brought the American ideal west /
by David McCullough.
Description: First Simon & Schuster hardcover edition. | New York:
Simon & Schuster, 2019. | "Simon & Schuster nonfiction original hardcover." |
includes bibliographical references and index.
Identifiers: LCCN 2018057066 | ISBN 9781501168680 | ISBN 1501168681 |
ISBN 9781501168697 (ebook)
Subjects: LCSH: Ohio River Valley—History—To 1795. | Pioneers—
Ohio River Valley—Biography.
Classification: LCC F483.M48 2019 | DDC 977—dc23 LC record available at https://
urldefense.proofpoint.com/v2/url?u=https-3A_lccn.loc.gov_2018057066&d=
DwlFAg&c=jGUuvAdBXp_VqQ6t0yah2g&r=zKAnnLSQltsYNuYGOgjF6SYJylp
wsS1CuoJqVbpsc2Q&m=Rm0RCSMcBQxc-xg3LzrGHXN0EiUAAW40bHj0llo
_yx0&s=h7kYaXnGsU-_hy2bdSilili8AS0L2WDOZU4ZjlsaMEl&e=

ISBN 978-1-5011-6868-0
ISBN 978-1-5011-6869-7 (ebook)

For Rosalee

The character ought to be known of these bold pioneers. . . . From whence did they spring? . . . For what causes, under what circumstances, and for what objects were difficulties met and overcome?

—EPHRAIM CUTLER

CONTENTS

PART I
1787–1794

1. The Ohio Country   *3*
2. Forth to the Wilderness   *35*
3. Difficult Times   *67*
4. Havoc   *91*

PART II
1795–1814

5. A New Era Commences   *121*
6. The Burr Conspiracy   *151*
7. Adversities Aplenty   *165*

PART III
1815–1863

8. The Cause of Learning   *195*
9. The Travelers   *221*
10. Journey's End   *241*

ACKNOWLEDGMENTS   *259*
NOTES   *265*
BIBLIOGRAPHY   *301*
INDEX   *315*

NORTHWEST TERRITORY

Lake Superior

WISCONSIN

Lake Michigan

Lake Hu

MICHIGAN

N
W E
S

Mississippi River

ILLINOIS

INDIANA

O

SPANISH LOUISIANA

Ohio River

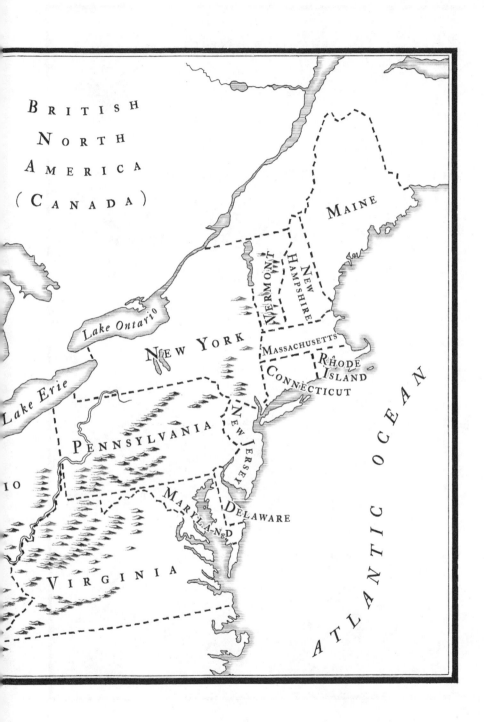

BRITISH
NORTH
AMERICA
(CANADA)

MAINE

Lake Ontario

NEW HAMPSHIRE

VERMONT

NEW YORK

MASSACHUSETTS

RHODE ISLAND

CONNECTICUT

Lake Erie

PENNSYLVANIA

NEW JERSEY

IO

MARYLAND

DELAWARE

VIRGINIA

ATLANTIC OCEAN

SOUTHEASTERN OHIO
AROUND
MARIETTA

Muskingum River

⊙ JOSEPH BARKER HOME
⊙ DEVOL AND BARKER
BOATYARD

OHIO

⊙ MARIETTA

Ohio River

EPHRAIM CUTLER HOME ⊙
'THE OLD STONE HOUSE'

BELPRE ⊙

⊙ PARKERSBURG

BLENNERHASSETT
ISLAND

VIRGINIA

N
W E
S

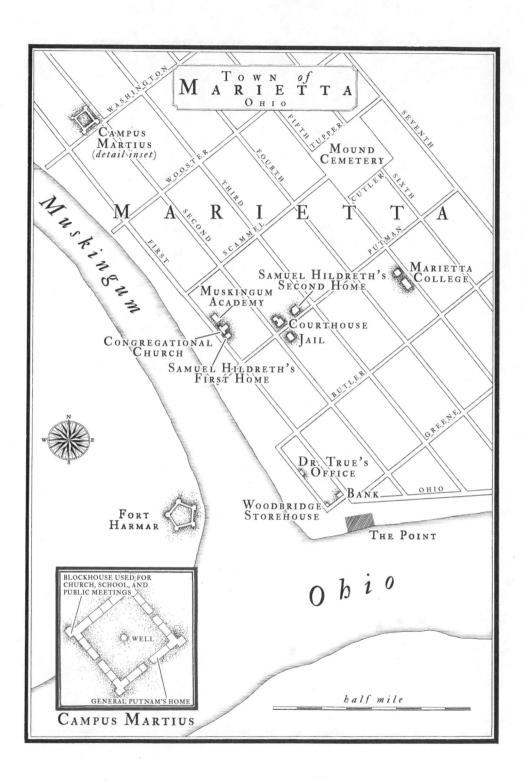

TOWN of
MARIETTA
OHIO

CAMPUS
MARTIUS
(detail inset)

WASHINGTON

WOOSTER

FIFTH

TUPPER

SEVENTH

MOUND
CEMETERY

CUTLER

SIXTH

FOURTH

THIRD

PUTMAN

MARIETTA

SECOND

SCAMMEL

FIRST

Muskingum

Samuel Hildreth's
Second Home

MARIETTA
COLLEGE

MUSKINGUM
ACADEMY

COURTHOUSE
JAIL

CONGREGATIONAL
CHURCH

SAMUEL HILDRETH'S
FIRST HOME

BUTLER

GREENE

N
W   E
S

DR. TRUE'S
OFFICE

OHIO

BANK

FORT
HARMAR

WOODBRIDGE
STOREHOUSE

THE POINT

Ohio

BLOCKHOUSE USED FOR
CHURCH, SCHOOL, AND
PUBLIC MEETINGS

WELL

half mile

GENERAL PUTNAM'S HOME

CAMPUS MARTIUS

PART I

1787-1794

The Ohio Country

The Ohio is the grand artery of that portion of America
which lies beyond the mountains. . . . I consider therefore
the settlement of the country watered by this great river as
one of the greatest enterprises ever presented to man.
—J. HECTOR ST. JOHN DE CRÈVECOEUR, 1782

I.

Never before, as he knew, had any of his countrymen set off to accomplish anything like what he had agreed to undertake—a mission that, should he succeed, could change the course of history in innumerable ways and to the long-lasting benefit of countless Americans.

That he had had no prior experience in such a venture and was heading off alone in his own one-horse shay appears to have been of little concern. If he was as yet unknown to those with whom he would be dealing, he carried with him letters of introduction from the governor of Massachusetts, the president of Harvard College, and some forty others. The day of his departure was Sunday, June 24, 1787.

Manasseh Cutler was forty-five years old and pastor of the First Congregational Church of Ipswich Hamlet, a tiny Massachusetts village not far from the sea, thirty miles north of Boston. He had been born and raised on a hilltop farm in Killingly, Connecticut, and given the biblical name of Manasseh after the oldest son of Joseph. Like most New Englanders, he was a descendant of those strong-minded English Puritans who had landed in America in the seventeenth century and proliferated ever since. James Cutler, the first of the family to arrive, had fathered twelve children. The Reverend Cutler himself was one of five and the father of eight.

He had attended Yale College, with classmates mainly from New England among whom a biblical name such as he had was by no means uncommon. He was distinguished for "diligence and proficiency," and finished with honors in 1765.

In less than a year he married Mary Balch of Dedham, Massachusetts, a small trim blonde said to have had a no less amiable disposition than he. Her father, the Reverend Thomas Balch, performed the wedding ceremony. When offered the chance to run a chandlery—a ship supply store—in Edgartown on the island of Martha's Vineyard, bride and groom moved immediately to the island and there remained for three years, time enough for two sons, Ephraim and Jervis, to be born, and for Manasseh to conclude that a mercantile life was not for him.

He resolved to enter the ministry under the tutelage of his father-in-law back in Dedham. His studies continued for nearly two years, during which he started preaching in one town or another. "Prosecuted my study," he wrote in his diary. "Began to make sermons. May God grant me his blessing and assistance in so important an undertaking, and make me serviceable to the cause of religion, and the souls of my fellow men."

He was offered the pulpit at Ipswich Hamlet. The day of his ordination, at age twenty-nine, the Meeting House was thronged so "exceedingly" that not more than half the people were able to attend.

A bit above average in height, stout but well-proportioned, the Reverend Cutler had a ruddy, healthy look, and dressed always in ministerial black—black velvet coat and breeches, black silk stockings. He would be described as a gentleman of "the old style, country type." But stiff-necked and somber he was not, any more than were most Puritans, contrary to latter-day misconceptions. Puritans were as capable as any mortals of exuding an affable enjoyment of life, as was he. Like many a

Puritan he loved good food, good wine, a good story, and good cheer. His black clerical attire, a professional requirement, by no means represented disapproval of bright colors in clothing or furniture or decoration. It was said he could out-talk anyone, and from numerous of his diary entries, it is obvious, too, that he had an eye for attractive women. But here again that was no violation of Puritan rules.

He had as well great love for his large family, his wife and children, and was ever attentive to their needs for as long as he lived.

In addition to all this, and importantly, Manasseh Cutler was endowed with boundless intellectual curiosity. It may be said he was a university unto himself, ranking high among the notable polymaths of the time, those "of great and varied excellence" who took an interest in nearly everything.

He had succeeded in becoming three doctors in one, having qualified for both a doctor of law and doctor of medicine, in addition to doctor of divinity, and having, from time to time, practiced both law and medicine. At one point he looked after some forty smallpox patients and seems to have gained a local reputation for his particular skill at coping with rattlesnake poisoning. He became an honorary member of the Massachusetts Medical Society, received a degree of Master of the Arts from Harvard, and was elected a member of the Academy of Arts and Sciences.

Further, to supplement his meager income as pastor—never more than $450 a year—he had added a third floor to the rectory and established his own private boarding school where the students were "prepared for usefulness in the world."

Most remarkable were his continuing scientific pursuits. He was at once an avid astronomer, meteorologist, and naturalist. Over the years, his modest income notwithstanding, he had acquired his own barometer, thermometer, telescope, spyglasses, and celestial globe, and was particularly esteemed among fellow scientists for his work in botany, and for having written the first-ever treatise on the classification of the flora of New England—a study of some 350 separate species. His knowledge of botany was probably surpassed by few if any Americans of his generation.

Year after year he carried on extensive correspondence with leading figures in all the sciences on both sides of the Atlantic. One letter concerning his studies of the aurora borealis, written in 1778 to Ezra Stiles, the president of Yale, went on for twenty-four pages.

Between times he studied French. Indeed, he seems to have been studying something nearly every waking hour. "Engaged in the study of botany," reads one diary entry. "This morning endeavored to observe the eclipse of the moon," reads another. "Studied," "studied hard," "studied very hard," he recorded one day after another.

Once, with a half dozen others, he climbed the highest peak in the White Mountains of New Hampshire, carrying a heavy barometer on his back in the spirit of wanting to bring back new knowledge—to compute the elevation at the summit, which he recorded to be 9,000 feet. That either he or the barometer had overestimated the height by some 2,600 feet did not in the least deter his zest for learning.

On the day of his departure on his unprecedented new mission, he brought with him the cabinet necessary for saving botanical specimens collected along the way.

He had a favorite quotation from Virgil that to his family seemed the key to his character, *"Felix, qui potuit rerum cognoscere causas"*— "Fortunate is he who understands the cause of things."

———————

The year before, on the morning of March 1, 1786, the Reverend Cutler and ten others gathered in Boston at the famous Bunch of Grapes tavern, at the corner of King and Kilby Streets. Their purpose was to launch a highly ambitious plan involving the immense reach of unsettled wilderness known as the Northwest Territory. They were a group of veteran officers in the Continental Army, as Cutler was considered also, having served six months during the Revolutionary War as an army chaplain.

At the peace treaty ending the war, signed in Paris in 1783, the American diplomats John Adams and John Jay had insisted that all the lands controlled by the British west of the Allegheny Mountains and northwest of the Ohio River east of the Mississippi, be ceded to the new United States. The British commissioners persistently urged making the Ohio River the westernmost boundary of the United States, but John Adams, it is said, responded indignantly, "No! Rather than relinquish our claim to the western territory, I will go home and urge my countrymen to take up arms again and fight till they secure their rights, or shed the last drop of blood." John Jay agreed and the British found it best to yield the point.

The land on the southern side of the Ohio was part of Virginia and already being rapidly settled according to the Virginia system, which allowed a man to take and mark for himself any unappropriated lands. By the New England system, so-called, the land lying north of the river was to be properly surveyed and sold, the establishment of settlements done by legal process, and lands of the natives to remain theirs until purchased from them.

Until that point the United States government did not own a single acre of land. Now, all at once, almost unimaginably, it had acquired some 265,878 square miles of unbroken wilderness, thus doubling the size of the United States. It was an unsettled empire north and west of the Ohio River, bigger than all of France, with room enough for as many as five more states and included access to four of the five Great Lakes, one of which, Lake Michigan, reached to its very center.

And then there was the Ohio River, itself a great natural highway west, *la Belle Rivière*, as the early French explorer René-Robert Cavelier de La Salle had called it.

The new realm was spoken of as "the back country," "the vast interior," "the howling wilderness," "the fair domain beyond the Ohio," or simply "the Ohio country." There were no roads as yet anywhere in all this wilderness, no bridges, no towns, churches, schools, stores, or wayside taverns. In New England there were more than a thousand towns, one about every five miles. But in all the immense territory to the northwest of the Ohio River, the territory from which five states were to emerge—Ohio, Indiana, Illinois, Michigan, and Wisconsin—there was as yet not one permanent legal settlement.

A few remote forts had been established and there were hunters, trappers, fur traders, and "squatters," those who settled wherever they chose and without legal claim to the land.

Much, too, was reported of forests teeming with wolves, bears, wild boars, panthers, rattlesnakes, and the even more deadly copperheads. And, as every easterner knew, there was the "Indian menace," the many native tribes who considered the Ohio country their rightful, God-granted domain. Much blood had already been shed in wilderness battles and atrocities committed by both natives and white men. These were realities well-known throughout the east and particularly on the minds of those gathered at the Bunch of Grapes.

Worst of all had been the infamous massacre by American militia of ninety-six peaceable Delaware Indians in central Ohio in 1782— Christian men, women, and children who knelt singing hymns as they were systematically clubbed to death, all because they were mistakenly thought to have had a part in the murder of a family of settlers. In revenge soon after, at Upper Sandusky, the Delawares stripped naked, tortured, cut off the ears, burned while still alive, and scalped a captured American officer, a friend of George Washington's, Colonel William Crawford. Delaware justice demanded a life for a life be taken, but they would give an enemy an opportunity to die well and honor his family during ritual torture. Crawford's dismemberment was also to insure that he would be a less formidable enemy in the next world. The story of Crawford's fate, the ultimate frontier nightmare, was told over and over back east.

Only the year before the Bunch of Grapes meeting, one of the group, General Benjamin Tupper, as part of a government surveying party, had been turned back from entering the Ohio country so severe was Indian resistance to the encroaching settlers.

Then, too, there was also the immediate reality of serious, mounting troubles right at home. Unprecedented financial panic had gripped the new nation since the end of the Revolutionary War. The resources and credit of the government were exhausted. Money, in the form of scrip issued by the government, was nearly worthless. The scrip the veterans received as compensation for their service was worth no more than ten cents on the dollar. Trade was at a standstill. In Massachusetts the situation was worst of all. Farmers were being imprisoned for debt. Only a few months earlier an armed rebellion led by a poor Massachusetts farmer and war veteran named Daniel Shays had to be put down by a force of loyal militia commanded by General Tupper.

As it was, the severe economic depression that followed the war would last longer even than the war. But out west now there was land to be had as never imagined—vast land, rich land where there was "no end to the beauty and plenty"—that could be made available to veterans at a bargain price in compensation for their service. West was opportunity. West was the future.

"As time progressed, the New England Revolutionary officers and soldiers interested in western immigration became more and more impatient to realize their hopes," as one settler was to write.

> They were poorer than their neighbors who had not been in the field; and if they had more of pride, that was only natural from the lives they had led, and surely they had a right to feel proud of the services they had rendered. One who was among them, and a close observer, says that they had a better and more dignified bearing than before the war, dressed more handsomely, and were improved in manners and conversation. . . . These men it must be remembered did not receive money in pay for their fatigue, exposure and suffering, but final certificates in settlement.

"The spirit of immigration never ran higher with us than at this time," Manasseh Cutler wrote to a member of the Congress, Nathan Dane, who happened also to be a Massachusetts neighbor.

The leading figure—the driving force—at the Bunch of Grapes gathering was a widely known hero of the Revolution and, in normal times, a farmer and surveyor, General Rufus Putnam. It was he who had called the meeting.

A commanding presence, he stood nearly six feet tall and spoke in a manner described as straightforward and impressive. One of his eyes had been disfigured by a childhood injury that "gave it an outward, oblique cast, leaving the expression of his face strongly impressed on the mind of the beholder." In his portrait he is shown in profile, with the intention, no doubt, to hide the bad eye. As would be said:

> He was not brilliant, he was not quick, but he was richly en-
> dowed with that best of gifts—good, sound, common sense, and
> he had, in unusual degree, that prescience that enabled him to
> skillfully adapt means to ends, so as thereby to accomplish what
> he wished. . . . His judgment was sound, he was patient and had
> great power of endurance. His integrity was never questioned.

He was also known to be full of jokes and loved to sing.

Most important to matters at hand, Rufus Putnam, before the end of the Revolution, had led 288 officers in signing what was known as the Newburgh Petition, whereby land bounties promised to veterans would be provided in the Ohio country in payment for their military services.

Then, at the war's end, he had written a long letter to Washington about the possibilities represented by the Ohio country, knowing Washington as a young man had seen that wilderness firsthand on surveying expeditions and, further, that Washington owned land there. He was already an Ohio land speculator.

> I am, sir [Putnam wrote], among those who consider the cession
> of so great a tract of territory to the United States . . . a very happy
> circumstance and of great consequence to the American empire.

Washington, though a Virginian to the core, had particularly high regard for the New Englanders who had served under his command. A great part of his military history had been made north of the Potomac, beginning in Boston.

Many there were in New England, Putnam assured him, waiting for the chance to head west as settlers, and there was "not the least doubt but other valuable citizens will follow their example."

In a letter to Congress, Washington strongly supported the idea, but

in a subsequent letter to Putnam he wrote, ". . . matters, as far as they
have come to my knowledge, remain in *statu quo*."

In 1784 Putnam wrote again to Washington to assure him settlement of the Ohio country still "engrosses many of my thoughts, and
much of my time," and that as soon as Congress made provisions for
granting land there, thousands from New England would emigrate.
Meanwhile, however, many were "growing quite impatient, and the general inquiry now is, when are we going to the Ohio?" It was being called
"Ohio Fever." Putnam preferred to call it "the Ohio cause."

In 1784 an ordinance for the government of the Northwest Territory
had been drawn up by several members of Congress including Thomas
Jefferson. It proposed, "That after the year 1800 . . . there shall be neither slavery nor involuntary servitude in any of the said States. . . ." The
ordinance passed but without any slavery restrictions, and without
them as would be said, it was "a dead letter."

Jefferson had since backed off from his position on slavery, having decided not to risk his political "usefulness" by maintaining such
a stand. Further, by this time he had resigned his seat in Congress and
departed for France to serve as the new American ambassador.

The plan set forth now at the Bunch of Grapes was to form an association or company to purchase from the government lands in Ohio and
establish a first settlement there. A "very pleasing description" of the
western country was provided by both Generals Putnam and Tupper.
Manasseh Cutler, too, took an active part in the discussions. He had
read nearly all that had been published of the writings of early French
explorers and like others had been moved especially by descriptions of
the land and the river by St. John de Crèvecoeur.

> It is, without doubt, the most fertile country, with the most var-
> ied soil, the best watered, and that which offers to agriculture
> and commerce, the most abundant and easy resources, of all
> those which the Europeans have ever discovered. . . .

Crèvecoeur also described the experience of giving oneself up to the
current of the Ohio River. "This sweet and tranquil navigation appeared

to me like an agreeable dream." (In a book he was soon to publish, *Notes on the State of Virginia*, Thomas Jefferson referred to the Ohio as "the most beautiful river on earth," though, like Manasseh Cutler, he had never seen it.)

Full agreement at the Bunch of Grapes gathering was reached with no difficulty and in the days that followed further details were seen to. It was to be called the Ohio Company of Associates and Rufus Putnam was to be its chairman. A fund of a million dollars would be raised. No one could purchase less than one share, or more than five. Payment for each share would be primarily the face value of the certificates held by the veterans, plus $10 in gold or silver. The cash raised by the $10 payments was to cover the company's operating expenses.

That the Ohio Company was also, apart from its noble intentions, a venture in land speculation went without saying. Those founders taking part at the Bunch of Grapes were to receive generous compensation. Rufus Putnam and Manasseh Cutler, for example, were each to receive four shares, or 4,692 acres of land.

Major Winthrop Sargent, another surveyor who had been to Ohio, was named secretary of the company, and Manasseh Cutler was chosen to negotiate with the Continental Congress in the purchase of the land. He was also to have a say in the enactment of a new Ordinance, whereby Congress would establish how the new states were to be laid out, and, importantly, the conditions under which they were to enter the Union. Such an ordinance was essential, for without it no purchase could be arranged. As would be said, "What would homes be worth to New England men without good government?"

That a national constitution had still to be resolved by the summer of 1787 meant there was as yet no president of the United States, only a Congress to deal with.

It was intended that this ordinance, now called the Northwest Ordinance, should stipulate that in the whole of the territory there would be absolute freedom of religion and particular emphasis on education, matters New Englanders considered fundamental to a just and admirable society.

Most importantly, there was to be no slavery. In the plan for the creation of a new state northwest of the Ohio River, the proposition put forth by Rufus Putnam and others at the time of the Newburgh Resolution, the total exclusion of slavery was an essential.

As would be observed by historians long afterward, the Northwest Ordinance was designed to guarantee what would one day be known as the American way of life.

———

Manasseh Cutler was to be the spokesman for the "Ohio cause" on the scene with the Congress in New York. The word "lobbyist" had yet to come into use. Rather he was the "agent" assigned to win congressional approval, and no fitter or more capable agent could have been selected.

His enthusiasm for the whole undertaking seemed to compound by the week. "The more I contemplate the prospect," he wrote to Winthrop Sargent, ". . . the more I feel myself inclined to take an active part in carrying on the settlement and to be one of the first emigrants." He was already contemplating the number of foreign vegetables that might thrive in land so rich.

II.

The day of his departure being a Sunday—"Lord's Day," as he liked to say—the Reverend Cutler preached a sermon before bidding goodbye to his wife and family and heading off "southward" to Cambridge, Boston, Providence, Rhode Island, and beyond, rolling along in his horse and buggy, making thirty to thirty-five miles a day and, to judge by his daily journal entries, in grand spirits.

He was bound first for New York, where the Congress sat, then Philadelphia, where for the past month the Constitutional Convention had been meeting in secret sessions. Crossing into Connecticut, he made a brief stop at the family farm in Killingly to see his father and found all well, his father, at age eighty, in better health than he expected, still able to help bring in the hay.

At Middletown, the traveling pastor was the guest of General Samuel Holden Parsons, one of the directors of the Ohio Company. A Harvard graduate, attorney, and noted officer in the Revolution, Parsons had traveled to the Ohio country only the year before as one of the commissioners appointed by Congress sent to the Northwest to negotiate a treaty with the Indians. He could speak from experience about the Ohio River, the great reach of the wilderness, the fertility of the soil. He and Cutler talked for the better part of a day. In addition, Parsons provided Cutler with still more letters of introduction.

At New Haven, he stopped again, this time to call on the president of Yale, the Reverend Ezra Stiles, a tiny sparrow of a man who, like Cutler, had enormous interest in practically everything.

It had been years since Cutler had been back to his alma mater and Stiles, happy to show him about, led a campus tour, introducing him to faculty and students, showing him the library and a collection of apparatus for the study of science. When Stiles insisted Cutler stay for a midday dinner with his wife and four daughters, Cutler could not resist. "I sent for my trunk," he wrote, "and showed the Doctor and his lady, and the young ladies, my botanical apparatus and books, with which they were all highly pleased, having never seen anything of the kind before." The previous day en route he had collected a number of flowers, all still perfectly fresh in his botanical box. With these in hand, he proceeded to deliver a short lecture on fructification, separating the parts at the same time, all to the delight of his audience. Only a call to dinner ended the performance.

Cutler could not have enjoyed the day more, but when urged to spend the night, he declined. He was on a mission and must keep on his way.

The roads were "very bad," or "excessively bad." He worried about his horse. A tavern at Fairfield, Connecticut, was "miserable, dirty." He wrote of crossing King's Bridge ("small, very narrow, and badly built") onto New York Island and of seeing the ruins of British encampments and fortifications on both sides of the road on his way down to the city, as well as the ruins of Fort Washington, Fort Independence, and other fortifications built by the Americans.

By mid-afternoon Thursday, July 5, having covered 302 miles in twelve days, he arrived at the Plow and Harrow in New York and from there, wasting no time, he set off to deliver his letters of introduction.

From that point on things moved rapidly. The days that followed were as full as any he had known. He was everywhere, busy every hour, meeting or conferring with, or being hosted by one figure of importance or influence after another. In his business with Congress he regarded success "a duty."

The morning of July 6, he went to New York's City Hall to deliver his introductions to several members of Congress. At eleven o'clock he climbed the spacious stairs to the Congress Chamber on the second floor. At the time only eight of the thirteen states were represented by delegates.

A member from Virginia, Colonel Edward Carrington, greeted Cutler and introduced him to other members to whom Cutler delivered his "petition" for purchasing land for the Ohio Company and proposed the terms and conditions of purchase. A committee of five was then appointed to agree on the terms and report to Congress.

He had made a good start, as no doubt he sensed. His manners in particular impressed three of the five members who were southerners. Never before, they said, had they seen such qualities in a northern man.

That the one who had come to persuade the members of Congress to accept a proposal of such monumental scale was neither a commercial proponent nor politician, but a well-mannered figure of high learning and culture, as well as a man of the cloth, was in itself a matter of considerable interest and importance. Clearly he was to be taken seriously.

In the days that followed, he dined in style several times, starting at the home of General Henry Knox, once a Boston bookseller, now secretary of war. Already an investor in the Ohio Company, Knox had great influence among veterans and was fervently urging Congress to act. Both the general and Madam Knox, as she liked to be called, with their love of lavish hospitality, had become quite large. (Secretary Knox weighed approximately 325 pounds.) Cutler described her as "gross" and thought her way of doing her hair, piled a foot high on top of her head, far from attractive.

But at a dinner hosted by an English social lion, Sir John Temple, the consul general of Great Britain, he was delighted to find Lady Temple "the greatest beauty, notwithstanding her age, I ever saw," as happily he recorded in his journal, and then went on about her "soft but majestic air" and smiles that "could not fail of producing the softest sensibility in the fiercest savage." One would suppose her to be no more than twenty-two, he wrote, when in fact she was forty-four and already a grandmother.

Attired as usual in clerical black, the Massachusetts pastor remained as courtly and socially active as always and filled his diary with each day's events and observations on those he was meeting. Such effort as he devoted to the diary alone would have been enough in itself to tire most people. Yet he was also faithfully writing home to his wife, Mary, and depending greatly on repeated word from her, as he would continually during times away from her for years to come.

On the afternoon of July 9 he went again to climb the stairs to the Congress Chamber and in the course of much discussion made his case. This time, however, the session did not go well. What exactly was said, he did not record, only that they "debated on terms but were so wide apart that there appears little prospect of closing a contract." With the meeting ended, several members of the committee were "polite enough" to point out to him the splendors of the great room, its fine furnishings, the grand, full-length portrait of George Washington, and drapery that "infinitely exceeds anything of the kind I ever saw before."

Clearly he had much work to do.

Earlier that same day he had made a most important call on the geographer of the United States, a military engineer and surveyor of long experience on the western frontier, Thomas Hutchins, to discuss the best possible site for settlement on the Ohio River. That afternoon they met again.

A veteran of the French and Indian War, Hutchins had laid out Fort Pitt at Pittsburgh, where the Monongahela and the Allegheny Rivers meet to form the Ohio. Later, in 1766, he had conducted a hydrographic survey down the Ohio, on an expedition led by the well-known Indian trader George Croghan. A great number of Shawnees and Delawares went too, the entire party with baggage filling seventeen canoes. They traveled the whole length of the ever-winding river, more than 1,000 miles from Pittsburgh to the Mississippi, with the result of the first published survey describing the river's depths, currents, bordering hills, and bottomlands.

More recently, Hutchins had been in charge of several surveys of the Ohio frontier under the protection of a military escort. He knew the territory as did very few white men and, as Manasseh Cutler learned, he had no hesitation about voicing his opinions on the subject. "He gave me the fullest information . . . and advised me, by all means, to make our location on the Muskingum, which was decidedly, in his opinion, the best part of the whole of the western country."

The great trees of the forests at the confluence of the Ohio and Muskingum would not only provide timber aplenty for houses and boat building, but were a sure sign of fertile soil. Further, a federal fort, Fort Harmar, had now been established close by and the native population in the vicinity was comparatively small, two highly important advantages.

Thomas Hutchins's advice was to be decisive.

The great Puritan leader John Winthrop, on board the ship *Arbella*, in 1630, on his way with the first Pilgrims to settle in Massachusetts, had famously declared, "For we must consider that we shall be as a city upon a hill." By all evidence, the Reverend Manasseh Cutler had decided where in the Ohio country the new City upon the Hill was to be located.

———•—•———

On July 10, he dined with an English immigrant, William Duer, who had distinguished himself as a member of the Continental Congress during the Revolution and later became involved in a number of commercial and financial projects whereby he had become quite wealthy. He lived in the style of a nobleman. "I presume he had not less than fifteen different sorts of wine at dinner, and after the [table] cloth was removed," Cutler wrote. Also present were Winthrop Sargent, who had come on to New York to work with Cutler, and another from Massachusetts named Samuel Osgood, who had recently been appointed one of the Board of Treasury.

To what extent Cutler discussed his conversation with Thomas Hutchins about the ideal location for settlement, if at all, is not known, but it would seem unlikely he could have kept Hutchins's opinions to himself. In any event, Duer, Sargent, and Osgood were all to play considerable parts in what followed.

Congress by then had come to an agreement on the form of government for the western territory and drawn up a bill, a copy of which was sent to Cutler, and with leave for him to make any remarks he wished and propose any amendments, which he proceeded to do that same afternoon of July 10.

That done, he decided the time had come for a visit to Philadelphia, to pay calls on Benjamin Franklin, Dr. Benjamin Rush, and several other notables in the fields of science and medicine. There was, to be sure, the expectation also of meeting and conversing with those members of Congress taking part in the Constitutional Convention in session there.

Early the next morning, he was on the road again.

———•—•———

Keeping his horse and buggy at a steady clip, covering ninety-five miles in just two days, he found himself "a little fatigued" by the time he arrived and checked in at the Indian Queen, an elegant Philadelphia inn on Third Street between Market and Chestnut. His third-floor room provided a broad view of the Delaware River and New Jersey beyond. A servant brought him tea and he was quite happy to have no plans for the evening.

THE PIONEERS • 19

But no sooner did he hear about the number of members of the Constitutional Convention staying in the house than his fatigue vanished and he "very agreeably" spent the evening meeting and conversing with a half dozen or more of considerable importance, including James Madison and George Mason of Virginia, Charles Pinckney of South Carolina, and Alexander Hamilton of New York, who, like Henry Knox, was already a stockholder in the Ohio Company, with no immediate interest in settling in the west, but great interest in it as a speculative venture. Not until one in the morning did Cutler retire.

He was to spend only two days in Philadelphia, but he had arrived just as a summer heat spell had broken and cooled the city. He also managed to pack more into his time even than in his days in New York, and from the many pages he filled in his journal, from his descriptions of so much that he saw and of the eminent figures he met and conversed with, the visit was like nothing he had ever experienced.

He breakfasted the first day with Elbridge Gerry of Marblehead, Massachusetts, one of the signers of the Declaration of Independence and a member of the Constitutional Convention, then toured the city with a noted physician, Gerardus Clarkson, covering twenty miles in a handsome four-wheeled, open carriage pulled by a pair of "very large and fine" horses.

He and Clarkson called on another signer of the Declaration of Independence and the most notable of Philadelphia physicians, Dr. Benjamin Rush, then moved on to meet the celebrated portrait painter Charles Willson Peale at the museum Peale had created. It was the first of its kind in America combining both art and natural history, and far beyond anything Manasseh Cutler had ever seen or even imagined.

> One particular part [he wrote] is assigned to the portraits of the principal American characters who appeared on the stage during the late revolution, either in the councils or armies of their country. . . . I fancied myself introduced to all the General Officers that had been in the field during the war, whether dead or alive, for I think he had every one, and to most of the members of the Congress and other distinguished characters.

In another part of the vast room was a great array of natural "curiosities" collected by Peale—all manner of shells, turtles, frogs, toads, lizards, water snakes—in addition to a variety of wild animals and birds of almost every species in America. What amazed Cutler most was that they were all real. It was hard to imagine Noah himself could have boasted a better collection.

From the Peale Museum, the tour moved on to the State House—Independence Hall—which Cutler thought "richer and grander in style" than any public building he had ever seen. Proceeding to the Mall outside, they confronted the city's prison, the one experience of the day Cutler did not care for. He thought the building sufficiently elegant. It was "its unsavory contents" he found objectionable. In the warmth of the July morning all windows were open.

> Your ears are constantly insulted with their Billingsgate language, or your feelings wounded with their pitiful complaints. Their long reed poles, with a little cap of cloth at the end, are constantly extended over into the Mall, in order to receive your charity, which they are incessantly begging. And if you refuse them, they load you with the most foul and horrid imprecations.

There were stops at the university and to view several churches of different denominations. Then, after a brief rest, they were joined by Elbridge Gerry to move on to what was to be the main event of the day, to the Market Street home of Benjamin Franklin.

As all knew, Franklin, at eighty-one, was taking part in the Constitutional Convention, but on this particular afternoon they found him in his garden, sitting under a large mulberry tree chatting with several gentlemen and ladies.

"There was no curiosity in Philadelphia which I felt so anxious to see as this great man," Cutler would write. In his imagination until then Franklin loomed considerably larger than life.

> But how were my ideas changed, when I saw a short, fat, trenched old man in a plain Quaker dress, bald pate, and short white locks,

sitting without his hat under the tree, and, as Mr. Gerry introduced me, rose from his chair, took me by the hand, expressed
his joy to see me, welcomed me to the city, and begged me to set
myself close to him.

At once they entered into a "free conversation" and most agreeably,
until one point when Franklin started to talk about some humorous
incident that had taken place earlier in the day at the Constitutional
Convention and had to be stopped by one of the other listeners and
reminded of the secrecy of all Convention matters.

By this time, as it was turning dark, everyone moved inside to Franklin's library where Cutler feasted his eyes, certain he was looking at the
largest and finest private library in America. And, of course, there was
more to be seen than books:

> He showed us a glass machine for exhibiting the circulation of
> the blood in the arteries and veins of the human body . . . a roll-
> ing press for taking the copies of letters or any other writing . . .
> his long artificial arm and hand, for taking down and putting
> books upon high shelves which are out of reach . . . his great
> armed chair, with rockers, and a large fan placed over it, with
> which he fans himself, keeps off flies, etc., while he sits reading,
> with only a small motion of his foot; and many other curiosities
> and inventions, all his own.

What Franklin wanted most to show his accomplished guest was a
large volume on botany, "which, indeed," wrote Cutler, "afforded me the
greatest pleasure of any one thing in his library."

The book was so large that only with great difficulty was Franklin
able to raise it from a low shelf and lift it onto a table. But as it often
was with old people, wrote Cutler, "he insisted on doing it himself, and
would permit no person to assist him, merely to show us how much
strength he had remaining." As Cutler's father could still help bring in
the hay, so the great doctor could still bring to the table weighty works
of the mind.

The book was *Systema Vegetabilium* by the Swedish naturalist Carolus Linnaeus, lavishly illustrated with large full-color cuts of every plant. "It was a feast to me," Cutler wrote. He wished he had at least three months to devote himself entirely to this one volume.

Franklin, too, as he said, loved natural history, and Cutler was amazed and "delighted with the extensive knowledge he appeared to have of every subject, the brightness of his memory, and the clearness and vivacity of all his mental faculties." Not until ten o'clock did Cutler and the others take their leave.

The day following, Saturday, July 14, he was up and dressed earlier than usual. Told that the City Market was among Philadelphia's greatest curiosities, he walked out the door to see for himself. It was still dark, yet people were converging from all directions.

The market was an open, one-story brick building nearly half a mile in length. By the time it was daylight the marketers had everything arranged. All that might be imagined was on display—fish, meats, vegetables of every kind, fresh fruit—and all in perfect order. No less a wonder was the crowd, people "of every rank and condition in life, from the highest to the lowest, male and female, of every age and every color."

He could hardly tear himself away, but another full day was in store. Taking no break for breakfast he and Dr. Clarkson were off again in the doctor's carriage, heading this time to the large homestead and famous gardens of the eminent naturalist William Bartram, several miles out of town on the banks of the Schuylkill River. There a considerable contingent of those attending the Constitutional Convention was already gathered and waiting, including Madison, Mason, Rutledge of South Carolina, and Alexander Hamilton.

Bartram was found busy hoeing in his garden without shoes or stockings, and at first seemed embarrassed by so large a delegation appearing so early in the day. But, as Cutler wrote, he soon got rid of his embarrassment and became quite sociable.

Like his time with Franklin, this summer morning visit with William Bartram was an experience Cutler would long treasure. They talked botany, toured the garden, then walked to the river between two great rows of immense trees to a summer house on the bank of the river.

About nine o'clock the group moved on to breakfast at Gray's Tavern also on the Schuylkill, and were treated to a tour of an even more lavish garden. For someone as passionate about flowers as Cutler, it seemed paradise.

At every end [he wrote], side, and corner, there were *summerhouses*, arbors covered with vines or flowers, or shady bowers encircled with trees and flowering shrubs, each of which was formed in a different taste. In the borders were arranged every kind of flower, one would think, that nature had ever produced, and with the utmost display of fancy, as well as variety.

On a path overlooking the river, they came to a fence, beyond which was a "view of one of the finest cascades in America. . . . A broad sheet of water comes over a large horizontal rock, and falls about seventy feet perpendicular. . . . Here we gazed with admiration and pleasure for some time."

As if he had not already done enough for one day, he next undertook an afternoon tour of the Philadelphia hospital with Benjamin Rush. It seemed the more there was for him to see and learn in the time available, the more people wanted to show him, the greater his curiosity and energy.

Rush led him first to the hospital's museum to see the finest collection of medical paintings in America. Then, along with twenty or so students, he took Cutler on his rounds of the sick. With each case Rush considered worthy of notice, he would address the students on the nature of the trouble at hand and the mode of treatment to be pursued, and on each of these occasions he would direct his comments to Cutler also, but always as though he, too, were a physician, which Cutler greatly appreciated.

They moved next to the floor below to see the cells of the "maniacs," a setting and experience about as different from the gardens of that morning as anything could have been. The cells were each about ten feet square and as formidable as those in a prison. Here were men and women, twenty or thirty in number, some fierce and raving, some nearly naked, others singing and dancing, or talking incessantly.

But as Cutler already knew, Rush was far ahead in his profession in his insistence on treating the insane as kindly as possible. "This would have been a melancholy scene indeed, had it not been that there was every possible relief afforded them in the power of man," he wrote. All was exceptionally clean—as it was throughout the hospital. To Cutler the hospital seemed more like a palace than a hospital.

Shortly after a midday dinner with Rush, the ringing of a church bell signaled that the library on the second floor of Carpenters' Hall—the historic place where the first Continental Congress had met—was open for receiving and returning books. It was to be Cutler's last stop in Philadelphia. As he told the others, he would be leaving for New York that evening.

Back at the Indian Queen, he said his goodbyes to those attending the Constitutional Convention he had come to know. To what extent he had discussed the Ohio project with them, or encouraged their involvement, is unknown. For all he wrote about his many activities in Philadelphia, he recorded virtually nothing concerning the great purpose he was so intent on serving.

That he considered his time in Philadelphia among the most stimulating experiences ever there is little doubt. In just two days, he had seen most of the city's main attractions and met and conversed with all the leading citizens he could have wished for.

Nor is there any doubt he himself had made an immensely favorable impression on those he met. When one of the other guests at the Indian Queen expressed amazement that the Reverend Cutler came to be in such demand in so short a time in a city he had never before set foot in, Cutler said it was the introductory letters that made the difference. But it had been much more than that.

As would be widely appreciated in time to come, that he had received "the most marked attentions" by figures so distinguished and of such prominence, was clearly "testimony to the worth and excellence of the character of Dr. Cutler."

Having settled his account at the inn and loaded his trunk onto the back of his one-horse shay, he was again on his way, knowing the moment of decision in New York was close at hand.

III.

"Called on members of Congress very early this morning," begins his journal entry for Thursday, July 19. "Was furnished with the Ordinance establishing a Government in the Western federal Territory."

He also learned a number in Congress were "decidedly opposed" to his terms—though what this was about, he did not say—and some to any contract whatever. Clearly, he needed to know how many were opposed, who they were, and if possible bring them around.

He was not at all sure about some of the New Englanders in Congress who worried that the lure of Ohio would take away too many of the home population. One was Congressman Nathan Dane, his neighbor from Ipswich—"Dane must be carefully watched," Cutler wrote, though exactly what concerned him is not clear.

Three Virginians were with him, he knew—Edward Carrington, William Grayson, and Richard Henry Lee—but a half dozen others could not be counted on. "If they can be brought over, I shall succeed; if not, my business is at an end." At a committee meeting he was told by the members they intended to make their report before the close of day.

The following morning, Friday, July 20, the secretary of Congress presented him with the ordinance agreed upon the day before, stating the conditions of the contract, and Cutler informed the committee that he could not agree to the terms proposed. "I told them I saw no prospect of a contract, and wished to spend no more time and money on business so unpromising."

At this point William Duer, secretary of the Board of Treasury, came to him with proposals from a number of principal characters of New York to "extend our contract" further down the Ohio to the confluence of the Scioto River "and to take in another company, but that it should be kept a profound secret." The plan, which also had the support of Winthrop Sargent, struck Cutler favorably.

Importantly, he had come to have high regard for Duer. "He is a gentleman of the most sprightly abilities, and has a soul filled with the warmest benevolence and generosity," Cutler would write. "He is made both for business and the enjoyment of life."

He also thought it best not to say anything further about Duer's proposal to Congress for now. As it was, the committee was "mortified" and seemed not to know what to say, but still urged another attempt.

Early the next morning, several members of Congress called on Cutler to report that on learning he was determined not to accept their terms and proposed leaving the city, Congress had "discovered a much more favorable disposition, and believed if I renewed my request I might obtain conditions as reasonable as I desired."

"This," as he wrote, "had the desired effect." The land purchase, he told them, would now be extended down the Ohio as far as the Scioto River. The Ohio Company's large purchase of land would provide Congress with funds of nearly four million dollars to pay down some of the national debt incurred during the Revolutionary War. "Our intention was an actual, a large, and immediate settlement of the most robust and industrious people in America; and that it would be made systematically, which must instantly enhance the value of federal lands, and prove an important acquisition to Congress." On these terms he would renew the negotiations, if Congress was willing.

July 22 being a Sunday, he attended three different church services and, to judge by his journal, dispensed with politics entirely until the next morning, when he, Sargent, and Duer "made every exertion in private conversation to bring over my opposers in Congress."

When the Reverend Cutler was repeatedly asked what civil office would be agreeable to him in the western country, he said he wished no such office, a response, as he wrote, that seemed surprising to "men who were so much used to solicit or be solicited for appointments of honor or profit."

In the days following a good part of his time was spent with the head of the Board of Treasury, Samuel Osgood, whom he had first met at Duer's dinner party and with whom he had much in common. A resident of Massachusetts and a Harvard graduate, Osgood, too, had great interest in science and was known for his piety, as well as his understanding of politics.

Cutler had been told Osgood was much in favor of the new terms Cutler had offered. Still, Cutler wrote, "such is the intrigue and artifice practiced by men in power, that I felt very suspicious, and was as cautious as possible." He had no scruples, however, about going over all of the Ohio Company's plans with Osgood. And Osgood, to Cutler's surprise, "highly approved." Indeed, he "thought it the best ever formed in America."

George Washington, as both of them doubtless knew, held to the strong belief that organized settlement of the frontier was the best way. "To suffer a wide-extended country to be overrun with land-jobbers, speculators, and monopolizers, or even scattered settlers, is, in my opinion," Washington had written, "inconsistent with that wisdom and policy which our true interest dictates, or which an enlightened people ought to adopt; and besides, it is pregnant of disputes, both with the savages and among ourselves."

"If we were able to establish a settlement as we proposed, however small in the beginning, we should then have surmounted our greatest difficulty," Osgood told Cutler. "Every other object would be within our reach, and, if the matter was pursued with spirit, he believed it would prove one of the greatest undertakings ever yet attempted in America," noted Cutler.

On Thursday, he, Sargent, and Duer did their best to pull every string they could. But Cutler's patience was nearly gone, which led the English diplomat Sir John Temple to remind him that were he to spend another month trying to get what he wanted he would be far more expeditious than was common for smaller matters through Congress, and that he should remember he was attempting something of unprecedented magnitude, exceeding any private contract ever made before in the United States. What was more, Temple told him, he had never seen anyone who "so warmly engaged" the attention of Congress as Cutler had. Nor had he ever known the members more pressing to bring an issue to a close.

Friday, July 27. I rose very early this morning, and, after adjusting my baggage for my return, for I was determined to leave New York this day, I set out on a general morning visit, and paid my respects to all the members of Congress in the city, and informed

them of my intention to leave the city that day. My expectations
of obtaining a contract, I told them, were nearly at an end.

At half past three that afternoon, he was informed that a new Northwest Ordinance had passed Congress "without the least variation," and
the Board of Treasury was directed to close a contract with the Ohio
Company. As the record of the vote on the Ordinance certified, eight
had been present.

By the agreement a grant of 5,000,000 acres of land had been ob-
tained for $3,500,000—a million and a half acres were for the Ohio
Company and the remainder for a private real estate venture, the Scioto
Company. "We are beholden to the Scioto Company for our purchase,"
Cutler would acknowledge. He and several other associates—Rufus
Putnam, Samuel Parsons, Winthrop Sargent—were to receive substan-
tial shares in the Ohio Company speculation.

Just as Sir John Temple had told Cutler, and as Cutler himself was
well aware, it was much the largest, most far-reaching contract in the
history of Congress. And immense as it was in monetary and geographic
scale, the clearly stated articles of the new ordinance—"An Ordinance
for the Government of the Territory of the United States, North-West
of the River Ohio"—were no less in their far-reaching importance.

The ordinance, as would be said, "created a machinery of government for immediate use," provided for the creation of new states, and
established a form of government meant to be of perpetual obliga-
tion. Not surprisingly, given the number of those from Massachusetts
involved, the new ordinance read much like the Constitution of the
Commonwealth of Massachusetts, the first constitution in the United
States, written in 1779 by John Adams.

Cutler knew Adams. He had dined with him, and had been present
for some of the sessions concerning the creation of the Massachusetts
constitution.

Particularly in the declaration of rights in both the new ordinance
and the Massachusetts constitution were the similarities most evident,
Article I of the ordinance, on freedom of religion in the territory, reading almost the same as that in the Massachusetts constitution.

In what he wrote, John Adams had left no doubt about his faith in education as the bulwark of the good society, the old abiding faith of his Puritan forebears. And so, too, in its Article III, the ordinance was quite clear on the matter. "Religion, morality, and knowledge, being necessary to good government and the happiness of mankind, schools and the means of education shall forever be encouraged."

That such emphasis be put on education in the vast new territory before even one permanent settlement had been established was extraordinary. But of even greater importance was the fact that outside of New England there was then no such thing in the United States as a system of state-supported schools of any kind, and even in New England students were poorly taught, housed, and hardly supervised in the least. Before the year was out, in a contract between the Ohio Company and the Board of Treasury, it would be specified that a section in each township be reserved for common schools and be "given perpetually to the use of an university."

To Manasseh Cutler the establishment of a university was of utmost importance as was plain to everyone concerned. It was "a first object," as he later told his oldest son, Ephraim, "and lay with great weight on my mind."

"Wisdom is the principal thing," read the ancient directive in Proverbs; "therefore get wisdom; and with all thy getting get understanding."

Importantly, the same Article III of the ordinance stated that the "utmost good faith shall always be observed towards the Indians; their lands and property shall never be taken from them without their consent . . . they shall never be invaded or disturbed, unless in just and lawful wars authorized by Congress."

But it was Article VI that set forth a tenet such as never before stated in any American constitution. "There shall be neither slavery nor involuntary servitude in the said territory." And, as was well understood, this had been agreed to when slavery existed in every one of the thirteen states. It was almost unimaginable that throughout a new territory as large as all of the thirteen states, there was to be no slavery.

Nothing written at the time indicated who had been most responsible for Article VI. In his journal Cutler said nothing on the subject.

Nathan Dane of Massachusetts would later claim credit for that part of the ordinance. But this seems unlikely. While he may have drafted certain parts, he was not the writer Manasseh Cutler was. As his own biographer would say, Dane had "no graces of style, either native or borrowed, neither did he ever seek for any."

Overall Manasseh Cutler had played the most important role by far. Years later he would tell Ephraim he had indeed prepared that part of the ordinance banning slavery and, as Ephraim also recorded, the reason for this, as well as the recognition of religion, morality, and knowledge as foundations of civil government, arose from the fact that his father was "acting for associates, friends, and neighbors, who would not embark in the enterprise, unless these principles were unalterably fixed."

In the opinion of the two grandchildren, William Parker Cutler and Julia Perkins Cutler, who would later edit and publish Manasseh Cutler's journals and correspondence, his way with the southern members of Congress had been the deciding factor.

In any event, the Northwest Ordinance of 1787 would prove to be one of the most far-reaching acts of Congress in the history of the country.

As one widely respected, later-day historian, Albert Bushnell Hart of Harvard University, would write, "Never was there a more ingenious, systematic and successful piece of lobbying than that of the Reverend Manasseh Cutler" and the great Northwest Ordinance of 1787 stands alongside the Magna Carta and the Declaration of Independence as a bold assertion of the rights of the individual.

———

Eager to be heading home, Cutler hurriedly packed, made a number of parting calls, took up the reins of his horse, and was on his way north, though, as he said, with some reluctance. The "attention and generous treatment" he had been shown in New York were "totally different from what I had ever before met with." He loved the city, loved its business, the grand buildings from four to six stories high, the straight, well-kept streets, the way people dressed, and the way they treated strangers. It was a city with a great future, he felt certain.

Not until past midnight Saturday, August 4, did he finally reach home. As he dutifully recorded he had traveled 885 miles. "Thus I completed one of the most interesting and agreeable journeys I ever made in my life . . . and may probably have reason to consider it as one of the most happy events of my life."

IV.

Through the rest of that summer and on into the fall there was much for the good pastor to attend to with his family, his parishioners, his boarding school, and, in addition, the hundreds of people now coming to his door to talk about the Ohio country and issues large and small to be settled as soon as possible in preparation for a first expedition to the distant wilderness. "Determined to send men this fall," he wrote in his journal at the end of August.

September 10–15   House full of Ohio people all the week
Sept. 21, 22   Ohio people here . . .
Sept. 24–29   Much engaged in the Ohio matters

Great care had to be taken to choose those who would be valuable in the community once it was established. By September 29, more than 150 had applied, and out of those, thirty-seven had been signed on.

In October, even though he had not seen the Ohio territory, the Reverend Cutler published a pamphlet on it, a work of considerable substance and effort in which he described the natural resources, soils, climate, the earlier enthusiastic judgments of an English engineer, and predicted that because of the great Ohio River and plentitude of fine timber at hand, shipbuilding would thrive there.

Further, he made his strongest statement yet on the subject of education and the important part it was to play. The field of science "may be greatly enlarged," he wrote, "and the acquisition of useful knowledge placed upon a more respectable footing here than in any other part of the world.

> Besides the opportunity of opening a new and unexplored region for the range of natural history, botany, and medical science, there will be one advantage which no other part of the earth can boast, and which probably will never again occur; that, in order to begin *right*, there will be . . . no inveterate systems to overturn.

And it was never too soon to get started on so worthy an aspiration. Even now, he wrote, "Could the necessary apparatus be procured, and funds immediately established for the founding of a university on a liberal plan, the professors could get started in their work."

For his father, this was "a season of the most arduous labor," son Ephraim would recall. It was his father's particular character that, after he had fully considered a matter and settled his mind to effect a purpose, nothing could discourage him; his energy and perseverance overcame all difficulties.

> General Putnam . . . [was] to take charge of the pioneer party; still, the men and means were to be sought for and provided, and in this he bore his full share. I well remember the extreme anxiety and toil it occasioned him. I was then only about twenty years of age, but I enlisted some of the first adventurers; many, however, of the most effective men were induced to come forward through my father's influence.

The thought that he, too, might go on to Ohio, had been on Manasseh Cutler's mind for some time, but with so much still to attend to there at home, he knew he must stay where he was. But if he could not go, his son Jervis, an adventurer by nature, was eager to take his place. At age nineteen he was to be one of the youngest men on the expedition.

The first pioneers—forty-eight men including surveyors, carpenters, boat builders, common laborers, and a blacksmith—were to go in two parties. One, numbering twenty and headed by a veteran officer, Major Haffield White, was to depart first from Ipswich Hamlet. The second, led by General Rufus Putnam, the overall head, or "superintendent," of the expedition, would leave soon after from Hartford, Connecticut.

Their tools, one ax and one hoe per man, as well as thirty pounds of baggage, were to be carried in the company wagon. In addition, each man was to furnish himself with one good musket, a bayonet, six flints, powder horn and pouch, priming wire and brush, half a pound of powder, one pound of musket balls, and a pound of buckshot. Wages were $4 a month.

By the time all was ready, December had arrived, hardly the best time of year to be setting off for the far wilderness. They would be traveling on foot the entire way until reaching the headwaters of the Ohio, so even under ideal conditions they would be moving at a speed of little more than one mile an hour, or about ten miles a day on an overland journey of some 700 miles that included the mountains of western Pennsylvania.

But spirits were high and the importance of getting there with the least delay possible was very much in mind. Once at the Ohio, time would be needed to build boats for the journey downriver—all to arrive in early spring, soon enough to get in a first planting of gardens and corn sufficient for survival.

Before sunrise the morning of Monday, December 3, 1787, a band of pioneers had gathered in front of the rectory, where they were to take an early breakfast. At dawn, they paraded in front of the house, and after a short address delivered by the Reverend Cutler, "full of good advice and hearty wishes," the men fired a three-volley salute, and marched off down the road, young Jervis among them, cheered by the bystanders and following a large covered wagon pulled by oxen.

The wagon had been a gift from Manasseh Cutler and he himself had painted the white inscription on the black canvas sides, *"For the Ohio."*

CHAPTER TWO

Forth to the Wilderness

*December 31, 1787—Monday—Set out from my own house,
in Rutland, in the state of Massachusetts, in the service of the
Ohio Company, for the mouth of the Muskingum River.*

—RUFUS PUTNAM

I.

Like so many born and raised on a New England farm in the eighteenth century and who served in the Revolutionary War, Rufus Putnam had known hard work and hardships, great sorrow and seemingly insurmountable obstacles most of his life. It was what was to be expected, just as one was expected to measure up.

His father, a good and "very useful" man, had, in the long family tradition, "pursued the occupation of a tiller of the earth" in central Massachusetts. But his father died when Rufus was only seven and when his mother remarried, it was to an illiterate tavern keeper who despised books and learning and, worse, ridiculed the boy for his ambition to learn. Because of this, Rufus was not sent to school. "After I was nine years old, I went to school in all only three weeks," he later wrote. To learn mathematics and spelling he had to earn his own money to buy the schoolbooks needed.

Mathematics he could handle, but spelling and grammar would remain lifelong mysteries. As he once wrote in a letter to a friend:

> Had I been as much engaged in learning to write, with spelling and grammar, I might have been much better qualified to fulfill the duties of the succeeding scenes of life. . . . Having neglected spelling and grammar when I was young, I have suffered much through life on that account.

As would be said, the "hardships of his early life were schoolmasters to fit him" for the life in store. He had joined the army at nineteen, spent three years serving in the French and Indian War. In 1761, at twenty-three, he was happily married to Elizabeth Ayres of Brookfield, Massachusetts, but she died in less than a year and only months later their infant son also died.

In 1765 he married again, this time to Persis Rice of Westborough and they were to have nine children.

His interest in, his need for the books he was denied as a boy never left him, and one book in particular played a key part in his service during the Revolution and in the course of the war itself. This concerned General Washington's decision to try to draw the British to attack the Americans on Dorchester Heights.

In the winter of 1776, Washington had put Putnam in charge of the defenses at Dorchester Heights overlooking Boston Harbor, where the ground was frozen so hard that ordinary breastworks could not be constructed.

Washington directed him to consider how this might best be accomplished, and to make a report to him immediately. What followed, Putnam would describe as one of "those singular circumstances which I call Providence."

Coming out of the meeting, he stopped to see another of Washington's command, General William Heath, and noticed a book lying on a table, lettered on the spine, *Muller's The Field Engineer.* He asked the general to let him borrow it. "He denied me," Putnam remembered. "I repeated my request; he again refused and told me he never lent his books." Putnam reminded him that it was he, General Heath, who had encouraged Putnam to undertake the role of military engineer, a role which, at the time, he had never read anything about, and that the general must let him have the book. "After some more excuses on his part and close pressing on mine, I obtained the loan of it," Putnam wrote.

Looking through the book the next morning, he saw the word "chandelier," something he had never heard of before. He read what it meant and almost immediately came up with the plan that would bring American success at Dorchester Heights and the withdrawal of the British from Boston—all from one word in a book.

Putnam created his own "chandeliers," heavy wooden-framed fortifications filled with facines (bundles of sticks) that could be moved about when necessary. Washington thought so highly of him that he became the chief engineer of the army. It was Putnam who marked out most of the fortifications in Brooklyn. Later still, he rebuilt the fortifications at West Point.

Since the end of the Revolution, he and his family had been living on a 155-acre farm in Rutland, at almost the precise geographical center of the Bay State. Their home, a large, white-frame, hip-roof house built by a wealthy loyalist, had been confiscated at the close of the war and so Putnam, who had by then achieved considerable success as a surveyor, was able to buy it on favorable terms.

There he did much of the thinking, planning, and correspondence needed for the Ohio venture, there he drew up the first plan for the town to be built on the chosen spot at the confluence of the Muskingum and Ohio Rivers. And it was there at the Putnam home on the last day of the year 1787 that, at age forty-nine, he said goodbye to his wife and family and started for the west.

To what extent he foresaw the difficulties and danger that lay ahead for him and those he was to lead is hard to estimate. Most likely it was considerable.

Because he felt obliged to settle certain matters in New York concerning the Ohio Company and Indian treaties, Putnam did not catch up with his unit of westward-bound pioneers until January 24, 1788, halfway across Pennsylvania at Hummelstown, on Swatara Creek, just short of Harrisburg.

As they moved on the weather turned worse. The wind-blown snow was eight inches deep, the traveling "excessive bad." In the days that followed, the going grew more difficult still. "So great a quantity of snow fell that day and the following night as to quite block up the road. . . . Our only resource now was to build sleds and harness our horses one before the other, and in this manner, with four sleds and the men in front to break the track, we set forward."

The "road," as he called it, was the Forbes Road, an old Indian trail that had been widened by the British General John Forbes for his expedition to the forks of the Ohio during the French and Indian War and was no easy pathway even under the best weather conditions.

There were twenty-two in the party. Among them were two in particular, both Rhode Islanders, whom Putnam knew he could count on to serve in ways the others were incapable of. Most conspicuous was Ebenezer Sproat, a surveyor who at six feet, four inches loomed over the rest like a giant. A highly respected officer in the war, he had afterward tried his hand at the importing trade, only to fail miserably, using all his own and his wife's resources. But by then Congress had ordered the first surveys of the Ohio territory under the direction of Thomas Hutchins. Sproat had been appointed the surveyor for the state of Rhode Island, and that fall joined in the operations. Though progress was limited because of Indian hostilities, he had nonetheless seen enough of the territory firsthand to know more about it than any of the others slogging west now under the command of Rufus Putnam. In effect, Ebenezer Sproat was second in command.

The other from Rhode Island, Captain Jonathan Devol, was a man of medium height whose reddish hair and strikingly clear blue eyes set him off as did his trade. As would be said, "Among that body of sterling men who were bold and hardy enough to make the first settlement in the wilderness where Ohio now stands, there was no more remarkable or useful man than Captain Jonathan Devol." Having learned the skills of ship carpentry at an early age, he had become widely noted for constructing "boats of a beautiful model, and famed for rapid sailing." It was understood by all that building boats in the wilderness would be essential to the success of the expedition under way, as well as the success of a settlement on the Ohio River. And that would depend greatly on those relative few who knew how to do it.

Others were mechanics, carpenters, and surveyors. The oldest of the party, William Moulton, a goldsmith from New Hampshire, was sixty-seven, while two others beside Jervis Cutler were still in their teens, Amos Porter from Danvers and Samuel Cushing from Hingham, Massachusetts.

Between them and the promised land of Ohio now were the Allegheny Mountains, a formidable barrier.

———·•·———

They crossed the Blue Mountain, Tuscarora Mountain, all on foot, the sleds loaded down with tools, baggage, and provisions. "Traveling both these days very bad. Men and horses much fatigued," wrote Putnam. The temperature kept dropping. "[The] cold last night and this day may be the coldest this winter," he recorded on February 5. At night they slept around huge, blazing fires. To what extent whiskey served to lessen their discomforts, he did not mention, though to judge from what would be recorded on the subject in days to come, it could have been considerable.

By the time they reached the westernmost of the Alleghenies—Laurel Mountain and the Chestnut Ridge—a thaw set in. Heavy rains fell and for a full day they could not proceed.

In the days following, progress improved. Finally, on February 14, they reached Sumerill's Ferry on the Youghiogheny River, thirty miles southeast of Pittsburgh, where Haffield White and his party were encamped. The journey for Putnam and his party over the mountains had taken nearly a month.

The situation at Sumerill's Ferry was not at all as wished. The

same severe weather, deep snows, and bitter cold experienced by Putnam's party had greatly delayed progress. As Putnam would report to
Manasseh Cutler, "No boats built, boards or planks in readiness, or
person capable of building a canoe, much less a boat." Waterpower for
the sawmill had been frozen. Five workers had taken ill with smallpox
through inoculation. Only with the recent thaw had the ice begun to
melt to the point where the sawmill could operate.

With the additional force of men now at hand and Putnam in
charge, a "new spirit was infused into the workmen" and with Captain
Devol overseeing work at the boatyard progress on the necessary "fleet"
moved forward steadily.

It took what remained of February and all of March to build a large,
roofed galley, forty-five feet in length and twelve feet wide, "strongly
timbered" and capable of carrying fifty tons. A smaller flatboat was also
completed, in addition to three dugout canoes, and, as would be said,
the burdens canoes could bear should never be underestimated.

Ebenezer Sproat and several others set off with packhorses to round
up the necessary provisions—flour, beans, pork, venison hams, bread,
butter, and salt. By the second of April, all was ready. And lest there be
any doubt of their seeing their journey as an extension of their heritage,
the big boat, at first called the "Adventure Galley," had been renamed
the "Mayflower." So early that afternoon the new *Mayflower* pushed off
carrying perhaps thirty men, the others, along with a large quantity of
tools, tents, and provisions, packed onto the smaller galley and canoes.

The whole flotilla drifted away with the current northward some
twenty miles to the point, at McKeesport, where the Youghiogheny
merged with the larger, muddy yellow Monongahela. From there it was
another twenty miles to where, at Pittsburgh, the Monongahela joined
the clearer, faster-flowing Allegheny to form the Ohio. (Even three miles
below the junction the waters of the Allegheny were to be distinguished
from those of the Monongahela.)

Pittsburgh at the time, a crude frontier settlement of no more than
150 log cabins and houses, was described as "an irregular poor built
place" alongside old Fort Pitt inhabited by "a lazy set of beings" and

where "money affairs" were at a low ebb. Its chief export was whiskey. But with its key location at the headwaters of the Ohio, Pittsburgh was the Gateway to the West and almost certain to have great promise.

Springtime, with the water level high, was the best of seasons to travel the river. In the heat of summer, it could dry up to half its usual size. Come winter it could clog with ice for weeks on end. In fall the water nearly always returned to its proper level. Still there was no time like spring and so in that respect the expedition was under way just when it should have been.

For thirty miles beyond Pittsburgh, the Ohio flowed not west but almost due north, past sparsely populated river settlements and the ruins of the Seneca village of Logstown, where Queen Aliquippa once held sway. Not far beyond, the river did indeed swing west until the mouth of the Beaver River, where it headed south-southwest. But then the river kept on twisting and turning. So "completely serpentine" was it that, in some places, as was said, "a person taking observations of the sun or stars, will find that he sometimes entirely changes his direction, and appears to be going back."

Islands and sandbars were past counting. (As later determined, there were in fact a total of ninety-eight islands.) There were besides sunken trees firmly embedded in the river bottom—"planters" as they were called—and "sawyers," sunken trees also, but with free ends that heaved up and down with the current, as well as ordinary snags.

For those on board the *Mayflower* who had long looked forward to being off at last on a shimmering, sunlit voyage on the legendary "Beautiful River," the disappointment could only have been great. It rained day after day, soft rain, hard rain, for hours on end. "A very disagreeable time," recorded a young surveyor with the party, John Mathews.

On Saturday, April 5, the boats "tarried" a full day at the mouth of Buffalo Creek, to take on additional supplies and a quantity of poplar boards for building temporary huts. More heavy rain followed the next day. Nonetheless, at half past eight, with everything aboard, the expedition continued past Wheeling on the left or "Virginia side" of the river. Though still only a tiny backwoods settlement, Wheeling was growing steadily, in contrast to the northern side where there was as yet not a single legal settlement. The Virginia wilderness was already thought to have a population of more than a hundred thousand.

Late in the afternoon that Sunday, the Putnam expedition tied up on the Virginia side of the Ohio River, at what was known as Round Bottom, a notable location of some 587 acres belonging to George Washington. The confluence of the Muskingum was by then sixty miles downstream, so, in order to arrive by daylight, the party rested there for five hours.

By this point they had traveled 140 miles on the rain-swollen Ohio. And though the celebrated charm of the river had been greatly diminished by the weather, one important, welcome change to be seen in the passing landscape was the arrival of spring. Back at Sumerill's Ferry and Pittsburgh the trees were still bare. Here they were in full green leaf, "delightsome," as said by one of the young pioneers.

"At half past nine got under way," recorded John Mathews, "and run all night without meeting with any accident."

Overcast skies and still more rain followed the next morning, visibility not at all what would be desired for such an anticipated arrival. The flotilla drifted on past a long, narrow island—Kerr's Island—that seemed to bend with the river, and at about this point Captain Devol remarked to General Putnam, "I think it is time to take an observation; we must be near the mouth of the Muskingum."

To make matters more difficult, the riverbanks were so overgrown with giant sycamores in full leaf that the incoming Muskingum on the north side of the river was practically concealed. As a result the party drifted on by and had to be pulled back upstream on ropes by soldiers from the garrison at Fort Harmar.

At last, about one o'clock, Monday, April 7, the galley tied up near the Point, as it was known, latitude 39° 25' North, longitude 81° 20' West. The pilgrims aboard their *Mayflower* had landed at Plymouth Rock.

As long and arduous as was so much of the journey, there had been no loss of life, nor, as plainly evident, no loss of spirit. "We arrived . . . most heartily congratulating each other on the sight of our new country," wrote one of them. The first to leap ashore, it would be said, was young Jervis Cutler, who grabbed an ax and cut down the first tree, which, as also said, was a buckeye.

On hand for the arrival were some seventy native men, women, and children led by a Delaware chief, Captain Pipe, neatly dressed in leggings and breechcloth and wearing large copper earrings. His name was not new to Rufus Putnam and the others. According to the widely known story of the torture and burning alive of Colonel William Crawford six years earlier, it had been Captain Pipe who painted Crawford's face black, the ceremonial sign of what was in store for him.

All the natives gathered at the Point seemed quite friendly. Pipe himself greeted the new arrivals as brothers. "As long as the sun and moon endured," he declared, the Delawares, Wyandots, and Yankees shall be friends and brothers.

Privately, Rufus Putnam thought it best to wait and see.

———·•·———

The new arrivals went right to work, unloading the boats, making camp among the trees, and on a bit of open land by the Muskingum, putting up a large tent, the "marquee," that was to be Putnam's headquarters. "They commenced with great spirit, and there is a prospect of it becoming a flourishing place in a short time," wrote an officer from Fort Harmar named Joseph Buell. To General Josiah Harmar it was already obvious these were "quite a different set of people" from the usual frontiersmen.

Only days later, Ebenezer Sproat and John Mathews, with their surveyors' chains and compasses and a crew of thirteen, set out to survey eight-acre lots Rufus Putnam had planned along what were known as the bottomlands by the Ohio and the Muskingum. Each settler was to be given both a small "in-lot" within the town for a place of residence and an "out-lot" of eight acres on which to grow crops.

With his commanding height, Sproat had caught the attention of the local Indians almost from the moment he stepped ashore and was given the name "Old Hetuck"—"Big Buckeye."

Six thousand acres were set apart for what in all-out optimism was called a "new city." Rufus Putnam had overall charge of the survey and all elements of the plan, residential lots, straight streets, and public squares, all as in a compact New England town. Indeed, it was and would remain his foremost intention to create a "new New England" in the wilderness.

The main streets were to conform to the course of the Muskingum and extend upstream a little more than a mile. They were to be ninety feet wide and crossed at right angles by others seventy feet wide. The main streets were designated by numbers, the cross streets by the names of officers of the American Revolution. One of these cross streets, a little north of the center of the plot, would be 120 feet wide, the widest, grandest of them all, and named Washington.

———•••———

The overriding, immediate tasks were clearing land and building shelter. Though accustomed as most were to hard work, few had had any experience in clearing virgin forests. Sometimes it took one man three to four weeks to chop down a single acre of hard-wooded forest, leaving the stumps in the ground. When it came to the largest of the trees, they had to be "girdled"—a ring of bark cut away around the trunk, so that the sap could not rise—and thus the tree would stand in place and slowly die. Many of the giant surviving stumps were to last for decades.

Huge, accumulating log heaps demanded weeks of laborious attention unless the weather remained dry, which it seldom did. To keep them from rotting, the logs required constant rolling together and re-piling—heavy, dirty work.

But persist the settlers did. In the words of an old Ohio Valley poem:

> *The axe, in stalwart hands, with steadfast stroke,*
> *The savage echoes of the forest woke,*
> *And, one by one, breaking the world-old spell,*
> *The hardy trees, long crashing, with thunder fell.*

The site chosen for the settlement was an elevated plateau three quarters of a mile back from the Ohio on the eastern side of the Muskingum. Fort Harmar, its flags flying, stood prominently on a cleared bluff downstream on the opposite, or western side of the Muskingum, at the confluence with the Ohio.

The fort had been built three years before, in 1785, on the orders of Josiah Harmar, not as protection against the native tribes but to protect them from the encroachment of illegal settlers, or "squatters," on government land, crossing into Ohio from western Pennsylvania, Virginia, and Kentucky. Many of these were of Scotch-Irish descent and, as said, "not strongly attached to government either of the royal or proprietary kind." Another characteristic was their "intense hatred of the Indians for whose treatment the extermination policy . . . was generally considered to be the proper model." To move into the Ohio wilderness the squatters had only to cross the Ohio River.

Of the two rivers, the Ohio and the Muskingum, the Ohio was much the larger, measuring about 400 yards from shore to shore in springtime. The natives called it "O-Y-O," Great River. The Muskingum was roughly 200 yards across, but clearer and smoother-flowing. Muskingum, in the native tongue, meant "elk's eye."

The waters of both rivers teemed with catfish weighing from three to as much as eighty pounds, buffalo fish from five to thirty pounds, sturgeon, and pike, and at the confluence of the rivers especially the fishing was ideal—all to the particular delight of the New Englanders.

Wild turkeys and passenger pigeons were in unimaginable abundance. White-tailed deer, otter, elk, buffalo, beaver, wolves, and bear filled the forests in all directions. So plentiful were squirrels that hardly a day passed without a few hundred being killed.

From the site of the new settlement the view, wherever visible through the trees, took in both rivers for at least three miles. In a letter to Manasseh Cutler, Rufus Putnam, never one to exaggerate, wrote that as a site for a future city it was the most beautiful he had ever seen.

But the measureless forest, the gigantic trees of every kind—hickory, beech, sycamore, tulip, ash, buckeye, oaks six feet in diameter that reached fifty feet before breaking out in branches—were the dominating reality. Of all these it was the sycamore that seemed, in the words of one observer, the king of the forest. "Their monstrous growth, towering height, and extended branches really fill the beholder with awe." And it was the immense task of clearing portions of open space that went on every day but Sunday, men working with "persevering industry." Teamwork counted greatly in clearing land, as it did in facing almost every challenge to be met on the frontier. At times there could be as many as six axes chopping away in unison to bring down one single giant of the forest.

Trees were the enemy standing in the way of progress. But clearly, too, in their immense size and variety, they spoke of rich, productive soil and could provide no end of firewood and logs for cabins and storage sheds. Yellow poplar was especially good for heavy planking. The buckeye was a favorite for making bowls, chairs, and cradles. Further, Rufus Putnam insisted, a new stockade for defense of the settlement had to be built without delay.

However friendly had been the welcome given by Captain Pipe and his people, Putnam had reason to be cautious. During his time in New York on the route west, going over former treaties made with the native tribes, he had become quite concerned. "I was fully persuaded that the Indians would not be peaceable very long, hence the propriety of immediately erecting a cover for the immigrants who were soon expected."

Fort Harmar across the way was a log pentagon that enclosed within its walls about three quarters of an acre. Whatever sense of security it provided as protection against the Indians would hardly be enough as the settlement grew. This that Putnam planned was to be considerably larger and more substantial, capable of being a safe refuge for the whole settlement should there be an attack.

Besides, the soldiers at Fort Harmar were not known for high standards of conduct. "Drunkenness and desertion" were prevalent evils, as Joseph Buell, one of the officers, recorded. The treatment of the soldiers was "excessively severe, and that flogging the men, to the extent of one and two hundred lashes, was an almost daily occurrence.

They seem to have been selected from the most worthless and depraved remnants of the revolutionary soldiers; men too lazy and idle to engage in any laborious employments, and as their wages were only three dollars a month, no sober industrious man would engage in the service.

As everyone knew, few were better prepared to design and build a fortification than General Putnam and the facility he created now in the wilderness was extraordinary, in that it went up in so little time, given all else that had to be done, and would serve so effectively as the bulwark of the settlement.

Located half a mile up the Muskingum from the Point, it was to be a great square structure with outer walls 188 feet in length and would have, when completed, strong blockhouses at all four corners, each surrounded by a watchtower, and walls of yellow poplar planks four inches thick, and thirty-six residences.

In all, it was designed to house 864 people. The front faced toward the Muskingum and in the center of the open court a well was dug to a depth of eighty feet, no small task in itself. Jonathan Devol was to supply the timber for the corner blockhouses. It was called Campus Martius (Latin for "Field of Mars") and referred to as a stockade, not a fort.

In addition, a good-sized timber wharf was erected on the Muskingum, opposite Fort Harmar, at which were moored the *Mayflower*, canoes, and a fine, new cedar barge for twelve oarsmen for General Putnam, this, too, built by Jonathan Devol.

A substantial bridge went up over the creek—Tyber Creek—that flowed into the Muskingum in the southern part of the settlement. The bridge was fully twenty-five feet high, ninety feet long, twenty-four feet wide, and covered with hewn planks four inches thick. It was the first bridge to be built in the Northwest Territory and was to stand for decades.

The whole while dozens of cabins large and small, and crude huts or worse, were going up, so great was the need for shelter. One young man chose to spend the better part of a year quartered in the hollow trunk of an ancient tree.

Jervis Cutler and another young pioneer, John Gardner, the son of a sea captain from Marblehead, Massachusetts, were clearing land together and making good progress. Gardner had come west, as did many others, in search of fortune and adventure. Then one morning, when Jervis was absent, as he sat resting on a tree stump, he was suddenly seized by a party of Shawnees who hurried him into the woods, where their horses were hidden. There they all mounted but one who walked and led the prisoner by a rope around his neck.

That night with his hands tied behind his back, he was bound to the trunk of a sapling that had been bent to the ground. After the weary march of the second day, his captors, feeling they were beyond the fear of pursuit, eased up somewhat, shot a bear and a deer, roasted both over a fire and offered him "a plentiful repast." They also tried to persuade him to join them, painted his face, cut off part of his hair, promised to make him "a good Shawnee," even provide a Shawnee wife. Still they secured him as before.

That night a light rain fell, making the thongs that bound him more pliable. By cautious and continued effort over several hours, he succeeded in releasing himself and slipped away into the dark forest. Walking all night and the following day in what he sensed was the direction of home, he slept the next night in a hollow log, then continued on the day after until finally he reached home, there to be "joyfully welcomed."

Though it is said that the next morning he and Jervis returned to their land clearing with renewed spirit, it is also true that John Gardner would soon depart for Marblehead and life at sea on his father's ship, "doubtless preferring to encounter the ills he knew, than those he knew not of."

———————

On an elevated plain just to the north of Campus Martius was a prominent, mysterious, and much talked about feature of the landscape that defied ready explanation except that it was the work of some ancient, vanished people. Spread across more than ninety acres was a variety of earthworks in direct lines, in squares and elevated mounds, including one dominant, conical burial mound thirty feet high. Rufus Putnam, who made careful maps of the area, called the entire system of earthworks the "Ancient Works." The conical mound was known as the "Great Mound."

Accounts of such earthworks were already exciting eastern scholars. Ezra Stiles, the president of Yale, thought they proved the descent of the Indians from the Canaanites expelled from Palestine by Joshua. Benjamin Franklin speculated such mounds might have been constructed by Hernando de Soto in his wanderings.

Three years earlier, in the winter of 1785, during his travels along the Ohio Valley, General Samuel Parsons had written to Ezra Stiles about what he took to be the remains of an ancient fortification at the mouth of the Muskingum, and that the size of the trees growing on top left little doubt that it had been abandoned long before America was discovered by Europeans. Not only was there a giant white oak more than three feet in diameter on top of the conical mound, but it appeared to have sprung from the remains of an earlier tree in the same place. So fascinated was Stiles with what Parsons had to report that he passed the letter on to Thomas Jefferson.

Jefferson, who was long fascinated by Indian lore, was intensely interested in the mounds, but remained open-minded. "It is too early to form theories on those antiquities," he wrote. "We must wait with patience till more facts are collected."

Rufus Putnam, who had studied every feature of the site, found "those works so perfect as to put it beyond all doubt that they are the remains of a work erected at an amazing expense perhaps some thousand years since, by a people who had very considerable knowledge of fortifications." They were besides, he decided, people of "ingenuity, industry, and elegance."

He was in awe of the achievements of these ancient builders, noting that the gradual ascent to the tops of the two largest mounds, "Quadranaou" and "Capitolium" as they were called by the newcomers, were like a beautiful flight of steps in the yard of the governor's house in Massachusetts. Nor was the gravel walk of the Boston Mall more regular than what was called "the covered way," a walkway that he had measured to be 231 feet wide, which led from the Muskingum to the great mound, Quadranaou, and was framed by parallel earthen walls rising some twenty-six feet.

What Putnam and the others did not know at the time was that the ancient ruins were as old as the ruins of Rome. As later archaeologists would determine, the whole complex was the work of what was known as the Ohio Hopewell culture and that the Great Mound was built between 100 BC, when the Hopewell began to occupy southern Ohio, and AD 500, making it more than 2,000 years old.

————•———

At home in New England concern over the fate of the pioneers grew steadily. There had been little at all in the way of communication. Only rumors were plentiful and fearsome more often than not, and ever-increasing worries among families and friends. Manasseh Cutler had not had a word from Rufus Putnam, nor from Jervis, since they set off for the Ohio country.

"It has . . . been currently reported here," Cutler wrote to Putnam on April 21, "that you and your whole party were cut off going down the river by the Indians and not one escaped to tell the doleful tale. Terrible stories are spread respecting the hostility and number of the Indians. Wish we may be favored with an account of the matter from you."

Nearly a month later, there was still no word. "Have not received a line from you since you left New England," Cutler wrote again to Putnam on May 15. All the same, Cutler assured him, the "spark for emigration" to the western country had "kindled into a blaze," and numbers of families were preparing for the exodus.

In a long letter dated May 16, 1788, that did get through to a friend back in Massachusetts named Isaiah Thomas, a publisher, Putnam gave a full description of the state of affairs there on the Ohio, and with the understanding that the letter could be published, which it was in the popular paper called the *Massachusetts Spy*.

All was going as hoped, Putnam wrote. "That part of the purchase I have been over, far exceeds my expectations." He had never seen soil so rich, trees of such size or so numerous. He described the views, the water supply, the favorable climate.

He reported, too, that "In laying out our city we have preserved some of the [ancient] works from becoming private property, by including them within lots or squares appropriated to public uses." It was a decision that can be rightly seen as a pioneering step in historic preservation.

Finally, concerning the natives, Putnam could say only that a treaty was being planned. He had met with Captain Pipe and told him he and other settlers hoped they could all live in friendship and that they would be glad to see them at all times. However, in a letter to Manasseh Cutler written the same day, Putnam did not rule out the possibility of an Indian attack. "At present, we do not think ourselves perfectly secure from them." Yes, the Delawares and Wyandots appeared very friendly, but he judged the Mingos, Shawnees, and Cherokees residing by the waters of the Scioto to be "a set of thievish murdering rascals."

Another letter that appeared back east at about the same time, this by an unidentified settler, expressed utmost wonder and joy, as though the promised land had indeed been reached at last.

This country, for fertility of soil and pleasantness of situation, not only exceeds my expectations, but exceeds any part of America, or Europe, I ever was in. The climate is exceedingly healthy; not a man sick since we have been here. We have started [startled] twenty buffaloes in a drove. Deer are as plenty as sheep [are] with you. Beaver and otter are abundant. I have known one man to catch twenty or thirty of them in two or three nights. Turkeys are innumerable; they come within a few rods of us in the fields. We have already planted a field of one hundred and fifty acres in corn.

Every now and then back home an occasional expression of doubt would appear concerning the "mania for Ohio immigration," as in a letter published that spring in the *Massachusetts Gazette*:

The delusive tales that have been told concerning the fertility of the western country have infatuated many of our citizens to such a degree that some of them have been led to harbor the idea that all the luxuries of life are to be had there in greatest abundance, without money and without price, and that with very little labor the fruits of the earth will yield most spontaneously. Inhabitants of Massachusetts, be not led away by such fairy tales, imbibe not such chimerical notions. Ever since our first parents were banished from the Garden of Eden, and God cursed the ground for Adam's sin, it is a fixed decree that man shall, "Earn his bread by the sweat of the brow." Ohio or no Ohio, this is a *serious* truth. . . . Stay at home, fellow citizens and till your farms, be industrious, and your labors will be crowned with success. Be not dupes to Ohio Quixotism.

But "Ohio Fever" was by no means limited to Massachusetts or even New England. As strong as any endorsements were those from George Washington. "No colony in America was ever settled under such favorable auspices as that which has just commenced at Muskingum," he wrote in one letter. "I know many of the settlers, personally, and there never were men better calculated to promote the welfare of such a community."

To the Marquis de Lafayette he wrote, "A spirit of immigration to the western country is very predominant. . . . Many of your military acquaintances, such as Generals Parsons, Varnum and Putnam, Colonels Tupper, Sproat . . . with many more, propose settling there. From such beginnings much may be expected."

———————

New settlers kept arriving. Dr. Jabez True was the first physician to land at the Point, Paul Fearing, the first attorney. Both were still in their twenties. Another young man, James Backus from Connecticut, was notable for his affluence, as made evident by the extensive quantity of clothing and other "necessities" he had brought along for his venture "into the woods.

Three shirts, two pair worsted stockings . . . one pair check trou-
sers, one pair leather breeches, one pair Indian stockings, one
pair shoes, one pair moccasins . . . twenty-six sheets of paper of
fine quality, vial of ink, one case of instruments, one waistcoat,
one silk handkerchief . . . two hatchets, one tomahawk, two Indian blankets . . . ten gallons whiskey . . . one red cedar box con-
taining a needle, a small file, a leather wrapper with thread and
needles.

During his first year in the new settlement he was to spend most of
his time building a frame house and "socializing" at teas and dinners
with friends.

Mary Owen, the first woman to join the settlement, arrived with her
husband, James Owen. She was a nurse accompanying one of the directors of the Ohio Company, General James Varnum, who was suffering
from a lung complaint.

Samuel Parsons, too, came down the Ohio on a barge carrying Josiah
Harmar, Winthrop Sargent, and some twenty-five others "pretty close
crowded" on board, along with two cows, two calves, seven hogs, nine
dogs, in addition to eight tons of baggage.

More followed week after week to the point that the adventurers on
the scene numbered nearly 100. And still more were expected. "Every
prospect as to the goodness of our lands and the facility of producing
the means of living, equal my most sanguine hopes," reported Samuel
Parsons to his wife back in Connecticut. He planned to begin work on
a house the next day.

The land was as good as to be found anywhere in the universe, as-
serted another of those who arrived on the same barge with Parsons. He
was John May of Boston and soon clearing land and, as a man of means,
had a crew working with him. "All hands clearing land . . . all busy . . .
still clearing land," he wrote repeatedly in his diary.

From the moment he had stepped ashore John May appears to have
taken heart from nearly everything he saw. The location "answers the
best description I have ever heard of it, the situation delightfully agreeable, well calculated for an elegant city." He was charmed by the Mound

and, like so many, amazed by the abundance and variety of food to be had. "I dare say not a market in the world can produce a greater plenty than we shall have this fall."

At the end of May, a young army officer named Ebenezer Denny, newly assigned to Fort Harmar, wrote in his diary with much admiration about the newly established pioneers and how much they had accomplished in only two months time.

These men from New England, many of whom were of the first respectability, old Revolutionary officers, had erected and were now living in huts immediately opposite us. A considerable number of industrious farmers had purchased shares in the [Ohio] company, and more or less arrive every week. A spacious city is laid out here. . . . About half a mile up the Muskingum, upon very commanding ground, the site of a very ancient and very extraordinary fortification, was erected a place of arms and security, called Campus Martius. Building put up of hewn timber, two stories high, forming an oblong square, with strong block-houses in each angle, leaving a considerable area [within]; here their stores, etc., were lodged, and some families perhaps more timid than others, reside, but generally both men and women appear enterprising.

"Those people," he further wrote, "appear the most happy folks in the world; greatly satisfied with their new purchase. But they certainly are the best informed, most courteous and civil to strangers of any people I have yet met with."

———————

But as the weeks passed, John May, like numbers of others, began discovering not all was perfection in the promised land by the Ohio. "Myriads of gnats" were eating him alive. Not only did they "bite surprisingly, but got down one's throat." After eight backbreaking days clearing land, he was "inflamed" with poison ivy. "Thunder and lightning all night, little sleep for me." Worst of all, his dog was shot at and injured so severely by a young settler that May had him killed and buried. "I tried to catch the fellow but he ran too nimble for me."

At night came the howling of wolves and "caterwauling" of panthers in the forests. Night and day there was the pungent, almost ceaseless smell of smoke in the air, from the fires that were kept going in the clearings, burning up giant heaps of brush and tree limbs.

One night Captain Pipe and the Delawares had "hellish Pow-wows" across the Muskingum that went on well into the morning. Tired as he was, John May could not get to sleep. "I have no doubt in my mind that Psalmody had its origin in heaven," he wrote, "and my faith is as strong that the music of these savages was first taught in hell."

Word came from the Virginia side of the Ohio that the settlement was about to be attacked by three strong parties of Chippewas, but that proved false. "At Boston," observed May, "we are alarmed with fires and inundations—here the Indians answer the same purpose—wherever we go we must expect to meet with trouble."

Even before the onset of summer, several of the pioneers had had enough. "A number of poor devils—5 in all took their departure homeward this morning," wrote May on June 15. "They came from home brainless and moneyless, and have returned the same, though not without my blessing in full."

The weather turned hot. The Ohio was running low, "sluggishly." All the same, the Muskingum "trips on as nimble as sprightly as a miss in her teens," May wrote. Early one Sunday morning, he plunged into the Muskingum for the first time. "It looked so tempting I could not refrain, and felt myself much refreshed."

———•·•———

On July 2, Ohio Company directors and agents gathered in General Putnam's tent for the first such meeting held west of the Allegheny Mountains and passed a resolution officially naming the settlement.

Skeptics back in Massachusetts had begun calling it "Putnam's Paradise." Manasseh Cutler had suggested it be named "Adelphia," for brotherhood. Those on the scene had been calling it Muskingum. Now it was officially to become Marietta, in tribute to Queen Marie Antoinette of France, who, the former officers in the Continental Army felt, had done more than anyone, including Benjamin Franklin, to persuade the King of France to lend support to the American cause with both financial and military help. As was said about the decision on the name, it was "a natural gush of feeling in the hearts of these old officers, to remember with gratitude their kind benefactress, and to perpetuate her name by connecting it with their infant city."

As for the name of the surrounding county, there seems to have been no need for discussion. It would be Washington County.

Despite periodic showers, the "infant city's" first celebration of July 4 took place under a sixty-foot-long green bower built for the occasion beside the Muskingum.

Some 150 people attended. Judge Joseph Varnum delivered a most flowery oration in which he complimented those gathered for their courage, "to explore . . . the Paradise of America" and declared "hope no longer flutters upon the wings of uncertainty." Then followed a spread of food and drink in ample quantity—wild meat, turkeys and other wild fowl, and a variety of fish, including, as none present would forget, a giant, 100-pound pike caught just downstream at the mouth of the Muskingum.

A seemingly limitless supply of punch and wine was at hand and patriotic toasts were raised one after another—to the United States, to Congress, the King of France, the new Federal Constitution, Captain Pipe, the wives at home back east—thirteen toasts in all.

"Pleased with our entertainment," recorded John May, "we did not separate till 12 o'clock." The next morning he was up at five and like everyone else back at work.

On July 9, General Arthur St. Clair, who had been president of the Congress at the time of the passage of the Northwest Ordinance, arrived at Fort Harmar to a national salute of thirteen guns, one for each state, and on July 15, on the other side of the Muskingum, in the same green bower where the Fourth of July celebration was held, St. Clair, with appropriate ceremony, became the first governor of the Northwest Territory, and thus civil government was now officially established.

While serving as the president of Congress, St. Clair had shown only lukewarm interest in the Northwest Territory, but as would later be written, "a change came over him when it was proposed to make him governor of the territory, and his warmest interest and endeavors were enlisted."

II.

In mid-August the Reverend Manasseh Cutler appeared on the scene, having traveled the full distance from Ipswich Hamlet, 751 miles in just twenty-nine days, a new record. Expecting to be absent from home and his pastoral duties for at least three months, he had relinquished his salary before setting off.

He had traveled as far as the Allegheny Mountains riding in a high-wheeled sulky, then by horseback over the mountains, then by barge down the Ohio. There had been rain and fog aplenty, "excessively" bad roads, steep, "anxious" ascents and descents, and barely tolerable roadside taverns. But it was summer the whole way, nothing like what Rufus Putnam and his party had experienced.

On his voyage down the "very romantic" Ohio, Cutler had the pleasure of the company of General Benjamin Tupper, his wife, their five children, and two grandchildren, as well as four other families, making thirty-six migrants heading for Marietta, including fourteen children.

They were the first group of families to arrive at the settlement and the fathers were all veterans of the Revolution, men whose experience, as they knew, had prepared them for the tasks ahead in a way nothing else could have. As another notable veteran, Joseph Barker, who was to follow later, would write, they had had "a second education in the Army of the Revolution, where they heard the precept of wisdom and saw the example of bravery and fortitude. They had been disciplined to obey, and learned the advantage of subordination to law and good order in promoting the prosperity and happiness of themselves and the rest of mankind."

At the Point a good crowd had gathered, people cheering, dogs barking. Rufus Putnam, Samuel Parsons, and Winthrop Sargent were among the welcoming committee. Not to be seen among the crowd, however, was Jervis Cutler, whose adventurous spirit, as his father already knew, had propelled him elsewhere for the time being.

First reactions by the newcomers to the realities of what was to be their new home in Campus Martius were mostly favorable, as one of the Tupper daughters would write. "Our buildings are decent and comfortable. The Indians appear to be perfectly friendly," she said, adding notwithstanding, "There is a guard placed every night."

In his usual energetic fashion, Manasseh Cutler was bent on seeing as much as possible and enjoying to the full the hospitality provided and the encouraging progress to be seen. "Cabin raisings" were taking place, joint efforts by neighbors to provide the newcomers places to live, and with many working together a cabin could go up in remarkably little time. The customary pay provided for such efforts was whiskey in generous quantity.

With Rufus Putnam, Cutler walked the "city lots" and a cornfield the size of which "astonished" him, as did corn already grown to an unimaginable fourteen feet high. One tulip tree nearly six feet in diameter he estimated to be over 400 years old.

Not surprisingly, it was the trees that commanded Cutler's greatest attention. He could be seen studying and measuring the stumps of those that had been cut down, carefully counting the circles. One sycamore, or buttonwood, measured twenty-one feet in circumference. On the stump of one elm he counted 336 well-defined circles.

With Generals Parsons and Varnum he inspected what was known as "the great tree," a giant, hollow black walnut just back from the Muskingum River. At two feet above ground the tree measured forty-one feet in circumference. Six men on horseback could parade inside it at the same time, Cutler was told.

As always, he took time to record every day's activities and with particular attention to the natural wonders to be seen. One day he carefully dissected a poisonous copperhead snake.

> Took off his head and examined his teeth. Took out seven teeth from the bladder on one side [of] his jaw. Found a circular bone, in which the teeth were inserted; this bone is connected with the jaw by a strong ligament.

Sudden and heavy rains by which he was "almost drowned," mist, fog, along with abounding mud, appear to have characterized a greater part of his visit. In compensation the women he met all struck him as bright and charming. Miss Anna Symmes was a "very well accomplished young lady." (She would one day become the wife of President William Henry Harrison.) Mrs. Harmar, the general's wife, was a "fine woman," and at a dinner given by Captain William McCurdy featuring squirrel pie, he found Mrs. McCurdy "very agreeable."

As might have been expected, Cutler was utterly fascinated by the Mound and loved conversing with others at length on the subject.

In the middle of one night, he was called on to visit the seriously ill child of one of the couples with whom he had traveled down the Ohio. But by the time he arrived, the child, thirteen-month-old Nabby Cushing, had died. Hers was the first death among the settlers of Marietta. The parents had six remaining children with them, and the mother was expecting another later in the winter.

The conspicuous presence of the natives of different tribes in the daily life of the community pleased Cutler no end. "We have had Indians to dine with us almost every day principally Delawares, Wyandots, one or two Shawnees, Mingos, Seneca, or Six Nations. No other nations come in." The Chippewas and Ottawas, he was told, appeared to be inclined for war. At one point he did complain that when he returned to his quarters at night, he found numerous Indians standing about, "the squaws mostly drunk."

On Sunday, August 24, the Reverend Cutler preached a powerful sermon before a large gathering at Campus Martius. He spoke at length, clearly having given it much thought. God and the Gospel figured prominently. So also did religious freedom and learning and the new nation at hand.

> It may be emphatically said that a new Empire has sprung into existence, and that there is a new thing under the sun. By the Constitution now established in the United States, religious as well as civil liberty is secured.
>
> Some serious Christians may possibly tremble for the Ark, and think the Christian religion in danger when divested of the patronage of civil power. They may fear inroads from licentiousness and infidelity, on the one hand, and from sectaries and party divisions on the other. But we may dismiss our fears, when we consider that truth can never be in real hazard, where there is a sufficiency of light and knowledge, and full liberty to vindicate it.

He was patriotic, high-minded, unmistakably brimming with pride and confidence in the community under way and its values, and optimistic about the future.

> Such is the present state of things in this country, that we have just ground to hope that religion and learning, the useful and ornamental branches of science, will meet with encouragement, and that they will be extended to the remotest parts of the American empire. . . . Here we behold a country vast in extent, mild in its climate, exuberant in its soil, and favorable to the enjoyment of life. . . . Here may the Gospel be preached to the latest period of time; the arts and sciences be planted; the seeds of virtue, happiness, and glory be firmly rooted and grow up to full maturity.

———•·•———

Traffic on the river grew steadily, with by far the greater part of it heading farther downstream to Virginia and Kentucky. The Kentucky-bound boats numbered ten or twelve a day. It was said that before the year was out more than 900 boats carrying more than 18,000 people had passed by the "New England settlement," as Marietta was sometimes called.

The variety in the shapes and sizes of the means of transportation on the river was a spectacle in itself—flatboats, rafts, barges of all sizes, and keelboats. The flatboat was a heavy, flat-bottomed, rectangular box eight to ten feet wide and thirty or forty feet long. It would be described "a mixture of log-cabin, fort, floating barnyard and country grocery" and was how the vast majority of the "floating pilgrims" traveled. John James Audubon, who embarked on the Ohio on his wedding journey, described passengers huddled together with their animals and poultry.

> The roof or deck of the boat was not unlike a farmyard, being covered with hay, ploughs, carts, wagons . . . [and] spinning-wheels of the matrons were conspicuous. Even the sides of the floating-mass were loaded with the wheels of the different ve-hicles which themselves lay on the roof.

At the end of their journey the flatboats would be broken apart, the lumber used for a variety of purposes.

The keelboat, on the other hand, was intended for travel both downstream and back up against the current. The keelboat, as said, "heralded a new era." It was a long, narrow craft, from fifty to seventy feet in length and had a fifteen- to eighteen-foot beam, shallow draft, was pointed at both prow and stern, and had a narrow running board from prow to stern on either side. The crew consisted of many men, a number of whom on the running boards, using long poles, would walk from bow to stern pushing the boat upstream. Or if not that, they would pull on oars.

Under certain circumstances it made sense to grab hold of the bushes and trees on the river's banks and pull the boat forward upstream. This was known as "bushwhacking."

There was no more grueling work in the new west than that of the keelboatmen and they were to become a long-standing, colorful element of life on the river, "a distinct class," with their red flannel shirts and wool hats set off with a feather. More often than not seasoned keelboat hands also carried one or two signs of their way of life after hours, a damaged nose or ear or face scars, of which they were quite proud. As one Ohio River historian was to write in understatement, "If a town had a really malodorous repute, it was to them, then, an excellent place to lie over and relax a bit. Their relaxing, of course, did nothing to quiet the scene of their repose."

On September 9, after a stay of three weeks, Manasseh Cutler started for home back up the Ohio. It was a sparkling, clear day and he was on a "fine, large" keelboat with ten boatmen pulling on oars. It was a boat belonging to a merchant from Pittsburgh returning from a trip to New Orleans who invited Cutler to be his guest. No sooner had they left shore than around Kerr's Island came a barge carrying more than fifty soldiers from Fort Pitt and some forty Indians in canoes lashed together. The soldiers were standing ramrod straight in immaculate uniforms and the Indians were in full dress. Among them was the celebrated Cornplanter, chief of the Senecas. The Indians, on their way to a treaty gathering, were carrying two small American flags. It was a spectacle Cutler was never to forget.

Plans were changed temporarily. Cutler's boat turned back to stop at Fort Harmar for several hours, during which Cutler had the chance to talk with Cornplanter. The chief was in his eighties, the son of a white Indian trader and a Seneca woman, and known as a strong leader and great orator. Cutler, as he later wrote, was "surprised to see a man of that age with so much sprightliness about him—his body erect, and countenance rather florid; and yet marks of senility were more evident on his body than in his mind." When Cutler asked Cornplanter about the origins of the Mound, Cornplanter said he did not know who made them, nor for what purpose. It was a mystery.

At about mid-afternoon, Cutler's journey upriver resumed. Any desire such as he had earlier expressed of becoming part of the settlement appears to have subsided. How soon he might return to Marietta for another visit, or possibly even to stay, was impossible to predict, given all he had to attend to at home.

With the passage of autumn and the days growing shorter, the work to be done was greater still. Winter was coming, winter in the wilderness, and much needed seeing to. Darkness fell earlier, but with the leaves gone from the trees, the stars and moon blazed in the night sky.

In mid-December some 200 members of different native tribes marched down the western shore of the Muskingum to Fort Harmar, a great number on horseback and those out front carrying the flag of the United States. As they approached the fort, they fired their rifles as a sign of friendship, and the salute was returned by several minutes of cannon and rifle fire from the fort. A guard of soldiers, with music, then escorted them into the garrison.

Thus commenced the procedures of a new treaty. The Delawares, Wyandots, and Ottawas had formed a loose confederacy. They had come in earnest and all "spirituous liquors" were prohibited on both sides. But the most important members of the confederacy, the Shawnees and the Miamis, had refused to attend the council. The leaders of the confederacy wanted rescinding of the cessions north of the Ohio River. The American government hoped that by a modest payment for the cessions, settlement could continue north of the Ohio without violence.

As the days passed, the Indians were slaughtering great quantities of game for their own subsistence, but as the chances of their getting what they wanted from the treaty seemed increasingly unlikely, they began killing all the game they could within a radius of twenty miles or more. Rarely could a deer now be seen where before a good hunter could kill from ten to fifteen a day. A settler later wrote that the natives said they meant to kill all the game and thus, "Destroy and starve out every white face north of the Ohio."

Captain Pipe and others of the tribes had become alarmed by the size of what was being built by the settlers and the numbers that kept arriving. The native people did not believe land was something to be owned. In the words of a Wyandot named Turk, "No one in particular can justly claim this [land]; it belongs in common to us all; no earthly being has an exclusive right to it. The Great Spirit above is the true and only owner of this soil; and He has given us all an equal right to it."

The treaty that was finally signed on January 9, 1789, would bring little change for the better. It was, as said, an "insincere and hollow affair." Rufus Putnam, who had kept closer watch than anyone on all that went on, wrote, "This treaty under all circumstances gave us no real security, or reason to relax in our precautions against a surprise."

The day following, on January 10, General Varnum, who had been suffering with consumption from the time of his arrival and had grown quite feeble, died at age forty.

From the start he had taken his responsibilities at Marietta quite seriously and, much to his credit, played an active part in promoting a resolution for the preservation of the ancient ruins of the Mound. But with the advance of his illness he had become a "very unhappy" man, and proved increasingly hard to deal with, taking issue with Rufus Putnam's land distribution policies and making life difficult for others. To Manasseh Cutler, who confessed that Varnum had given him "much uneasiness," it was as if his death had been an intervention of divine providence.

———•—•———

Meanwhile two notable advances had been made in the life of the settlement. A first school was established in one of the blockhouses at Campus Martius, and a first general store opened on the Point, the enterprise of the affluent young James Backus from Connecticut, in partnership with another young man from Connecticut, Dudley Woodbridge. In their inventory of stock at hand, the first thing listed was fifty-seven gallons of whiskey.

As the year's end approached the population of Marietta numbered

132 people, including fifteen families, and, it may be said, nearly all were still optimistic.

Winter "set in cold," in mid-December. One cold day after another was followed by "very cold days" or "still very cold" days. The Ohio River became choked with ice to the point that no boats moved up or down-stream and the settlers, who had so recently enjoyed such a wondrous abundance of food, now found themselves hard pressed for enough to eat.

Jediah Bagley was an itinerant fiddler who moved about among the settlements playing for parties, weddings, and funerals. Trudging through the snow along the Muskingum one freezing afternoon, he was chased by wolves and just barely succeeded in climbing a willow on the riverbank. Gripping the tree with his legs, he managed to get the fiddle off his back and out of its case and began to play for the wolves on into the night, until they finally "saw fit" to leave him.

The next morning, it was said, he continued on through the snow playing one tune after another until at last he reached Marietta. True or not, the story would help a great many get through much that was to come.

CHAPTER THREE

Difficult Times

Spit on your hands and take a fresh holt.

—EARLY SAYING

I.

"The little provisions which the settlers had provided was soon spent. Their flour entirely," remembered Ichabod Nye. "Very few had laid in any salted meat of any description, the season for venison was gone by. Turkeys scarce, beef and cattle there was none."

Ichabod Nye from the Bay State had been among those settlers who arrived the first summer. The son-in-law of General Benjamin Tupper, he had made the overland journey with the general and the rest of the family, including his wife, Minerva, and their children, and had had an extremely hard time almost from the start. He wished he had never agreed to go west, "for the long and unknown adventure to a wilderness among savages and prowlers of the forest." But of this he said nothing. "I never made one word of complaint. The die was cast and I made the best of it."

At Sumerill's Ferry, where the others "tarried" ten days, while a boat was made ready, he was charged with driving a stock of twenty worn-out horses through the wilderness on the Virginia shore of the Ohio to Marietta, a task such as he had never before undertaken or even imagined.

On arrival he had been appropriately greeted by Rufus Putnam. But he would not have gotten by until the arrival of the family had it not been for a new acquaintance named Dean Tyler, who had a cabin on the east side of Campus Martius, which he offered to share in return for help with his patch of corn and cucumbers.

Tyler, too, was from Massachusetts, a Harvard graduate who had come west as a way of coping with the death of a young lady with whom he had been much in love. If most agreeable in manner and known to be brilliant of mind, he was also thought a bit eccentric, the sort who had been "exclusively confined to handling books and found it difficult to become familiar with the axe handle and the hoe." And as Ichabod Nye soon learned, he and Tyler were to subsist mainly on their meager corn and cucumber production. With the arrival of Nye's wife and children, they, too, moved into the Tyler cabin.

When, in November, the shortage of food had become all too apparent, Tyler, with funds provided by the Ohio Company, acquired a flatboat and set off upstream to Pittsburgh for a supply of flour. But then the river froze. Tyler was stranded at Pittsburgh, and at Marietta, as Nye wrote, "We were all starving for bread."

The fortunes and fate of the settlement, it had become increasingly clear, were much at the sufferance of *la Belle Rivière.*

General Tupper and his family, meanwhile, established themselves in one of the houses within Campus Martius, or the stockade, as it was commonly known, and were making do as best they could. The general became actively engaged with Rufus Putnam in the management and interests of the Ohio Company, but had suffered severely from the economic depression back home and was consequently "without funds."

Among the others also residing at the stockade was Winthrop Sargent, who had earlier made a concerted effort to introduce himself to Ichabod Nye, when Ichabod first arrived, and who did no less now in welcoming the Tupper family.

Sargent was impressive if not altogether likable. Tall and slender, always elegant in attire, he had the erect military stance of a high-ranking officer that seemed a bit out of place on the frontier and a voice that could turn somewhat harsh even when discussing matters pleasing to him. Particularly to those not from New England, he seemed the perfect stiff-necked Yankee and would doubtless remain so. But then, like Manasseh Cutler, he was an avid botanist and took serious interest in Marietta's prehistoric mound. As a gardener he surpassed everyone in the settlement.

Sargent had grown up in Gloucester, Massachusetts, the son of a wealthy merchant, and while a student at Harvard ran into trouble. As recorded in a faculty report, he had chosen to entertain two women of ill fame who were seen at his chamber early the next morning "in such circumstances as indicate a strong presumption that they were kept there the whole night." On other occasions, the report continued, he fired pistols in the town of Cambridge "in such a manner as to endanger the lives and property of the inhabitants." Dismissed from Harvard, Sargent was soon readmitted to the class of 1771 after his father made a substantial contribution toward the restoration of Harvard Hall.

The next four years following graduation were spent at sea on his father's ships. He then served as an officer in Washington's army through the Revolution, after which he returned to Gloucester to find the family fortune ruined by "the fickleness of privateering."

In his role as secretary of the Ohio Company Sargent had received an annual salary of $750. At Marietta came another $750 a year as second in command with the title of secretary of the territory.

In little time, he began actively courting General Tupper's twenty-two-year-old daughter, Rowena, and apparently with the full approval of her family, except for Ichabod Nye, who had by now decided Sargent was "a consummate tyrant and raskale."

Others, though, heartily approved the match. On hearing of a pending wedding, Manasseh Cutler wrote to offer his congratulations to Sargent for choosing such an "amiable and agreeable young lady." Matrimony, he had thought, was the only prospect that could frighten Sargent. "But true bravery rises superior to every hazard. The young lady has certainly done herself great honor in the conquest she has made."

On February 6, 1789, at the stockade, with Rufus Putnam presiding, Rowena Tupper and Winthrop Sargent were married at what was thought to have been the first formal wedding ceremony among the settlers known to have taken place in all the Northwest Territory. But no sooner were they married, according to Ichabod Nye, than Sargent put on his true character, turning ever more "imperious and haughty." He broke off all contact with General Tupper and the family, which was "most mortifying and trying" to the general, who doted on his daughter.

That General Tupper liked to drink was no secret, nor by any means an unusual or unacceptable indulgence on the frontier at all levels. But Sargent had no tolerance for such indulgence. Tupper was a "slave to whiskey," Sargent informed Manasseh Cutler in a letter in which he also turned quite unkind in what he wrote about Rowena. While crediting her for her devotion to his happiness, he went on to describe her as plain, nor "so graceful or accomplished as many fine ladies of my acquaintance," but then, he implied, what was one to do there in the backwoods with so little to choose from?

Meantime, he had built a comfortable house for her, where sadly less than a year after their marriage, on January 29, 1790, Rowena Tupper Sargent died in childbirth, as did the child.

———————

Despite the lack of flour and the Indians driving off the game, the settlers survived. With the return of spring the gloom of the wilderness winter soon vanished. In the words of Ichabod Nye, "Spring opened with much activity." The return of traffic on the river not only meant the return of food supplies, but the return of the tide of humanity. New emigrants kept arriving in considerable numbers, which meant more farmers to clear and prepare more land, but also an increasing supply of skilled carpenters, gunsmiths, saddlers, glassmakers, weavers, boot makers, blacksmiths, all much in need.

William Moulton alone, a blacksmith from New Hampshire, as an example, fulfilled a multitude of essential needs. As one scholar of frontier life has written:

> The blacksmith was gunsmith, farrier, coppersmith, millwright, machinist, and surgeon general to all broken tools and implements. His forge was a center of social as well as industrial activity. From soft bar iron, nails as well as horse shoes were forged as needed. . . . Chains, reaping hooks, bullet molds, yoke rings, axes, bear and wolf traps, hoes, augers, bells, saws, and the metal parts of looms, spinning wheels, sausage grinders, presses and agricultural implements were a few of the items either manufactured or repaired in his shop.

Moulton served also as a goldsmith, Captain Joseph Prince a hatter, Moses Morse a sign painter whose tavern signs were all noted for featuring a black horse. It was said his road from New England to the Ohio River could be traced all the way by tavern signs he painted, thereby paying his traveling expenses.

Most importantly there were more women now to share in the endless work and hardships of life on the frontier. Pioneering demanded joint effort in just about everything. In the words of an old folk song:

> *Tis I can delve and plough, love,*
> *And you can spin and sew,*
> *And we'll settle on the banks*
> *Of the pleasant Ohio.*

As Ichabod Nye would write, "The women put up with all these inconveniences with spirit and fortitude not often excelled by men."

The center of pioneer life was the home, where, in the old saying, a woman's work was never done, from first light to setting sun. There were no days off, no vacations.

Besides cooking, baking, cleaning, and the full-time role of wife and mother, there were cows to milk, gardens to tend, candles and soap to be made, butter to churn. As would be said, "Working butter with wooden paddles in the large wooden bowl, molding it, and cleaning the pails and utensils was as much a part of women's work as washing dishes." Butter was a major element of the frontier diet and making good butter was a skill in which women took particular pride.

Then there was yarn to spin, wool to weave, clothes to make for large families, clothes to wash, mend, and patch. And just as the man of the house had his ax, plowshare, long rifle, and those other tools necessary for the work to be faced, so, too, did the woman of the house—knives, needles, spoons, paddles, hickory brooms, spinning wheels, and most important, the bulbous, heavy iron pots to be seen in nearly every cabin that were used more for cooking than any other item and led to count-less aching backs by the end of the day.

In contrast to the many surviving letters and journals by the men who came west, first-person accounts by the pioneer women are disap-pointingly scarce, and even they record little of the struggles and hard-ships faced. There was, it would seem, widespread reluctance on the part of women to subject those they loved back home to any of their troubles or fears or regrets.

One notable exception was Lucy Backus Woodbridge, who, over the years, wrote quite often to her parents and others of her family in Con-necticut. But even then it was primarily to say how intensely she missed them.

She had been one of those who arrived at Marietta in the autumn of 1789. Her husband, Dudley Woodbridge, a Yale graduate, with James Backus, had been the two who established Marietta's first general store. She was thirty-two and the mother of six children, the youngest four of whom had come west, while the older two remained in Connecticut to continue their education.

She had grown up in a family of some means and in one of the larger, more luxurious houses in the town of Norwich, and in little time in Marietta, the general store prospered. So the struggle for survival on the frontier was not for her as it was for so many. But when she wrote as she did of her longing for home and her family there, she was speaking for many another woman. When her younger brother, Elijah, who had also come west, reported the adversities of age their parents were going through, she wrote to tell them, "I never so severely felt the pain of being separated from you . . . your confinement and suffering excites sensations that are never to be expressed."

About all she could offer in the way of her own outlook was to say she was confident her prospects there on the frontier were "much better than I had any reason to expect had I continued in New England."

In conclusion, she said simply what so many New Englanders were raised on and was taken to heart by so many of the women there on the banks of the Ohio: "I will not afflict you with complaining."

As things were to go, it would be nearly two years later when she could honestly report, and with apparent surprise, that she had come to like "this country." As she wrote to a brother "I am happy to feel my attachment for this place and its inhabitants strengthen [with] the affectionate attentions I have met from my old neighbors."

Conspicuous loafing, loafing of almost any kind was as yet unknown. Everyone worked, including children. It had to be so for survival. Come spring there were crops to be sown. Through summer and into fall, there were crops to be harvested, and always more land needed to be cleared. Winter was a struggle in itself.

The attire of women was invariably all-of-a-kind homemade, plain and simple of necessity. The male pioneer, too, dressed as called for, often as not in the same work clothes he had worn back in New England, but increasingly, as time passed, the wardrobe evolved into that of the frontiersman, consisting primarily of a long linen shirt and pantaloons produced by wives or daughters or female friends. The rest was nearly all buckskin—moccasins, leggins or gaiters (these for defense against rattlesnakes), and hunting shirt. Hats varied, but were mainly of the broad-brimmed kind.

The impression the settlement at Marietta made on those seeing it for the first time often depended on the eyes of the beholder. One of those newly arrived was overcome with disappointment, even despair, by what he saw:

On ascending the bank of the river to look at the town we had been nearly three months toiling to see, a very cheerless prospect was presented to our view. A few log huts were scattered here and there, raised only a few feet above the tall stumps of the sturdy trees that had been cut away to make room for them. Narrow footpaths meandered through the mud and water from cabin to cabin; while an occasional log across the water-courses afforded a pedestrian a passage without wetting his feet.

However, John May, who returned to Marietta that summer of 1789 after an absence of a year, saw things differently. Astonished by all the improvements, he spent the whole of one Saturday "reconnoitering" the settlement. "I find about 60 good buildings, many of which are large and handsome," he wrote. There were at least 400 acres of corn "as good as ever was seen," and would, he estimated, produce 20,000 bushels of grain.

On Sunday, he attended a public service to hear the new pastor, a slender young man from Massachusetts, the Reverend Daniel Story, who had been selected for the role by Manasseh Cutler, and who, May was happy to record, provided "a very good performance."

But as May also recorded, he found himself growing weary of "the howling wilderness," and when, on reuniting with his family back east, he was told they had no desire to settle in Ohio, he, too, gave up on the idea and did not return.

Ichabod Nye, by now, had "come to the end of his rope." Having concluded he would "never amount to a hill of beans," he had taken stock of the little he had left in the way of material assets—two old horses, one old watch, two barrels of flour (purchased from Dean Tyler), and some twenty-five pounds of shoe leather. These, he would write, were "all the resources which I could bring into action for the maintenance of my family." So he had decided to make the best of his hands and took up patching and making shoes, little knowing at first how to go about it or where it might lead. In fact, as neither he nor anyone else could have imagined, it would lead to great success with Marietta's first tannery.

Ichabod Nye, the man who had so wished he had never come west, was soon writing to a brother back home, urging him to pack up and come join him.

———·•·———

With all the concentrated activity, the tangible progress to be seen, there still remained the hard realities of the frontier. The life left behind back east, families and friends, was as distant, as out of reach as ever. Not only were letters from home rare, but news of any kind was still rare, still painfully slow to arrive. The news that in April on a balcony at Federal Hall in New York George Washington had taken the oath of office as the first president of the United States took more than a month reaching Marietta.

Measureless wilderness on all sides and the continuing fears and uncertainties over the native peoples so close at hand remained a constant presence. It was the great overshadowing fact of life on the frontier and was made even more unnerving by two events that summer of 1789.

In early July, a surveying party led by John Mathews working the lower part of the Ohio Company's purchase suffered the loss of two packhorses, which apparently had strayed off into the woods, with the result that the party also suffered a serious loss of provisions. The men had to get by on meat alone, or what little there was to be found, until, after nine or ten days, they were forced to return to Marietta.

On the trip back up the Ohio they met with Generals Tupper and Parsons and a number of others coming downstream on a reconnoitering expedition and who requested that Mathews and his party turn back and complete their unfinished work. To make this possible, they sent a messenger to Marietta for provisions.

As would be said of John Mathews, his energy always increased with the difficulties of his situation. He knew that, in the frontier expression, he and his men were "in danger pretty considerable much." He had been told many times by old scouts that anyone who ventured continually into dangerous country would, sooner or later, run into trouble. He was also well aware of the particular hostility Indians had for surveyors, knowing they were the ones preparing the way for still more white invaders.

All the same, Mathews and his party, which included a number of soldiers, returned to their assignment only to have another horse disappear. This time, however, they discovered moccasin tracks in several places. The explanation was clear.

Early the morning of August 7, as Mathews was sitting on his blanket undressed, two guns were fired by an unseen enemy. One of his men, sitting beside him, was shot through the chest. "Oh God, I am killed!" he exclaimed. At that instant a second volley was fired at a cluster of six or seven soldiers, all but one of whom were killed.

As a swarm of Indians rushed upon their victims on one side of the camp, Mathews and three others of his men fled off on the other side.

In a later account, Mathews is described as having escaped with nothing on but his hat and shirt. He and another comrade ran for their lives. Seeing Mathews's condition, the other man offered him his coat, which Mathews managed to pull on by slipping his legs into the sleeves.

They raced on for seven or eight miles, until Mathews's bare feet were so torn and blistered he could only walk and then in searing pain.

After reaching the banks of the Ohio, they had almost succeeded in building a raft out of old logs bound together with grape vines, when an Ohio Company boat and crew came in sight and took them on board and back to safety.

One week later, Mathews and a party of armed men returned to the scene of the calamity to recover the remains of nine dead soldiers.

> He found them lying near where they fell [an old account continues]. . . . The flesh was all eaten from their bones by the wolves, except that on the palms of their hands and soles of the feet; to which parts of the human body they, as well as dogs, seem to have an instinctive aversion.

To which tribe the killers belonged was never determined for certain, but they were thought to have been Shawnees.

The second event, or incident, though far from so tragic in its consequences, nonetheless made a lasting impression among those who heard about it, and particularly on the mothers of overly adventurous children.

It involved a party of only one, Jervis Cutler, who had returned to the settlement that fall after more than a year back in western Pennsylvania teaching school. He had joined another surveying party between the Big Hockhocking River and Raccoon Creek. That he had been one of the first pioneers to land at Marietta—indeed by reputation the first to have leapt ashore—made what happened now such a surprise, and to him no less than to others.

Having "quite a relish for hunting and an expert with the rifle," as he himself said, he had set off into the woods one morning accompanied only by a small dog, and to his surprise soon found himself altogether lost. And so it remained until nightfall and all through the following day, as well as the day after and the day after that. Because of his skill with a rifle, he and the dog survived on one deer, a turkey, and "a little half-starved opossum." But not for fully eight days did he finally find his way out of the woods and back with the surveyors.

Not surprisingly, the story spread far.

———•———

As serious as had been the need for food through the previous winter, concern over the problem seemed to have slipped out of mind. The spring and summer of 1789 proved ideal for growing just about everything. Turnips, cabbages, and radishes were up in gardens as early as March. The midsummer corn crop was all that could be hoped for. Beans, tomatoes, and potatoes were in abundance, and a second crop of corn was doing as well or better than the first.

Normally, Indian summer was the prime time of the year. But not this year. On the first day of October an early frost struck throughout much of the Northwest country killing most of the corn when it was not quite out of the soft succulent stage called "the milk." Many thought that if dried out, it could make good bread. Instead, it produced sickness and vomiting. It could not even be fed to animals with safety.

Were this not enough, in November came a serious outbreak of measles in Marietta that would take the lives of a number of children.

The year had started with the death of General James Varnum. Now, in mid-November, General Samuel Parsons was killed trying to shoot the rapids in a canoe on the Beaver River, which joined the Ohio northwest of Pittsburgh. A companion in the canoe, Captain Joseph Rogers, escaped with his life.

As a soldier, patriot, lawyer, as a director of the Ohio Company and chief judge of the Western Territory, General Parsons had been a figure of considerable importance through much of his life. For the pioneers of Marietta his death was an altogether unexpected blow.

II.

Joseph Barker was twenty-four years old. Raised in New Hampshire, he was descended from a long line of weavers, saddlers, and farmers. His father, Deacon Ephraim Barker, was a highly respected "housewright" and church builder, and for years served as deacon and musician in his church in Amherst, New Hampshire.

The second of ten children, Joseph had been sent away to school until age fourteen when he was brought home again to begin work as his father's apprentice. Thus it was that the carpenter's trade became his own and he had become exceptionally skilled at it.

Tall and strong, he was also known for his athletic abilities, his humor, and cheerful outlook. He loved to read and in time was to show considerable skill as a writer, though, like Rufus Putnam and numerous others of the time, proper spelling was more than he could handle. He spelled canoe, "canoo," large, "learge." The word "excellent" he did with no "c" and only one "l," thus it came out "exelent." "Seldom" became "sildom," which may have been how he pronounced it. But apparently none of this mattered much to him, or to others.

In September 1789, Joseph married nineteen-year-old Elizabeth Dana of Amherst, the daughter of Captain William and Mary Bancroft Dana. Less than two years earlier, his financial state shattered by the depreciation of the currency, Captain Dana had set off with two of his sons for the Ohio country to see about settling there. When Captain Dana returned to bring the rest of the family west, Joseph and his bride decided to go with them.

The journey proved more difficult than they had imagined. At times, crossing the Alleghenies, progress became so slow, their wagons had to be taken apart and the separate pieces carried by hand over impassable barriers of rocks and ledges.

After crossing the mountains to Sumerill's Ferry and waiting for an unwieldy boat to be built for them, they proceeded down the Ohio. Instead of landing at Marietta, they went on to a newly established settlement of about two dozen families downstream on the Ohio side of the river called Belpre. There Captain Dana's land was located, but on arrival they found the cabin he built the year before had, by accident, burned to the ground. As a consequence, young Joseph decided to stay for the time being at Marietta where carpenters were much in demand.

Winter had set in by then and troubles were all about. As serious as had been the shortage of food the previous winter, this one was to be worse—the "Starving Year"—and the suffering extreme. Because of the slaughter of the wild game by the Indians, the woods were still bare within a radius of twenty miles. There were other explanations as well—the clearing of the forests and the hunting by the settlers, and as Joseph Barker put it, a large majority of the emigrants had "strewed all their money" on the mountains of Pennsylvania "and in the enjoyment that they had got to the land of promise, they forgot to provide for the future."

In fact, there were many causes of the "hungry year," as it was also called and in many other sections of the country, including New England, most of them not readily apparent in Ohio. France had been importing unprecedented quantities of wheat and flour from the United States. Then there was the devastating effect of the insect called the Hessian fly on wheat production. Climate historians would later attribute a large part of the problem to major volcanic explosions in Iceland and Japan that blew millions of tons of particles into the upper atmosphere, thereby reducing the warming of sunlight on a good part of the globe.

What saved the settlement was generosity. To Barker it was a power-ful lesson in life. "Where poverty, improvidence, and scarcity meet," he wrote, "charity and benevolence only could give relief."

Later, Marietta's earliest historian, Samuel P. Hildreth, was to write, "In this great scarcity it was wonderful how little there was of selfish-ness, and how generally kindness and good feeling abounded. Those who had more resources, lent, or gave, to those who had less."

One family in particular came to the rescue in a way never forgotten. Isaac and Rebecca Williams, emigrant farmers from Pennsylvania, who had settled on the Virginia side of the Ohio across from Marietta, were known and admired for their consistently abundant harvests. To those now starving Mr. Williams sold his corn at the usual price of 50 cents a bushel, instead of the then going price of $2.50. To the desperately poor, he let them have it without payment. To speculators who offered to buy all he had, he refused to sell even a bushel.

Joseph Barker, in his later reminiscences, would recount how two heads of families told Williams they had no bread and had come to get what corn they could with the little money they had.

> "How many is there of you?" said Mr. Williams [in Joseph Bark-er's account]. "Rising of twenty," was the reply. "*Dang it!*" says the old man, "there is a heap of you but you must have half a bushel a piece," and they had.

> "Those who had cows," wrote historian Hildreth, "divided the milk with their neighbors, especially where there were children.

> Sugar, or molasses, they had little of, as they had not kettles to boil the sap of the maple. . . . The Ohio Company, with a liberal-ity worthy of all praise, assisted many poor families with small loans of money, or the suffering would have been much greater: with this they could occasionally get provisions from boats de-scending the Ohio. . . .

> The matrons of the colony, in a little sober "chit-chat" over a cup of spice-bush tea, without any sugar, and very little milk,

concluded if they lived ever again to enjoy a supply of whole-some food for their children and selves, they would never com-plain of their fare, be it ever so coarse and homely.

That November came an outbreak of measles in Marietta that would take the lives of still more children. To add further to the miseries, a sick man and his family were put ashore from a boat heading downriver to Kentucky and his trouble proved to be the ever-dreaded smallpox, which had not made its appearance until then.

A town meeting was called at the stockade. A separate log cabin was quickly put up for the sick man, and nurse Mary Owen, the first woman to settle in Marietta, took up her duties, only to contract the disease herself.

When the sick man died, another town meeting was hurriedly called and more cabins went up farther off, in back of the big cornfield on the plain, where more people could be inoculated and cared for, and among them was Joseph Barker. To his wife, Elizabeth, who remained in Belpre, where it was thought to be safer, he was happy to report, "I am living in a little, clean log-cabin that is six feet wide, seven feet long, and four and a half high. We make out to sit up, but cannot stand straight." Complaints he had none. "We lodge very well."

Six more died of the disease. Two of the hundred or more inoculated also died. Much to the relief of the many who knew her, Mary Owen recovered to live many more years, though with evidence of what she had been through marking her face.

Joseph Barker, too, lived on.

———•·•———

At the start of the new year, 1790, Governor Arthur St. Clair took up residence with his family in the southwestern blockhouse of the stock-ade, newly finished quarters with, as carpenter Barker proudly noted, "good, smooth poplar floors, doors, casings, etc., and a brick chimney with three fireplaces below and three above."

With the return of spring, families scoured the woods for edible weeds and herbs—nettles or purslane, which was preferred. They collected the tender shoots of pigeon berry and potatoes. Then came the earliest of the garden vegetables—peas, beans, radishes, squash—followed by what turned out to be a bumper crop of corn.

By early July the famine had ended, the settlement had survived, and for all the difficulties still to be faced the supply of food was not to be one of them ever again. Rather, there were to be continuing ample surpluses to sell.

That March, Rufus Putnam had been appointed territorial judge by President Washington, as the replacement for General Samuel Parsons, and this along with the bright prospects that returned with spring, led him to conclude it was time at long last to bring his family west to the settlement. A handsome, new, decidedly New England–looking home with clapboard siding, brick fireplaces, four bedrooms, and attic was ready for them at the stockade.

In June he headed back to Rutland to lead another westward expedition, including this time his wife, two sons, and five daughters, as well as some fifteen others who had contracted "Ohio Fever," two men hired as teamsters, two wagons, two yoke of oxen, and half a dozen cattle. One of the Rufus Putnam wagons was loaded with as many as fifty varieties of apple seeds, as one of the requirements of the Ohio Company stipulated that settlers plant an orchard of that many apple trees.

While in Massachusetts Putnam had written to Manasseh Cutler urging him to come to Marietta. "Your company is much wished for by the best people." But Cutler, immersed in his pastoral duties, his school, his numerous intellectual pursuits, was not to return, then or ever again.

The journey of Putnam and his family took eight weeks. "At length we arrived at Marietta about nine in the morning," remembered one of the party. "All the settlers gave us a hearty welcome."

———·—·———

For Joseph Barker, family life was just getting started. His wife, Elizabeth, who was still living downriver at Belpre with her father and mother, had given birth to a son, Joseph Jr., and that spring he had moved them to be with him in Marietta. Fully employed now by Rufus Putnam, he was building pickets at the stockade where, in December 1790, he and his family moved in.

Also, as was expected of all men fit to serve, Barker had joined the Marietta militia. The territorial law made it the duty of the troops to assemble at the stockade parade ground for inspection every Sunday morning at ten. After this, with fife and drum, Generals Putnam and Tupper and Colonel "Big Buckeye" Sproat in the lead, sword drawn, would march to the place of public service in the northwest blockhouse.

As he was proud to explain, Barker had been made orderly sergeant. It was his role to keep attendance, "Call every man's name, examine their arms and ammunition . . . note down and report delinquencies." In case of an alarm, those who were armed among the congregation were to rush out of the meeting to face the danger.

In remarkably little time, a matter of mere months, young Barker had taken a notable place in the community as both a highly skilled worker and a dutiful citizen.

III.

Serious trouble of a different kind had been festering beneath the surface for some three years, all the way back to the agreement reached with Congress on the Northwest Ordinance of 1787, that, in addition to the Ohio Company, there would be a speculative real estate venture called the Scioto Company involving more than four million acres farther down the Ohio to the confluence of the Scioto River. In the time since the Scioto Company had come under suspicion.

For some unknown reason, William Duer, the secretary of the Board of Treasury and originator of the Scioto idea, put in place as the company's sales agent a gentlemanly Connecticut lawyer, Joel Barlow, who was also known as a poet. Barlow went off to France to market the Scioto land and there took on a business partner named William Playfair, whom he described as "an Englishman of a bold and enterprising spirit" and "a good imagination." As it turned out, Playfair did not play fair.

In Marietta were several people, like James Varnum, who had been angry at Manasseh Cutler, not because the Scioto Company was a mistake or an enterprise of questionable integrity, but because they had not been included, and told him so.

Deeply offended, Cutler insisted he had done nothing inappropriate and by all evidence he had not. In a heartfelt letter to Rufus Putnam dated November 18, 1788, Cutler declared, "I view my character as much dearer than my life. And the man who would deprive me of it I consider infinitely worse than a highway robber—for it is what cannot be restored especially in a matter of public trust."

In France, Barlow and Playfair prepared a "prospectus" on the rivers Ohio and Scioto and including Cutler's earlier pamphlet along with numerous additions and embellishments. Playfair's "good imagination" had been put to work. Not surprisingly, no mention was made of freezing winters or starvation or smallpox or the threat posed by the native tribes. Instead, it was a climate altogether "wholesome and delightful, frost even in winter almost entirely unknown." There was "venison in plenty, the pursuit of which is uninterrupted by wolves, foxes, lions, or tigers." Added to that, there were "no taxes to pay, no military services to be performed."

In 1789, France was in the early throes of revolution, and as a French geographer would write, "Nothing was talked of in every social circle, but the paradise that was opened to Frenchmen in the western wilderness; the free and happy life to be led on the blissful banks of the Ohio."

Sales of Scioto land went fast, and in February 1790, some 600 French emigrants—men, women, and a few children—believing they owned land in the Ohio paradise, boarded five chartered ships and sailed for America. After three months at sea they landed at Alexandria, Virginia, on the 1st of May, only to discover they had been defrauded.

The Scioto Company owned no land in Ohio and had no money to pay Congress for it. William Playfair had made off with the money they invested and disappeared. Joel Barlow, it seems, had also been duped by him.

So the land belonged still to the government of the United States. The Scioto Company and William Duer had failed. Only Duer could be held accountable and when President Washington intervened to tell Duer something must be done at once, Duer arranged for Rufus Putnam to prepare to receive the emigrants on Ohio Company lands, to erect the necessary buildings, and, in addition, provide sufficient provisions for a year, which they, Duer and Putnam, were to wind up paying themselves out of their own funds.

In mid-October, after an arduous journey overland and downstream on the Ohio on six Kentucky flatboats, the French pilgrims, literally "strangers in a strange land," arrived finally at Marietta. Some would choose to stay, the rest proceeded downstream to a point three miles below the mouth of the Kanawha River, which was to be their new home.

To the local populace, not surprisingly, they were an immense curiosity. Exhausted, out-of-sorts, they grumbled on effusively in rapid French such as never heard in Marietta. "There might have been more tongues at Babel," commented Joseph Barker, "but they never went faster."

Wanting no delay in the establishment of the new colony downriver, Rufus Putnam brought in a crew of forty men to make a clearing and build eighty rough log cabins in four rows, twenty to a row, and a high stockade fence with two-story blockhouses at each corner. It was, as said, a primitive little frontier village facing the river. The cabins had dirt floors only. Deep forest closed in on three sides.

Much there was still to be done and in background and working skills, the emigrants who came ashore were hardly prepared. They were French artisans, artists, craftsmen, jewelers, hatters, watchmakers, silversmiths, city people from Paris and Lyon. A few were noblemen. Hardly any had ever held an ax or a gun before, or skinned an animal.

But if they knew nothing of gardening, some had brought books on the subject from France.

Still, most were optimistic and with pride named their settlement Gallipolis, "City of Gauls," or French Town, as Americans would refer to it. Whether it could survive remained to be seen. When it came to clearing more of the land back from the river their initial struggles to find the best way were to be long remembered by locals.

"I have seen half a dozen at work in taking down a tree," wrote one witness, "some pulling ropes fastened to the branches, while others were cutting around it like beavers." Several of the Frenchmen were killed when crushed by trees they were cutting down.

Though many of the French would give up and move on to settle elsewhere, far more remained, grateful for the new life, given what they had left behind, and confident, even optimistic about the future. As one wrote, "To some the surrounding woods might appear frightful deserts; to me they are the paradise of nature; no hosts of greedy priests; no seas of blood to wade through; all is quiet."

The Scioto Company left the French settlers largely to fend for themselves. William Duer, creator of the Scioto Company, would wind up in debtors' prison until his death in 1797.

Meantime, significant changes had taken place in Marietta. Arthur St. Clair had decided to move the office of the territory governor farther west, down the Ohio, to a village known as Losantiville, meaning "town located opposite the mouth of the Licking," a name St. Clair promptly changed to Cincinnati in honor of the famous Revolutionary officers' society. There also the army had begun construction of Fort Washington, as a base of operations against the Indians.

Winthrop Sargent, too, as secretary of the territory, now chose to make his home in Cincinnati, a move he was to regret, finding the cost of living and uncultured, low moral tone of the place hard for him to bear. To compensate, it would seem, he took greater interest than ever in botany and the historic mounds of Cincinnati, and spent time with increasing correspondence with the naturalist Joseph Bartram and the Massachusetts Historical Society.

On Monday, December 20, 1790, Rufus Putnam sat down to write a long and important letter to President Washington.

"It was as late as the 5th of November before I arrived here with my family, since which I have been so busily engaged in preparing for the winter that I have not been able to attend minutely to any other subject, but in general I have observed that our crops have been very fine, that the spirit of industry and enterprise among the people is as great as ever, and the improvements and buildings which have been made are truly surprising."

He reported also that the emigrants from France had arrived and were settling in, but it appeared they were not "calculated for the *meridian of the woods.*"

From there he moved on to what had become his overriding concern.

As to Indian matters we are fearful that the spring will open by a general attack on the frontiers unless prevented by Government carrying a war into the enemy's country. It is possible that the Shawnees etc. may be for peace but I consider it very doubtful. From all the circumstances which I have been able to collect respecting the late campaign I do not believe the Indians have had sufficient drubbing to induce them to ask a peace, and every day I am more and more confirmed in this opinion by the Delawares and other Indians keeping aloof.

The "late campaign" referred to had taken place that fall well to the west on the Miami River and had been a disaster that only made the situation worse. A makeshift frontier army of almost 1,500 men, regulars and militia, under the command of General Josiah Harmar, had set out to punish the Miami and Shawnees. Harmar was known to be a drinker, prone to "indulge . . . to excess in a convivial glass," as his friend Secretary of War Henry Knox expressed it. Both Knox and President Washington had been greatly concerned about this and as it turned out Harmar and his men were soundly defeated by a much smaller force led by the Miami war chief, Little Turtle. Of the regulars and militia 183 were dead or missing. The Indian loss had been fewer than a dozen.

One regular officer called the militia's behavior "scandalous." Many of the militiamen, he said, "never fired a shot but ran off," and left a few regulars to be sacrificed. Some of them never halted until they crossed the Ohio.

Even more ominous to Rufus Putnam, as he stressed to the president, was the vanished presence of the numerous Delawares and Wyandots who for so long had been part of the everyday life in the settlement. Except for two familiar women, none was to be seen any longer, and word was they had reason to move north, some eighty miles up the Muskingum. Trouble was coming. Of this Putnam was certain.

"When or where it will fall God only knows," he continued in his letter to the president, "but I trust, Sir, that in the multiplicity of public concerns which claim your attention, our little colony will not be forgotten. . . .

> I believe you will not think me vain and presumptuous when I say that the inhabitants that compose this settlement have as great a claim to protectionism as any under the Federal Government. A great proportion of us served our country through the war . . . and being good subjects in general, as well as [being] disposed to live in friendship with our savage neighbors if possible.

Less than two weeks later, on Sunday, January 2, 1791, a calamity such as Rufus Putnam so feared took place on the eastern bank of the Muskingum, thirty miles upstream from Marietta.

———

The location was called Big Bottom, for the generous size of the rich bottomland at that point along the river, which gave it great appeal as a place for a settlement. Even so, Putnam and others of the Ohio Company strongly opposed any venturing out that far at this time. Moreover, those determined to establish themselves there were young and little acquainted with native warfare. But impatient to get started and confident in their ability to cope with whatever they had to face, the young settlers went ahead.

All were single men from New England, except for one Virginian, an experienced hunter with a wife and two children. They put up a log blockhouse that, in an emergency, could accommodate them all, and in doing this made the first of several crucial mistakes. They failed to chink the building between the logs. That the weather was extremely cold, the river frozen, may explain this in part.

The second mistake was posting no sentry after dark, and for this there was no excuse. Nor had any dogs been left outside to sound an alarm. There was little or no order. Rifles were left lying about in different places. No system of defense had been worked out.

Two nearby cabins housed four other men, Francis and Isaac Choate in one, Asa and Eleazer Bullard in the other.

It would be said that the raiding party of Delawares and Wyandots that arrived on the old path on the opposite side of the river on the afternoon of Sunday, January 2, had not been aware of there being a settlement at Big Bottom.

> From the ridge [reads an account by Samuel Hildreth] they had a view of all that part of the bottom, and could see how the men were occupied, and the defenseless condition of the block house. After completing their reconnaissance and holding a council as to the mode of attack, they crossed the river on the ice a little above, and divided their warriors into two divisions; the larger one to assault the block house, and the smaller one to make prisoners of the men in the upper cabin without alarming those below.

The plan was skillfully arranged and promptly executed.

At the Choate cabin the raiders found those inside at supper. A few of the Indians stepped through the door in a friendly manner and were offered something to eat. They at once pounced on and bound the settlers and told them they were prisoners.

At the blockhouse the slaughter took but minutes. One stout Indian smashed open the door and stood by to keep it open while others outside opened fire through the unchinked logs.

The inhabitants had also been at supper. One man, Zebulon Troop from Massachusetts, was frying meat and fell dead in the fire. Several others fell at the discharge. The Indians then rushed in and killed the rest with tomahawks.

Everything happened so fast there was no resistance, except for the wife of the Virginian Isaac Meeks, a stout backwoods woman who, seeing her husband shot dead and her children killed with tomahawks, seized an ax and in rage struck a blow at the head of the Indian who opened the door. Only a slight turn of the head saved his skull and her ax sliced through his cheek and into the shoulder. She was instantly killed with the tomahawk of another of the Indians.

A young man named John Stacy tried to escape out a window. When spotted by Indians outside as he clambered onto the roof, he begged to be spared, saying he was the only one left. They shot and killed him.

After the slaughter ended, the scalps taken, and the raiders proceeded to round up the plunder, sixteen-year-old Philip Stacy was discovered hiding under a pile of bedding in the corner of the room. He, it was decided, would be spared and along with the two Choates taken away as captives.

As for the Bullards, they, at the first sound of the Indians near their cabin, had snatched up their rifles and barely escaped out the door and into the woods. It was they who would sound the alarm.

Fourteen people had been killed in the attack. Before leaving the scene the raiders piled up the bodies and lit the blockhouse on fire, and expecting all traces of what had taken place to go up in flame, they went on their way. But it was a building of still green logs, and except for the floor and roof, it did not burn. Neither did the bodies, though most were charred and blackened beyond recognition.

———— • ————

Word of the massacre spread rapidly and struck terror as nothing had since the first settlers came ashore at the Point. The time had come, said Rufus Putnam, "to prepare for the worst."

CHAPTER FOUR

Havoc

Beware of surprise! You know how the Indians fight us.

—GEORGE WASHINGTON

*The sad and dreadful havoc of our army at the
westward cast a gloom over us all.*

—ABIGAIL ADAMS

I.

For more than three years Rufus Putnam had devoted all he had
in time and strength to his frontier settlement on the Ohio and
despite continuing setbacks and adversities of every variety he
had seen progress such as had, until then, been only talked about or
dreamed of.

Now, suddenly, all seemed threatened with annihilation. The Indians were claiming that by the time spring arrived there would be no
more smoke coming from a settler's cabin anywhere along the Ohio.
As Putnam himself said, "A horrid savage war stares us in the face."

How or where it would begin, how long it might go on, there was no telling.

The situation at Marietta was critical. Most of the troops stationed at Fort Harmar had been sent downriver at the time of General Harmar's unfortunate attack on the Indians, leaving behind only a small detachment comprised mainly of invalids. But Putnam also knew that in the face of adversity the people of Marietta had, as said, "spunk to the backbone."

On January 5, he called a special meeting in the northwest blockhouse, where it was resolved that additional fortifications were necessary for the safety and defense of the settlement, these to be built without delay on the Point at Marietta, and at Belpre, and that six experienced backwoods hunters be hired as rangers or "spies" to go out daily into the surrounding wilderness over a route of roughly twenty miles to watch for any signs of a surprise attack. Meantime, all who could in Marietta were to take up residence after dark inside the stockade, which itself was to be much improved by additional defenses.

Under orders from Governor St. Clair, Campus Martius was to be kept under strict discipline. The men, divided into squads, were called to their posts at daylight, while through the night four other squads kept watch at the bastions. Sentries were set and the watchword cried every half hour. Cannon were mounted in the northeast and southwest blockhouses, and especially to be fired as alarm signals to residents at home or at work in the surrounding fields, who were then to go directly to their alarm posts within the walls.

Rufus Putnam was said to have had a stormy temper—it was thought to have been one of his few human flaws—but seldom if ever seen. Then on January 6, in a letter to the governor of Massachusetts, Caleb Strong, the general exploded in outrage at the apparent indifference back home to the situation in which he and the people of Marietta found themselves. Because of "the prudence of our people, the friendship with which we treated the natives, we remained in a state of general quiet without any apprehension from the Delawares and other tribes, till the [Harmar] expedition. . . .

"If therefore we had no claim to the protection of government before, I trust we have now.

> For a parent to invite his children to gather plumbs under a hornet's nest, and then beat the nest without giving them notice to get out of the way or covering them, while he provokes the hornets, has something so cruel in its nature that the mind revolts at the idea. . . . I ask are not allegiance and protection reciprocal? Have we not given the most unequivocal proof of our allegiance and love of our country with constitutional government, through the revolution and ever since? Why then in the name of God will you not protect us?

Two days later on January 8, Putnam sent another frantic letter, this time to President Washington. The situation had become "truly critical," he wrote. The garrison at Fort Harmar, consisting by then of little more than twenty men, offered no protection, the number of men in the settlement capable of bearing arms did not exceed 287, and many of these were badly armed.

> The situation of our people is nearly as follows:
> At Marietta are about 80 houses in the distance of one mile with scattering houses for three miles up the Ohio; a set of mills at Duck Creek four miles distant and another mill two miles from Marietta; up the Muskingum 22 miles distant is a settlement of about 20 families; and on Wolf Creek about 18 miles from Marietta is a set of mills where are five families. Down the Ohio and opposite Little Kenhawa, commences the settlement of Belpre, which extends on the bank of the river with little interruption about twelve miles, and contains six blockhouses and can muster about sixty fighting men. Before the late disaster [Big Bottom] we had several other settlements which had commenced, and are now entirely abandoned. . . . [I] beg leave with the greatest deference to observe that unless govern-

ment speedily sends a body of troops for our protection we are a ruined people.

. . . and only observe further, that our present situation is truly distressing. I do therefore most earnestly implore the protection of government for myself and friends inhabiting these wilds of America. To this we consider ourselves justly entitled and rest assured that so far as you, sir, have the means in your power, you will grant it.

In yet another letter written the same day, to Secretary of War Henry Knox, Putnam said much the same as he had to the president, but adding, "better that [the] government disband their troops now in the [Northwest] country, and give it up altogether than be wasting the public money in supporting a few troops totally inadequate to the purpose of giving peace to the territory."

———·•·———

The weather was cold and miserable, with ice on the Ohio and extreme tension everywhere as work on the defenses proceeded with all possible speed. Still, nothing out of the ordinary happened as the weeks passed, nothing until March.

On Sunday, March 13, two of the rangers employed to keep watch against surprise attack, Captain Joseph Rogers and Edward Henderson, on return from duty up the Muskingum were suddenly attacked a mile north of the stockade. Four Indians rose up from behind a log and shot Rogers through the chest. As he fell Rogers told Henderson to run for his life, he himself was "a dead man."

Henderson managed to escape, but Rogers was later found both dead and scalped and there was to be much talk about him and the ominous dream he had had the night before.

Rogers was a veteran soldier from Pennsylvania in his fifties who had seen much. He it was who had accompanied General Parsons in the canoe when Parsons was killed trying to shoot the rapids on the Beaver

River. Calm by nature, he was not one known for flights of fancy, but as he had told others earlier that morning, he was much shaken by a dream he had had the night before that he was to kill an Indian that day, or be killed himself. On his way out the gate he had remarked to the guards, "Well, boys, today we take a scalp, or lose one."

Alarm guns and cannon were fired at the stockade. It was not just that Rogers had been killed but that the Indians were said to have chased Henderson all the way to the gate.

"All was consternation," wrote Joseph Barker, who, with his family, was still quartered in the garrison, and who went on to describe the scene in his own distinctive way:

> Everyone made immediately for his alarm post. . . . The first person for admittance at the central blockhouse was Col. E. Sproat with a box of papers, then came some young men with their arms, then a woman with her bed and children, then came old Mr. William Moulton, from Newburyport, aged 70, with his leather apron full of old goldsmiths tools and tobacco. His daughter Anna brought the China teapot, cups and saucers. Lydia brought the great Bible, but when all were in mother was missing. Where was mother? She must be killed. No, says Lydia, mother said she would not leave a house looking so, she would put things a little to rights, and then she would come. Directly mother came, bringing the looking glass, knives, forks, and spoons, etc. . . . All returned to their homes in the morning and a party from the Point and Campus Martius went out about 10 o'clock, and brought in Capt. Rogers and buried him.

———·◆·———

With the advance of spring more scouts were ambushed on duty. Indians killed Benoni Hurlburt at Belpre, James Kelly at Bellville, and captured his small son, Joseph. On the Virginia side of the Ohio, seven miles from Marietta, four white men were killed, three others taken prisoners. On

June 16, just above the mouth of the Muskingum, the elderly Mathew Kerr from Ireland, one of the earliest of Marietta settlers, was gunned down and scalped.

It was a loss deeply felt in the settlement and shortly afterward that summer of 1791, Kerr's son, Hamilton, and several others happened on a party of six Indians near Mill Creek and, as would be said, Hamilton was unable to resist the opportunity to gratify his revenge. He not only shot and killed an Indian but cut off his head, fixed it to the end of a pole, and marched it back to the stockade.

Horace Nye, one of Ichabod Nye's several sons, would remember as a small boy going out the gate with his mother and seeing Kerr and others bringing home the trophy. "Some whites are more savage than the Indians," Horace would write recalling the scene.

In Philadelphia, meantime, President Washington made certain Congress became well aware of General Putnam's call for help. There was talk of raising an army of 4,000 or more.

On May 3, Congress, having decided something had to be done, authorized Governor St. Clair to raise a force of 2,000 to put down the native confederacy and to do so without delay. The major general appointed to command the army was Arthur St. Clair, who was also to remain governor of the territory.

It was a tall order. The government had virtually no troops or money and the Ohio frontier, "the far west," was in itself no easy matter to contend with, Indians or no Indians. And then there was the choice of St. Clair to take command.

A native of Scotland who had come to America as a young officer in the British Army, he had married an American, Phoebe Bayard of Boston, and with money inherited from her estate purchased 4,000 acres in the Ligonier Valley of western Pennsylvania, making him then the largest resident landowner west of the Allegheny Mountains.

At the start of the Revolution he had enlisted at once in the American army. Rising rapidly from the rank of colonel to brigadier general, he was with Washington at the battles of Trenton and Princeton. However, when put in command of Fort Ticonderoga, a stronghold widely believed to be impregnable, he ordered its evacuation, a decision that, as said, "filled the public mind with much dismay." Though exonerated by a court-martial that followed, he was to receive no further assignment of consequence for the remainder of the war.

Many on the frontier thought him arrogant and overly determined to dominate. Further, by that spring of 1791 he was at fifty-five noticeably aged, overweight and in poor health, suffering from ague and gout. Much of the time the pain of swelling joints caused by gout was such that he could hardly walk.

In early May during a visit to Fort Washington at Cincinnati he found the quantity of arms and other military supplies available insufficient for a major campaign.

Many of those on hand were hard at work. Indeed, the fort had "as much appearance of a large manufactory on the inside, as it had of a military post on the outside." An armory had to be built since the arms of the detachment were nearly all in bad order. Blacksmiths, carpenters, harness makers, colliers, wheelwrights were all in great need.

The expedition was supposed to have been under way by July 10. With time running out, it became even more apparent how much had still to be done. Weeks passed. Pressure from Philadelphia grew greater. "The President of the United States still continues anxious that you should at the earliest moment, commence your operations," wrote Secretary of War Knox to St. Clair on August 4. Again on August 11 and again on August 25, Knox wrote to say how greatly the president lamented the delays.

The new troops left much to be desired as to material for an army soon to embark on a campaign into the unfamiliar wilderness of enemy country. They consisted largely of men collected from the streets and jails of eastern cities bribed into service with money and whiskey. Many of the officers, too, were seen to be "totally unacquainted with the business in which they were engaged." The quartermaster and contractors in place were clearly well below standards.

To General Josiah Harmar, it was "a matter of astonishment . . . that the commanding general [St. Clair], who was acknowledged to be perfectly competent, should think of hazarding . . . the lives of so many others." But General Harmar was out of favor with the president and secretary of war and his views were no longer considered.

The plan was to proceed north some 170 miles to the Maumee River, building a road through the dense forest as they went, all of which was certain to be slow-going. But one of the few positive lessons learned from the Harmar expedition was that building such a road was possible.

Little or nothing was yet known of the size or makeup of the native forces to be confronted, or who was in command. General St. Clair was known to have little knowledge of or interest in Indians, and had given the matter no serious attention. His attitude seems to have been that so long as he did not encounter the enemy he need not worry. The problem could be dealt with if and when the occasion should arise.

Until then the worst defeat ever suffered by an army in battle with American natives occurred in 1755, during the French and Indian War. The British general Edward Braddock, in command of some 1,400 British regulars and 700 American provincials, including young George Washington, had been ambushed and slaughtered in a heavily wooded ravine about eight miles from Pittsburgh, then the French Fort Duquesne.

Thirty-three years later, when on the way to Marietta to take up his role as the first governor of the Northwest Territory, General St. Clair had been escorted from Pittsburgh to Marietta by young Ebenezer Denny. But before departing down the Ohio, Denny took St. Clair for a visit to Braddock's Field, where the bones of the victims were still to be seen scattered through the woods.

As St. Clair's new command was now organized, Denny was to be with him almost constantly. Whether they ever recalled together their long past visit to the scene of Braddock's defeat neither is known to have recorded.

But months earlier, back in Philadelphia, at the close of a meeting between Washington, Knox, and St. Clair, just as St. Clair was about to return to Ohio to assume command, Washington's parting words to him, as Washington would recall, had been, "Beware of surprise! You know how the Indians fight us."

As St. Clair organized his command, Winthrop Sargent, now to be Colonel Sargent, was his adjutant general, Major Denny, his aide-de-camp, and so it was to be three from Marietta largely in control.

Most worrisome to Winthrop Sargent was the obvious lack of the essential "stamina of soldiers" so evident in the army itself.

> Picked up and recruited from the offscourings of large towns and cities; enervated by idleness, debaucheries and every species of vice, it was impossible they could have been made competent to the arduous duties of Indian warfare. . . . An extraordinary aversion to service was conspicuous among them. . . . They were, moreover, badly clothed, badly paid and badly fed.

They had signed on for $2 a month, plus a whiskey allotment.

By early September the greater part of the assembled troops were encamped on the banks of the Great Miami River, some twenty miles north of Fort Washington, where St. Clair began construction of another fortification to be named Fort Hamilton.

By the end of September, the expedition that was supposed to have been under way by July 10, had still to get started, and morale among the troops grew worse by the day. On the night of October 3, one sergeant and twenty-five men deserted. The day after nine more followed.

Finally, on October 4, with a great roll of drums, St. Clair's army was on the march from Fort Hamilton, though not until noon because of certain "deficiencies" in packhorses.

The army that was supposed to have numbered more than 4,000, then 2,000, now comprised approximately 1,700, and with it went some 200 camp followers, consisting of wives, mistresses, washerwomen, prostitutes, and a scattering of children with pets.

II.

The advance proceeded with much racket of drums, barking dogs, cattle bellowing, and innumerable undisciplined soldiers shouting and cursing, in addition to the constant crashing of trees being felled ahead. The clamor was intended, in the hope that a lot of noise and show made on the march might deter the enemy from daring to attack so mighty a force.

Progress was slow. Not only was the forest dense with giant trees, but it was a part of Ohio about which little was known. St. Clair would later explain, "We had no guides, not a single person being found in the country, who had ever been through it, and both the geography and topography were utterly unknown."

The army crossed the Great Miami with little delay, the river in that season being quite low. But beyond the river, clearing a way for a cavalcade of packhorses, oxen, troops, and artillery proved extremely difficult. By day's end they had progressed all of three miles. On the second day, the woods everywhere were so "compact" as to make the opening of a road most "tedious." Even when marching single file they had to cut their way every step.

Fair weather followed day after day. Still the advance remained no better than about four miles a day, the country getting even "rougher," crowded with giant oaks, hickory, ash, walnut, sugar maples, and "a considerable portion of beech," all, as Winthrop Sargent noted, indicating a "very rich land."

Not until October 12, after more than a week on the move, were the first signs of Indians seen, many tracks and the traces of camps old and recent.

The day after, the army having advanced only a mile, General St. Clair called halt, having decided they had reached an acceptable, if not ideal location on a low knoll for another fort. By this time they had come sixty-eight miles from Fort Washington, forty-four miles from Fort Hamilton. There the army would remain encamped for another ten days.

Two hundred men were put to work clearing land and laying a foundation. It was to be a small, square log fort.

The good weather did not hold. Late in the day of October 14, heavy rains fell and continued through the night, the next day, and the following night. "Cold and wet." "Weather very bad," recorded Major Denny.

The night of October 21, came a "very severe" frost and "ice upon the waters a half inch thick."

The troops, having been issued substandard tents, suffered severely. The substandard shoes issued were by now falling apart. Food was running low, their supply of bread nearly gone, due, as Denny noted, to "unpardonable mismanagement" in the provisions department. Of no small concern, too, was a serious decline in liquor.

To face the emergency all the horses with the army were to be sent back to Fort Washington for supplies. When some of the men were asked to go with the horses, their reply was that if sent they would not return.

On October 23, two artillery men who intended to desert to the Indians were, on orders from General St. Clair, tried, sentenced, and promptly hanged. Another man was hanged for shooting a comrade, and two more found sleeping on duty were subjected to fifty lashes each.

All such miseries and suffering were greatly compounded by the physical incapacities and sufferings of the commander himself, whose physical condition had worsened. The excruciating grip of the gout had gotten to the point where he could no longer walk and had to be lifted onto his horse.

On October 28, with the new fort nearly completed, a caravan of seventy-four horses loaded with 12,000 pounds of flour arrived, along with a few more horses loaded with clothing, and all to "good effect."

Clearly, the time for a decision had arrived—to push on to confront the enemy, about whom nothing was known, no matter the condition of morale or inexperience of the army, or call off the campaign and make an orderly withdrawal while that was still possible.

"Our prospects are gloomy," wrote Sargent, ". . . with the difficulties of transportation every day increasing by the season and to become still greater, as we add to our distance, may make events fatal to the whole army."

To what degree Sargent and Denny voiced such grave concerns to St. Clair is not known, but with so much at stake, it seems unlikely they would have held back. And just as surely, St. Clair's past decision to abandon Fort Ticonderoga and the disapproval it had brought down on him must have figured now in his decision to push on, which, as he confided to Sargent, he saw as the one and only way to hold the army together. It was his secret design, he said, to get them deeper into enemy country, where the men "may be afraid to return."

———•·•———

As they were soon to learn, the force that lay in wait was large, highly experienced in wilderness warfare, and led by two exceptional commanders: the Miami war chief Little Turtle, who had so roundly defeated General Harmar, and the Shawnee war chief Blue Jacket, regarded by his contemporaries as a leader of exceptional wisdom and courage. In addition, they were thoroughly supplied with information about the advancing army by an ample number of scouts that included the young Shawnee warrior, Tecumseh.

In total, the native force numbered some 1,000 warriors, representing eight more tribes other than the Miami and Shawnee—Delawares and Wyandots, Ottawas, Kickapoos, Chippewas, Pottawatomies, Mohawks from Canada, and Creeks from the south. Among them also, reportedly as an observer only, was the infamous Revolutionary War "turncoat," Simon Girty, who had been captured in boyhood by Senecas, raised by them, and was still in the employ of the British.

"The Indians were never in greater heart to meet their enemy, nor more sure of their success," Girty wrote. "They are determined to drive them to the Ohio."

———•·•———

Incredibly, for General St. Clair, the unseen enemy was still a matter of little concern. On the first day of November, in a dispatch to Secretary

Knox, he was happy to report, "The few Indians that have been seen were hunters only, who we fell upon by accident."

The army by then was again on the move, having pushed on in fair weather the morning of October 30. A small contingent of soldiers ("all men unable to march") had been left to maintain the new stockade, Fort Jefferson. In one day, October 31, no fewer than sixty of those on the march deserted.

As troubling as almost anything was the specter of the commander whose physical condition had so deteriorated that he now had to be carried like a corpse in a litter strung between two horses.

During the march of November 2, in bitter weather all day, the army, hungry, cold, reduced by sickness and desertion, made eight miles. On November 3, in a "small flight of snow," it marched another eight miles through low, damp woodlands, to a cramped piece of rising ground close by a branch of the Wabash River, and there the advance came to a halt.

During the course of the night detachments of soldiers were supposed to have gone out to determine the enemy's whereabouts and strength, but did not, on the excuse they were too tired. As the night passed separate shots were heard, fired "principally by our own sentinels, sometimes, no doubt, at the enemy," wrote Winthrop Sargent, "but oftener, probably, without any object whatever."

III.

The following morning—Friday, November 4—was intensely cold, but as Sargent recorded, the sky "unclouded." The sun was not yet up. Campfires were blazing.

The troops had already paraded as usual and been dismissed for breakfast, when, only minutes after sunrise, the woods to the front on the other side of the Wabash suddenly erupted with the yells of Indians, a sound that most of the soldiers, including Colonel Sargent, had never heard until then. "Not terrible, as has been represented," Sargent thought, "but more resembling an infinitude of horse bells suddenly opening to you than any other sound I could compare it to."

All at once, a great number of painted warriors burst from cover and started firing, and almost at once the militia positioned several hundred yards in front, beyond the river, turned and fled. Then, Sargent wrote, "Close upon the heels of the flying militia followed the Indians," estimated to have numbered at least 300.

The rest of the troops were under arms almost instantly and "smart fire" was returned just as fire from the enemy began coming in from all sides. It was like nothing the army had been prepared for. Such was the noise, smoke, and speed of all that was happening, that all sense of order or direction vanished in an instant.

"The enemy from the front filed off to the right and left, and completely surrounded the camp, killed and cut off nearly all the guards, and approached close to the lines," wrote Ebenezer Denny.

> They advanced from one tree, log, or stump to another, under cover of the smoke of our fire. The artillery and musketry made a tremendous noise, but did little execution. The Indians seemed to brave everything, and when fairly fixed around us they made no noise other than their fire, which they kept up very constant and which seldom failed to tell.

At one point, they took possession of part of the encampment, but on being exposed on what was comparatively clear ground, they were soon repulsed by troops led by General St. Clair himself on foot, despite all his agonies.

When the attack came he had been in his camp bed. He had hurriedly put on his cocked hat, and greatcoat, and tottered out of his tent. With the help of three or four men, he had tried to mount a horse, but the animal, frightened by the gunfire, kept bolting, then was shot in the head and instantly killed. When another horse rushed into place, it, too, was shot and killed before St. Clair could be hoisted into the saddle. Refusing to wait any longer, he hobbled off on foot, his pains forgotten, he later claimed.

The battalions in the rear charged several times, but the attackers, utterly fearless, only turned and fired back. "Indeed, they seemed not to fear anything we could do," wrote Ebenezer Denny.

> They could skip out of reach of the bayonet and return, as they pleased. They were visible only when raised by a charge. The ground was literally covered with the dead.

Atrocities were to be seen everywhere. Wounded men had been scalped while still alive, then flung onto campfires. Dead settler women lay scattered, some of their bodies cut in two, breasts cut off, then heaped on campfires.

"The Indians fought like hellhounds," said another soldier. But then so, too, did a number of soldiers. When an Indian fell wounded and tried to crawl away, a colonel named Darke, his sword drawn, rushed after him and cut his head off.

Ohio, with its promise of the Garden of Eden, had suddenly become Hell on Earth.

"I wish I could describe that battle," one rifleman later wrote, "but I have not the power. . . . It seems like a wild horrid dream in which whites and savages . . . were all mixed together in mad confusion . . . melting away in smoke, fire, and blood amid groans, shouts, yells, shrieks."

The wounded were taken to the center, where it was thought to be most safe, and where many of those who had quit their posts unhurt had crowded together.

General St. Clair, with others of the officers, tried to rally these men, and twice succeeded in moving them back to the lines, where, being left with few experienced officers, they gave up the fight and crowded back to the center again.

Denny, who was in the thick of it, would write about all that he saw. Nothing, it seems, could induce those concentrated at the center to do anything in their own defense.

> As our lines were deserted the Indians contracted theirs until their shot centered from all points, and now meeting with little opposition, took more deliberate aim and did great execution.

Exposed as to a crossfire, men and officers were seen falling in every direction. The distress, too, of the wounded made the scene such as can scarcely be conceived.

A retreat had to be called. The battle had become a one-sided slaughter. A few minutes more and it would be too late. In Denny's words, "Delay was death."

The only hope was that the savages would be so taken up with plunder of the camp as not to follow after. No preparation could be made. Numbers of brave men must be left a sacrifice, there was no alternative.

Shortly past nine o'clock St. Clair gave the order. In a matter of minutes the army was in full desperate retreat, a scene of utter panic and chaos. Guns, ammunition, knapsacks were thrown aside, littering the road for miles.

A great number of the wounded were left behind, including General Richard Butler, who had been notably harsh with Indians in previous treaty negotiations and who had often been criticized for knowing so little about the Indians. Too severely wounded to be moved, Butler was left propped against a tree. Found by several of the warriors, he was tomahawked, scalped, and reportedly his heart cut out and divided into pieces to be distributed among the different tribes that fought in the battle.

Many more of the wounded left behind—men, women, and children—were massacred, their bodies desecrated.

One of the Delaware chiefs taking part in the battle was old Captain Pipe, who had once given such a warm welcome to Rufus Putnam and the others on their arrival at Marietta. According to his own account, he now distinguished himself differently, slaughtering white men until his arm was "weary with the work."

The hope that the enemy might pursue the army a short distance only, so exultant would they be over their triumph and the spoils left behind at the camp, proved to be what happened. The escaping survivors of the battle were pursued little more than a few miles and by only a few Indians, though those rushing headlong to get away were unaware of this.

Winthrop Sargent had been hit three times by gunshot and was to carry two musket balls in his hips for the rest of his life, yet he had kept in the thick of the battle the whole time.

As, too, had General St. Clair, who came through bearing no sign of it except that eight musket balls passed through his coat and hat. So exhausted and in such pain was he that he could barely sit straight, let alone stand. He had been hoisted onto the back of a comparably exhausted packhorse that could move no faster than a walk, and so the general had no choice but to follow at the rear of the desperate march. He, too, saw the whole scene as a total disaster. But then what could be done?

Having fought in and survived a battle lasting nearly four hours, having had little or nothing to eat since the night before, many of them suffering from wounds, the men moved on, hour after hour, mile after mile for twenty-nine miles to reach Fort Jefferson just after dark, only to find no supplies of food or medicine at hand, which left no choice but to keep going.

Those of the wounded or others unable to go on were lodged as comfortably as possible within the fort. "Accordingly," recorded Ebenezer Denny, "we set out a little after ten and continued our route [through the night] until within an hour of daylight, then halted and waited for day and until the rear came up.

> Moved on again about nine o'clock; the morning of the 5th we met the convoy [from Fort Hamilton]. Stopped [to provide] a sufficiency to subsist us to Fort Hamilton; sent the remainder on to [Fort] Jefferson under an additional escort of a captain and sixty men; proceeded, and at first water [creek] halted, partly cooked and ate for the first time since the night preceding the action. At one o'clock moved on, and continued our route until nine at night, when we halted and made fires within fifteen miles of Fort Hamilton. Marched again just before day [November 6], the General soon after rode on to the fort [Washington]. Troops reached [there] in the afternoon.

The battered, pitiful soldiers found little room awaiting them in the barracks. Told to set up camp nearby, they found themselves provided with almost nothing in the way of tents or food. So they moved in to the village of Cincinnati. "Every house in this town is filled with drunken soldiers and there seems one continued scene of confusion," reported Winthrop Sargent.

For days wounded soldiers kept staggering into camp, some in horrid condition. One was without his scalp, his skull crushed in two places by a tomahawk. General St. Clair was being housed within Fort Washington, so weak and exhausted he would not leave his room for two weeks.

———•—•———

St. Clair's Defeat, as the battle came to be known, had been a total disaster, worse than any suffered by the American army during the entire Revolution, and the greatest defeat of an army at the hands of natives until then, including Braddock's Defeat.

According to the count tabulated by Ebenezer Denny, the army losses numbered 623 dead, including 39 officers. In addition an estimated 200 others, men, women, and children, were killed. In all only three women survived. This made a total of 1,094 dead and wounded or well over half of the 1,400 Americans present at the scene.

The Indians lost no more than 21 dead and 40 wounded.

They had also acquired from the soldiers' abandoned encampment some 1,200 muskets, 163 axes, eight cannon, baggage wagons, and a mountain of camp equipment.

Exhausted and distraught as he was, Major Denny tried to determine in his mind why the massive effort had gone so wrong, and kept coming back to the warnings that General Harmar, with all his experience with failure, had voiced at the start. On November 9, in the privacy of his journal, Denny wrote at length on the matter and while never fixing the blame on General St. Clair by name, clearly he saw it as a case of repeated bad judgment and bad decisions made one after another from the beginning.

Well before the St. Clair campaign got under way, General Harmar had seen "with what material the bulk of the army was composed," and that with such recruits defeat was inevitable.

Men collected from the streets and prisons of the cities, hurried out into the enemy's country, and with the officers commanding them, totally unacquainted with the business in which they were engaged; it was utterly impossible they could be otherwise. Besides, not any one department was sufficiently prepared; both quarter-master and contractors [were] extremely deficient. It was a matter of astonishment to [Harmar] that the commanding general [St. Clair], who was acknowledged to be perfectly competent, should think of hazarding, with such people, and under such circumstances, his reputation and life, and the lives of so many others, knowing, too, as both did, the enemy with whom he was going to contend, an enemy brought up from infancy to war, and perhaps superior to an equal number of the best men that could be taken against them.

For one officer only did Denny voice praise and that was Winthrop Sargent, the Revolutionary officer, who remained "constantly on the alert," and "took upon himself the burden of everything."

But, he wrote, there was one further, most important matter that if not entirely neglected, should have had far more serious attention. *"This was a knowledge of the collected force and situation of the enemy; of this we were perfectly ignorant."*

What was left of the miserable army remained encamped in front of Fort Washington. There were days and nights of cold rain, then snow. Such officers as were sufficiently capable were busy making payrolls and preparing for their men's discharge as quickly as possible.

An official dispatch reporting the defeat had gone off to Secretary Knox from General St. Clair, but whether it had been received was unknown.

After another week it was decided that someone who had been through the ordeal had to take the news in person to President Washington. The choice for this unpleasant task was Major Denny, and on the evening of November 19, carrying a copy of the earlier dispatch to Secretary Knox, he departed on board a fourteen-oar barge back up the Ohio.

Though Marietta and vicinity had suffered no attack by the Indians, there had been cause for considerable, unrelieved tension and misery for many, including a return of smallpox and scarlet fever, which carried off fifteen to twenty children. Jonathan Devol and his wife as one example, had suffered the loss of three of their children.

When Major Denny brought the news of St. Clair's Defeat to Marietta, during a stop there, so alarmed were many there was talk of evacuating the settlement. But, as said, "these evil forebodings began to subside, and by the calm deportment and resolute counsel of the more influential and experienced men, a better spirit prevailed."

Foremost and most important of such men was, most obviously, Rufus Putnam, who several days afterward was to write at length to Washington about the state of conditions in Marietta, but make no mention of St. Clair's Defeat, fully conscious, as he would have been, that the first word to the president had to come from Denny. But even absent of any mention of the massive defeat of the army, it was a powerful expression of what was also being experienced day after day by many on the Ohio frontier. The letter was dated December 26, 1791.

"When I consider the multiplicity of business which necessarily engages your attention, it is with great reluctance I address you on the affairs of the people settled in this quarter," he began.

After describing the improvements of the local fortifications that had been established, he went on to list the numerous murders committed by Indians in the near vicinity since the massacre at Big Bottom. Was it not to be feared, he asked, that "the enemy's late success" would bring on more bloodshed?

People were leaving daily.

Our numbers are few and daily decreasing. Some families and many young men have left us already, and more are going, because they can get employ[ment]. Nor are we able to prevent them. All resources by which we retained them the last year are at an end, and we are scarcely able to subsist ourselves and families, much less to pay men for labor or military service. So, that unless we can be assured of government protection, self-preservation dictates the propriety of getting away as soon as possible.

He then proceeded with what was clearly a sore subject.

"But however surprising for you to hear and painful for me to relate, these people think they have very little hope from Governor St. Clair. They believe that both the Governor and Mr. Sargent have, for some reason or other, conceived a prejudice against them." More than this, however, he did not express, except to say that for all the recruits stationed at Pittsburgh and Wheeling, "indeed all stations on the Ohio" of any consequence, only Marietta had received no protection of any kind.

"I do not wish to entertain groundless jealousies nor frighten myself with imaginary evils; but it must be allowed that a black cloud hangs over us, and God only knows when, or on what devoted spot it may break."

IV.

As Denny was to learn on arrival in Philadelphia, the earlier dispatch had already reached Knox, who wasted no time sending it by courier to the president's residence, where the president was entertaining guests at a private Sunday dinner and wished not to be disturbed. But the president's private secretary, Tobias Lear, entered the room and whispered in the president's ear, whereupon Washington excused himself, left the table, and after reading the dispatch, rejoined the gathering as though nothing had happened.

Only later would Tobias Lear recount how, after the guests had left, Washington paced up and down the room, then exploded in a fury.

"It's all over," he said. "St. Clair's defeated—routed; the officers nearly all killed. . . . Here," he continued, his anger growing, "on this very spot I took leave of him. . . . You have your instructions, I said, from the secretary of War. I . . . will add but one word—beware of surprise! You know how the Indians fight us. . . . He went off with that as my last warning. . . .

> And yet, to suffer that army to be cut to pieces, hacked, butchered, tomahawked by a surprise—the very thing I guarded him against! Oh God, Oh God, he is worse than a murderer. How can he answer it to his country! The blood of the slain is upon him, the curse of widows and orphans, the curse of Heaven!

Tobias Lear had never heard such an outburst of rage, at the end of which Washington collapsed on a sofa and sat silent. Then, his voice softened, he told Lear, "This must not go beyond this room. General St. Clair shall have justice. . . . I will receive him without displeasure. I will hear him without prejudice; he shall have full justice."

—•—

During his journey from Cincinnati, Ebenezer Denny tried to banish from his mind, as much as that was possible, every idea of the slaughter and defeat of the army. To talk at all on the subject was an "unpleasant task" for him. At Pittsburgh old friends there seemed to view him as having escaped from the dead.

Meanwhile, word of what happened spread rapidly throughout the east and public rage kept mounting. As early as December 10, the New York *Gazette of the United States* carried a letter from Shippensburg, Pennsylvania, on the Ohio, reporting news of "our army being totally defeated and 600 privates killed." The Philadelphia *National Gazette*, the Boston *Columbian Centinal*, and the *Massachusetts Spy* all carried reports of "dreadful carnage" and chaos. Some of what appeared was inaccurate. The *Gazette of the United States*, on December 17, described General St. Clair lying ill of the gout the whole time the battle raged and how his guards, "by dint of the bayonet had prevented the Indians getting into his tent to butcher him."

The horror and alarm over the news felt by people in all walks of life

was powerfully expressed in a letter written December 18 by Abigail
Adams, wife of the vice president, to an old family friend back in Boston.

> The sad and dreadful havoc of our army at the westward cast a
> gloom over us all. Some of the best officers who remained to us
> after the Peace have fallen here. All our Boston youths who were
> officers are amongst the slain. . . . Not even Braddock's defeat is
> said to have caused such a slaughter. A poor gouty, infirmed gen-
> eral, always unsuccessful, a miserable banditry of undisciplined
> troops—an excellent choir of officers—who I am told went out
> like lambs to the slaughter, having no prospect of conquering—I
> apprehend much uneasiness will ensue.

Arriving in Philadelphia late in the day on December 19, after more
than a month of extremely difficult travel through rain and snow nearly
the whole way, Denny reported immediately to the secretary of war.
The next morning he was received by the president with "attention and
kindness," and following a breakfast with the president and his family,
he and Washington talked at length in privacy.

To what extent and in what detail he talked of all he had seen and
knew remains unknown, but doubtless he reported a great deal, including
the full death toll of the massacre and retreat, he being the one who made
the count. In the earlier dispatch St. Clair had mentioned by name only
five of the officers killed, and said nothing of the 593 enlisted men, about
whom Denny was obliged to report and no doubt did all that was known.

General St. Clair did not arrive in Philadelphia until two months
later, and was received by Washington with the same degree of courtesy
and respect that Denny had been given. Formally resigning his command, St. Clair asked for an investigation by Congress into the cause of
his defeat, and this led to the first congressional investigation in American history.

Ebenezer Denny returned to Pittsburgh, where he had a number of
friends and which he saw as a city with a future. He resigned from the
service and would go on to a highly successful banking career in Pittsburgh and was to become the city's first mayor.

St. Clair would eventually be exonerated from blame for what happened by Washington and by a committee of the House of Representatives, which praised his bravery under fire. He was also to remain the governor of the territory.

But the horrors and disgrace of St. Clair's Defeat were not forgotten. Nor would the fact that the military situation even before the campaign got under way was hopeless. One bad decision by St. Clair as commander followed another, starting with that of proceeding with the campaign in the first place. Far better it would have been to have abandoned the whole thing, just as he had once abandoned Fort Ticonderoga.

Then, too, the timing had been off. It all got going too late in the year, and no one, it would appear, including Washington and Knox, seemed capable of learning from the disastrous experience of General Harmar.

———————

On the morning of February 1, 1792, Winthrop Sargent rode by horseback with a small detachment of soldiers combining a burial party to the scene of the slaughter. As he wrote, the memory of the disaster that filled his mind bore no resemblance to the scene before him.

The whole "melancholy theater" was covered with twenty inches of snow, yet with every tread of the horses' hooves dead bodies were exposed to view, "mutilated, mangled and butchered with the most savage barbarity; and, indeed, there seems to have been left no act of indecent cruelty or torture which was not practiced on the occasion, to the women as well as the men."

Looking over the lay of the ground, he thought, it, as an encampment, very strong and certainly defensible had it been held by regular troops. However, the dense woods, thick bushes, and old logs in such abundance close by were exactly the ideal cover for an Indian attack.

What struck him most, riding around the line, was the amazing effect of the enemy's fire. "Every twig and bush seems to be cut down, and the saplings and larger trees marked with the utmost profusion of their shot."

Removing the bodies proved extremely slow and difficult. It was not just that they were buried in deep snow and had to be uncovered but were frozen hard down to the ground and would break to pieces when being torn loose. The solemn task and rendering last rites would require more than a day.

V.

Wasting no time in taking what were considered the steps necessary to carry on the campaign against the Indians, President Washington used the "unfortunate affair" of St. Clair's Defeat to press Congress into increasing the size of the army as well as military pay, a program that would cost the government more than a million dollars, a colossal sum. And this time the necessary preparations and training were to be gone about in the right way. The one great still unanswered question was who would take command?

Also in Philadelphia at this time were the Reverend Manasseh Cutler and Rufus Putnam, too, who had come as representatives of the Ohio Company to lobby Congress for an additional land grant and a reduction in land prices, as a way of compensating for the economic fallback the company was suffering because of the Indian Wars. Most encouraging had been the reception they received from many members of Congress and in particular from Vice President John Adams.

On the evening of March 4, 1792, Cutler was invited to dine with Adams and his family at their home on Bush Hill, overlooking the Schuylkill River.

"When I came to his house I found that Mrs. Adams was dangerously sick with a fever," Cutler wrote to his wife, Mary. "He told me he refused all invitations to dine abroad, and that he received no formal company at home, but very politely desired me to come and take a family dinner with him every day while I was in the city . . . in short, to make his house my home."

The day following Cutler called again at the Adams home to inquire after Mrs. Adams, and wound up spending the next several hours "closeted" with the vice president, talking about Ohio Company issues and more.

As he reported to his wife, "It gave me much pleasure that I had this favorable opportunity to mention to him General Putnam as a proper officer to command the force to be raised and sent against the Indians. He is much dissatisfied with the conduct of St. Clair, and highly approves of the command being given to Putnam."

Adams then encouraged Cutler, at earliest opportunity, to converse with General Knox, as well as members of the Senate and House about Putnam.

It seems to have been an especially active day for Cutler, who later ran into General St. Clair, whom he described as "now hearty and well," and, from some of what he said, seemed to presume he would continue in command.

"It is said that the people in the western country universally wish Putnam may take command, and I believe were it to be decided by Congress he would have a generous vote," Cutler also noted. The problem was Putnam. "He does not wish for it."

As Putnam made clear in a letter to Secretary of War Knox, he had "not the remotest wish" to enter again into military service. His private affairs and family situation forbade it, not to say his advanced age.

The decision was finally made by Washington in mid-April 1792. The man in command this time was to be Anthony Wayne—General "Mad Anthony" Wayne—who had a reputation for the tenacity and aggressiveness needed to lead an army and was anything but mad.

One anecdote about Putnam's health problems at this time that he loved to tell concerned the return trip he made back up the Ohio that September, after concluding a treaty of peace with the Wabash and Illinois Indians.

While on his barge rowed by U.S. soldiers, he suffered an attack of severe fever and ague. A doctor also on board "debarred" him from all food and drink. When they put ashore to camp for the night and the others treated themselves to a banquet of bear meat, venison, and turkey, "the very fumes of which were a feast," Putnam lay as peaceably as his cravings would allow. But when at last the rest of the party was asleep, he crept to the camp kettle and feasted on what remained of the bear meat and venison and, as he later loved to report, he experienced no more of the fever and ague.

———•◦•———

The cloud of fear that had hung over Marietta and its neighboring settlements ever since the Big Bottom massacre had begun to clear to a degree. Word had come down the Ohio from Pittsburgh of the new army being recruited and properly trained under General Wayne to settle the threat of Indian attacks once and for all—an army said to number 8,000 men. By early spring 1793 the army was on its way, and if numbering closer to 2,000, it was there to be seen passing by on flatboats down river to Fort Washington at Cincinnati.

Difficult as they had been, the years of confinement at Campus Martius had given rise to a very different way of life, and, to the surprise of many, what evolved had proven quite enjoyable. To enliven the off-hours within the stockade a variety of games and sporting events—foot races, boxing matches—had become a mainstay in which old and young engaged. Dancing was another diversion practiced by the youth, and encouraged by their elders as affording healthy exercise in which females could take part. No distinctions of family or official positions were then made. All activities were open to everyone. As would be written:

> They were united in bonds of friendship like one great family, bound and held together in a common brotherhood by the perils which surrounded them. In after years, when each household lived separate in their own domicil, they looked back on these days with satisfaction and pleasure, as a period in their lives when the best affections of the heart were called forth and practiced towards each other.

The absence of a single violin in the garrison to enliven events was made up for by an elderly man, a sailor in his youth, known as "Uncle Sam," who "with the aid of the enlivening beverage," could sing all night, often tiring out the dancers sooner than they him. When, before day-light, he became a bit drowsy, a few kind words and another dram set him going again.

Some worried this change in the settlement's way of life would have long-range, detrimental effect. But they were a decided minority.

One year later came word from the northwest corner of Ohio on the lower Maumee River that on August 20, 1794, General Wayne and his army had won an overwhelming victory over some 2,000 native war-riors again led by Blue Jacket at the battle of Fallen Timbers. Unlike the forces under General Arthur St. Clair, Wayne's troops, foot soldiers and cavalry, fought with great discipline and fury, and though the Indians, too, fought with great bravery, they were quickly routed.

Wayne's losses were minor, 33 killed, about 100 wounded, while the losses by Blue Jacket's warriors were twice that.

The victory, as Rufus Putnam said, was decisive. Its importance could "scarcely be over-estimated." It ended more than four years of bit-ter frontier fighting.

At Marietta, the cloud of fear lifted at last. The settlers could come out of their blockhouses and return to their farms or trades at their pleasure. The entire community could get on with much that needed doing.

In another year, on August 3, 1795, American officials and scores of Indian representatives signed the Treaty of Greenville, establishing a treaty line above which, north and west of the line, the Indians were confined. As the noted Ohio historian George W. Knepper was to write, "Compared to any previous effort to separate Indian and white in Ohio, the Treaty of Greenville was effective, though at the Indians' expense. It opened the way in eastern and southern Ohio for a renewed flood of settlers anxious to clear and cultivate lands that had never known the axe and the plow."

PART II

1795-1814

CHAPTER FIVE

A New Era Commences

*Thus we left the scene of my early life, and started
on this then hazardous journey and perilous
enterprise. We had with us our four children.*

—EPHRAIM CUTLER, JUNE 15, 1795

I.

Young Ephraim Cutler and his father were much alike in a number of ways. Both were vigorous, affable, well-intentioned. Both were devoted family men with a strong allegiance to their Puritan values. At approximately six feet in height, Ephraim stood a bit taller than his father, and was, as said in the family, more strongly built and quite handsome, with dark gray eyes.

But Ephraim's childhood had been altogether different from that of the other Cutler children and he was different as a result. He had been named for a younger brother of his father's who had been thrown from a horse and killed the year before Ephraim was born. At age three, on a visit to the Cutler grandparents at their farm in Killingly, Connecticut, they had, as he later wrote, "earnestly entreated that I should remain with them, and in some measure supply the place of the son of whom they had been so unexpectedly bereaved." And so he had been left to their care, and there he was to stay.

Only once, when his father was ordained, was he taken by his grandfather to visit Ipswich Hamlet. His parents came to see him, but he did not go again to Massachusetts to see them until he was sixteen. Instead, he grew up knowing firsthand the ceaseless hard work of a farm.

If he harbored any resentment that he had been passed off to his grandparents, and thus denied the childhood provided his brothers and sisters by their parents, he is not known ever to have said as much.

Though it had been his grandfather's intention that he be educated at Yale as his father had, the troubled economic state of the country following the Revolution made that "impracticable." He had, as he said, "a strong propensity to read" and thus gained a good understanding of history and geography quite early.

By age sixteen, because of his grandfather's advancing age, he had had to take charge of the whole business of the farm, which included cutting and hauling wood, driving sheep and cattle to market, and once, driving a rafter of turkeys about twenty-four miles to Providence.

The Cutler farm was spread across a high hilltop with a sweeping view of the western horizon and memorable skies at sunset. What influence, if any, the presence of such a panorama may have had on the attraction of the west to both Manasseh and Ephraim no one can say for certain, but it could have been considerable.

At the urging of the pastor of the church in Killingly, the Reverend Elisha Atkins, Ephraim studied on his own mathematics and surveying, which were to prove important to him. But he knew that was not enough. "It has always been to me a source of regret," he later wrote, "that I was deprived of a liberal education." Try as he would, he could never master proper spelling or punctuation, a deficiency his father was to call to his attention all too often.

In 1787, the year of his father's success with the Northwest Ordinance and the year his younger brother Jervis set off with the first pioneers to leave for Ohio, Ephraim, "before I had attained my twentieth year," as he said, married Leah Atwood of Killingly and in the years that followed, with a young family to support, he struggled to succeed with several enterprises that failed and felt himself ever more ready to join the move west.

Jervis, meanwhile, had given up in an attempt at farming near Marietta, sold his land, returned home to New England, and was married in 1794. He wished to go back to Ohio he told Ephraim—"I should esteem it one of the greatest pleasures of my life," he wrote—but his wife feared the dangers and privations of pioneer life.

Reports on the situation in Ohio, while rarely providing much in detail or with consistent accuracy, were in reasonably good supply in the Philadelphia, New York, and Boston newspapers. Most likely Ephraim turned to the *Massachusetts Spy* for the latest word from beyond the mountains in accounts datelined Pittsburgh. And by the end of August 1794, like everyone in the east, he knew of General Wayne's victory.

———•••———

On the 15th of June, 1795, all necessary arrangements completed, Ephraim and his wife said goodbye to old friends and departed for Ohio.

Leah had been in poor health and many who pressed around her on parting expressed their fears that she might not survive the journey. She answered cheerfully, saying she had committed herself to God and should not "suffer herself to be disheartened," and especially since several physicians had advised a change of climate.

With them were their four children, ages seven through one, two horses, and one cow to provide an abundance of milk on the way. Their "conveyance" was a wagon drawn by a yoke of oxen. Also traveling with them were a number of Putnams of all ages—part of the family of the famous, highly colorful Revolutionary War general, Israel Putnam—with two large wagons, four oxen, four horses, and three cows.

Ephraim, of course, knew a great deal about Ohio and a number of those with whom his father had long been associated, and Rufus Putnam in particular. But he did not yet know Rufus Putnam or anyone else at Marietta. Nor did he have any clear idea of what he might do once there, or what opportunities might arise.

The journey as far as the mountains of western Pennsylvania went without difficulty. Beyond there, the road was no better than it had long been and the struggle mile after mile was no less than ever.

On reaching the Monongahela River, Ephraim had a boat built and on this the party proceeded past Pittsburgh and onto the Ohio where the current carried them steadily on downstream at about three miles per hour.

Somewhere short of Beaver Creek, tragedy struck. The Cutlers' youngest child, one-year-old Hezekiah, took ill and died. A halt was made at a single cabin by the shore where the owner had already buried some of his family and there Hezekiah was laid to rest.

"Again we moved on in the usual slow way, the river very low," Ephraim wrote. "Below Wheeling we saw but few openings on the banks . . . no one living for fifty miles." For all that had been written and said about the thousands pouring into Virginia and Kentucky no sign of that was to be seen. All was an unbroken wilderness.

Then, after leaving Wheeling, the Cutlers' oldest child, Mary, age seven, became violently ill with bilious fever and she, too, quickly died.

She had been her father's favorite and her death a blow such as he had never known. "To add to our distress," he wrote, "we had no alternative but to commit her to the earth in the dreary wilderness." Nothing could be worse, he recorded.

Their sufferings were by no means over. Farther on, Leah Cutler, while stepping down a plank to get onshore, slipped and fell and suffered two broken ribs. About the same time Ephraim was struck by an attack of dysentery and "much weakened" before landing at Marietta, the morning of September 18, fully three months after leaving home. As he would write, it was a bleak beginning:

We had landed sick among strangers, with no well-known friend to meet us with kindly greeting, and myself destined to be confined to a bed from which, for a time, there seemed little hope that I should ever rise in health. Such was our introduction to pioneer life.

Where or with whom the Cutlers stayed their first days after landing is not clear, but their response to the setting as it had so often been for so many others was one of wholehearted approval. "There is probably no more beautiful and pleasant location to be found on the banks of the Ohio River," wrote Ephraim, who cited as well a number of "principal inhabitants" whom he had already met, including Rufus Putnam, Ebenezer Sproat, Paul Fearing, and Dr. Jabez True.

He also went on to describe how the years of Indian troubles and the ways of those confined to garrison life had brought a change in the established way of life, how as he was told, it had "broken up former fixed habits of industry, and led to a fondness for sports and social meetings where drinking was practiced, and hours spent in jovial conviviality." But there appeared to be little need for excessive concern. Those New Englanders who first settled there had come with habits of industry, respect for order, and strict subordination to law, and clearly that outlook still prevailed. Indeed, it would be difficult, Ephraim had already concluded, to collect a more intelligent and refined society than could be found at Marietta.

Ephraim made his first visit to Waterford, twenty miles up the Muskingum, soon after recovering his health. Several of the Waterford settlers who were also from Killingly came with a canoe and took him back up the Muskingum. Once there, he decided Waterford was the place to locate.

One particularly generous man, a Revolutionary War veteran, Captain Daniel Davis, offered Ephraim and his family half of his home— which Ephraim estimated to be the best log house in that part of the wilderness—in which to spend the winter.

Waterford by then consisted of thirty-two families spread along the east side of the Muskingum and once settled, the Cutler family found themselves, even with the onset of winter, far more comfortable than they had been at Marietta.

To Ephraim's great surprise the weather proved quite mild. His team of horses "found employment" plowing unfrozen ground through the entire season. In addition Rufus Putnam hired him to work surveying some 50,000 acres of land there at Waterford, mostly east of the river, and the $100 he received in payment proved "a great relief to me in my then needy circumstances."

That spring he moved his family into an empty cabin near Fort Frye and purchased four acres of rich bottomland. On his own he managed to clear it of its giant beech and poplar trees, which to a green-hand, as he acknowledged, was a severe labor as the condition of his hands bore witness.

The corn he planted produced a fine crop and that summer he built a cabin. By fall he and the family had moved in.

That the son of Manasseh Cutler had come to Ohio and brought his family with him, and that he so clearly had come to stay, did much to lift the spirits of the earliest of the settlers. Now, before the year was out, he received a thick packet which on opening was found to contain three commissions from Governor St. Clair—one as captain of the militia, another as justice of the peace, and another as judge of the first Court of Common Pleas. His astonishment was "overwhelming."

He felt himself inadequate to fulfill the duties involved and until Dean Tyler—the same scholarly Harvard graduate who had been of help to Ichabod Nye when he first arrived—observed that though it was most likely the appointments had been made owing mainly to his father's character, he ought not hesitate in accepting them.

And so he did.

———

When he left New England to head west, Ephraim had expected that most likely he would make farming his way of life and was encouraged to do so by his father. The more he saw now of the lands to the north of Marietta, the more convinced he became that his initial plan had been the right one and again he was encouraged by his father.

"I have earnestly wished you to have a good farm, to establish if possible a good landed interest in preference to trade, or any other object," Manasseh Cutler advised in a long letter, for there is nothing in this country that will render a man so completely independent and secure against the difficulties which arise from the changes which the times, the state of the country, and other contingencies may occasion, and which are and always will be taking place in the world.

"Human life is short and uncertain," he continued, "the sooner such a work is undertaken the better."

In 1797, two years after his arrival, Ephraim purchased 600 acres some twenty miles into the wilderness northwest of Marietta. By selling 100 acres each to two other men, along with a gift to each of an additional 100 acres, he set out with them to commence a new settlement. But not until early 1799, because of various "circumstances," did the clearing of land get under way. With one acre cleared, a log cabin went up, and on May 7, Cutler, his wife and children, who by then numbered three, made the twenty-mile trek through the forest with loaded pack-horses to take up residence in their new home.

With the help of the two other men, who with their families had established their own cabins, Ephraim set about preparing more ground for planting.

The timber was large, principally beech and sugar-tree, all of which we cut down and piled, and burned the most of it [he would later recall]. Four acres were cleared ready to plant by the fifteenth of June. . . . From this patch of ground I raised that year one hundred and fifty bushels of corn that ripened well.

The wilderness to the north and west was a favorite hunting ground of the natives, which in the hunting season they still occupied in large numbers. "They sometimes visited us," Ephraim wrote, "but did us little injury, except stealing two horses."

Buffalo and elk were still to be seen. Deer and bears were "abundant," wild turkey "innumerable." Wolves and panthers also "infested" the woods. From the Cutler cabin to those of the other pioneer families was a mile or two.

On June 17, 1799, the day after finishing the planting, Ephraim made his way back through the woods to Marietta to attend court. Starting then he was to be called away to serve as a judge four times a year and had to spend two weeks or more each time.

Court sessions were customarily held at Campus Martius, but also quite often at a considerable distance from Marietta in what was still wilderness, areas in which one of the court's most difficult duties was to prevent illegal occupations by newcomers. As said in one account, "In those early times, notwithstanding the primitive state of society, the judges had proper ideas of the sanctity of law and the dignity of a court."

At the trial of one land case, at which Ephraim and another judge named Alvan Bingham presided, "the leaders of the disorderly class came forward and threatened violence; the magistrates ordered them to leave the room, which they did, but uttering threats to put a stop to such courts." In the words of one old account, "The judges, determined to vindicate their judicial dignity, instantly issued warrants, and ordered the sheriff to arrest the parties immediately, and take them to Marietta.

> They were arrested accordingly, and it is not easy to conceive of men more frightened; the idea of being taken to Marietta, to be tried by a court that had established a reputation throughout the territory for firmness and strict justice, filled them with terror.

Judge Bingham's brother, Silas Bingham, a deputy sheriff and a man known for great shrewdness and dispatch in the role, as well as "unconquerable humor," did nothing to ease their fears, but told them a better way would be to come into court and get down on their knees and ask for forgiveness and promise amendment.

The ringleader of the offending party replied, "It was too bad to be compelled to kneel down and ask forgiveness of two Buckeye justices; but he concluded to submit, rather than be taken to Marietta."

The judges received no per diem or travel expenses. In all the years Ephraim served in the Court of Common Pleas, he did not receive a cent. Often, coming and going, he had to camp in the wilderness. Yet he never failed attending a single session.

II.

By the autumn of 1795, by dint of hard work and consistently high performance over the years since he first arrived at Marietta, Joseph Barker, at age thirty, had achieved notable importance. He was a man of many interests and skills, an independent thinker who read widely. Moreover, he was a happy man, much liked by everyone, and blessed with a family now numbering three children.

In 1792, he had spent the better part of the year building a new blockhouse at the Point. The year after, hoping to avoid smallpox, he had moved with his family downriver to Belpre, where, part of the time, he taught school. Then, in February 1795, for his services during the Indian Wars, he received a grant of 100 acres seven miles up the Muskingum at what was called Wiseman's Bottom. That spring, with the help of his two brothers-in-law, he began clearing two acres of giant black walnut and sugar maples, planted an apple orchard, the whole time feeling compelled, as he put it, "to hold his scalp on with one hand while he dug holes for the trees with the other." By December, he had also completed a 16 x 16-foot log cabin. One week before Christmas, he and his family established themselves on the farm that was to be their home for nearly half a century.

As would be said, "The fortitude and perseverance requisite to meet the hardships and privations of a settlement in the wilderness, were found centered in this family." Barker's wife, Elizabeth, too, was credited with all the patience, resolution, and good sense needed in no small degree. Their nearest neighbors were seven miles away back in Marietta.

In the year that followed, three more families, including that of Captain Jonathan Devol, moved to Wiseman's Bottom. Barker cleared more land, enlarged his orchard with 200 peach trees, and put up a larger, hewed log house with a brick chimney, a "refinement" rarely attained by pioneers before the passing of several years.

He also helped develop a salt spring on the other side of the Muskingum. Clearly he had achieved success in ways he had never imagined. At home, the Barker children were being raised, as one daughter, Catherine, would remember, "to be useful, to be pleasant with our playmates, respectful to superiors, just to all, black or white, good to the poor not showing pride or selfishness but kindness and good will . . . and to see to it that we looked to our own, more than to others' faults."

She would also, much of her life, like to quote words to the wise that were most frequently repeated by her mother, and that could have served for the motto of most of the community:

> *Count the day lost at which*
> *the setting sun*
> *sees at its close*
> *no worthy action done.*

But as with so many on the frontier, life was not without its worries and blows. Catherine would also recall, "I sometimes thought it terrible, to live in the woods, and hear tell of snakes, and wolves, and panthers, and when I went to the spring, was afraid I should see some of them."

One of the Barker children, a boy named William, drowned in the Muskingum River at age three.

When fire destroyed the first log cabin Barker had built, which he had since converted into a workshop and storage place for the great stock of tools he had brought from New England, all of which were destroyed, along with a quantity of food, he went back to work as both carpenter and builder.

As it was, the demand for such skills as he had mastered had grown greater than ever. With the Indian War ended, Marietta had sprung back to life. The revival of river traffic, and abundance of food supplies, trade goods, and a steady flow of new emigrants—families in quest of a new life—had resumed almost instantaneously. Marietta was growing and prospering once again.

A new post office was established and a first school, Muskingum Academy, under the leadership of Rufus Putnam. A first school build-ing, a modest frame house went up on Front Street. A first courthouse was built on the corner of Second and Putnam Streets, and stood two stories high, with walls three feet thick made of hewn yellow poplar logs.

Log cabins were being replaced by more comfortable houses with glass windows. A visitor from Massachusetts only a few years later would note in his journal that Marietta had "ninety-one dwelling houses, sixty-five of which are frame or plank, eleven of brick, and three of stone."

Much work went on and the demand for such skills as Barker, the master builder, offered only grew greater. Indeed, he had so pursued his interest in and study of architecture by this time and perfected his skills that he could rightly be called the first architect in the Northwest Terri-tory and was to design and build homes for the Reverend Daniel Story, the lawyer Paul Fearing, and others.

But a magnificent mansion, a structure like nothing else to be seen anywhere along the whole length of the Ohio River, would upstage everything Barker or anyone else had accomplished until then and would remain the subject of much talk for a long time to come, as would its owners.

———————

Harman Blennerhassett and his wife, Margaret, were like no other cou-ple yet to appear on the Ohio frontier. No one dressed as they did or conversed so readily on so many subjects. Or spent so much money so lavishly or appeared so entirely out of place.

Both were new to America. He was of Irish aristocracy, a graduate of Trinity College in Dublin, and heir to a fortune. She was seven years younger than he, English and though of limited means, well-educated, well-read, and as cultured as her husband. That she was also his niece had played a significant part in their decision to depart for America where they would be less likely to be ostracized for so scandalous a marriage and particularly in the new territory of the remote west.

They arrived in Marietta in the fall of 1797 and began looking about. After seeing a beautiful island twelve miles below the mouth of the Muskingum, opposite Belpre—an island that was part of Virginia and near land once owned by George Washington—Blennerhassett decided it was the place for him. For the upper portion of the island, a stretch of some 169 acres, he paid an unprecedented sum of $4,500 to the then owner, Elijah Backus, the brother of Lucy Backus Woodbridge.

He then proceeded to have much of the ground cleared for buildings and gardens. Meantime, the couple moved in to live temporarily in an old abandoned blockhouse on the property which was where their first child, a boy, was born. In no time they became a most conspicuous element locally, a twosome such as had not been seen before, or even imagined.

He was a tall, thin, gangling man, prematurely gray-haired, and slightly stooped. He dressed in the old English style, with scarlet or buff-colored breeches and silver-buckled shoes. Severely nearsighted, he could read only by putting his face so close to a book that his rather large nose nearly touched the page.

He was also highly intellectual, fond of experimenting in chemistry and electricity, a classics scholar, an accomplished violinist. As soon became apparent, he was as well quite eccentric, absentminded, a touch snobbish, and easily rattled. On the approach of a thunderstorm, he would close all the doors and windows and huddle in the middle of a bed, to avoid "the accidental effects of the electric fluid."

Then, too, notably, he was not always sensible about how he spent his money, and thus was easily duped by some of the locals known for dishonesty. In the days before limestone quarries were opened, river clamshells were calcined on log fires and used to plaster rooms. In bargaining with one noted cheat, Blennerhassett was told that collecting the shells was a difficult task, in that it was necessary to dive into water six or eight feet deep, and therefore the charge was 50 cents a bushel, when in truth any quantity of shells could be found in water only inches deep. Blennerhassett paid five times what the shells were worth.

Among those he dealt with locally he was known, half in affection, half ridiculed, as "Blanny."

Margaret, however, drew ever more attention, and particularly as she appeared far more often in public. Though not beautiful—her neck was a bit too long, her mouth a bit too small—she was tall and stately, a young woman, as said, of "the most perfect proportions, her eyes dark blue, sparkling with life and intelligence." She rode a white horse superbly and on frequent excursions to Marietta sported a scarlet dress with brass buttons and a white beaver hat festooned with white ostrich feathers and she moved fast. Fluent in French, she was also known for reading Shakespeare aloud with all the vitality of a great actor. At home she often wore a bright yellow or pink silk turban.

It should be added that her money sense was no better than her husband's, and the fact that she was his niece was not to become known for several years.

Because their island—Blennerhassett Island, as it was known—was part of Virginia, eight black slaves were purchased to serve as cooks, waiter, grooms, and to operate ferry service back and forth to the island. This last, most important position was filled by a young black man, Micajah Phillips, known as Cajoe, who had been taught to read and write by Margaret Blennerhassett.

The total outlay for the house and improvements of the grounds—which featured an extensive English garden laid out and tended by an English gardener named Peter Taylor—would come to an unheard of $50,000, or perhaps more.

It was clear nothing was to be spared in the way of expenses and that once completed, their home would far exceed in size and elegance any structure to be seen the length of the Ohio Valley. In such a wilderness setting it seemed at first sight totally incongruous and unreal, as did its owners, who, in a land where everyone worked exceedingly hard of necessity, did nothing but whatever suited their pleasures.

To no one's surprise the builder chosen for the task was Joseph Barker, who drew up the plans for the house and would be credited, then and later, as the architect, though doubtless others, too, including Blennerhassett, would have been involved in the design.

Barker laid down substantial boat landings for a sizable workforce and the volume of stone, lumber, and other supplies needed, no small task in itself.

The house was to be of Palladian design, with a large, two-and-a-half-story, wood-frame main section from which were to extend two portico wings curved like arms reaching out, at the ends of which were to be two other buildings or "dependencies." The main house, with its ten rooms, would measure 39 x 54 feet and contain fully 7,000 square feet, while the dependencies, though small by contrast, were each 26 x 26 feet, or about the size of the average Ohio cabin.

The building at the end of the left wing was to be the summer kitchen and servants quarters, that on the right, Harman Blennerhassett's study.

Pressure was on to finish as soon as possible, the Blennerhassetts having no wish to wait any longer than necessary to take up residence in their dream palace. As it was, the work went on for two years, and given the scale, the quality, the attention to detail achieved that, too, was remarkable.

Meanwhile, giant crate-loads of exquisite mirrors and massive furniture, much of it from abroad or custom-made in the east, kept arriving. In good weather, the numbers of visitors to the site grew steadily.

Everything about the finished interior was done to perfection, with the finest of woods and craftsmanship—from its domed entrance hall to the great dining room and banquet table, to the downstairs drawing room, which, with its polished black walnut paneling floor to ceiling, was considered the finest room of all. Shining brass doorknobs, gold moldings, marbled wallpaper, a giant Venetian window, and well-stocked library upstairs were all further evidence of elegance of the kind one might find only in England or Europe. Yet there it stood on the Ohio frontier.

One of the many visitors was to describe the house and gardens as "a scene of enchantment, a western paradise, where beauty, wealth, and happiness had found a home." Others were to call it "the Enchanted Island," an "Earthly Paradise."

The house had cost a fortune. And most happy was the Blennerhassett family, by now increased by two children, when they took up residence. Parties were put on for young people from Marietta and Belpre, and extended social gatherings for the older "more sedate" portions of the community invited to spend several days and nights on the island. Guests came by canoe or rowboat, or most often by the Blennerhassetts' own ferry service, operated by the ever cordial Cajoe. In the summer when the river was low, many came on horseback.

Ephraim Cutler was among those who came in social contact with the Blennerhassetts and in later years liked to talk about Mrs. Blennerhassett, describing how she could ride the wildest horses, but he had also known her to walk from her Ohio River landing to Marietta and back in the same day, a distance of twenty-four miles.

The way of life, the privacy and pleasures of convivial society that Harman and Margaret Blennerhassett had hoped to attain in their wilderness paradise would continue for several years largely as they had envisioned, neither they or anyone else imagining what was to come and that they were, as said, to figure prominently "under the spotlight of history."

———·—·———

With startling suddenness, just at the close of the eighteenth century, death had come to George Washington. A heavy cold had turned suddenly to pneumonia, and after the struggle of twenty-four hours, he died at his home at Mount Vernon on December 14, 1799. He was sixty-seven years old. His last words were said to have been, "Tis well."

The nation, said President Adams in a formal message to Congress, had lost "her most esteemed, beloved, and admired citizen. . . . I feel myself alone, bereaved of my last brother."

In Marietta, among the many veterans who had served under Washington during the war, the feeling was much the same.

———·—·———

With a new century under way, the times were changing nearly everywhere, including Marietta where a promising new enterprise was taking hold.

In 1800 a merchant named Charles Greene had a 110-ton brig built there on the riverbank by Stephen Devol, an oceangoing square-rigger christened *St. Clair*, which set sail down the Ohio at the end of April 1801, when the river was at its ideal springtime height. In command was Commodore Abraham Whipple, the famous Revolutionary War naval officer and a new resident of Marietta. It was to be a commercial voyage to New Orleans, then on to Havana, and Philadelphia.

Along the entire length of the Ohio, from Pittsburgh to the Mississippi, there was only one difficult—even dangerous—stretch, and that was the "Falls" or "Rapids" at a bend in the river at Louisville, Kentucky. There a ledge of rocks extended across the river over a distance of about two miles, and the river cascaded down in whitewater rapids some twenty-six feet.

When the river was high, the fall was made apparent only by the increased speed of the vessel. If the river was low, the rocks came into plain view and the passage became quite dangerous.

There was a choice of three channels. One on the north side called the Indian chute was the main channel. Another, the middle chute, was considered safe and easy in all heights of the water above middle stage. The third on the south side, called the Kentucky chute, was passable only with the water high.

Under the right conditions the Falls could be passed without great difficulty by canoes, flatboats, and keelboats. There were also experienced pilots regularly on hand to conduct boat traffic over the rapids. But how well a square-rigger the size of the *St. Clair* might do was a subject of much speculation.

As it turned out, Commodore Whipple, with his abilities as a seaman, negotiated the challenge himself in his own way and with perfect success. He went over the Falls backwards—stern first—dragging two anchors from his bow to keep to the center of the channel and control the descent.

He then sailed downstream and on to the Mississippi to New Orleans and out to sea.

At Wiseman's Bottom on the Muskingum, Joseph Barker's friend and neighbor, Jonathan Devol, had started building a ship of 400 tons for a Marietta merchant named Gilman, the entire vessel made of the black walnut that grew in such abundance along the river. The year following, Devol built two more ships, brigs of 200 tons, and Barker, too, established his own shipyard on his farm by the Muskingum and in 1802 built two ships on order, one a brig for Harman Blennerhassett, the other a schooner for Edward White Tupper.

The orders for these ships had come through an active young Marietta merchant, Dudley Woodbridge, Jr., the son of Lucy Backus and Dudley Woodbridge, Sr., who had become something of a business partner with Blennerhassett, and had worked with Barker in supplying materials needed for the building of the Blennerhassett mansion.

In a letter to his father dated March 18, 1802, Ephraim Cutler wrote, "I am . . . fully convinced that this is by far the most eligible place to build [ships] within the United States. At any rate there are ten vessels of from one to three hundred tons burden to be built here this summer."

On the evening of May 4, 1803, the brig *Mary Avery* of 130 tons, built at Marietta, set sail and like other vessels built at Marietta provided a spectacle for the people of the town who saluted with cheers on the shoreline and small cannon fired.

Serious shipbuilding on the Ohio, a dream long held, had become a reality and the reach of Joseph Barker's involvement and influence in the community had increased still more, along with his circle of friends, among whom now were the Cutlers. One of the Barker daughters, Catherine, would later write at length of the Cutlers as a family "highly respected for their moral worth and standing," and of her own particular affection for one of the Cutler daughters, Sarah, who became a "cherished" friend.

The Barker family, too, had expanded by now to number nine children and Barker had decided it was time for a larger home of his design, work on which was to go on for several years.

Built on higher ground farther back from the Muskingum, it was to be a large, brick house in the Federal style, with a handsome front door flanked by recessed side windows and an elliptical fanlight overhead. Two large windows to either side of the front door had twenty-four panes (twelve over twelve) each, as did the windows above on the second floor, which were also recessed in brick arches, an architectural touch that was to distinguish most of the buildings designed by Barker. Once completed the whole house was painted white, and soon became, as intended, a "distinguished seat of hospitality."

III.

The year 1800 had been one of unprecedented political turmoil at the national level, with the Federalist president, John Adams, challenged for reelection by the Republican (or Democratic) candidate, Thomas Jefferson, who proved the victor.

Then, too, in 1800, and to his immense surprise, the Reverend Manasseh Cutler, at age fifty-eight, was elected to Congress as a Federalist. As he explained in a letter to Ephraim, when the previous representative had announced only that November that he no longer wished to serve, the principal leaders of the towns around had held a meeting and decided he should be the nominee.

"It was so sudden, and to me undesirable, that I wished to decline," Manasseh confided to his son. "I conceived, myself, that there was no probability I should be elected, but the event proved very different from my expectations." As he would also report, he won every town by large majorities, but added that he viewed it as "very unpleasant business."

Thus Manasseh Cutler—doctor of divinity, doctor of law, doctor of medicine—had become Congressman Cutler and since his town had lately been renamed, he was Congressman Cutler from Hamilton, Massachusetts.

He departed Hamilton for Washington early the next year, and that same year, 1801, Ephraim, too, entered politics for the first time at thirty-four, elected as a delegate from Washington County to Ohio's territorial legislature.

Ames, the settlement Ephraim had started on Federal Creek, could now claim, as he proudly reported to his father, a population of 161 souls. He himself had never been so involved with the community, in addition to his own enterprises.

He also continued buying and selling land and profitably, all this much to his father's approval it would seem. Yet the elder Cutler could not help but lodge his fatherly disapproval of certain of his son's failings, almost as if Ephraim were still a boy.

In the same letter in which he reported to Ephraim his election to Congress, he concluded as follows:

> I cannot close this letter without suggesting some little inaccura-
> cies in your letters which I wish you to attend to and which you
> must necessarily correct. I find in almost every one of your let-
> ters, you begin . . . on the wrong side of the sheet of paper. Look
> at my letters, you will find every letter is begun on the side of the
> sheet with the fold to the left hand. You will observe the same in
> every letter you receive from any man who knows anything of
> letter writing. . . . Your spelling is also bad. If you have no English
> dictionary I wish you, by all means, to receive one. Good com-
> position looks ill if it is badly spelt. By looking your words up in
> a dictionary as you write you will soon spell right.

His punctuation was also not what it should be, the father went on. His question marks sometimes appeared where there were no ques-tions. It was as if the eminent master of his rectory school were lectur-ing one of his slower students.

In response Ephraim wrote to his father, "I thank you for your ad-vice respecting my pointing [punctuation], writing etc. I will attend to it as much as in my power, but till lately, it was rare that I took a pen in hand to write, except to you, and I write so bad a hand and am so unac-quainted with grammar, that I feel so ashamed of my performances in this way, that I almost wish a letter burnt as soon [as] was written."

During his time in Washington, Manasseh was to write often to Ephraim and other members of the family, describing what he was seeing and people he was meeting. To his surprise, he found the city far more appealing than expected, the weather "remarkably pleasant," as he wrote to his daughter Betsy.

> The block in which I live contains six houses, four stories high, and very handsomely furnished. It is situated east of the Capitol, the highest ground in the city. . . . Mr. [Nathan] Read and myself have, I think, the pleasantest room in the house, or in the whole city. It is in the third story, commanding a delightful prospect of the Capitol, of the President's house, Georgetown, all the houses in the city, a long extent of the river, and the city of Alexandria.

Only the Capitol was a disappointment. He thought it "a huge pile . . . very heavy in its appearance without, and not very pleasant within." The president's house, on the other hand, was both "well proportioned and pleasingly situated."

The house in which he lodged was owned by a couple named King, whose "very handsome" seventeen-year-old daughter, Anna, played the piano with "great skill." Two or three evenings a week, he and the other lodgers would gather to hear her perform. As he wrote to Betsy, "After we have been fatigued with the harangues of the [Congressional] Hall in the day, and conversing on politics, in different circles (for we talk about nothing else), in the evening, an hour of this music is truly delightful."

For his fellow lodgers, all members of Congress, he had only praise. Three were from Connecticut and fellow Yale graduates. John Davenport was "a very pleasant, agreeable man"; John Cotton Smith, the son of a clergyman, and a man "of very sprightly and distinguished talents"; and Elias Perkins, "a man of very handsome abilities." As for Nathan Read, Manasseh's roommate, a Harvard graduate, who was also from Massachusetts, he could hardly say enough.

"Were I to have made my choice among all the members of Congress for one to have lived in the same chamber with me, all things considered, I should have chosen Mr. Read." Like Manasseh, Read, too, had great interest in science.

Remarkably all these gentlemen were professors of religion and members of churches. "An unbecoming word is never uttered by one of them, and the most perfect harmony and friendliness pervades the family."

As usual, Manasseh was to keep an extensive diary in which he recorded the ups and downs of Congress, days of "very little done," days of "debates long, warm, and acrimonious," days of "nothing very interesting."

Besides, as did few others, he recounted occasional added experiences of particular interest such as a visit to Mount Vernon made with a small delegation of fellow representatives to have breakfast with Martha Washington. She appeared much older than when he had last seen her in Philadelphia, but she "conversed with great ease and familiarity, and appeared as much rejoiced at receiving our visit as if we had been her nearest connections. . . . We were all Federalists, which evidently gave her particular pleasure."

She spoke of "the General" with great affection, viewing herself as left alone, her life protracted to the point where she felt a stranger in a strange world. She repeatedly remarked on the blessings bestowed on her. But as Manasseh also recorded, she talked of the election of Jefferson, whom she considered "one of the most detestable of mankind" and "the greatest misfortune our country had ever experienced."

To this Cutler added that such unfriendly feelings toward Jefferson were to be expected, given the abuse Jefferson had directed to General Washington, while living and to his memory since, though what exactly Cutler had in mind, he did not say.

Several weeks later, with a number of others, he was a guest for dinner at the president's house and afterward recorded only that Jefferson was "social," then went on to describe all that was served in some detail. Indeed his diary entry would be the only known record of the full menu of one of the many famously sumptuous Jefferson banquets.

Rice soup, round of beef, turkey, mutton, ham, loin of veal, cutlets of mutton or veal, fried eggs, fried beef, a pie called macaroni, which appeared to be a rich crust with the strillions of onions, or shallots, which I took it to be, tasted very strong, and not agreeable. Mr. [Meriwether] Lewis told me there were none in it; it was an Italian dish, and what appeared like onions was made of flour and butter, with a particularly strong liquor mixed with them. Ice-cream very good, crust wholly dried, crumbled into thin flakes; a dish somewhat like a pudding—inside white as milk or curd, very porous and light, covered with cream sauce—very fine. Many other jimcracks, a great variety of fruit, plenty of wines, and good.

All was going better for Manasseh than he had expected. "Before I came," he confided to Ephraim, "I was apprehensive that as I was a clergyman I might meet with some unpleasant things on that account. I viewed myself a *speckled bird*, because I presumed I should be viewed so by others. But the case has been far otherwise."

President Jefferson paid him more particular attention, he believed, than any one Federalist in either the House or Senate. "From members of Congress I have received every civility I could desire, not with our own party only, but I often converse freely with those of the opposite side, and in the most cordial manner." As for the work itself, he had to say, it was "trying indeed."

———·•·———

In early spring of 1802, Ephraim made the long journey from Ohio to Washington to spend some time with his father, though exactly why neither was to say. Their first day they enjoyed a spring stroll together down the shores of the Potomac as far as Alexandria, dined there in a public house, "rambled" a bit around the town, then took a boat back to Washington.

In the days that followed, Manasseh wrote of the weather, of attending committee meetings, but said nothing of consequence until May 4, but even then he recorded only, "At five o'clock took leave of my son Ephraim, who set off for the western country." Of their conversations, of issues on their minds, political or personal, he said not a word. Nor would Ephraim. But almost certainly a great deal of what was said was

taken up with Ephraim's new role in Ohio politics now that the new
Ohio legislature was under way.

With Ephraim no longer keeping him company and the daily tedium
of so much of the congressional life, Manasseh began writing ever longer
letters home to his wife, Mary, urging her to write to him more often, so
greatly did he miss her. In another month or two, the evening of the same
day he received a letter from her, he writes, "I rejoice to hear you are well."
Then went on again at length about much that he faced in Washington.

In still another letter he was beside himself in an effort to express his
longing for her.

> Your very affectionate letter of the 6th has touched my heart
> and excited the most tender sensations. The sincerest love has
> always rendered a long absence from you extremely irksome and
> painful. . . . Be assured, my dearest love, my kind and affection-
> ate wife, that I now anticipate with anxious expectation, if it may
> please Heaven, the day when I shall have the pleasure of seeing
> you again. And then we may converse on subjects which I do not
> wish to commit to paper.

IV.

By order of Congress the town of Chillicothe, about 100 miles west of
Marietta on the Scioto River, had become the capital of the Northwest
Territory in 1800. Ephraim Cutler, a new member of the legislature, had
been appointed to a committee to create a road from Marietta to Chillicothe, and with the help of Rufus Putnam he had spent two weeks plotting a route through the woods.

At first the new territorial legislature commenced its sessions in
a two-story log house that also served as a popular tavern. Two years
later, the legislature relocated to what was reputed to be the first public
building built of stone in the Northwest Territory. It was there, during
an Ohio state constitutional convention convened in November 1802,
that the two delegates from Washington County, Rufus Putnam and

Ephraim Cutler, both new to politics, stood firm on an issue of utmost importance that they, like others, had thought long since settled—the question of slavery in Ohio.

In the election selecting Rufus Putnam and Ephraim Cutler as delegates to the convention, a black servant of Colonel Israel Putnam, Christopher Malbone, also known as Kit Putnam, was permitted to cast his ballot in the District of Marietta. It was considered to have been the first vote cast by a free black African in the Northwest Territory.

<hr />

The political picture at home in Marietta had greatly changed, just as in so much of the country since Jefferson's victory over John Adams. The time when Revolutionary War veterans, nearly all staunch Federalists, had control in Marietta had passed. Jefferson Republicans were claiming predominance. The whole makeup and nature of political rivalry had changed, and as Ephraim wrote to his father, and no doubt discussed with him during their time together in Washington, there was cause for serious concern. Political parades and gatherings were filled now, as Ephraim wrote, with "dirty, drunken, newly imported Irishmen," some quarreling, others singing the praises of their leaders, a scene "worthy of the attention of a Hogarth," he thought.

The immediate issue at Chillicothe centered around what was to be Article VIII of a new constitution, and a first preliminary discussion of the matter took place at the home of a Dr. Edward Tiffin, a resident of Chillicothe and a Jeffersonian, who was speaker of the Ohio House of Representatives.

The subject was the question of whether Ohio permit or exclude slavery. Immediately the chairman of the committee, John W. Browne, proposed a section that would define the issue quite simply: "No person shall be held in slavery, if a male, after he is thirty-five years of age; or a female, after twenty-five years of age." In other words, the tenet of the Northwest Ordinance of 1787 stating in no uncertain terms that there would be no slavery was to be eliminated. Slaves would be permitted in Ohio up to certain ages, which meant Ohio was to be a slave state.

1 General Rufus Putnam, Revolutionary War veteran and leader of the first expedition of pioneers to the far distant wilderness of "the Ohio country." In the 1840s, artist Sala Bosworth of Marietta painted this portrait in profile in order to hide Putnam's right eye, which had been disfigured in a boyhood accident.

City Hall on Wall Street in New York (later Federal Hall), where the
Continental Congress passed the Northwest Ordinance.

The Northwest Ordinance of 1787 (right), one of the most important, far-
reaching acts of Congress in history, established by law the fulfillment of
American ideals in a way nothing yet had, and was passed even before the
Constitution. It guaranteed, in the first article, freedom of religion. The
third article stated the need for education, and in the sixth article, most
important of all, it declared there would be no slavery. Until then, despite
the claim that "all men are created equal," slavery continued throughout
all of the thirteen states. Now, in five new states, a territory as large as the
original thirteen, there was to be no slavery.

An ORDINANCE for the GOVERNMENT of the TERRITORY of the UNITED STATES, North-West of the RIVER OHIO.

BE IT ORDAINED by the United States in Congress assembled, That the said territory, for the purposes of temporary government, be one district; subject, however, to be divided into two districts, as future circumstances may, in the opinion of Congress, make it expedient.

Be it ordained by the authority aforesaid, That the estates both of resident and non-resident proprietors in the said territory, dying intestate, shall descend to, and be distributed among their children, and the descendants of a deceased child in equal parts; the descendants of a deceased child or grand-child, to take the share of their deceased parent in equal parts among them: And where there shall be no children or descendants, then in equal parts to the next of kin, in equal degree; and among collaterals, the children of a deceased brother or sister of the intestate, shall have in equal parts among them their deceased parents share; and there shall in no case be a distinction between kindred of the whole and half blood; saving in all cases to the widow of the intestate, her third part of the real estate for life, and one third part of the personal estate; and this law relative to descents and dower, shall remain in full force until altered by the legislature of the district. ——— And until the governor and judges shall adopt laws as herein after mentioned, estates in the said territory may be devised or bequeathed by wills in writing, signed and sealed by him or her, in whom the estate may be, (being of full age) and attested by three witnesses; — and real estates may be conveyed by lease and release, or bargain and sale, signed, sealed, and delivered by the person being of full age, in whom the estate may be, and attested by two witnesses, provided such wills be duly proved, and such conveyances be acknowledged, or the execution thereof duly proved, and be recorded within one year after proper magistrates, courts, and registers shall be appointed for that purpose; and personal property may be transferred by delivery, saving, however, to the French and Canadian inhabitants, and other settlers of the Kaskaskies, Saint Vincent's, and the neighbouring villages, who have heretofore professed themselves citizens of Virginia, their laws and customs now in force among them, relative to the descent and conveyance of property.

Be it ordained by the authority aforesaid, That there shall be appointed from time to time, by Congress, a governor, whose commission shall continue in force for the term of three years, unless sooner revoked by Congress; he shall reside in the district, and have a freehold estate therein, in one thousand acres of land, while in the exercise of his office.

There shall be appointed from time to time, by Congress, a secretary, whose commission shall continue in force for four years, unless sooner revoked, he shall reside in the district, and have a freehold estate therein, in five hundred acres of land, while in the exercise of his office; it shall be his duty to keep and preserve the acts and laws passed by the legislature, and the public records of the district, and the proceedings of the governor in his executive department; and transmit authentic copies of such acts and proceedings, every six months, to the secretary of Congress: There shall also be appointed a court to consist of three judges, any two of whom to form a court, who shall have a common law jurisdiction, and reside in the district, and have each therein a freehold estate in five hundred acres of land, while in the exercise of their offices; and their commissions shall continue in force during good behaviour.

The governor and judges, or a majority of them, shall adopt and publish in the district, such laws of the original states, criminal and civil, as may be necessary, and best suited to the circumstances of the district, and report them to Congress, from time to time, which laws shall be in force in the district until the organization of the general assembly therein, unless disapproved of by Congress; but afterwards the legislature shall have authority to alter them as they shall think fit.

The governor for the time being, shall be commander in chief of the militia, appoint and commission all officers in the same, below the rank of general officers; all general officers shall be appointed and commissioned by Congress.

[...] one room, shall have authority by joint ballot to elect a delegate to Congress, who shall have a seat in Congress, with a right of debating, but not of voting, during this temporary government.

And for extending the fundamental principles of civil and religious liberty, which form the basis whereon these republics, their laws and constitutions are erected; to fix and establish those principles as the basis of all laws, constitutions and governments, which forever hereafter shall be formed in the said territory;—to provide also for the establishment of states, and permanent government therein, and for their admission to a share in the federal councils on an equal footing with the original states, at as early periods as may be consistent with the general interest:

It is hereby ordained and declared by the authority aforesaid, That the following articles shall be considered as articles of compact between the original states and the people and states in the said territory, and forever remain unalterable, unless by common consent, to wit:

Article the First. No person, demeaning himself in a peaceable and orderly manner, shall ever be molested on account of his mode of worship or religious sentiments in the said territory.

Article the Third. Religion, morality and knowledge, being necessary to good government and the happiness of mankind, schools and the means of education shall forever be encouraged. The utmost good faith shall always be observed towards the Indians; their lands and property shall never be taken from them without their consent; and in their property, rights and liberty, they never shall be invaded or disturbed, unless in just and lawful wars authorised by Congress; but laws founded in justice and humanity shall from time to time be made, for preventing wrongs being done to them, and for preserving peace and friendship with them.

Article the Sixth. There shall be neither slavery nor involuntary servitude in the said territory, otherwise than in punishment of crimes whereof the party shall have been duly convicted: Provided always, that any person escaping into the same, from whom labor or service is lawfully claimed in any one of the original states, such fugitive may be lawfully reclaimed and conveyed to the person claiming his or her labor or service as aforesaid.

Be it ordained by the authority aforesaid, That the resolutions of the 23d of April, 1784, relative to the subject of this ordinance, be, and the same are hereby repealed and declared null and void.

DONE by the UNITED STATES in CONGRESS assembled, the 13th day of July, in the year of our Lord 1787, and of their sovereignty and independence the 12th.

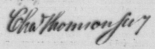

4   The Reverend Manasseh Cutler of Massachusetts, who, against all
odds, almost singlehandedly persuaded Congress to pass the Northwest
Ordinance. Artist unknown.

The first covered wagon sets off for the west from in front of the Reverend Cutler's church and parsonage in Ipswich Hamlet, Massachusetts, on the morning of Monday, December 3, 1787.

LEFT: General Rufus Putnam and the first pioneers being greeted on arrival near the Point by the Delaware chief Captain Pipe and some seventy native men, women, and children, as artist Sala Bosworth imagined the scene. Fort Harmar is seen in the distance.

BELOW: Campus Martius on the Muskingum River, measuring 188 feet in length, had an interior court and strong blockhouses at all four corners. Designed by Rufus Putnam as the bulwark of the settlement, it was built to house 864 people.

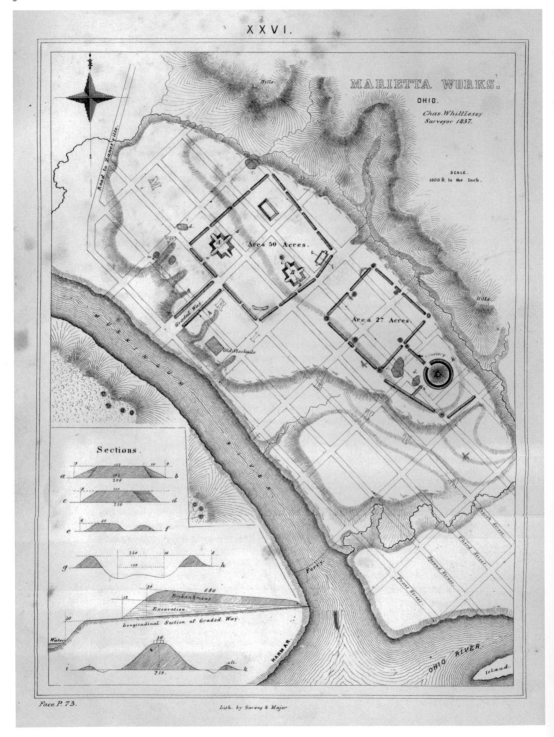

Early map of Marietta's ancient earthworks, constructed by what was known as the Ohio Hopewell culture and built between 100 BC and AD 500.

The grand sweep of the ancient earthworks with Campus Martius in the distance. Painting and drawing below both by Charles Sullivan.

The Great Mound, a thirty-foot-high ancient burial site, was to become the central feature of the cemetery of the Marietta settlement, in part as a way of protecting the historic Mound from destruction from future developers, a far-sighted decision for which Rufus Putnam was largely responsible.

Greatest and most formidable by far of the many initial challenges to be met was clearing the forests, the gigantic trees of every kind, and all by hand. Food supply in the form of white-tailed deer, wild turkey, and fish was available in quantity such as never imagined. But so, too, were wolves, panthers, black bears, and rattlesnakes.

STIZOSTETHIUM VITREUM.   WALL-EYED PIKE.

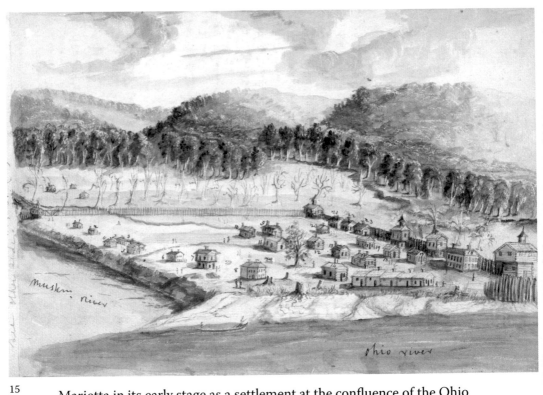

15   Marietta in its early stage as a settlement at the confluence of the Ohio and Muskingum Rivers, the area known as "The Point." Artist unknown.

16   The classic Ohio River flatboat would be described as a mixture of log cabin, floating barnyard, and country grocery. Colored lithograph based on an unsigned Ohio folk art painting.

General Arthur St. Clair, whose little knowledge of or interest in Indians, combined with notably poor judgment, led to one of the worst defeats ever of the American army in a battle by the Wabash River on November 4, 1791, to be known only as St. Clair's Defeat.

17

Colonel Winthrop Sargent, who, with so much going wrong on every side, proved himself a highly able and steadfast officer. Sketch by the great American portrait painter of the time, John Trumbull.

18

The native force of some 1,000 warriors was commanded by the Miami tribe chief Little Turtle and Shawnee chief Blue Jacket, and included the young Shawnee warrior Tecumseh (left). All were highly experienced in wilderness warfare.

19

Like Sargent, Major Ebenezer Denny proved himself a highly admirable officer in the chaos of defeat.

20

21

With the defeat of the Shawnee chief Blue Jacket and his warriors by another American force, this commanded by General Anthony Wayne, at the battle of Fallen Timbers in 1794, came the end of four years of bitter frontier fighting. At Marietta the cloud of fear lifted and life for many returned to the main task of clearing and burning trees. Painting by George Harvey.

To Ephraim there was no mystery as to who was behind the move. "The handwriting, I had no doubt, was Mr. Jefferson's." Another member of the committee, Thomas Worthington, a Virginian by background, told Ephraim that Jefferson had confided to him that he hoped such an article would be introduced into the Ohio convention, and that he hoped there would be no further effort made for the exclusion of slavery from the state.

Ephraim at once spoke up to say that those who had elected him to represent them were "very desirous" to have this matter clearly understood, and to avoid any excessive "warmth of feeling," he moved to have the matter tabled until the next meeting and he hoped very much each member of the committee would prepare a statement clearly expressing his views.

———

The following day Ephraim made the case for his position that there must be no slavery as strongly as he could and at some length, and when the issue came to a vote by the committee, "the Jeffersonian version," as he called it, "met with fewer friends" than he expected.

For some time he had not been feeling right, but the day after, the day when the issue was to be voted on by the committee of the whole convention, he had become quite ill. The nature of his ailment is not clear, but he had little or no strength to get out of bed.

Then Rufus Putnam came to his room and exclaimed, "Cutler, you must get well, be in your place, or you will lose your favorite measure."

According to one account, Putnam and another man carried him to the convention on a stretcher, but there is no reliable evidence of this. Cutler himself wrote only, "I went to the convention and moved to strike out the obnoxious matter, and made my objections as forcibly as I was able."

It was an act of wholehearted fortitude and the result was never to be forgotten. "It cost me every effort I was capable of making," he wrote, "and it passed by a majority of one vote only."

Fully fifteen years after his father's success in championing passage of the 1787 Northwest Ordinance abolishing slavery in the territory, he had carried the same banner of abolition and with success.

It was a landmark moment. As would be written in time to come, "To Ephraim Cutler, more than to any other man, posterity is indebted for shutting and barring the doors against the introduction into Ohio of the monstrous system of African slavery."

Nor was Ephraim's opposition to slavery ever to fade.

Partly for speculation and partly to encourage settlers to come to Ohio, Ephraim had purchased a "considerable" amount of land from proprietors in New England on credit, and which he sold to new settlers on credit, then waited on them until they could raise cattle to pay him. No fewer than 200 families were thus furnished with farms.

This had led him into the "droving business," which meant driving a herd of eighty or more cattle back over the mountains of Pennsylvania to markets in the east, no small or easy task. As he would explain, "There was no other means of raising funds to pay my debts, and it resulted in placing many poor families who had nothing to buy land within very flourishing circumstances."

The first such drive occurred in 1800 and was the first ever out of Ohio and he kept at it annually for thirty years. "These trips over the mountains were attended with much anxiety and fatigue," wrote his daughter Julia.

Sometimes he realized a profit upon his cattle, perhaps as often a loss was experienced. For some years the roads over the Mountains were infested by men of desperate character who laid in wait for drovers and many robberies were committed, and several murders perpetrated by them. From these dangers, father, although several times placed in circumstances of known peril, was mercifully preserved.

It was on such a drive a few years after his vote on slavery that Ephraim crossed paths with a party of slave drivers and masters, with two or three "droves" of Negroes, and, as he wrote, he "gave one of the drivers and the master who rode in a carriage, a lecture they will be likely to remember," adding, too, that he felt better for it. "I felt some energy, and what little humility I possess was roused at this shocking sight."

———•·•———

Another of the noblest of those objectives championed by the original pioneers, including most prominently Manasseh Cutler and Rufus Putnam, was higher education. In January 1795, at a meeting held in Marietta, the directors of the Ohio Company determined that two townships be reserved for the creation of a university and that a surveying party under Rufus Putnam and a guard of some fifteen men set off on the Hocking River to determine the site.

Manasseh Cutler would write,

> This was a strange introduction of the higher classics to the Northwest. In a fleet of canoes, propelled by the power of the setting pole against the swift and narrow channel of the Great Hocking, accompanied by armed guards against the lurking savages, and carrying with them the pork, beans, and hard tack that made up their rough fare, the committee of old veterans of three wars proceeded to fix, with compass and chain, the boundaries of the University lands. There was little of culture and polish in the undertaking, but rifles, canoes, and salt pork were never put to a better use.

And in this same cause now Ephraim and Rufus Putnam took the lead at Chillicothe in the signing of a charter to establish a state university at the location first surveyed on a series of hills overlooking the Hocking River. With the same brightly optimistic spirit that had inspired Putnam and others to call Marietta a "city," the little college town that was to emerge in the wilderness by the Hocking would be called Athens, and while it was Manasseh Cutler's idea to name the new institution the "American University," the name chosen was Ohio University.

But there was still more to be done in the cause for learning. From Athens to the settlement Ephraim had helped establish at Ames was approximately seven miles, and there in Ames at about this same time, as

Ephraim would write, "the intellectual wants of the neighborhood" became the subject of much conversation. And so it was decided to establish a public library there in the wilderness that would become famous as the "Coonskin Library."

A library society of some twenty-five members was organized, each of whom was assessed $2.50. The first name on the list and first librarian was Ephraim and the library was to be located in his house. To cover the cost of the books, it was decided to collect raccoon skins and proceeds from the sales of these back in Boston made possible the purchase of some fifty "choice books" selected appropriately by Manasseh Cutler.

———•———

Life for the Cutlers on their Federal Creek farm, meantime, had changed greatly. In November 1801 Ephraim's brother Jervis had appeared on the scene once again, and in the month following their younger brother Charles, too, arrived and moved in with the family.

Charles was twenty-nine, a Harvard graduate and schoolteacher, and he had come to take the place of the one previous teacher in the Ames community who had proven unacceptably "intemperate." Charles had long suffered from poor health and so had headed west also in the hope of benefiting from a change in climate. But Charles also, it seems, was an alcoholic, and had long been a worry back home. Details of his troubles during his time with Ephraim and the family are few, but tragically three years later Charles died there at age thirty-two. The sorrow felt was great indeed, and particularly by his father. Because of the great western adventure he had helped set in motion, two of his grandchildren were buried on the banks of the Ohio River. Now one of his own children was gone.

"It is painful indeed to reflect that he should fall a victim of his own imprudence," Manasseh Cutler wrote to Ephraim on receiving the news. "It is not possible for me to express the distress and anxiety of my mind for him—nor the extreme disappointment after I had struggled with almost insurmountable difficulties to get him through college, that the prospects that which early opened for usefulness and respectability, should prove abortive. But the will of God is done."

Brother Jervis, by contrast, seems to have taken hold quickly and in impressive fashion, having hired a shop in Marietta and set himself up in the tinning business. "He is in great spirits and has the reputation of an uncommon industry," Ephraim was pleased to report to their father. In another year or so he had branched out to an active fur trade in Chillicothe.

The momentum of change seemed only to increase all the while and there was no question that the hand of Jefferson, in Ephraim's expression, brought it on. He had removed and replaced Arthur St. Clair as governor, a move long overdue. At age sixty-eight St. Clair was in poor health and often out of touch. On a recent visit to Chillicothe he had gotten quite drunk. He would retire to his properties in Ligonier, Pennsylvania, where he was to die impoverished and living in a log cabin.

Jefferson also removed Rufus Putnam from the office of surveyor general of the United States, a position to which President Washington had commissioned him. As Ephraim would write, "no man in the territory more entirely deserved and enjoyed the respect and confidence of the people than General Rufus Putnam."

The Ohio legislature completed a state constitution, and it was carried to Washington, to Jefferson, who sent it on to Congress, where it was approved by both the Senate and House. It was then returned to the president, who signed it into law, and thus on February 19, 1803, Ohio became the seventeenth state of the Union and the first state established in the Northwest Territory.

Later in 1803, on an infinitely grander scale Jefferson brought about great historic change with the purchase by the United States from France of the vast Louisiana Territory west of the Mississippi. Further he commissioned Meriwether Lewis and William Clark, both experienced soldiers, to explore what had now suddenly become the new and far vaster Northwest Territory.

On the evening of September 13, the reality of this was brought home to Marietta, when Meriwether Lewis and his crew on their way down the Ohio stopped there to lay over for the night. But as everyone in town was soon to learn their progress was delayed several hours the next morning when it was discovered that two of the crew had gone ashore during the night and gotten so drunk they were of no use.

With the pull of the west growing greater than ever, the number and variety of those appearing on the scene at Marietta on their journeys on the Ohio was bound only to increase.

Among the great many who were altogether inconspicuous was a family from Leominster, Massachusetts, not far from Rutland, Rufus Putnam's hometown. Their name was Chapman and they took up frontier life in Washington County, in a log cabin on Duck Creek, fifteen miles north of Marietta, and seven miles from the nearest neighbor. They were there to stay, except for one eccentric, thirty-year-old son named John, who could not remain anywhere for long and was to become famous as Johnny Appleseed.

Like Rufus Putnam, he had a great, lifelong love of apple trees and had committed himself to supplying settlers with apple seeds or young trees, while, at the same time, he spread the gospel according to the Swedish theologian Emanuel Swedenborg. Much would be written and said about Johnny Appleseed, including much that had little or no bearing on the truth. But as for his appearance there is no doubt. It was described as outlandish even on the frontier.

> He was quick and restless in his motions and conversation; his beard and hair were long and dark, and his eyes black and sparkling. He lived the roughest life, and often slept in the woods. His clothing was mostly old, being generally given to him in exchange for apple trees. He went barefooted, and often traveled miles through the snow in that way. . . . He was welcome everywhere among the settlers, and was treated with great kindness even by the Indians.

His wanderings, almost entirely in Ohio, were to go on for more than forty years. The legend would last far longer.

CHAPTER SIX

The Burr Conspiracy

Your talents and acquirements seemed to have destined you for something more than vegetable life . . . it would seem there has been, without explanation, a sort of consent between our minds.

—AARON BURR TO HARMAN BLENNERHASSETT, APRIL 15, 1806

I.

Any thought that Blennerhassett Island could suddenly figure as the focal point of a national crisis, or that the affluent, rather odd owner of the island would be at the center of the drama, would have been utterly inconceivable to those who made Marietta their home and way of life—or that the arrival on the scene of one single public figure would set it all off.

The first appearance of Colonel Aaron Burr and his means of travel were not to be forgotten. He arrived on board as luxurious a flatboat as yet seen on the Ohio River, a "floating house," as he liked to say, built to his specifications at Pittsburgh. It was sixty feet in length, fourteen feet wide, flat-bottomed, squared-off, roofed from stem to stern, and included a dining room, kitchen with fireplace, two bedrooms, and windows of glass. A slender stairway led to the rooftop, which served as a promenade where one might enjoy the passing river scenery or evening air. That a craft so large should carry a man quite so small made the spectacle all the more memorable.

The date was May 5, 1805. Less than a year earlier, on the morning of July 11, 1804, Aaron Burr had shot and killed Alexander Hamilton in a duel and it had been only a matter of months since he ceased to be vice president, all of which was well-known in Marietta.

He was denounced as a murderer and by all conventional rules a ruined politician. He, however, did not see it that way. He had come west to explore some new and mysterious pursuits and as Hamilton himself had once said, he was "bold enough to think no enterprise too hazardous and sanguine enough to think none too difficult."

Though he stood only about five feet, six inches and at age forty-nine was going bald, Aaron Burr, still trim and handsome with luminous, almost hypnotic hazel eyes, had a way of charming nearly everyone, male or female. As his first biographer, James Parton, would write:

> He succeeded best with young men and with unsophisticated elderly gentlemen. . . . Many young men loved him almost with the love of woman, and made him their model, and succeeded in copying his virtues and his faults. He, on his part . . . succeeded in so imprinting his own character on theirs, that their career in life was like his—glorious at the beginning, disastrous, if not disgraceful, at the close.

Both Hamilton and Jefferson had called him the Catiline of America, referring to the unprincipled ancient Roman notorious for scheming against the republic.

His lineage was highly distinguished. His grandfather on his mother's side was the great New England divine Jonathan Edwards. His father, Aaron Burr, a scholar and theologian, was the president of the College of New Jersey at Princeton. Burr himself had graduated with distinction from Princeton when he was only sixteen.

He served as an officer in the Revolution, married, took up the law and New York politics and succeeded in both rapidly and conspicu-ously. In the words of a satiric poem of the time:

> *Tho' small his stature, yet his well known name,*
> *Shines with full splendor on the rolls of fame.*

Ultimately, running as a Republican—or Democrat—against Thomas Jefferson he wound up tying with Jefferson in the 1800 presi-dential race against John Adams, and by a painfully drawn-out decision by the House of Representatives became vice president. In the mean-time his most trusted political ally, his wife, Theodosia, had died.

What exactly his intentions were on his expedition west was hard to say, since he left a number of different impressions wherever he went, depending on whom he was talking to. To some he implied he had come primarily to learn as much as he could about the western country to determine his next undertaking. To others it seemed he wanted to stake out a new settlement farther south down the Mississippi. Then there were hints and rumors of founding a vast empire in the provinces of Mexico, and there were discussions, too, about the probability of a sepa-ration of the western states from the Union. But again it depended on with whom he was conversing.

According to one observer, when Burr spoke, it was "with such ani-mation, with such apparent frankness and negligence, as would induce a person to believe he was a man of guiltless and ingenuous heart." Burr also implied secrets and high, even risky adventure to come. There was no human being, the same observer continued, more "mysterious and inscrutable."

Rumors and fearful speculation about a "Burr conspiracy" kept growing. The impression among many was that he hoped for hostilities between the United States and Spain along the Louisiana-Mexico bor-der to detach New Orleans from the United States and establish a new independent country.

"How long will it be," asked an editorial in Philadelphia's *United States Gazette*, "before we hear of Colonel Burr being at the head of a revolutionary party on the western waters? . . . How soon will Colonel Burr engage in the reduction of Mexico?"

On landing at Marietta he made a visit to the ancient Mound, which seems to have interested him greatly, as did the Marietta shipyards. Much the most important stop followed, when the little Colonel stepped ashore on Blennerhassett Island on the balmy evening of May 5. With him was a single traveling companion named Gabriel Shaw, a wealthy New York law client.

As someone who happened also to be deeply in debt and in need of all the financial support possible for his grandiose schemes, whatever they might be, Burr already knew something about the Blennerhassetts and their wealth. On seeing their "castle in the wilderness" and the way of life there, he had no doubt he had come to the right place.

Many there were in Marietta, however, and especially among the veterans of the Revolution, who looked on Burr with considerable suspicion if not utter contempt, as the murderer of Hamilton, one of the heroes of the war, as well as a major stockholder in the Ohio Company. To those like Rufus Putnam and Ebenezer Sproat, as later said, Burr's arrival at Blennerhassett was "an evil hour" in which he, "like Satan in the Eden of old," visited this "earthly paradise, only to deceive and destroy."

The one surviving eyewitness account of the visit was written long afterward by the Blennerhassetts' son, Harman Jr., a small boy at the time. Burr was received with "the usual hospitality of the island," he wrote, and his father in particular was "much taken with the accomplished manners and agreeable wit and conversation of the ex–vice president."

When, at about eleven o'clock, Burr and Shaw were invited to spend the night, they politely declined, saying they preferred to sleep on the boat. The Blennerhassetts then walked them to the boat. On approaching the mooring, Burr slipped on the sandbank and fell. He immediately recovered himself, it is said, though not without observing, "That's an ill-omen!"

The morning after, he cast off downstream, heading away on his mysterious mission.

What all had been discussed or learned or revealed to his hosts during the course of conversation the evening before, no one ever said, but the months following gave rise to considerable correspondence between Burr and Harman Blennerhassett, in which Burr, in one beguiling letter, expressed the view that Blennerhassett deserved a more active, engaged life than the one he was leading, surrounded only with comforts and pleasures, all a merely passive existence. Far better, Burr said, that someone of such marked intelligence and talent as he get action, take part in the world, particularly for a man with a growing family and a gradually diminishing fortune.

It appears also that at some point the evening before, Burr had put forth to Blennerhassett the prospect of a takeover of Mexico with Burr as the emperor and Blennerhassett as his ambassador to Great Britain.

The ever-gullible Blanny had been taken as never before, and the result was all Burr could have desired. In a long letter to Burr dated December 21, 1805, Blennerhassett declared himself ready to pursue a full change in life. "I hope, sir, you will not regard it indelicate in me to observe to you how highly I should be honored in being associated with you, in any contemplated enterprise you would permit me to participate in."

With mail as slow as it was, and with Burr ever on the move, he did not respond for more than three months, but in a letter from Washington dated April 15, 1806, he expressed his "utmost pleasure" in learning that Blennerhassett was to return to the real world. He congratulated him for giving up his "vegetable life" for one of activity. "Your talents and acquirements seemed to have destined you for something more."

But as much still depended on certain "contingencies," Burr said, the business at hand could not be explained by letter, and must be deferred until private discussion was possible.

On August 27, 1806, almost a year from his first visit, Aaron Burr reappeared at Marietta and made a contract with Dudley Woodbridge, Jr., for the building of fifteen large flatboats capable of transporting 500 men, the recruits to be gathered for his mysterious expedition southward down the Ohio and Mississippi. As Woodbridge would later testify in court, "I immediately made a contract with Colonel Barker to build the boats."

Contracts were made as well for large supplies of provisions to the amount of $2,000 and Harman Blennerhassett was to cover the cost, boats and all. Of the boats to be built, one for him and his family was to have separate rooms, a fireplace, and glass windows. All was to be ready by December 9, rather late in the year, given the quantity of ice usually gathered on the river by then.

Speculation and rumors about Burr's shenanigans increased by the day along the Ohio, and particularly as Blennerhassett Island was so clearly to be the main staging ground. As reported back in Massachusetts, in the *Republican Spy*, "Letters from Marietta in Ohio state that the public mind is considerably agitated in that quarter by political intrigues, the ultimate object of which is not discerned, nor comprehensible." In public statements, Burr refused still to say no more than that it was "a laudable undertaking."

To Dudley Woodbridge, Jr., and hence to Joseph Barker, Burr confided that his expedition had secret government approval. Only days after Burr's visit, Blennerhassett confided to a neighbor that "under the auspice . . . of Colonel Burr, a separation of the Union was contemplated."

———·•·———

It was that same autumn of 1806 when a gifted, but as yet unknown young doctor from Massachusetts, Samuel P. Hildreth, arrived in Marietta for the first time. He was twenty-three years old. In time to come he was to distinguish himself as one of the outstanding physicians in all the Northwest Territory, but also as the great chronicler of Marietta's pioneer history and of the principal figures in that history, including that of the Blennerhassetts.

His first stop the afternoon of his arrival was for something to eat at a new brick tavern house at the upper end of town kept by an elderly Englishman, John Brough—a sign over the door featured the British lion. There, too, at a ball not long after, Hildreth had the pleasure of meeting the Blennerhassetts.

What struck him particularly about the couple, he recorded in his diary, was that while the husband, who did not dance, only sat and watched, she was "quite the most attractive figure and active dancer on the floor."

In little time Hildreth heard much talk and numerous opinions about Burr, the little Colonel, and what he was up to with many of the young men in Marietta and the vicinity. They were being told, Hildreth learned, that no injury was intended to the United States and that President Jefferson was not only aware of the expedition but approved it. Later on, Hildreth was to state with absolute conviction, "Not one of all that number enlisted on the Ohio would have harkened for a moment to a separation of the western from the eastern states."

Soon a series of astonishing articles by Harman Blennerhassett began appearing in *The Ohio Gazette, and Virginia Herald*, a newly established Marietta newspaper, owned by the same Elijah Backus who had sold him the island. Blennerhassett chose to write under a pseudonym, "The Querist." The pioneers of the frontier west of the Appalachians were being unfairly disregarded, overtaxed, and commercially exploited by the mercantile Atlantic states and the federal government, he insisted at length. The answer was western independence, a break from the Union.

The article drew much attention far beyond Marietta. "That he [Burr] has formed, and that he is now employed in executing, a scheme highly injurious to the interest, the tranquility, and the well-fare of the U.S. we have the strongest ground to believe," read an article in the *Richmond Inquirer* that had already appeared in the *New York Commercial Advertiser.*

From information recently received, we have been induced to believe that now powerful efforts will soon be made to sever the western states from the Union, connect them with Louisiana, and form a whole into a distinct empire with Col. Burr at its head.

Many there were, the article continued, who were "needy, unprincipled and ready at all times to embark in any desperate enterprise that holds out a prospect of accumulating a fortune. If this be the object, it is hoped that the government will be vigilant, and ready to crush with a strong arm any attempt at such a nefarious measure."

By November speculations and rumors had turned to a strong sense of alarm nearly everywhere in the country, including the White House. Jefferson had been receiving anonymous warnings for nearly a year. One dated December 1805 began:

Sir

Personal friendship for you and the love of my country induce me to give you a warning about Colonel Burr's intrigues. You admit him at your table, and you held a long and private conference with him a few days ago <u>after dinner</u> at the very moment he is mediating the overthrow of your administration and what is more conspiring against the State. Yes, sir, his aberrations through the Western States <u>had no other object.</u>

A sentence from Jefferson's Cabinet Memoranda of October 22, 1806, left no doubt of the seriousness of the Burr intrigue. During the last session of Congress, it read, "Colonel Burr who was here, finding no hope of being employed in any department of the government, opened himself confidentially to some persons on whom he thought he could rely, on a scheme of separating the Western from the Atlantic states, and erecting the former into an independent confederacy."

On November 3, 1806, Jefferson himself wrote, "Burr is unquestionably very actively engaged in the western preparations to sever that from this part of the Union."

Then came a letter to the president dated November 12 from James Wilkinson, general-in-chief of the armies of the United States and governor of the Louisiana Territory. Wilkinson, a stout, hard-drinking veteran of the Revolutionary War, had, as Burr said, "a propensity for intrigue." In fact, Wilkinson and Burr, for more than a year, had been conferring privately about possible plots. Now Wilkinson had chosen to turn on Burr, telling the president:

> This is indeed a deep, dark and widespread conspiracy, embracing the young and old, the democrat and the Federalist, the native and the foreigner, the patriot of '76 and the exotic of yesterday, the opulent and the needy, the Ins and the Outs, and I fear it will receive strong support in New Orleans.

The letter was hand-delivered to Jefferson by a Quaker merchant chosen by Wilkinson for the mission.

Why Jefferson, who loathed Burr, had delayed so long in doing much of anything about the intrigues would remain a question. But now he dispatched a trusted Virginian named John Graham, a former ambassador to Spain, who understood relations between Spain and the United States, to investigate what was happening in the west.

On reaching Marietta, Graham dined with Harman Blennerhassett at a local tavern, where Blennerhassett, under the impression that Graham had come to volunteer for the expedition, talked freely with him about plans to invade Mexico and how he was busy recruiting young men who were single, without families, and how they would be armed. When Graham told Blennerhassett he was an agent for the president to stop the expedition, Blennerhassett got up and walked out the door.

From Marietta, Graham rode swiftly on to Chillicothe, where he met with the governor of Ohio, Edward Tiffin, and convinced him that immediate action had to be taken against the conspiracy.

On Tuesday, December 2, the governor went before the assembled legislature, where the lawmakers, after two days of secret sessions of the two houses, unanimously authorized the governor to call out the militia. But as there was still no hard evidence against Burr, the legislature also transmitted a message to the president saying, "We trust that public rumor has magnified the danger, but should the design in agitation be as destructive as represented, we have no doubt that all fears will shortly be dissipated before the indignation of our citizens."

In and about Marietta those who had taken interest in the Burr venture all but disappeared. As Samuel Hildreth was to write, "When the act of the Ohio Legislature was passed, to suppress all armed assemblages, and take possession of boats with arms and provisions . . . they, almost to a man, refused to embark further in the enterprise."

A six-pound cannon was mounted on the bank of the Ohio at Marietta and every boat heading downriver was examined. Regular sentries and guards were posted with orders to stay on duty until the river froze over and all navigation ceased.

Numerous jokes were played on the militia all the while, such as setting an empty tar barrel on fire and sending it off on a raft in the dark of night. The sentries, after hailing and receiving no answer, opened fire. Then men went out to board and take possession, only to find it all a hoax.

II.

Winter had arrived at Marietta, with several inches of snow, bitter winds, and ice building up on the rivers. On the morning of December 9, an express rider from Chillicothe appeared with orders from the governor for the local militia to "take forcible possession" of the fifteen boats being built for Burr and at dusk the authorities intercepted Joseph Barker and ten of the boats already headed down the Muskingum. The rest were seized at the Barker boatyard.

What all Barker may have said or done, unfortunately remains unknown.

News of the seizure reached Blennerhassett almost immediately, as did word that a warrant was out for his arrest. On the Virginia shore the local militia was getting ready to take over the island. Clearly, it was time for Harman Blennerhassett to make his exit.

It became, as said, a night of acute "hubbub and confusion" on the island with Cajoe and other slaves moving steadily back and forth in the dark from the mansion to load boats at the river's edge, where a great bonfire blazed.

Fires, burned too, on the other side of the river, where the Ohio militia was camped and keeping watch.

A number of Marietta merchants were on hand, settling accounts with Blennerhassett before he got away, including most notably Dudley Woodbridge, Jr. To wind up all he and Blennerhassett had to settle took fully two hours.

Not until past midnight was all ready for Blennerhassett to push off with a flotilla of four boats carrying at most only thirty men, instead of the thousand or more expected. Not one man from Marietta was aboard.

Margaret Blennerhassett and the children were to follow after.

———•——

At daybreak the next morning, Saturday, December 13, she made a hurried trip by skiff to Marietta, hoping to persuade the Ohio authorities to release the family houseboat so she and her sons might depart. She was refused.

On returning to the island, she found her home had been taken over by a horde of Virginia militia raiding the larder and liquor supply, and noisily ransacking the house, while outside still more were tearing up fence rails to build fires and forcing slaves to cook for them or be imprisoned.

In her absence, only hours before, a number of young men who had been recruited by Burr in Pittsburgh also appeared on the scene by boat and were at once arrested and held captive.

Margaret angrily protested such an outrage on her property, only to be told by those in charge that as long as they were on the island the property absolutely belonged to them.

As two of the young men from Pittsburgh would recount, "There appeared to us to be no kind of subordination among the men; the large room they occupied on the first floor presented a continued scene of riot and drunkenness." The furniture appeared ruined by bayonets, and one of the militia fired his rifle through the ceiling of the large hall, the bullet passing through the chamber upstairs, near where Margaret and the children were sitting.

In another few days, the adventurers from Pittsburgh were tried in the mansion and acquitted for lack of evidence. On Wednesday, December 17, Margaret and her children departed with them on their boat.

Her Eden in the wilderness, now a scene of ruin, was to be hers no more. She was granted permission to take only some silver and books of her choice, and a few pieces of furniture. Not for another month traveling down the Ohio and Mississippi was she reunited with her husband at the mouth of the Bayou Pierre, a tributary on the Mississippi north of Natchez.

At the time of her departure from Blennerhassett Island, in the midst of all the excitement, the slave Cajoe decided the north side of the Ohio was the place for him and so managed to escape across the river and make his way to the home of the English gardener, Peter Taylor, who lived some twenty miles away on Wolf Creek. As a free man, Cajoe stayed on in Ohio, married, had children, became widely popular as a preacher, and lived until well past the age of 100.

III.

On February 18, in the village of Wakefield on the Tombigbee River in the Mississippi Territory, Aaron Burr was arrested on the orders from President Jefferson. To disguise himself, Burr was unshaven and wearing a weather-stained, broad-brimmed hat and an old homespun blanket coat, with a tin cup strapped to one side, a scalping knife to the other. But it was the eyes that "sparkled like diamonds" that gave him away.

For a month, under arrest, Burr traveled by horseback through Mississippi, Georgia, South Carolina, and North Carolina to Richmond, Virginia, where he was to be tried for treason.

Harman Blennerhassett, too, was later arrested and would make the journey under arrest to Richmond with the onset of summer, leaving Margaret behind in Mississippi.

Since Blennerhassett Island, part of Virginia, was considered "the scene" of Burr's conspiracy, Richmond had been chosen as the proper place for the trial, and there, on March 3, Burr was brought before Chief Justice John Marshall in the United States district court of Virginia.

Judge Marshall's first examination of the accused took place in the Eagle Tavern, but so large was the crowd that came to watch the proceedings that the sessions following were held in the Virginia Hall of Delegates, a notably stately structure designed by Jefferson, but which at the time was "bare," "dingy," and "dirty."

On June 24, Burr was indicted for treason. A free man no longer, he was consigned at first to the vermin-infested Richmond jail, then out of consideration of his having been the vice president of the United States, moved to three-room quarters on the top floor of the state prison, where guests were permitted, then moved again to a private house. When Harman Blennerhassett arrived in Richmond on August 3, he, too, was confined to the three rooms at the state prison.

The oppressive heat of the Virginia summer bore down heavily as the trial continued week after week.

Dudley Woodbridge, Jr., was among the many to be put on the witness stand and provided a memorable observation on how the people of Marietta and the vicinity regarded Harman Blennerhassett.

"Is he esteemed a man of vigorous talents?" he was asked.

"He is; and a man of literature," Woodbridge said. "But it was mentioned among the people in the country, that he had every kind of sense but common sense."

On the last day of August, Chief Justice Marshall of the United States Supreme Court handed down a lengthy decision. An act of treason, an act of war, "could not be levied without the employment and exhibition of force," he said. "His intention to go to war may be proved by words, but the actual going to war is a fact which is to be proved by open deed." The overt act must be proved by witnesses. "It is not proved by a single witness."

It took Marshall three hours to read his opinion. The next morning, Tuesday, September 1, 1807, the jury reached its verdict in twenty-five minutes. Burr had been acquitted, due to lack of evidence. It was a landmark decision. He and Blennerhassett were both to go free.

In the years that followed, Aaron Burr lived for a time in Europe, where he wrote notes to Napoleon, offering to overthrow the American government, then returned to New York where, after more than twenty miserable years he died in 1836, at age eighty, unrepentant to the end.

The Richmond trial over, Harman Blennerhassett returned to his wife and family in the Mississippi Territory, where with what little money they still had, he purchased a 1,000-acre plantation. There they would remain for ten years during which additional children were born. Forced by ever-mounting debt he had to sell the plantation and move the family to Montreal.

The governor of the province, an old friend, had led him to believe he might attain a post on the bench. But, as would be said, "Misfortune having marked him for her own," soon after his arrival his friend died and all Blennerhassett's expectations died with him.

He moved on again, this time to England and Ireland, in search of almost any kind of employment, only to fail.

He and the family were saved only when an elderly, unmarried sister, Avice Blennerhassett, took pity and invited them to live with her. They moved to the Isle of Guernsey off the coast of France, where the cost of living was less and the climate more beneficial. It was there Harman Blennerhassett died in 1831 at age sixty-five.

Margaret remained at Guernsey another seven years, until, following the death of Avice, she returned to New York. She died penniless in a home for destitute Irish women.

The fate of the two older sons was to be no less bleak. One died of cholera in New York. Another, an alcoholic, disappeared in the wilderness near St. Louis.

In the meantime, in 1811, the dream home she and her husband so loved on Blennerhassett Island had accidentally burned to the ground.

CHAPTER SEVEN

Adversities Aplenty

*Town property, as well as farms, sunk in value; a stop was put to
improvements in building and Marietta, the oldest town in the
state, retrograded as fast as it had ever advanced.*

—SAMUEL HILDRETH

I.

Through the summer of 1807, with the attention of so much of
the country focused on the Burr trial in Virginia, the people of
Marietta, indeed people along hundreds of miles of the Ohio
River Valley, were far more preoccupied with serious trouble there on
home ground—an outbreak of deadly fever.

Only two years before, in 1805, Philadelphia and several other eastern cities suffered a yellow fever epidemic that took about 400 lives,
and among those now stricken in the Ohio Valley there were some
cases "resembling very nearly the yellow fever of the Atlantic cities."
As young Dr. Samuel Hildreth was to observe, most were bilious fever,
or influenza. The symptoms included "pain in the head . . . bad taste in
the mouth, pain in the back . . . followed by fever, attended with more
or less delirium." In Belpre, where he was the only doctor in residence,

Hildreth suddenly found himself responsible for no fewer than 100 cases.

The Marietta death toll was such as had never been known. Scarcely a family had not been struck by the fever and for those still in good health, the worry over family and friends, and the grief over the losses, was dreadful, as expressed in a letter written by William Woodbridge, a son of Lucy Woodbridge, to his brother Dudley Jr., who was away.

> Maj. Lincoln is dead and his wife is at the point of death. Holt is dead. Old Thornily and his wife are dead, a girl that lived at old Mrs. Gilman's is dead. Mr. Fearing is very sick. Miss Gilman has been dangerous and her brother also. . . . Mr. Munn is very sick. . . . Mrs. Brough, Moses McFarland and his wife are all supposed [to be] at the point of death.

Somewhere between fifty and sixty men, women, and children died.

Of the 100 cases under young Hildreth's care at Belpre, only two or three were to die, and his reputation soared. He earned an unimaginable $1,400 in fees.

———

The son of a physician, Samuel Prescott Hildreth had grown up with five sisters and a younger brother in the small town of Methuen, Massachusetts. For a time he attended Phillips Academy at Andover, a six-mile hike from home, where in addition to his concentration on Latin and English grammar, he "paid considerable attention to drawing and painting in water colors" and became quite accomplished at both.

Thanks to an uncle who had an extensive private library, he also became "extravagantly fond of reading" and in the course of four or five years read nearly all the books the library contained.

He was also, as he would later say, "passionately fond" of amusement, and "indulged" himself at every opportunity. He loved parties, loved to dance. He was never to forget the three black musicians who lived nearby and provided "very fine music," one on the bassoon, another the clarinet, the third on the violin. "All combined, they animated our youthful hearts with such life and spirit as made even the heaviest feet light."

At age eighteen, with the encouragement of his father, he began the study of medicine, first with his father, then, along with five other young men, under Dr. Thomas Kittredge of Andover, a much celebrated surgeon and "a perfect model in dress and manners of a New England gentleman of that day."

"I generally read about ten hours every day," Hildreth would recall. "The last year of the pupilage we were allowed to ride with the doctor in his practice, our journeys extending into all the neighboring towns, especially in surgical operations."

In the winter of 1803–04 he taught school to some 120 students, "a severe task." He also kept up with his medical studies, reading six hours a day, and to do this had to rise at four in the morning and read by candlelight.

In the fall of 1804, he began an eight-week course of medical lectures at Harvard (what he called Cambridge College), and the following February, examined by the Massachusetts Medical Society, he received a diploma to practice physic and surgery. That spring he was trying to figure where to "cast my lot." In New England there was an oversupply of medical practitioners.

He was in fine health, of medium height, physically strong, noticeably handsome, and of cheerful disposition, clearly a young man of promise, and he was ready to move on. A local pastor named Wardsworth, whose advice he greatly valued, told him to go west, and that as the country grew, he would grow with it.

Another older man he knew and liked, the keeper of a general store named John True, told him about a brother of his, a doctor, Jabez True, who lived in Marietta, and spoke of it as a most favorably growing town and a good place to practice medicine. After a short while Dr. True invited Samuel to come west, promising to help him get started.

As it happened, Samuel had heard about Marietta since boyhood, when his father, encouraged by the Reverend Manasseh Cutler, purchased two shares of Ohio Company land, and so, like the many others before, he made up his mind.

He gathered what money he had, some $120, and after paying his bills, still had $50, which along with his horse and all the clothes he could jam into his portmanteau, he said goodbye to his mother and father, sisters and brother, and on September 9, 1806, at age twenty-three, headed off on his own. In Boston, he stopped briefly to purchase a brace of pistols for $9.50, thinking he might need them on the road.

The journey took twenty-five days, during which he experienced one violent rainstorm, lost his way several times, spent one night by the Susquehanna River in a bed that was not only highly uncomfortable but well-stocked with bugs, rode forty miles another day, passed another night in the Allegheny Mountains in what he judged to be the dirtiest house he ever saw, "the beds most wretched and sheets very black."

He spent another night in a backwoods farmhouse watching two old cronies drink more Monongahela whiskey at a single sitting than he had ever witnessed and listened happily as they went on about their adventures of earlier days.

At Wheeling, at about noon the first day of October, he first saw "the beautiful Ohio." As he rode on down the banks of the river, his horse's back became extremely swollen and tender, so he let the horse walk free much of the way. He reached Marietta Saturday, October 4, about mid-afternoon, and stopped first for something to eat at the Englishman John Brough's new brick tavern.

He knew not a soul. He had no relatives or friends of his parents who had come to Marietta before him, no friends of his own from home. Not a familiar face was to be seen. But the welcome he received from Dr. Jabez True that evening was all he could have hoped for.

Dr. True, Marietta's first physician, had a long-standing interest in the advancement of young people. For a number of years, at the time of the Indian Wars, he had taught school students the fundamentals of reading, writing, and arithmetic at one of the blockhouses on the Point.

The day after Hildreth's arrival, a Sunday, Dr. True took him to the Congregational services held in the academy building where the young newcomer saw plainly that most Mariettans were New Englanders like himself. He even shared acquaintances with some he met.

Dr. True told Hildreth of the need for a physician at Belpre and the following day rode with him down the river to look Belpre over, and on both the ride down and the ride back talked with him on a wide range of subjects.

———•—•———

Despite all the stress and tragedy of the epidemic summer, the flow of life quite naturally went on, and even for the young physician. That same August at Belpre he was married to Rhoda Cook, the beautiful daughter of a proper "New England lady" who kept the boardinghouse where he was staying.

Not only had he acquired a partner for life, he had purchased from the sale of Harman Blennerhassett's library six volumes of the *Medical Repository.* They were his first purchase for what was to be his medical library. They were also his first exposure to the most important scientific periodical of the time and the one in which he was to publish and distinguish himself throughout his profession with scores of his own contributions, the first of which, published in 1808, was about the influenza epidemic at Belpre.

In little time he and his bride began thinking about leaving Belpre and talked of moving downriver to Cincinnati, but as her mother was opposed to the idea, they concluded to settle in Marietta, where all seemed to be going well, and where the New England atmosphere was much to their liking.

———•—•———

Though Marietta had still to go a long way to become the idealized "City upon the Hill," the same plan of the town as laid out by Rufus Putnam held in place. Welcome improvements were to be seen nearly everywhere and the growth of the economy, if not up to that of Cincinnati, remained strong. Openly pleased by all he saw, one visitor from the east was to declare, "Marietta may be considered as New England in miniature."

Far the most conspicuous evidence of this was the importance shipbuilding had become to the whole way of life, just as it had for so long in New England and just as Rufus Putnam and Manasseh Cutler and others had foreseen. "Shipbuilding will be a capital branch of business on the Ohio and its confluent streams," Manasseh Cutler had written in 1787, now twenty years past.

In the six years since Commodore Whipple sailed the first fully rigged ship, the *St. Clair*, down the Ohio to the Mississippi and on to New Orleans, the shipyards at Marietta and upstream on the Muskingum had continued to produce and prosper, just as traffic on the river increased steadily, as did the volume of trade, the main items of which were: flour, whiskey, apples, cider, peach and apple brandy, beer, iron and castings, tin and copper wares, glass, cabinet work, Windsor chairs, boots, shoes, millstones, grindstones, bacon, beef, pork, lumber, and nails. The main articles brought up the Ohio in keelboats were cotton and furs, hemp and tobacco.

The Marietta shipyards, along with Greene & Company, which built the *St. Clair*, were those of Jonathan Devol, Joseph Barker, Benjamin Ives Gilman, Colonel Abner Lord, and were all highly active. It had become an enterprise of greatest importance. "This part of the country owes much to those gentlemen, who, in a new and experimental line, have set this example of enterprise and perseverance."

In addition three rope-works were in operation to supply rigging and cordage. The summer of 1807 saw two ships, three brigs, and two schooners being built at one time.

The local supply of the best timber, all that was needed, remained at hand. Jervis Cutler, still active in the fur trade and now an officer in the Ohio militia, had studied closely the situation on the Muskingum while at work on his ambitious *A Topographical Description of the State of Ohio, Indiana Territory, and Louisiana*, particularly the work at Captain Devol's shipyard. Jervis would write admiringly that "the workmanship and timber of these vessels are said not to be inferior to any that have been built in the United States.

> Their frames were black walnut, which is said to be as durable as the live oak and is much lighter. The plank of these vessels are said to be of an unusual length and firmness. The forests here abound with the best of timber, such as white oak, black walnut and locust, and the prodigious height and size of the trees, admit of the selection of any dimensions which can be wanted. Excellent masts of yellow pine are easily procured.

Nor was there any reason to doubt that the need for such resources and productivity would continue far into the future. As said, "Ship building was carried on with considerable spirit."

But then, in the last weeks of the year 1807, came still another blow, this like no other before it.

President Jefferson, with the immediate support of Congress, had put through the Embargo Act, in the hope of strangling English commerce at sea, as a way of avoiding all-out war. American ships were now forbidden to carry exports. The act went into effect immediately with the result that shipbuilding on the Ohio and Muskingum came to an abrupt halt.

One of the prominent local shipbuilders was to inscribe for his children on a page of the family Bible what he hoped would "bear testimony against the cruel policy of Jefferson . . . which has been destructive as to our interest and lives." Shipbuilder Abner Lord himself had been so hard hit by the blow he gave up his enterprise and moved away.

The local economy went into a slump from which it was not to recover for several years. Nor did the east escape the blow. A number of small eastern seaports like Newburyport, Massachusetts, and New Haven, Connecticut, suffered severely.

Marietta was extremely hard hit. Town property, as well as farm land, sank in value. A halt was made in the improvement of buildings. As Samuel Hildreth was to write, Marietta "retrograded." Cincinnati was now seen as the future "Queen City" of the west.

But if Hildreth and his wife, Rhoda, then or later, had any second thoughts about having chosen Marietta over Cincinnati as their home, there is no evidence of it. Their love for the town and attachment to its surroundings only increased and there he would achieve an outstanding role as a dedicated local physician and loyal citizen, but was also to become a ranking trailblazer in the field of natural history, as well as one of the pioneer American scientists of the time.

For $70 a year the Hildreths rented the large, comfortable house in Marietta that had been the home of Colonel Ebenezer Sproat, "Old Buckeye," who had died quite suddenly and "in the full vigor of health," in 1805.

On April 20, 1808, an advertisement on the front page of Marietta's *The Ohio Gazette, and Virginia Herald* announced:

> Physician and Surgeon—Samuel P. Hildreth—respectfully informs the inhabitants of Marietta and the vicinity, that he practices in the above branches. The strictest attention will be paid to all who may favor him with their commands and as little expense as possible. He may be found at any hour by calling at the mansion of the late Col. Sproat.

In May the Hildreths' first child, Mary Ann, was born. He had become a father, Hildreth would write, and felt that "new responsibilities had fallen upon me. It also strengthened the bond of union between me and my wife, making it still more tender and enduring." Five more children were to follow.

As a way of getting to know his new location and also out of natural inquisitiveness, Hildreth worked up his own concise description of the town and its surroundings.

"Marietta, at present, contains about 180 dwelling houses, and nearly 1500 inhabitants," he noted.

> Many of the houses are large and elegant, and nearly half of them are brick. About 20 houses have been built within a year. The public buildings are a court house, jail, academy and two meeting houses; one of wood, large and very elegant; the other of brick, not finished—both begun since 1807. The public offices are, a post office, a receiver's office, and recorder's office. A bank, the capital which is $100,000 was established in 1807.

As he did not record, and most likely because he was too new to town to know, the "very elegant" new Congregational Church was both planned and in good part paid for by Rufus Putnam, who generously contributed $800 and purchased thirty pews sold at auction. In keeping with the town's emphasis on the New England look and ways, this handsome structure was an almost exact duplicate of the Hollis Street Congregational Church in Boston, designed by the great Charles Bulfinch, with the twin towers providing the most recognizable similarity. It stood on Front Street overlooking the Muskingum and was already a town landmark. It would be completed in 1808.

In his survey, Hildreth went on to describe the more prevalent diseases of the area, the local climate, the crops grown, the weather, the medicinal plants to be found, the minerals, clays, the variety of stones. His curiosity about nearly everything was boundless.

The flow of humanity westward down the Ohio River bound for Virginia or Kentucky beyond kept growing. "Ohio Fever" had become epidemic. In a single decade, from 1800 to 1810, the population of Ohio grew from 45,365 to 230,760. Noticeably greater, too, were the number of professionals joining the migration. Even in Marietta, which was not growing anything like Cincinnati, but remained still a small community, there were now five doctors besides Samuel Hildreth.

Even so, despite the competition, he developed in no time an extremely busy and lucrative practice as a frontier physician. He was constantly in demand, rarely still, treating diseases of all kinds, tend-ing wounds of every size, origin, and seriousness, broken bones, burns, snake and insect bites, infections, and never-ending childbirths.

"Whoever pursues the healing art . . . is no longer master of his own time, nor of his own person, but his time and himself are at the call of another," Hildreth would write.

He could be only just sitting down at the table to enjoy a meal with his family, or have only laid his head on the pillow after an exhausting day and be called at a moment's notice. There was as well the further burden, the constant anxiety, felt by anyone with heart that went with the responsibility of lives.

His house calls, so called, often required going by horseback twenty miles or more into the dense forest and often at night. One of the first of many of these calls was to visit a patient across the Ohio River in the wilds of Virginia thirty-two miles from Marietta, most of the journey made after dark with the help of a guide. When they arrived at last at a miserable cabin about midnight, the man in distress died only minutes later.

On another occasion he had to ride sixteen miles no fewer than three times to help deliver a child, all because of the expectant mother's false tally on her "notching stick," her way of keeping count of the months of her pregnancy.

Few saw how extremely primitive life remained outside towns like Marietta or Belpre and fewer still put down on paper such firsthand accounts as did young Dr. Hildreth. Among the most memorable of these was a visit to a patient some thirty-four miles from Marietta, on the headwaters of Duck Creek. The settlement was quite new, clusters of log huts occupied primarily by people from the backwoods of Virginia, most of whom had the same family name.

"The roads were deep and muddy," Hildreth was to write, "and towards the end of the journey the trace was a mere bridle path, marked out by blazes on the trees. The streams of water had to be forded, as bridges then were of rare occurrence."

He arrived just at nightfall. The patient was a young woman, about sixteen or so and "much emaciated" from the discharge of a large ulcer on the bones of the sacrum, the posterior side of the pelvis, as a result of an accident of several months before. Of his method of treatment, he wrote nothing, rather the focus of his account was the crowd that gathered.

"Soon after my arrival, quite a number of the settlers, living within three or four miles of the cabin, assembled to see the strange doctor, and where they had any disease, to get advice, as I was the first who had visited the settlement."

He described their attire, both men and women wearing either homespun linsey-woolsey, or dressed deer skins, their feet protected by moccasins. Every man wore his hunting shirt, secured by a leather belt, on which hung a large knife with a stout buckhorn handle. Caps made of the skins of raccoon or fox topped their heads, with the tail attached behind.

The cabin in which all were gathered consisted of "a single room, about sixteen feet square, built of rough logs, with a puncheon floor. . . .

Two or three rough wooden stools supplied the place of chairs, and as the neighbors came in the men took seats on the floor, Indian fashion, with their backs to the wall, all round the sides of the room; while I was making my prescriptions, and answering the inquiries of these simple minded people, the good woman of the cabin was preparing the evening meal. It was quite instructive to see how few comforts and little furniture a family could live and the business of housekeeping be conducted.

He went on to describe the cooking apparatus, the common cast iron "bake oven," a heavy black kettle with an iron cover. Filled with slices of fresh venison and salt pork, it went on top of a huge fire in the fireplace until sufficiently cooked, after which it was poured into a large brown earthen platter and set down on the hearth. The kettle was then refilled with the dough of Indian meal, put back on a bed of hot embers, and allowed to bake into "pone bread." That accomplished, the kettle was again employed to make a hot drink of spring water and maple sugar and the guests were invited to take seats or stand at the table.

"There were no plates," Hildreth wrote, "but each one had a fork or his hunting knife, with which he speared up pieces of meat from the platter, conveying them to his mouth, with occasional bites of nice pone bread, in the most natural and easy manner."

As the evening grew late, those who lived nearby left for home, while those who lived farther off were invited to spend the night, including Dr. Hildreth.

Above all it was the medical profession that figured foremost, that he had "the blessed means of rescuing a father, mother, or a child, of some distressed family, from the grasp of death," that was the physician's "richest compensation to be prized far above gold, however necessary it may be to our wants and is his best, if not often his only reward for many a long and weary ride, and many a sleepless night."

The country physician had inevitable adversities to face but as Hildreth was to emphasize in one of his articles, he himself had his own source of compensation, of enjoyment. On his solitary rides the physician need not be downcast or feel alone, not with such wonders of nature all about him.

> During the spring, as he traverses the woodlands and prairies, he can collect for his herbarium the choicest gifts of flora, and select such medicinal plants as will be useful in [treating] diseases. In the summer, endless species of insects, offering the most charming specimens for his entomological collection, cluster around him and beset his path on every side. Many of the most rare and beautiful in my cabinet were collected in my country rides. Has he a taste for conchology, various species of land shells are strewed along the way, and in every rivulet he crosses, contains varieties of bivalves. In autumn the hill sides and the banks of streams, offer continual subjects to exercise his skill in geology; while the frosty nights of winter, in the sparkling stars and heavenly constellations, afford the sublimest views for his contemplation.

There seemed no end to his interests, or the reach of his appeal among the many with whom he came in contact and the respect they had for him. "He observed and noticed," one friend remembered, "everything that came within the range of a capacious mind."

In the fall of 1810, when a number of his Republican friends placed him on the ticket as a representative of Washington and Athens counties in the state legislature, he suddenly found himself, at age twenty-seven, the youngest member of Ohio's House of Representatives.

His political career "terminated" after two sessions. As he would explain, "I never had any talent for oratory." And so he returned to his professional duties and private life without the least regret, "fully satisfied with my trial to become a noted public character."

Nonetheless, he had drafted and succeeded in getting passed a first bill for the regulation of the practice of medicine.

Along with everything else, he somehow found time to draw and paint and with stunning results, and particularly with his exquisite watercolors of speckled caterpillars morphing into dazzling butterflies. He had been fascinated with butterflies since a boy. "I have not language to express the delight afforded to me from the sight of rich colors, especially those of a small butterfly commonly seen on the blossoms of the thistle. I never tired of looking at them."

But then he never seemed to tire of looking at almost any form of nature. The love of natural science, as he said, had followed him all his days, and served as "a never failing source of enjoyment amidst the perplexities of life."

Asked how it was that he could do so much and accomplish so much, he said, "I've learned to use every one of all the odds and ends of the time."

II.

For Ephraim and Leah Cutler it had become an extremely difficult time. Her health, a concern even before they first came west, had taken such a downward turn that to give her the help and attention needed Ephraim had ceased serving in the legislature.

The situation became such that it was decided Leah must be nearer proper medical attention. So they had leased the wilderness farm they had worked so hard to establish near Ames and in the last week of December 1806 departed in two wagons. After three days of slow-going twenty-seven miles through the woods, they reached the banks of the Ohio to settle temporarily in a rented house at Belpre in what was to become the township of Warren.

With the passing of winter Ephraim began clearing land to build a new home on high ground beside the river farther upstream six miles below Marietta.

He was far from alone in his concern about Leah, who had the "decided symptoms" of consumption. "We feel extremely anxious about her," his father wrote from Hamilton. "We rejoice that you have left your farm so that she will be freed from so much [to] care [for]. I would recommend to her to abstain from all labor, to use an easy, generous diet and have her mind as easy and quiet as possible."

Because of an extremely rainy spring in Ohio, progress on the new house went slowly and Leah's condition grew worse to the point where it became clear she had little time left to live.

Leah died on November 3, 1807, at the age of forty-two. It was the worst blow of Ephraim's life.

But in her final days, she had offered some advice. For his own good and that of their four children, she had insisted, he must remain single a short time only and remarry. She even went so far as to name the person she thought best suited for him. It was an act of genuine, selfless good intent, and of courage.

The woman she had in mind was not someone she knew, only heard about. Her name was Sally Parker and she was also unknown to Ephraim. Thirty years old, or ten years younger than he, she had been born and raised in Newburyport, Massachusetts, before coming west with her family at age eleven. They had left their home in the summer of 1788. Her father, William Parker, had a proprietor's share in the Ohio Company of over a thousand acres, but on reaching western Pennsylvania decided he did not want, not yet at least, to risk his wife and family to the realities of life on the Ohio frontier. Instead he purchased a small farm in western Pennsylvania. Not until 1800 did they continue on to Ohio. By then Sally was twenty-three.

On March 11, 1808, a matter of only a few months after Leah's death, Ephraim sat down to write Sally Parker a letter. "It is with great diffidence I presume to address you on a subject which to me is of the highest importance," he began.

I am at this time destitute of that solace of the heart a female friend to whom I can disclose my cares or who can alleviate my sorrows, assuage my grief or share my joys. The author of our natures has given your sex the most unlimited faculties and powers in all those respects and has said that it is not good, for a man to be alone. I am not insensible of the hard terms which I have to offer you and in consequence a total rejection of my suit is what I have a right to expect. . . . I have nothing to give as a compensation for this but my love and respect, but I find the impetuosity of my passion has carried me too far. I will then only ask the favor to address you and cultivate an acquaintance. As I am very anxious to know my fate I must ask the favor that you will condescend so much as to convey to me your sentiment in such a way as you may think proper.

Four days later came her reply. She felt herself in an "awkward predicament," knowing nothing of his "person, manners, taste and sentiments," but given his reputation as a gentleman: "If a personal interview is consistent with your desire, I am induced by the principles of politeness to accede thereto." When or where they met for the first time was not recorded.

Ephraim felt a great need for advice from his father, who by this time because of health problems had retired from Congress and returned home to Hamilton and his responsibilities as pastor of the First Congregational Church.

In a letter dated April 4, Ephraim wrote to tell his father about

Sally Parker and to say he had marriage much in mind and without delay.

"She is a person of excellent character and of a refined and cultivated mind and manners," he wrote, but added that he could not count on any fortune to come with the marriage. "Her father is a good liver with a handsome property, but has eleven children. Of course each one's share will be small."

That same day, April 4, Ephraim also wrote what appears to have been his first all-out love letter to Sally. "The heart when full to over-flowing seeks a vent and nothing relieves it so effectively," he began, "as to pour out our thoughts to [the] one we love."

He was busy every day, at work on his new house, but thinking of her constantly.

> The lonely hours I pass, altho' I am surrounded by noisy work-men and trifling neighbors are tedious. Indeed, there is none to whom I can divulge my thoughts. . . . You may well conceive then the pleasure I take in flying to my pen for relief. . . . You will my dear, pardon me when you consider that my heart has been a long time, as it were, on the rack, its feelings have been strained on the highest cord of grief, sorrow and joy and love, it now wants a repose and how can it enjoy repose when every-thing that is dear, to it is at such a distance. Oh my sweet girl, how can it be possible for one to live without you. I have felt the rapture of the most refined love. . . . O my dear every little pleasure I enjoy, every beauty of nature I see loudly tells me who is absent.

His father's reply from back home, dated May 6, was all Ephraim could have hoped for. "I have no hesitation in advising you to do it," wrote Manasseh Cutler, "and so far as I am acquainted with your cir-cumstances, I should conceive it best for you to do it as soon as you can make it convenient. It is true, a decent respect ought to be paid to the memory of a very valuable deceased companion, but I never thought that propriety in this respect rendered long delay necessary especially where the circumstances of a family required the forming a new connection.

> You are sensible [he continued] I can give no advice with respect to the individual you name, as she is a perfect stranger. Your choice might be left to your own judgment and the advice of friends who are acquainted. But a person pointed out by your late excellent wife, I think you must prefer, if all other instances accord, much before any other. This would certainly have weight in my mind. I think her advice that you should not remain single long is a strong proof of the correctness of her judgment.

But by then Ephraim and Sally were already man and wife. They were married on April 13, Ephraim's forty-first birthday.

In his reply to his father to tell him the news so his new bride would not remain "a perfect stranger," Ephraim provided a first full-scale description:

> She is tall and of a very agreeable figure. Her countenance is very striking, it is perfectly engaging without having that regularity which distinguishes great beauties, a native dignity and elegance of manners added to this intelligent and serene countenance with a modest air which tells the beholder she is well bred, cannot fail to be interesting.

Since leaving Massachusetts at age eleven, she had had no "benefit from schools," Ephraim continued, but well aware of the importance his father put on education, he quickly added with emphasis that, nonetheless, she was "well acquainted with history, geography, poetry, and music," largely because of her mother and her own "ardent thirst for knowledge." Her taste, he said, particularly her love of reading and appreciation of nature, was congenial to his own.

Finally, knowing how it would delight his father, he added, "She would indeed make an excellent botanist in a short time under your tuition, for nothing [would be] more pleasing to her than to trace things to their secret springs and to look through nature up to nature's God."

Sally proved almost at once to be a highly welcomed addition to the Cutler family, warm-spirited, well-mannered, and witty. As one of Ephraim's daughters, Julia, would one day write, "She not only superintended and participated [in] the labors of the large household, but by her systematic methods found time to direct, in their early years, the studies and hear the recitations of her children."

Ephraim and Sally were to add five more children to the family, the first of whom was born a year after their marriage, the second a year after that.

Ephraim finished building their new home, a handsome, two-story stone house facing the Ohio River at what was to become the town of Warren, named for one of the heroes of the Revolution, General Joseph Warren, who was killed at the battle of Bunker Hill.

The house had taken longer to complete and cost more than he had expected. It "absorbed all my means," as he would write, and he had already been in debt. Indeed, if Ephraim Cutler had one failing, it was his seeming inability ever to be out of debt and remain so. Nonetheless he and Sally were to make the new home a center of hospitality in all seasons.

As daughter Julia was also to recount, "A free hospitality characterized the early settlers of Ohio, and in few houses was its exercise more constant than at the Cutler homestead." New Englanders who came west to see for themselves, proprietors of shares in the Ohio Company, plus any number of others, would stop for a rest from the fatigue of their travels.

"Travelers, or persons visiting Marietta often had letters of introduction to father, or were brought by gentlemen of that place to see him," Julia wrote. "And an impromptu dinner party of well informed and agreeable people was no rare occurrence and not infrequently the visit was prolonged until the next day. My mother and father were both eminently social and good talkers, and often on these occasions friendly, delightful intercourse continued into the small hours of the night."

But, as she also added, "Sometimes it must be confessed the pleasure of this free hospitality had its drawbacks. Disagreeable people would occasionally take advantage of it, in several instances prolonging their stay two to three months."

Local veterans of the Revolution, many among Ephraim's best friends, were always welcome guests for dinner or an overnight stay. Ministers passing through or visiting would preach a sermon in the house, and for nearly a year the front sitting room served as the first school in the community.

When, after a time, Ephraim returned to service in the state legislature, all manner of politicians, attorneys, pleaders for one cause or another kept coming and going.

III.

The winds of change, the unexpected blows of nature, and unexpected developments taking place elsewhere kept striking and with pronounced repercussions for the people of the Ohio Valley. In 1807 it had been the influenza epidemic, then Jefferson's Embargo Act.

But it was also in 1807, on August 17 in New York, that Robert Fulton's new steamboat made her memorable voyage up the Hudson River to Albany and back, attaining a speed of five miles per hour.

Four years later in the 1811 edition of an Ohio River guidebook called *The Navigator*, published in Pittsburgh, appeared a most important item.

> There is now on foot a new mode of navigating our western waters, particularly the Ohio and Mississippi rivers. This is with boats propelled by the power of steam. This plan has been carried into successful operation on the Hudson River at New York, and on the Delaware between New Castle and Burlington. It has been stated that the one on the Hudson goes at the rate of four miles an hour against wind and tide on her route between New York and Albany, and frequently with 500 passengers on board.

From these successful experiments there can be but little doubt
of the plan succeeding on our western waters, and proving of immense advantage to the commerce of our country.

A Mr. Rosewalt [Nicholas Roosevelt], a gentleman of
enterprise . . . has a boat of this kind now on the stocks at
Pittsburgh, of 138 feet keel, calculated for 300 or 400 tons
burden. . . . It will be a novel sight, and as pleasing as novel to see
a huge boat working her way up the windings of the Ohio, without the appearance of sail, oar, pole or any manual labor about
her—moving within the secrets of her own wonderful mecha-
nism, and propelled by power undiscoverable! This plan if it suc-
ceeds, must open to view flattering prospects to an immense
country, an interior of not less than two thousand miles of as
fine a soil and climate, as the world can produce, and to a people
worthy of all the advantages that nature and art can give them.

In late October 1811 the first steamboat on western waters, the
New Orleans, under the command of its builder, Nicholas Roosevelt,
departed from Pittsburgh and proceeded down the Ohio at an astonishing speed of 12 miles per hour. Fifteen people were on board, including
Roosevelt, his wife, and their two-year-old daughter. After a brief stop
at Marietta, where they were greeted by a cheering crowd, they traveled
on down the full length of the Ohio and on to the Mississippi, then all
the way to New Orleans, 2,000 miles in fourteen days.

The age of steam had arrived on western waters.

After the *New Orleans*, in a matter of only a few years, would follow
the steamboats *Comet, Vesuvius, Enterprise, Aetna, Dispatch, Buffalo*,
and more. The moving of produce and supplies, as well as countless passengers both downstream and back, was never to be the same.

In mid-December 1811, Marietta was hit by a major earthquake. It happened at night. Doors and windows rattled loud enough to wake people
from a sound sleep. Many instantly sprang from their beds thinking it

an Indian attack. A neighbor of Samuel Hildreth grabbed an ax and stood ready at the door until he was nearly frozen, having put on no clothes.

Elsewhere in town chimneys toppled. Downriver the shaking was even more pronounced. "The first shock was at half-past two o'clock [A.M.]," Ephraim Cutler recorded, ". . . the floors and joists made a noise much like a frame house in a violent wind; as our house is stone, and we never perceive the least motion in the hardest winds, we were of course alarmed."

About sunrise came another shock. At eight o'clock the house began to shake again and this time for forty-five minutes. In the course of the day ten distinctive shocks were felt.

As was soon to become known, what happened there on the Ohio was mild compared to the great earthquake that hit at the same time in Missouri territory. There huge riverbanks collapsed. Islands in the river disappeared, and great gaps burst open in the earth engulfing trees, rocks, and whatever else was on the surface. Many took it to mean Judgment Day was upon them.

With the new year came more quakes. In February 1812, Ohio was hit again and even harder than before. Ephraim Cutler happened this time to be in Zanesville. He was serving again in the state legislature, and the state capital had by then been relocated there from Chillicothe.

"On the 3rd of February I was . . . in the senate chamber about nine o'clock in the morning, when the court house in which we were shook to that degree that nearly all the people, perhaps three hundred, rushed out. I felt a giddiness and nausea, which I found was the case with many others." The spire on the courthouse vibrated a good twelve inches.

———•——

Less than six months later, the United States was at war with Great Britain. The War of 1812, as it was to be known, was far from popular in the country, and among Federalists especially.

New England was the section most strongly opposed and outspoken on the subject. Manasseh Cutler in a letter to Ephraim stated his views on both the war and President Madison in no uncertain terms. The war was "unprovoked, unnecessary, and abominably unjust," he wrote. "Nor will it ever be much otherwise, until there is a commander-in-chief who is fit for the station. . . . In this quarter, the distresses of the war are most sensibly felt. Commerce has almost totally ceased."

The war was unpopular everywhere and in Marietta, too. In the July 6, 1812, edition of a new Federalist newspaper, *Western Spectator*, edited by a Marietta lawyer named Caleb Emerson, appeared the following editorial statement titled "Our Manifesto":

> As war is declared, we must necessarily wish success to the army of our own country; of that country in whose welfare of all we shall hold dear in this world. But a state of war is the last situation in which we will be induced to be silent on the acts of an administration which we deem unfit to manage the concerns of our country.

In a letter to Caleb Strong, a former United States senator and governor of Massachusetts, Rufus Putnam would write that though different opinions were to be found there in Marietta, he had little hope for the present foolish administration. "No sir, nothing that is generous candid or honest in the conduct [of our] present administration toward the British have I seen or expect to see from Mr. Madison." Rufus Putnam and Ephraim Cutler were at the center of Ohio's opposition to the war.

Of the many concerns in Ohio, greatest and most immediate was that the British would rekindle the "Indian menace" and particularly in the northwest corner of the state. "The savages may now be expected to attack our frontiers in every direction," warned the *Western Spectator.* Of extreme worry was news that the great Shawnee chief, Tecumseh, with some of his followers had joined the British Army, in the belief that an English triumph would allow him to establish the Indian state he envisioned.

In August the British commander on the Canadian side of the border convinced the American in command at Detroit he must surrender

Detroit or face a massacre. The elderly American commander, General William Hull, surrendered.

And then there was the presence of a British fleet on Lake Erie. Clearly Ohio was very much in harm's way.

To add to this came a flood on the Ohio River such as no one had yet imagined. As early as 1755, a writer had said the river, as the winter thawed by warmth or rains in the spring, rose in vast floods, in some places exceeding twenty feet in height, but that rarely anywhere did it overflow its banks. Thomas Hutchins, the geographer of the United States, whose advice had been decisive in the Ohio Company's choice of Marietta as the best of locations on the river, had stressed in a book published in 1778 that the Muskingum was "a fine, gentle river, confined by high banks, which prevent its floods from overflowing the surrounding lands."

The water began rising at Marietta in late January 1813, less than a year after the war had been declared. The river had been covered in ice, the ground in snow, when the weather suddenly turned warm and rain fell in torrents.

Samuel Hildreth, with his unceasing fascination with nature, was to take close notice of it all. "In twenty-four hours after the commencement of the rise," he would record, "the water was over the banks and rising at the rate of 8 inches per hour."

It was a spectacle such as he had never seen and he was thrilled to behold:

> The interest and grandeur of the scene was greatly augmented by the immense bodies of ice which covered the river from shore to shore, and of a thickness varying from 12 to 18 inches. . . .
>
> In the night, the rushing of the waters and the crashing of the ice against the dwelling houses in the streets near the river, was truly alarming and terrific. The water continued to rise until Thursday, 6 o'clock A.M., the 28th, when it ceased; and about 12:00 or one o'clock P.M., began falling slowly. . . . The banks of the river were left piled up with ice, to the height of six or eight feet.

At the Cutler homestead, even at its presumably safe elevated location, the fast-rising water came high enough to flood the first floor. The family had to move quickly upstairs.

As recorded in an old Cutler account book,

The rise was rapid beyond any before known—so sudden as to prevent us from getting our stock off to a place of safety. We drove the cattle to the hill early in the morning, but had to carry our sheep off in a boat. . . . We got the hogs into the house, in the course of the night, except eight or ten that were drowned. We also lost two sheep and two calves; one was drowned, and the others perished in consequence of the cold and snow.

Elsewhere on both rivers great damage had been done to orchards and fences and quantities of hay and grain. Farmers who had neglected to drive off their horses and cattle had lost all their stock.

The sufferings of the whole community were much increased. With the rising of the water, many had fled to higher ground and built make-do temporary camps. When the waters subsided and they could return to their homes, the destruction they saw was like that left by an invading army.

The height of the flood was estimated to have been forty-five feet above the low-water mark, or a full twenty feet higher than earlier estimated.

———

In September 1813 came big news from Lake Erie. A young American naval officer, twenty-eight-year-old Oliver Hazard Perry, had succeeded in building a stout fleet of small ships on the lake, and on September 10, in a battle at Put-in-Bay, defeated the British Lake Squadron. In a succinct dispatch that was to become famous, Perry announced, "We have met the enemy, and they are ours."

"GLORIOUS NEWS!" ran one Marietta headline. The whole town

was illuminated in celebration and "every demonstration of joy expressed."

In October in Ohio's northwestern corner American forces under General William Henry Harrison won another decisive victory over British forces and Tecumseh and followers in a battle in which Tecumseh was killed and his following dispersed.

With these victories the war moved elsewhere. Not until the following summer did news from the conflict in the east stun the country in a way nothing yet had. On the evening of August 24, 1814, a British expeditionary force had seized Washington, burned the capitol, burned the White House, where the British officer in command personally directed the piling up of White House furniture that was put to flame.

President Madison and Congress had been forced to flee.

Americans everywhere, including a great number of those who opposed the war, were outraged. In Marietta, the *Western Spectator* asked in an impassioned editorial, "Shall we repose in apathy when our liberties are not only threatened, but openly assailed. Shall we cherish a lethargic sleep when the enemy is at our doors? Americans! . . . Awake . . . !"

An American peace commission sent to Ghent in Belgium seemed to be making little progress.

Then in January 1815, came the stunning news that an American army under General Andrew Jackson had won a crushing victory over the British in a battle at New Orleans. On top of that came word that the war had ended. Peace had already been signed at Ghent on Christmas Eve.

"PEACE," proclaimed the *Western Spectator* headline.

In the little community of Warren, the Ephraim Cutler home became the scene of a long-remembered celebration. As one of the old pioneers in the community would write,

The house was brilliantly illuminated, the word PEACE shining from the upper windows, and the judge came out upon the doorsteps and made us a capital speech, to which we responded with hearty cheers and patriotic songs, and the discharge of our guns,

after which we were invited into the house to partake of a bounti-
ful repast spread in the long hall, to which we did ample justice.

———·+·———

In early February 1815, just after the close of the war, Samuel Hildreth
decided to make a trip back to Massachusetts for a visit. It was, as he
well knew, the worst time of year to cross the Pennsylvania mountains
on horseback, but there was also a winter lull in his professional de-
mands. He had been in Ohio nine years by then and longed to see his
mother and father, sisters and brother. The trip proved quite as difficult
as expected all the way to the end, when he rode the last eight miles in
a blinding snowstorm.

"I reached my father's house just at dusk, went in and asked if I could
stay all night with them," he would later write in a most memorable,
good-hearted account.

> Not one of the family recognized me, not thinking of my being
> nearer to them than Marietta, as I had not written to notify
> them of my visit. My father said there was a tavern not far off
> and that they did not entertain travelers. . . . I replied, that it was
> so stormy I disliked going out again and thought they had better
> keep me. He then asked where I was from. I said Ohio. "Oh, I
> have a son there, living in Marietta." I replied, "I know him well,"
> and began to smile at the curious blind play going on; this smile
> recalled some slight recognition of who it might be, and mother
> said it must be cousin Warren Hildreth, whom I resembled and
> who they thought was thus amusing himself at their expense.
> At length my father said it must be their son "Sam" but mother
> thought I looked too old and dark complexioned for him. The
> snow had tanned my face very much and made me several shades
> darker than usual. At length to settle all doubts my mother said if
> it was really "Sam" I must have a large scar on the top of my head
> on which there was no hair.

(At the time of his birth, Samuel had had a large abscess near the top of his head, which his physician father had removed leaving a scar three inches long and nearly an inch wide.)

I submitted my head to her inspection and she soon found the mark of recognition indelibly stamped and as fresh as when I left home nine years before. At the sight of this, all doubts vanished and I was heartily welcomed to the bosom of the rejoicing family and gladly allowed to pass the night. This scene served for a frequent subject of amusement during my visit.

His "visit" stretched on into April, during which he purchased from his father the balance of his father's Ohio lands, roughly 1,500 acres at 75 cents an acre, and with a credit of four years to pay it. Near the close of the visit, his younger brother, Charles, then seventeen, decided he, too, wanted to go to Ohio and perhaps study medicine under Samuel, to which Samuel happily agreed.

"We reached Marietta the seventh day of May, I think," Samuel concluded his account of the expedition, "and found the family all well and greatly rejoiced to see me and my brother."

He was both extremely glad to be home and full ready to get back to work.

PART III

1815–1863

CHAPTER EIGHT

The Cause of Learning

If ignorance could be banished from our land, a
real millennium would commence.

—EPHRAIM CUTLER

I.

The home ground Dr. Hildreth returned to that spring of 1815 was in many ways, as was being said, a "new Ohio." With the end of the War of 1812 came a great sense of relief that the threats of British invasion and native resistance were over, and almost at once came a pronounced surge of optimism and in the economy, production, investments, and confidence in the future.

The Ohio River had become "one of the especially great thoroughfares," the traffic greater than ever, the flow of freight in both directions such as never seen. The mass movement of American settlers heading west now numbering in the thousands, seemed to grow by the week, and was supplemented by unprecedented numbers of immigrants from England, Scotland, Ireland, and Germany.

By 1815 Ohio's population was approximately 500,000 and still growing. Cincinnati had become the fastest-growing city in America.

But still more of the settlers traveling the river were bound for the territory beyond. In 1816, with a population of about 65,000, Indiana would become a state. In 1818 Illinois, too, would become a state, its population having reached approximately 35,000.

More steamboats traveled in both directions, their "chugging" engines, and whistles, an increasing noise, had become a part of the scene. At Pittsburgh, Wheeling, and Cincinnati still more and larger steamboats were in production. One being built at Wheeling called the *Washington* would be, at 201 tons, the largest steamboat yet on the western rivers, the first double-decker and driven by a stern paddlewheel fully twelve feet wide, which was thought remarkable. It also had two smokestacks instead of one, a pilot house, elegantly appointed cabins, and included a "commodious" barroom.

On Monday June 3, 1816, the all-new much anticipated *Washington* left Wheeling on her maiden voyage down the Ohio, with Captain Henry M. Shreve, her part owner and builder in command. On June 4, she anchored off Point Harmar. Then, the next morning, Wednesday, June 5, with steam up and all hands on deck weighing anchor, the boiler at the stern exploded with tremendous force sending scalding water over many of those on deck and blowing Captain Shreve and a number of the crew overboard.

"It was terrible beyond conception," declared one contemporary account. A half dozen or more of the victims were nearly skinned from head to foot. In stripping off their clothes their skin peeled off with them. The screams and groans of the agonizing sufferers made the scene even more horrible. Several people died, and more died later from the severity of their wounds.

It was the worst steamboat disaster in the country until then. Yet except for the boiler that exploded there had been no damage to the ship and in only a few weeks the *Washington* continued on down the Ohio and the Mississippi, to New Orleans. Even more remarkably, the *Washington* made the trip back up the river in the record time of twenty-four days.

Nor was there any letup in steam traffic on the rivers or the building of more steamboats. Or any end to steamboat accidents. The importance of the Ohio as a highway, indeed as a way of life, continued only to expand. In a matter of three years, there would be sixty-three steamboats on the river.

Such boats could do about fifty miles a day, or more than twice the fastest-moving barge or keelboat. In another few years some of the newest steamboats on the Ohio could travel 100 miles in a day.

II.

The rapidly growing state's capital had been moved once again to a new location. This time it was a new town called Columbus at the center of the state. There was nothing especially impressive or inspiring about the new capitol, a modest, two-story brick building clearly intended to serve the purpose for the time being only, as all taking part seemed to understand.

Ephraim Cutler arrived there on December 5, 1819, and was at first most pleasantly surprised by just about everything.

"Several friends called on me that evening and gave me a welcome I did not expect," he wrote to his wife, Sally. Almost immediately, with no trouble whatever, he found lodging in a house "very pleasantly situated" and all much to his liking. "No other member boards with me, but there are fifty within a few steps. I have the benefit of retirement in the midst of bustle and noise." He urged her to write soon and let him know "every feeling of your heart," and "if my dear children ever think of their father."

Writing to Sally two weeks later, Ephraim said he had found some agreeable, respectable men among the members whose company he enjoyed, but that "on the whole there is an unaccountable procrastination which is disgusting to me." Nothing of a public nature had yet been accomplished.

As would be said of Ephraim Cutler, he always wanted to do what was right. And as he had in his earlier years in the legislature battled to keep slavery out of Ohio, so now he had returned to politics determined to make possible the establishment of a public school system for the state. He felt it essential and long past due and he intended to make it happen.

On December 24, he was extremely pleased to report to Sally, "I am appointed on a very important committee, who have under consideration a bill to regulate schools." Already he was drawing up a bill "which I hope will be so constructed as to pass, and to produce a good effect."

Then suddenly, in a matter of days, and greatly to his surprise, all seemed to change. On the evening of December 29, in the privacy of his room at the boardinghouse, he poured out his anger in a long letter to Sally over the "thick-headed mortals" and "knaves" of politics.

> I have just returned from attending a meeting of our committee and all is hushed in slumber in the adjoining rooms. The difficulty in making thick-headed mortals understand plain questions is sometimes vexing, but this evening our committee has had to contend with art and avarice combined. There is nowhere to be found knaves more designing than at a legislature, where designing scoundrels lurk and with specious words and demure looks they calculate to entrap the unwary and like blood-suckers leech and suck the public.

He was fed up, "truly tired" of it. "My head, hands and even heart are engaged in the labors before me."

But by no means did he consider giving up. With his New England background, his devotion to the cause of learning was no less than ever. "I am not without hopes," he assured her, "of effecting a change in our system of taxation and of getting a law passed for establishing school districts and encouraging schools."

On the matter of taxation he had already had to combat, alone, all who spoke out in the House. When it came to the first vote, twenty-two others voted with him and forty against. On the second vote it was clear his side was making progress, twenty-eight for and thirty-two against.

Among those who spoke out in favor of public schools was Joseph Barker, who had also become a member of the House. As his daughter would one day recall, his speech had been written in the hope that the poor as well as the rich might receive the advantage of education.

Well into the new year, on January 21, 1820, Ephraim wrote again to his wife to express little hope for the public school bill.

> I am oppressed with the responsible situation which I am in. . . .
> There is a bill before the House for regulating schools, on which
> I have spent many painful thoughts and hours of labor. I expect
> to lose it and dread the day when I must exert all my poor ability
> to again defend it.

He went on to say a bill for building a canal from Lake Erie to the Ohio River was before the House and another source of anxiety for him. He opposed it and felt alone in that position. "But I must do the best I can."

Sally, too, had much on her mind, much to contend with at home, but wanted him to know she understood the situation he was in and that he had her support.

"As to the frequent use of your oratorical abilities," she wrote on January 23, 1820, "I have only to say, if by exercise, they brighten, pray continue to pour forth your eloquence. If not, desist.

> Nor vainly think the merit of your cause, unless ably, and smartly,
> defended, will have any effect on such opponents, as I fear you
> have to deal with. Men who will waste their breath, and prosti-
> tute their talents to deprive a fellow mortal of *that* which is their
> birth-right.

Three days later, on January 26, she wrote again to say she hoped he would be home soon to transact business at home himself to more advantage. "I can truly say I am tired of it. . . . A constant fear of doing something wrong continually perplexes me."

How did the thought of home affect him, she asked. "Your children all love, and long to see their father. As for myself, you know my feelings better than I can describe them."

On January 28, Ephraim was writing to her again, this time in an entirely different spirit.

"The act for regulating schools, which I originated, and that I now feel gratitude to God for sustaining me in carrying through, has passed the house—yeas forty, nays twenty."

An editorial in the *Cincinnati Inquisitor*, one of the most influential newspapers in the state, voiced strong approval of a public system of education, saying that advantages to be gained were too generally known to need comments.

"We seek no further proof in favor of schools supported by law than the estimation in which they are held by older states of the Union. Wherever they have been admitted they have never been abandoned, but are universally cherished."

Ephraim's active involvement with the creation of Ohio University had also become greater than ever. In 1816 work was proceeding on the first building on the campus, on the high ground of the College Green as it was called.

On August 27, 1818, writing to Ephraim from Hamilton, his father bemoaned the "total neglect" he had received concerning the part he had played in the founding of the university. He went on about it at some length, reminding Ephraim that the establishment of a university was "a first object and lay with great weight on my mind."

Age and failing health were increasing realities for Manasseh. His wife, and Ephraim's mother, Mary Balch Cutler, had died three years before at seventy-four. "Her death was as surprising to me as if she had been in perfect health," Manasseh had written to Ephraim, ". . . but have the firm hope that my loss is her infinite gain. I think I can say the will of the Lord be done."

"I am just going off the stage," he now told Ephraim, "and any mark of respect that can be shown to me in this world, I consider of very little consequence to myself, but may be of some to my posterity. . . . Such as the name of some building," he wrote, reminding Ephraim that this was long the custom in all the colleges in New England.

The new building, now nearly finished, was a fine, three-story red-brick structure with a tall clock tower referred to only as the College Edifice. What Ephraim may have written to his father in response or how much say Ephraim may have had in the naming of the building is not known.

The wait for a decision went on and sadly Manasseh Cutler would not live to hear his wish fulfilled. Not until 1914 would the centerpiece of the university officially become Cutler Hall in his honor.

He had been suffering severely for years from lung disease, asthma, with spasms of difficulty in breathing and excruciating pains in the chest. Yet he maintained his customary cheerfulness and interest in life.

In his diary on September 11, 1821, he wrote, "This day it is fifty years since I was ordained in this place. My state of health renders it impracticable to take any public notice of the day. How wonderful that my life should be prolonged to this day! How much I have to be thankful for! And much to be humble for!"

Finally, after fifty-two years at the pulpit, he had to step down. He died on July 28, 1823, at the age of eighty-one.

An old friend, the Reverend Benjamin Wadsworth, preached his funeral service before a full church. Long obituaries appeared in papers throughout New England, many listing at length the numerous citations and awards conferred on him, the honorary degrees received from Harvard and Yale for work he had done in medicine and the natural sciences. Yet for all that little or nothing was said of the all-important part he had played in the creation and enactment of the Northwest Ordinance of 1787 and the settlement of Ohio.

One notable exception would not appear until much later in a national publication, *The American Naturalist*, calling Manasseh Cutler not only "a pioneer in a new country, not merely a pioneer in science, but a pioneer for truth and civilization in every form" and credited him for the clause in the Northwest Ordinance declaring there would be no slavery.

Meanwhile, life went on in Marietta. A steady flow of news good and bad filled the pages of the *American Friend*, a local paper. There seemed no end of weddings, divorces, fires, crimes committed, including murder, and tragic accidents.

> Drowned on Thursday the 30th . . . Mr. Samuel McClintock, a
> respectable citizen of this town. . . .
> Drowned . . . on Friday last Jane Murry . . . aged between two
> and three years.
> Drowned, on Sunday the 16th inst, in the Ohio River . . .
> Mr. John Walsh, a native of Canada.

Rewards were announced by Sheriff Timothy Buell for a criminal prisoner who broke out of the Marietta jail, one Samuel Berry, described as about five feet, eight inches tall with dark, small eyes, who "like an experienced villain will betray you with a smile."

As for public announcements of marriages, separation, or divorce, the standard form published in the paper would declare, "Whereas my wife Eliza has left my bed and board without any just cause, this is to warn all persons against harboring or trusting her on my account, as I will not pay any debts of her contracting, from the time of her leaving me."

Then followed Eliza's response:

> Reader!!! I WILL STATE that you [are] wrongly informed, for I have neither left bed nor board. *My bed* I took with me, and board I had none. He neither provided me with victuals or drink more than one half the time since we were married. He came home on Saturday, and Sunday morning he could not think of returning back to work, without expressing some of his kind affection to me; so he whipped me, and kicked me out of doors, without any provocation. He immediately sold his farm, and put the rest of the property out of his hands, and of course I had

neither board nor home; therefore, my husband ELIUD has absconded; and I forbid all persons trusting or harboring him on my account, for I will not pay any debts of his contracting. I will give ONE HALF CENT reward for said Eliud Thomas, but neither thanks or charges.

There were reports of counterfeit five dollar bills making an appearance in town, of course thievery, even a bank robbery and the reward of $1,000 offered, after the cashier of the Muskingum Bank, one David J. Maple, made off with $15,000 to $20,000. (A description was provided of both the culprit and the small sorrel horse he rode away on.)

Warnings, too, were posted on a habitual "abscounder," calling himself Seth Lothrop, a cabinetmaker who had taken off leaving his creditors unpaid. "This running away has been so often repeated," said the announcement, "as to have become a habit, and the good people of Ohio would do well to be upon their guard. It may well be said of him, that he,

> Run so long, and run so fast,
> No wonder he ran out at last,
> He run in debt and then to pay,
> He distanced all and run away.

The summer of 1820 was distinguished by uncommon heat and lack of rain. The temperature on August 10 was 98 degrees in the shade. The summer of 1821 was no better. By the summer of 1822, the "mighty" Ohio River had become a mere brook, lower than ever known at Marietta. The water, nearly stagnant in some places, produced a "noxious" smell in the air that became a cause of much concern. As Samuel Hildreth was to write, in this "poisonous gas, no doubt, the seeds of fever were contained."

Potato bugs were in multitudes such as never seen. Toward autumn the country was overrun with gray squirrels, their "line of march" from north to south. "No obstacles obstructed their course; often passing through, or over the houses of the inhabitants, and swimming the Ohio River in its widest places," Samuel Hildreth recorded.

In the later part of June fevers began, typhoid in particular. Then followed a full-scale influenza epidemic, "a terrible visitation of burning fever, wild delirium, and deathly chills." No family and few individuals escaped. More than 500 people took sick and more than seventy in Marietta died, including many children.

All business stopped. The town's newspaper, *American Friend*, shut down because of illness to the staff except for one boy, which probably explains why there had been no obituary of Manasseh Cutler in the paper. Physicians were overworked. Samuel Hildreth, who had more than 600 patients under his care, refused to take any payment for his services.

Paul Fearing, the first lawyer among the earliest settlers, and who became a widely respected judge of the Court of Common Pleas, and his wife were both victims of the epidemic. Dr. Jabez True, the first physician, whose friendship had meant so much to Samuel Hildreth, was another who died.

Ephraim and Sally Cutler and their family were sick and recovered but for one son, twelve-year-old Manasseh, who died that October 1822. The grief in the family was overwhelming, and for Sally most of all. Three months later, in a letter to Ephraim, who was back at Columbus serving in the legislature, she wrote that she could not stop thinking of and longing for "our dear departed son.

> I think I see his animated countenance, his noble mien. The arms of maternal tenderness are extended in vain to embrace the beloved child. The next moment my gloomy thoughts are transported to the silent grave where he sleeps in the dust. The sorrows of a mother are beyond all human consolation.

The epidemic had proved so dreadful it became widely assumed that, once over, nothing like it would strike again for a long time. Even Samuel Hildreth, when his father expressed a desire to come out to Ohio for a first visit the following spring of 1823, saw no reason for him not to.

"My father concluded to make a visit to Ohio, not only to see his son in Marietta, but also to view the rich valleys of the west which had for many years excited his curiosity," Hildreth later wrote.

> His journey out was performed very comfortably in a small covered one-horse wagon. The visit was very pleasant to him, and the time passed rapidly away until the fore part of August, when the country became the seat of a violent epidemic fever. The year before had been very sickly, but this year it was still worse.

As one resident wrote, "At Marietta the people at last thought no more of seeing a corpse go on the street than seeing a dog run. . . . One house they took out a man's wife and buried her. When they came home from the funeral and found her husband was dead, the people set to and made a coffin and buried him."

The elder Hildreth fell victim to the epidemic and died on August 6, 1823. "His health was generally firm and good," his son wrote, "and but for this attack he might in all probability have lived a number of years."

He was buried in the Mound Cemetery.

But for Marietta greatest was the loss of the most notable and admired of the first pioneers, General Rufus Putnam, who died, not of epidemic fever, but old age, at eighty-six, on May 4, 1824.

No one had played so important a role in the creation of the settlement or shown such leadership, perseverance, and strength of character without fail.

Word of his death moved the community in ways nothing had. His obituary—in effect a full biography—ran in installments for days in the *Gazette*. So, too, did news of his death and tributes to his life appear in numerous papers in the east. He was hailed as "the fast friend of Washington," and "the pride of the army." One particular acclamation that appeared many times said simply, "He did honor to human nature."

He was rightly lauded as the originator of the whole idea of a new future in Ohio country beginning with the Newburgh Petition before the end of the Revolution. He it was who led the way from the first meeting at the Bunch of Grapes tavern in Boston that gave rise to the Ohio Company, who drew his own early map of the area, drew up the plan for the "City upon the Hill," and who led the first of the New England pioneers. Through every variety of adversity and struggle, through every step forward to the ideals of a new start, he had maintained his strong sense of purpose.

He would widely be remembered for having once issued a directive to deliver to a Delaware woman, the widow of a murdered Indian, "such goods as she shall choose to wipe away her tears to the amount of five dollars."

He had designed and built Campus Martius and wanted always to be fair in his dealings with the native tribes, and he provided much needed, sound leadership through the dark time of the Indian Wars.

He had led the way in establishing Marietta's first school, its first church, first bank, served in the state legislature as an ardent supporter of the first state university, and with Ephraim Cutler stood firm against the acceptance of slavery in Ohio.

He would be admired and long remembered, too, for his way of life, how he "surrounded his modest, but commodious dwelling with fruit trees of his own planting" and that "finer, or more loaded orchards than his, no country could offer.

In the midst of rural plenty, and endeared friends, who had grown up around him—far from the display of wealth, the bustle of ambition and intrigue, the father of the colony, hospitable and kind without ostentation and without effort, he displayed in these remote regions, the grandeur, real and intrinsic, of those immortal men, who achieved our revolution.

In a book Samuel Hildreth was to write on the pioneers of Marietta, a collection of thirty-eight biographical sketches, the first and longest by far was that of Rufus Putnam, with whom Hildreth had spent many hours in conversation. Along with so much else that was admirable, the general was highly interesting, "possessing a rich fund of anecdote, and valuable facts in the history of men" and that the "impress of his character is strongly marked on the population of Marietta, in their buildings, institutions, and manners."

After the death of his wife, Persis Rice Putnam, in 1820, their eldest, an unmarried daughter, Elizabeth, kept house and looked after him in the same family home he had built as part of Campus Martius. Sarah Cutler Dawes, the daughter of Ephraim Cutler, would later recall staying there overnight. The general shook her hand a long time and said, "And are you Ephraim Cutler's daughter!" and kept shaking her hand. "He was quite deaf . . . feeble with age," but also "erect in his carriage and dignified in manner.

> He asked a blessing at table, standing himself at the head of the table while we all stood up by the side of our chairs. At night he had family prayers. We all stood up during the service, which was conducted by the General.

She saw him, too, at church service. "He would walk up the aisle with great dignity, and all the people seemed to pay him deference."

On the matter of advancing age, he liked to say, "My sun is far past its meridian."

More than half a century later in 1881, historian H. Z. Williams would write in his *History of Washington County, Ohio* a concise, highly insightful tribute to both Manasseh Cutler and Rufus Putnam:

> Dr. Cutler and General Putnam were from first to last the leading spirits of the Ohio company, the office of the former being principally the management of the difficult and delicate negotiations with the General Government, and that of the latter the superintendency of the internal affairs of the organization.
>
> The relations of the two men were intimate and cordial. Each seems to have entertained the most thorough respect for the other. Yet they were as dissimilar as two men well could be. One was thoroughly educated, cultured, accomplished; the other a strong, rugged man, almost entirely lacking in knowledge, save by the kind acquired little by little in the experience of life, but full of wisdom, possessing the genius of uncommon common sense, great strength of purpose and vast executive ability. Either

of these men would undoubtedly have made a failure in the position of the other. But in the places which they did occupy no men could have been more efficient.

As General Putnam had requested there was no public event commemorating his life, only a funeral service at the Congregational Church, where a large crowd attended. He was buried at the old Mound Cemetery, where a plain but substantial marble tombstone was erected. He was survived by three daughters and two sons, thirty grandchildren, and twenty-one great-grandchildren.

In his last will and testament, he gave 348 acres of land to three grandsons and left money for the "education of poor children in Marietta . . . and for the support of missionaries to preach the Gospel in places destitute of a settled minister or among the Indian tribes."

The modest inventory of items he owned at his death included:

One old black horse
One musket
One axe
One broad axe
One surveyor's chain
One hoe
One pitch fork
One plough
Six cider barrels
One grindstone
Two old scythes
One hand saw

The contents of his library of more than seventy books included:

One Bible
Two volumes of *The Lewis and Clark Journals*
A copy of the *History of the First Settlement*

Two psalm books and two singing books

One copy of the Constitution of the United States

One French grammar

Milton's *Paradise Lost*

One copy of *The Art of War*, a treatise on fortifications and a
    military dictionary

Two volumes of *The Letters of George Washington*

The summer following Rufus Putnam's death, the Marquis de Lafayette arrived at Long Island, New York, to begin a nationwide tour of the United States like nothing ever before or since. The symbol of a heroic past he was to be celebrated at age sixty-seven, wherever he went one stop after another.

Nearly a year later, on the morning of May 23, 1825, a small steamboat, the *Herald*, was heading upstream on the Ohio carrying Lafayette on the last leg of the tour. Until then it was generally understood that Marietta was not to be part of the itinerary and no preparations had been made.

Two or three miles below town a gun was fired on the *Herald*, which was supposed to signal that Lafayette was on board, and as the boat approached the landing a sign could be seen across the bow, "General Lafayette," that put aside all doubt.

More cannon were fired as Lafayette came ashore, bells rang as virtually the whole town flocked to greet him, "all eager," as said, "to seize his hand and welcome him to the soil he so nobly defended." The crowd arranged itself in two lines, down which and back Lafayette passed to shake hands with each and all. Grasping the hands of the few veterans of the Revolution there to pay their respects, he seemed unwilling to let go.

A list of nearly fifty military officers who had been among the pioneers who settled Marietta was read to him, including most prominently General Rufus Putnam. "I knew them well," Lafayette said. "They were the bravest of the brave."

At the conclusion of this, saying he could stay no longer, Lafayette departed on the *Herald* and, as it was reported, "practically the whole population of Marietta cheered on the shore."

———•—•———

Of the many residents of Marietta and the surrounding towns and farms and cabins in the woods for whom Samuel Hildreth served as the family physician, the Joseph Barkers counted high among his favorites. He and Barker had discovered quickly how much they had in common, and particularly in their love of books and history.

Hildreth convinced Barker that he was a natural writer and must put down on paper his story and in his own way. Hildreth had also been extremely grateful during the recent epidemics to have had Barker's daughter, Catherine, come stay with the Hildreth family in Marietta and help serve as a nurse. The doctor was then working sixteen to eighteen hours a day, attending more than 600 patients.

Also, like so many others, Hildreth was a great admirer of Barker's talents as architect and builder. And so to Barker he turned to design and build a new Hildreth residence for an enlarged family, now counting five children, as well as a new doctor's office.

In the years since his work on the Blennerhassett mansion and boats for Aaron Burr, Barker had been extremely busy designing and building more houses, as well as a second courthouse on Putnam Street, the old courthouse having become too small for the growing town.

The Hildreth project was a major undertaking, one of the largest houses in Marietta and located beside the new courthouse. The cost would be covered in large part by labor donated by patients of Hildreth's unable to pay for the care he had provided during the epidemic. Work began the summer of 1824 and became the subject of considerable attention. The house was to have much the look of Barker's other houses, built of brick and in the Federal style, with large recessed windows, a front door with fluted columns, a fanlight over the door and the windows above. It was three stories with a two-story wing to the rear. Grander in scale than any of his previous in town houses, it more than qualified as a mansion. Once finished, in 1826, it counted as one of the town's showpieces.

One young lady from New England, a teacher new to the town, who was invited by the Hildreths for an afternoon visit, would write at length about the pleasure of sitting in their spacious garden.

"We passed nearly an hour," she wrote.

> It is filled with peach, quince, pear and apple trees loaded with fruit, a great profusion of grapes of ten different kinds, flowers of indigenous and exotic origin, comprising a variety of 200, and under the shade of the grapevines, a number of beehives. Loaded with flowers and invitations to come again . . . we bade them good night, very much pleased with our call.

As time went on the house was also to become known as a center of medical and scientific collections and innovative ideas, the production center of countless medical and scientific articles by the doctor, as well as works of history, not to say a professional medical office. But primarily it was a home and there Hildreth was to live for almost forty more years.

III.

In the fall of 1823, at the age of fifty-six, Ephraim Cutler had been re-elected to the state legislature, only this time to the Senate, and by a resounding margin. He arrived back in Columbus that December and in a letter to Sally reported that while he was as yet little acquainted with the new members, he thought favorably of them.

"So far as I am able to form a judgment, there is as much talent, harmony, and industry as is usually assembled in the legislature." His main purpose was to achieve as much as possible in the cause of education, in a state public school system and the university. "I have a strong hope we shall accomplish something."

Two weeks later he could report that never in his life had he been placed in a situation so arduous and difficult as he had faced this whole session. He had first wanted to attain Senate backing for increased financial support for the university and found himself "put constantly on the defensive and had to parry, answer, and sometimes retort attacks." But he succeeded. The vote was a decisive 23-to-10 in favor of an appropriation of $3,000.

He was also serving on the school committee and as chairman of the revenue committee, two of the most important roles of that session, and had already finished one report on the subject and had another nearly ready, and he was exhausted.

Two others on the committee he found he greatly liked, both fellow New Englanders who felt as he did about the critical need for public schools. Caleb Atwater, the chairman of the committee, had been born in North Adams, Massachusetts, and graduated from Williams College. He had come to Ohio in 1811 and settled in Circleville, about twenty-three miles to the north of Chillicothe, where he practiced law and served as postmaster. Nathan Guilford, senator from Hamilton County and a resident of Cincinnati, had grown up in Spencer, Massachusetts, and Ephraim thought highly of him, "a fine man" and "most efficient supporter."

As the three of them were quite aware, the reality of education in Ohio was far from the ideal expressed in the Northwest Ordinance, that "schools and education shall forever be encouraged." The gap between the dream and the reality was immense. Ohio was in fact without a school system, except for a few "enterprising" towns like Marietta, as well as Cincinnati and Cleveland, where schools were local creations. In the northeastern corner of the state on Lake Erie, Cleveland had a population of little more than 1,000 but also one of the best harbors on the lake and was growing rapidly.

That the master of the academy in Marietta, David Putnam, the grandson of General Israel Putnam, and a graduate of Yale, taught classes ranging from penmanship to astronomy and grammar in English, Greek, and Latin, was hardly representative of Ohio teachers in general. Good teachers were hard to find. A great many were just ordinary or less, someone of little or no training or prior experience, and who made an agreement "to keep school." Those who sent their children to attend usually paid a fee of one to three dollars a year.

In towns and villages classes were taught in private homes or over places of business, in basements and churches. In the countryside vacant cabins and abandoned barns often served the purpose. The usual school building or schoolhouse was no more than a one-room log cabin, "extremely simple and uncomfortable," measuring about 15 x 28 feet, with a dirt floor.

> The furniture consisted principally of rude benches without backs made of splitting logs lengthwise into halves and mounting them, flat side up, on four legs or pins driven into the ground. Desks similarly though less clumsily made were sometimes furnished to the "big boys and girls." The room, or at least one end of it, was heated with an immense fireplace. There was no blackboard, no apparatus of even the rudest description to assist the teacher in expounding the lessons.

The curriculum consisted of reading, spelling, writing, and arithmetic, and in some districts a rule in force prohibited the teaching of anything more. Reading and spelling were the great tests of learning. To master arithmetic as well was to have "acquired an education."

Settlers who had been educated in the east often saw their children growing up illiterate. But great, too, were the number of settlers who had no wish to see their taxes raised. Among the German immigrants were many who disliked the very idea of their children learning to read English.

For Ephraim, as it had been for his father, the cause of education, like that of excluding slavery from Ohio, was a cause never to be abandoned. But also, as with Rufus Putnam and Joseph Barker, it was because he himself had had such a "scanty" education and well knew the barriers that could present.

That there was nothing limited about his vocabulary is evident throughout; words like "discretion," "mitigate," and "inestimable" appear frequently and naturally. But then he read constantly and had built his own substantial library. Spelling, however, remained a continuous problem as he knew. He wrote of "the hollow compliments or blarney which I sometimes meat with hear," or "times of difficulty." The word "get" invariably appears as "git" or "gitt." (In years to come, in a book prepared largely from his letters and journals by his daughter Julia, mis-spelling and syntax were all touched up.)

In what had been his first love letter to Sally, written seventeen years before, Ephraim had told her that the heart when full to overflowing seeks a vent and that nothing relieved it so effectively "as to pour out our thoughts to one we love." Now he was pouring them out to her full force in letter after letter.

He was laboring "incessantly," allowing himself no more than four hours sleep a night for three weeks. Friends told him he looked sick, but his bodily health was fine, he assured her, "Not only my reputation, but the good of my country is at stake, and much depends upon how I am able to discharge my duty."

Two nights later, at the end of another exhausting day, he wrote again. He was still struggling with the tax laws.

> You know when my mind is intensely engaged, I can neither eat nor sleep. One cup of coffee in the morning, one of tea at sup-per, with little else, and an equally light dinner. . . . I regret that I undertook this immense labor. I despair of effecting the passage of these laws this session, but some good may, hereafter, grow out of bringing the subject fairly and fully before the public.

Still, again, two days after that, he was declaring himself "entirely insufficient" to sustain the load he carried. If he had more sensibility, he would undoubtedly sink under it.

> For one person, alone, to attempt to change the whole revenue system of a great and powerful state, almost without a hint from another, and to have the temerity to think that his crude and,

perhaps, badly digested notions can be made to succeed, may well be considered by a sober, reflecting mind to border on madness.

But he felt himself on a mission of high purpose and he would not give up.

Your husband has undertaken this unpromising thing, and that he feels the pressure of such a "mountain" you may well imagine. I am encouraged by believing that the cause is one of the highest importance to my country, and that from its success great benefits will result, in relieving the poor from their burdens, by providing an equitable way to call forth the revenue of the state, and thus provide for the support of schools and seminaries of learning; and for making roads, canals, etc.

She worried intensely about him. As she would write, "To say that I am concerned about your health would be but a faint expression of my uneasiness on that account.

I regret that it is not in my power to attend on you, and administer those little offices of kindness which is so necessary in your situation and which delicacy forbids you to ask of another. It seems as if Providence has designed we should not live much together, to this I must quietly submit, although it is, and ever has been a source of regret and uneasiness.

Though he knew how his absence from home compounded the difficulties Sally had to contend with herself, as she confided in her correspondence, he often failed to respond as quickly or sympathetically as he could have, so preoccupied, so totally distracted could he become with his situation of the moment.

It was a side of him memorably illustrated by an incident that took place during a stay at Athens when he had gone there to take part in a transaction of important business for the future of the university. One morning he was seen by others at the house where he was staying sitting down by himself after breakfast for the perusal of the Bible. According to one account, he continued to read "in an absorbed silence hour after hour until late in the forenoon, when it occurred to his friends that he might be regarding the day as the Sabbath." Following dinner, he seated himself once more with his Bible, but before night, he was told directly it was Friday not Sunday. He had, he said, been a little troubled in his mind that the church bells did not ring.

In a letter written February 12, 1824, as the legislative session was about to end, Ephraim could report to Sally only that his expectations regarding appropriations for Ohio University had been "dashed to the ground" by the House of Representatives. "These matters," he said, "will be themes of discussion between us, if Providence kindly permits me to return to my home once more."

———

The next session of the legislature convened at Columbus on December 6, 1824, and Senator Ephraim Cutler was full ready to get back to work.

A canal bill and a new system of taxation were now the absorbing subjects. The prospect of building a canal from the Ohio River to Lake Erie, a massive and extremely costly project, had great appeal to many. The need for an equal system of taxation was for Ephraim the "favorite wish of my heart," along with, no less than ever, statewide, state-financed public education.

Caleb Atwater, who knew as well as anyone what he had been through, sent him a heartfelt note of praise of the kind one never forgets:

> Dear Sir—You are doing nobly; press forward with your equal taxation, the school system, and the canals, and immortalize this legislature. What must be your sensations on the prospect you

now have of carrying into effect the three greatest objects ever presented to our legislature! Press forward, I say, in your career of doing good. Posterity will call you blessed.

Now, in return for their vote on the canal bill, the representatives from Marietta, led by Ephraim Cutler, demanded a new tax to support statewide public education. And unpopular as a school tax was, a bargain was struck.

"I have little doubt the revenue law will be made to my mind, and also a free school system," Ephraim wrote to Sally on January 23, 1825, adding, "The canal bill will, of course, pass, which is also important."

All three bills—on equal taxation, on the canal, and on the school tax—passed in both houses.

On the day the school bill finally passed in the house, Ephraim, deeply anxious over the fate of the bill, was present to witness the moment. Standing beside him, equally interested, was Nathan Guilford, the senator from Cincinnati. When the result was announced, Ephraim turned and raising his hand said, "Lord, now lettest thou thy servant depart in peace, according to thy word; for mine eyes have seen thy salvation."

———•——

Through all this, meanwhile, Ephraim had been giving additional attention and effort to furthering the cause of higher education. At a meeting with other trustees of the university held in Columbus in 1824, he had taken part in the selection of a first president of the university, the Reverend Robert G. Wilson, a Presbyterian pastor from Chillicothe. When the inaugural ceremonies took place at Athens, it was he who presented the keys and the university charter to Dr. Wilson, then delivered the welcoming address, citing the university as a fulfillment of the high hopes of the original pioneers for "the blessings of an enlightened education."

In early 1829, Ephraim Cutler's youngest son, William, would enter Ohio University as a freshman.

No annual event in Marietta compared to the Washington County Agricultural Fair. It was the biggest, most high-spirited community gathering of the year, with all ages, trades, professions, every walk of life in attendance, and the Agricultural Fair of the year 1829 was the biggest yet and included a speech by Ephraim Cutler that was to be long remembered and talked about.

The day was fair but unusually cool for the time of year, as reported in the *American Friend and Marietta Gazette.* Attendance was full and included "a considerable number of strangers." All seemed happy, a good sign.

> The hilarity and good feeling exhibited on such occasions cannot but be productive of beneficial effects to society. The sober, steady, and industrious citizens of our own county are so little accustomed to periods of relaxation, or holidays and we have so few of them generally as a nation, that it is no wonder that foreigners on their first arrival amongst us should view us with astonishment, as a people whose sober and grave faces were never lighted up with a smile, and whose thoughts were wholly given to business or something of more serious import.

The fair itself included exhibits and contests aplenty. Some of the first Merino sheep ever seen west of the Alleghenies were on display. There were rugs and beautiful woolen blankets, "the snowy whiteness and handsomely ornamented corners [of which] would lose nothing in comparing with the very best of imported articles of this kind."

There were highly popular plowing matches contested "with great spirit and skillful exertion." As few were to forget, one mammoth yellow squash on display weighed ninety-six pounds and measured five feet eleven inches and was twenty-four inches in circumference.

Among the awards bestowed was one to Joseph Barker, Jr., for his apples and to Colonel Ichabod Nye for "the best sole leather."

Ephraim Cutler's speech was delivered to a full gathering in the Congregational Church. The fact that there was no written history as yet of the founding of the Marietta settlement, and that most of the original pioneers had by now passed on, led him to address the subject as no one yet had. He spoke at length and with deep feeling.

"It is said that certain epochs in the history of nations will always attract to themselves a lasting interest," he said. "Among other things, their origin awakens a lively curiosity. From whence did they spring? At what period was their country settled? For what causes, under what circumstances, and for what objects were difficulties met and overcome?

> The toils and misfortunes incident to new settlements; the slow progress of even successful effort [he continued]; the patience, fortitude, and sagacity by which evils are overcome or diminished; the causes which quicken or retard their growth, all furnish lessons which improve the wise, correct the rash, and alarm the improvident.

He went on to describe the veterans of the Revolution who founded the Ohio Company, talked of General Putnam, Colonel Sproat, Captain Jonathan Devol, and the others who led the way, seven of whom, as he said, were still alive. He quoted the tribute spoken by "the good Lafayette" during his visit to Marietta.

Then, in conclusion, he said there was another subject he wished he had the powers of eloquence to enforce, and that was "the importance of cultivating the mind." For the purpose of improved cultivation of farms, great and lasting advantages could be gained from scientific knowledge. A knowledge of geology and chemistry would enable the farmer to learn the nature of the soil he possessed.

Forty-one years earlier, during his one visit to the new western settlement, the Reverend Manasseh Cutler had preached a powerful sermon at Campus Martius, in which he said that with the establishment of religious freedom and learning a new nation was at hand.

Now, speaking from the Congregational pulpit, Ephraim expressed his earnest wish that "this enlightened audience will all join me in de-

claring that if ignorance could be banished from our land, a real millennium would commence."

—•—

Less than six years later would follow the founding of Marietta College,
"a natural outgrowth" of the settlement. The purpose was to establish a
"genuine college of the New England type." In time to come, members of
the faculty and the board of trustees included graduates of Dartmouth,
Amherst, Yale, Princeton, and Harvard. Members of the Putnam and
Cutler families would take part, along with Samuel Hildreth and Caleb
Emerson, serving on the board and as substantial donors. Its first grad-
uating class of 1838 numbered only four, but it was to keep growing.

CHAPTER NINE

The Travelers

*The use of traveling is to regulate imagination by reality, and
instead of thinking how things may be, to see them as they are.*

—SAMUEL JOHNSON

I.

O f the many descriptions of passage on the Ohio few would
surpass that by an American named Timothy Flint. A missionary and writer from Massachusetts, he started down
the river with his wife and children on a perfect fall afternoon in
1816.

"The autumns of every part of our country are beautiful," he wrote,
"but those of the western country are pre-eminently so. Nothing result-
ing from beauty of sky, temperature of air, and charm of scenery, can
surpass what was now above us and around us."

He wrote of the wide, clear sandbars that stretched for miles, the
flocks of wild geese, swans, sandhill cranes, and pelicans stalking along
them. The height and size of the corn was in itself alone a matter of
astonishment.

There is something, too, in the gentle and almost imperceptible motion, as you sit on the deck of the boat, and see the trees apparently moving by you, and new groups of scenery still opening upon your eye, together with the view of these ancient and magnificent forests, which the axe has not yet despoiled, the broad and beautiful river, the earth and the sky, which render such a trip at this season the very element of poetry.

Many another expressed the same pleasure, including an increasing number of travelers from abroad who had come for the specific purpose of seeing America.

"Our passage down the river was extremely agreeable," reported one British writer, J. S. Buckingham, of his journey on the Ohio. "The weather was like the brightest English day in the middle of May, with a perfect calm, which made the surface of the stream like a mirror, in which were reflected the lofty hills on either side, with the occasional log cabins."

Much that the travelers would see and experience was not to their liking. But the great river seldom proved a disappointment.

Harriet Martineau, another English writer, who paid a long visit to the United States, described the experience of descending the Ohio as fully equal to her expectations:

and when we had put out into the middle of the river, we found ourselves in the way of a breeze which enabled us to sit outside, and enjoy the luxury of vision to the utmost. The sunny and shadowy hills, advancing and retiring, ribbed and crested with belts and clumps of gigantic beech; the rich bottoms always answering on the one shore to the group of hills on the other, a perfect level, smooth, rich, and green, with little settlements sprinkled over it; the shady creeks, very frequent between the hills, with sometimes a boat and figures under the trees which meet over it; these were the spectacles which succeeded each other before our untiring eyes.

Even Frances Trollope, an aspiring English writer who was to become famous for her mockery and unabashed criticism of America and American ways, was openly moved by her first encounter with the Ohio River:

> truly does "La Belle Rivière" deserve its name; the Ohio is bright and clear; its banks are continually varied, as it flows through what is called a rolling country. . . . The primeval forest still occupies a considerable portion of the ground, and hangs in solemn grandeur from the cliffs; but it is broken by frequent settlements, where we were cheered by the sight of herds and flocks.

"And were there occasionally a ruined abbey, or feudal castle, to mix the romance of real life with that of nature," she decided, "the Ohio would be perfect."

Frances Trollope, a short, plump, plainly dressed English woman in her forties, arrived in America in 1827 accompanied by a son and two daughters and chose to try life in Cincinnati. Pressed for a way to earn a living, she created an odd-looking public entertainment hall, or arcade—partly Greek, partly Gothic-Egyptian in architectural style—that included a theater, lecture rooms, coffeehouse, and bazaar. "Trollope's Folly," as it became known, continued only to lose money. Eventually she gave up and returned to England, there to write a travel book titled *Domestic Manners of the Americans* that appeared in 1832 and became an immense success more than a decade before the works of another of her sons, Anthony Trollope, achieved his great fame.

As for finding fault with Americans, their ways and outlook, she had no trouble. She deplored the "reality" of slavery and the way the sins of Jefferson with slave women were "spoken about openly by all." She discounted the sacred American phrase, "All men are born free and equal," as no more than "mischievous sophistry."

J. S. Buckingham, who wrote no fewer than eight volumes on his American experience, also expressed at the start his ardent opposition to slavery. He also thought Americans ate far too much too fast and had disgusting habits in the use of tobacco—namely constant spitting.

If the condition of the average American worker was no better than that of the average English peasant, claimed Mrs. Trollope, that of his wife and daughters was worse, so hard was the life they led. It was rare, she claimed, to see an American woman reach the age of thirty without losing "every trace" of youth and beauty. She wrote, too, of "the detestable mosquitoes" and of feeling absolutely done in by how boring Americans could be.

"There is no charm, no grace in their conversation. I very seldom during my whole stay in the country heard a sentence elegantly turned, and correctly pronounced." Perhaps, she thought, it was a result of how hard they worked, in the sense that "all work and no play would make Jack a dull boy."

Charles Dickens, when he arrived with his wife in America in 1842, had much the same reaction. "I am quite serious," he wrote, "when I say that I do not believe there are, on the whole earth besides, so many intensified bores as in these United States."

Dickens was then not quite thirty years old, but already the author of a half dozen novels immensely popular at home—including *The Pickwick Papers* and *Oliver Twist.* As it had been for Mrs. Trollope, his steamboat, the *Messenger*, did not stop at Marietta and so it was not to be part of the western American experience for him.

He was heading for Cincinnati, and could hardly believe the company he was keeping. At mealtime, nobody said anything.

> All the passengers are very dismal, and seem to have tremendous secrets weighing on their minds. There is no conversation, no laughter, no cheerfulness, no society, except in spitting, and that is done in silent fellowship round the stove when the meal is over.

The people were all alike. He found no diversity of character. "All down the long table there is scarcely a man who is in anything different from his neighbor."

J. S. Buckingham and Charles Dickens were both struck by the immense and lamentable difference between life on the northern and southern sides of the Ohio River. Buckingham saw in Kentucky "the general absence of neatness and cleanliness," for "the great bulk of laborers were negro slaves, whose air, dress, and general appearance, sufficiently manifested their indifference to everything but their own ease, and their desire to escape from labor."

Dickens said succinctly, "Where slavery sits brooding . . . there is an air of ruin and decay."

Still another foreign traveler of note, Alexis de Tocqueville from France, who was to write one of the most brilliant studies of the American character, would conclude that if there were dark times ahead for the new country and its people, they would be brought about by the presence of slavery. "They will owe their origin, not to the equality, but to the inequality of condition."

Another subject of continual fascination, puzzlement, and frequent amusement among the first-time visitors was the range and oddities of local expressions and vocabulary to be heard on all sides. Words like "et" (for ate), "yourn," "hisn," and "hern," for example, were part of everyday discourse, as were "dunk" (for dip), "fair to middlin" (for fair), "crick" (creek), "disremember" (uncertain), or "red up" (tidy up), "lolly gagin," "tom cattin," and "a chip off the old block."

Dickens was particularly taken by the many duties served by the word "fix."

You call upon a gentleman in a country town, and his help informs you that he is "fixing himself" just now . . . by which you are to understand that he is dressing. You inquire on board of a steamboat of a fellow passenger, whether breakfast will be ready soon, and he tells you he should think so, for when he was last below, they were "fixing the tables," in other words, laying the cloth. You beg a porter to collect your luggage, and he entreats you not to be uneasy, for he'll "fix it presently"; and if you complain of an indisposition, you are advised to have recourse to Doctor So-and-So, who will "fix you" in no time.

Correct pronunciation or too much fuss over diction were ranked by local people in the same category as fancy dress and considered "stuck-up." Tall tales and practical jokes were much in favor. If asked by a stranger, "Where does this road go?" the local answer might be, "Don't go nowhere, mister, stays right here."

Like so many travelers, both foreign and American, Frances Trollope was astounded by the degree to which "ardent spirits" were consumed on all sides and "often to the most frightful excess." Whiskey, rum, peach brandy, hard cider, and mint juleps, all plentiful and cheap, had long been an accepted part of frontier life, as an essential to celebrations and ordinary camaraderie, as well as relief from physical pain, injuries, toothaches. Nor were those who consumed to excess a rarity, as everyone knew.

The Philadelphia clergyman John A. Clark wrote of "the free and unrestrained use of ardent spirits" as "fearfully prevalent" on river travel especially.

> Usually on board these western steamboats whiskey is used just as freely as water. All drink. The pilot—the engineer—the fireman—all drink. The whiskey bottle is passed around several times a day, and then the dinner table is loaded with decanters.

The plain truth, as one early chronicler of life in Ohio country, Henry Howe, would write, was that alcoholic liquids were long considered a "necessity of life."

Dr. Samuel Hildreth would write of the time when his physician father owned a tavern for a while and of the large part drinking had played in the New England way of life. Cider—hard cider—he called the national beverage, and any farmer who furnished water in place of cider for his work hands was accounted a close-fisted, stingy man. While few farmers became drunkards, wrote the doctor, ". . . their red noses, blotched cheeks, and sore eyes, betrayed the constitutional effect of their favorite beverage."

In his research for his history of the Ohio Valley, Hildreth had come upon the journal of the young surveyor, John Mathews, Rufus Putnam's nephew, who had been one of the original pioneers to land at Marietta in 1788, but had also taken part in an earlier surveying expedition in the valley in 1786 and in his journal provided a memorable description of the part alcohol could play on the frontier, as experienced during a night spent in one log cabin.

> Here I found a number of neighbors seated in social glee around a heap of corn. The inspiring juice of rye had enlivened their imaginations, and given their tongues such an exact balance, that they moved with the greatest alacrity, while relating scenes of boxing, wrestling, hunting, etc. At dusk of evening the corn was finished . . . many of them took such hearty draughts of the generous liquor, as quite deprived them of the use of their limbs. Some quarreled, some sang, and others laughed, while the whole displayed a scene more diverting than edifying. At ten o'clock, all that could walk went home, but left three or four around the fire, hugging the whiskey bottle, and arguing very obstinately on *religion*; at which I left them and went to bed.

Come morning, Mathews found those who had "tarried all night, still at their cups" and about eleven others came in to assist in drinking up what whiskey still remained.

The scene Mathews witnessed and so "graphically described," wrote Samuel Hildreth, would lead one to conclude that great as was the need for surveyors in the west was the need for those to "rebuke the vices" of the west as it was in the older settled portions of the country near the Atlantic coast.

The fact was by then the amount of drinking in the entire country had increased markedly. Consumption of hard liquor per capita by the 1820s had reached five gallons per year, the highest ever and at that same time the temperance movement had gotten under way, a crusade against drunkenness that was taking hold everywhere, including the Ohio Valley.

Charles Dickens found that even more distressing than the boredom of the company he had to endure on board the steamboat *Messenger* was the total absence of any ardent spirits. "At dinner," he wrote, "there is nothing to drink upon the table but great jugs full of cold water." Apparently it depended on which boat you happened to be aboard.

The temperance movement, too, had taken hold in Marietta and vicinity and among its most earnest advocates was Ephraim Cutler. Having suffered the loss of his own alcoholic brother Charles, Ephraim well knew the extreme miseries excessive drinking could bring to a family. As his daughter Julia would write, he had banished all intoxicating drinks from his house and farm and on the Fourth of July as well, and in private and in public urged others the "propriety and necessity of total abstinence."

———•••———

For all that so many of the prominent travelers found fault with, there was also more than a little they did like and for which they openly expressed approval.

Dickens was astonished and delighted to find Cincinnati "beautiful . . . cheerful, thriving, and animated. I have not often seen a place that commends itself so favorably and pleasantly to a stranger at first glance as this does." He found Cincinnatians "intelligent, courteous, and agreeable," and, "with good reason," were proud of their city. He was amazed to learn that the population had reached 50,000, and that the city was rightly famous for its free schools.

By the time of his visit, in 1842, Cincinnati had become a great center for meatpacking, breweries, distilleries, boat works, soap plants, shoe and beet factories. The population would steadily increase, due in substantial part to the thousands of immigrants arriving every year as a consequence, in good part, of the potato famine in Ireland and revolutions in Germany.

From his hotel window Dickens watched a temperance parade pass by and was "particularly pleased" to see the Irishmen in the march.

[They] formed a distinct society among themselves, and mustered very strong with their green scarves; carrying their national Harp, and their portrait of Father Mathew, high above the people's heads. They looked as jolly and good-humored as ever; and working [here] the hardest for their living and doing any kind of sturdy labor that came in their way, were the most independent fellows there, I thought.

Dickens was also pleasantly surprised during his visit that no man sat down until the ladies were seated or omitted any small act of politeness that would contribute to their comfort. "Nor did I ever once, on any occasion, anywhere, during my rambles in America, see a woman exposed to the slightest act of rudeness, incivility, or even inattention."

Harriet Martineau, too, thought the manners of Americans the best she ever saw and showed to their greatest advantage "as to the gentlemen in traveling."

The presence of music in one form or other, and that of the fiddle in particular, was another part of American life at all levels with much appeal to many of the travelers, a number of whom were glad to join in.

A well-traveled Englishman named Fortescue Cuming, who happened also to play the violin, was a notable early example. He crossed Ohio in 1807, and on a night spent in a farmhouse near Chillicothe had to sit and listen to the farmer's sons as they "scraped away without mercy" on "two shocking bad violins, one of which was of their own manufacture."

But the next day, in threatening weather, he stopped at the home of an immigrant Irishman, whose daughter had married a young shoemaker named Irons. Cuming decided to linger to have his shoes mended and,

found a dozen of stout young fellows who had been at work repairing the road, and were now sheltering themselves from the increasing storm, and listening to some indifferent music made by their host on a tolerably good violin. I proposed taking the violin while he repaired my shoes. He consented and sat down to work, and in a few minutes I had all the lads jigging it on the floor merrily. Irons himself, as soon as he had repaired the shoes, jumping up and joining them.

If there was a reality of American life that Frances Trollope, Charles Dickens, and others found most disgraceful and unacceptable, it was the removal of the native tribes to more remote reservations to the west, brought on by the members of Congress. "If the American character may be judged by their conduct in this matter," wrote Mrs. Trollope, "they are most lamentably deficient of every feeling of honor and integrity." It was "impossible for any mind of common honesty not to be revolted by the contradictions in their principles and practice."

Dickens encountered firsthand one of the last phases of the "removal." It occurred in northeastern Ohio, still mostly wilderness, as he and his wife were heading by stagecoach toward Niagara and ultimately home to England. At Upper Sandusky, a Wyandot village on Lake Erie, they stopped for the night.

Upper Sandusky was one of about sixteen locations where the tribes of Ohio—more than 2,000 Shawnee, Seneca, Delaware, Ottawa, and Wyandots—had been forced to remove, as a result of the Removal Bill enacted in 1830.

At breakfast the morning after his arrival, Dickens listened to the federal agent for the Wyandots, Colonel John Johnston, deliver "a moving account of their strong attachment to the familiar scenes of their infancy, and in particular to the burial places of their kindred; and of their great reluctance to leave them."

"We met some of these poor Indians afterwards, riding on shaggy ponies," Dickens continued. They looked to him like gypsies.

Later that summer the Wyandots departed for Cincinnati, where they were to go by steamboat to reservations farther west. They were the last of the natives to leave Ohio.

Only the Indian names were to remain—names like Chippewa and Chillicothe, and Cuyahoga, Ottawa, Muskingum, Sandusky, Scioto, and Seneca, as well as the name of the state and the great river.

II.

In the spring of 1839, Samuel and Rhoda Hildreth decided that for them the time had come for travel in the opposite direction—back east to their home ground.

Twenty-four years had passed since Samuel had made his surprise appearance at his parents' doorstep in Massachusetts, while for Rhoda it had been more than forty years since she had said goodbye to her Massachusetts home at age ten. Both were now in their fifties. Their children were nearly all grown.

Their son George, now twenty-seven, had become a doctor and, still single, lived at home and worked as a partner with his father, and so he would look after the practice in his father's absence.

Samuel and Rhoda would travel by a system of transportation un- imaginable until then—by private carriage, river steamboat, canal boat, railroad car, and one oceangoing steamboat, covering in all some 1,700 miles round-trip. The day of their departure by private carriage was Monday, May 6, and, as usual, Samuel was to keep a journal the whole way.

Because he was to speak at a gathering in Cleveland, the convention of the Physicians Society of Ohio, of which he was the president, they headed north, overland by carriage to Zanesville, instead of taking the usual route back upstream on the Ohio. At Zanesville they would stop overnight with their son Charles, who like his father and grandfather and brother had also become a doctor.

The route to Zanesville was highly picturesque and much changed. The countryside had become well-cultivated, whereas only a few years past it had been covered with dense forest. Samuel remembered riding twelve miles or more without seeing a clearing or cabin. Now from an elevated ridge the view reached as much as twenty miles to the horizon.

From Zanesville they moved on by steamboat on the Muskingum to a tiny town called Dresden and there "shipped on board" a canal boat to Cleveland. The cost of passage, he dutifully recorded, was 5 cents a mile, or $7.50 total to Cleveland.

Cleveland was dazzling. If ever evidence was needed of Ohio's transformation, he felt, here it was, with its 8,000 or 10,000 inhabitants and buildings equal in splendor to those of any other city of its size in America, its wharves swarming with life, and the bustle of an active seaport.

"In the short space of 55 years," he wrote, "the gloom and silence of the wilderness has given place to civilization, with the arts of agriculture and commerce which follow in its train."

No fewer than fifty steamboats now navigated Lake Erie, he was told, and the lake itself he thought spectacular.

> To a person unacquainted with the grandeur of the sea, the first view of the lake has a sublime and imposing appearance. The wind blew strongly from the north-east and heavy surf was breaking on the shore with all the tumult of the ocean. The white foam of the curling water, glancing on the sunbeams, were seen as far as the eye could reach.

The lake was subject to sudden storms, he went on to explain, the calm, placid surface of a morning could turn into "angry billows" by midday and navigation was considered more dangerous even than in storms on the Atlantic Ocean.

The next day being a Sunday, they attended church and "rested from our labors." The day after was taken up touring the city and the day following, May 14, Samuel delivered his talk at the Medical Convention at Council Hall, to a gathering of approximately fifty Ohio physicians.

His subject was the diseases of Ohio and the history of medicine in the early settlements. As a naturalist he also took particular pleasure in describing how, in 1788, the Ohio Company established one of the first settlements, "one dense, continuous forest covered the whole region" and went on to recall the variety of giant trees.

It was, in its way, his hymn to the vanished wonder of the wilderness and to the natives for whom it had so long been their kingdom. He described:

> On the bottoms, or alluviums, and on the north sides of rich hills, the beech, sugar maple, ash, and elm, were the prevailing growth;

while the sycamore (Platanus occidentalis) lined the borders of the rivers, where its roots could be refreshed by the running water. Along these streams the red man pushed his light canoe, rejoicing in the wild freedom of the forest, and happily unconscious of the approaching fate which threatened his race, and was soon to banish all but his name from the face of the earth.

At nine the following morning the travelers were on their way again on board the steamboat *Erie* heading east on the lake to Buffalo at an amazing 14 miles per hour. "Arrived at the harbor of Erie at 7 P.M.... We left Erie at 9 P.M. and arrived at Buffalo at 5 o'clock the next morning." Later in the morning they went by rail to the village of Niagara. "As we approached the falls," Hildreth wrote, "the noise of 'many waters' was heard in awful majesty." The spectacle of the falls was all that had been said of them.

On Friday, May 17, another short train ride to Lockport, New York, where they changed to a canal boat on the Erie Canal which, overnight, carried them to Rochester. After another overnight on the canal, they arrived at Syracuse on May 19, four days after departing Cleveland. It being another Sunday, they again rested and attended church.

On reaching Utica by a canal the next day, they boarded a train to Albany, traveling part of the way at an unimaginable 30 miles an hour, "or a mile in two minutes, a little like flying," Hildreth wrote.

Then, it was on to New York, on board another steamboat down the Hudson River, past West Point, the view of which was "very grand," past the majestic Palisades, landing at the city about 6 P.M., having run the distance of 160 miles in eleven hours, as Hildreth also noted with amazement.

The U.S. Hotel, where they stayed, was an immense seven stories high. But the continual noise and confusion of the streets were also "very striking and annoying to strangers," and "especially to those from the back woods."

The next morning, Friday, May 24, "a very pleasant day," as Hildreth noted in his journal, they took passage on a steamboat named *Splendid* for New Haven, Connecticut.

For Hildreth the stop at New Haven figured as one of the highlights of his life: The chance to visit Yale, by then the largest university in the country and one with a curriculum that included geology, chemistry, theology, art, and medicine—all that so mattered to him—meant worlds. Even more important he would, at last, meet Benjamin Silliman. If he, Hildreth, ranked among the pioneers in American science at the time, Silliman, "The Path Finder," was the most prominent and influential scientific American during the first half of the nineteenth century.

Important, too, to Hildreth, was the part Silliman had played in establishing the Medical Institution at Yale, at a time when only five medical schools existed in the United States.

In addition to the articles Hildreth had been writing for the *American Journal of Science*, the first of the kind, a successful publication that Silliman had started in 1818, the two of them had been carrying on active correspondence for some time, Hildreth reporting on the shells he had found by the Ohio River, or on the abundance of Isabella and Catawba grapes he was growing with great results.

In 1835, after six years of intensive research and field management, Hildreth had written a major paper for the *Journal* on bituminous coal deposits in the valley of the Ohio. It was a subject certain to appeal to Silliman, the first to teach geology at Yale or anywhere else in America, and who had since become the leader of American geology.

The article was abundantly illustrated with a map, numerous drawings of plants and shells, and views of interesting scenery.

In 1836 another treatise appeared in the *Journal*, this titled, "Ten Days in Ohio; from the Diary of a Naturalist," which placed him among the nation's foremost geologists. He put forth a highly important theory, his belief that it had taken a "vast period of time to hollow out the local valley between the hills, in which the Ohio now meanders, and to deposit that vast bed of alluvial earth which constitutes its present fertile and rich bottoms." In fact, as would be acknowledged by later-day geological scholars, Samuel Hildreth was the first American geologist to "recognize the enormous amount of sub-aerial [on the surface of the earth] erosion that had taken place throughout the region and that the Ohio River had carved out its own channel." Among those of his own time who immediately grasped the importance of what he had written, and told him so, was Benjamin Silliman.

When the steamboat *Splendid* docked at New Haven that same day the town of New Haven struck him immediately as one of the most beautiful he had ever seen, in its setting and the "classic neatness" of its buildings, but most of all its broad avenues lined with "noble elms." No town in America, he decided, was so beautifully provided with shade trees.

He wrote of the three "imposing" churches near the center of the common and of the college buildings extending along the whole length of the back side of the common.

At age sixty, Benjamin Silliman was just four years older than Hildreth, and as would be said, "richly endowed by nature physically as he was mentally . . . a man of striking appearance," tall, well-proportioned, handsome, and courteous. In his years at Yale he put science on an equal to the arts, something no one had yet done, but also maintained an active interest in the arts.

Professor Silliman greeted the Hildreths at their lodgings and to start things off he took them on a stroll through the lovely, historic Grove Street Cemetery, just off the campus. ("Death loses half its terrors" Hildreth wrote, "when we reflect that our bodies are to be laid quietly in such a beautiful spot.")

That evening was spent with Silliman, his wife, two daughters, and a son at their handsome home on Hillhouse Avenue, a street of many handsome homes. It was there that Hildreth found Silliman to be the most affable and good-humored of men. Also part of the family, much to Hildreth's surprise and delight, was the celebrated painter John Trumbull, who was Mrs. Silliman's uncle, then eighty-six and living with the family.

A few years earlier, finding himself "without ready means of support," Trumbull had offered to give Yale his collection of his work, if Yale would grant him an annual income of $1,000 for the rest of his life. Silliman then succeeded in raising the money to build a Trumbull gallery on campus designed by Trumbull, the first art gallery on any campus in the country.

Hildreth found Trumbull "very interesting" and enjoyed looking at a number of Trumbull paintings that decorated the Silliman parlor. He also spent a good part of the evening enraptured with Silliman's rare books on natural history. Seldom if ever had Hildreth been surrounded by so much that so intensely interested him. Silliman's private library filled a "very large" separate building attached to the house and was to Hildreth a perfect wonder.

When the Sillimans invited the Hildreths to spend the rest of their time in New Haven as their guests, the Hildreths happily accepted.

Most of the next day was spent touring the Yale campus, starting with the Trumbull Gallery, where, among the many Trumbull masterpieces were his *Declaration of Independence, Death of General Warren at the Battle of Bunker's Hill*, and *General Washington at the Battle of Trenton*, as well as numerous miniature portraits, including one of Rufus Putnam.

For Hildreth, who in his professional life had cared for so many veterans of the Revolution, and was himself an accomplished artist, to be seeing all this as he stood beside Trumbull himself could only have been an experience like no other.

Further, he was greatly moved by the conditions Trumbull had insisted on in making the gift to Yale. "All the avails of the exhibitions of this gallery," Hildreth noted in his journal, "go to the support of indigent students in the college, so that the labors of his pencil will continue to bless and to charm mankind for ages after his death."

From the gallery, the group moved on to the great Gibbs Cabinet of minerals, the gift to Yale by a Colonel George Gibbs, who had collected some 10,000 species in Europe. Hildreth had not a doubt that he was looking at a collection "superior to that of any other in America."

Before the tour ended, it also included a stop to see a display of the anatomical collection at the medical college, and another of "exceedingly rare and beautiful" birds sent from China by a missionary.

What Rhoda Hildreth thought of all this, and whether she stayed with the group the whole tour, unfortunately remains unknown. No letter or travel journal in her hand has survived.

The day following, Sunday, May 26, they attended church at the chapel of the college, where about 350 students were present, or most of the student body. That evening, as Hildreth was proud to record, he went with Silliman to pay his respects to the remarkable Noah Webster, the great lexicographer who had demanded there be an American language and who ranked high among Hildreth's heroes, and lived nearby the Yale campus. "He is now 84 years old," Hildreth wrote in amazement, "but active in body and nearly as brilliant in mind as he ever was. I consider this man as first in American literature, and as having done more for the enduring fame of the country in letters, than any other person."

———————

The next morning, May 27, they were on their way again, this time by stagecoach to Hartford, and they would keep on the move for two months, visiting relatives, sisters and brothers, old friends in Boston, museums, libraries, and historical societies. Samuel also took time to witness an operation performed at the Massachusetts Hospital and to examine the "very extensive" collections at the Boston Natural History Society.

They traveled as far north as Portland, Maine, to visit a Hildreth sister, Harriet, and as far south in Massachusetts as Fairhaven, near New Bedford, where Rhoda Hildreth was born and raised. "My wife is highly gratified with the visit," wrote Samuel, "and recognizes many of the scenes of her childhood."

On a visit to Methuen, his birthplace, they found the old family home much as he remembered it. "Examined with much interest the room in which I was born and the one where I slept when a boy, for many years. . . . Happy, happy days, never again to return."

By the first week of July, the time had come to start the return to Ohio. There was a stop again in New York, with still more visits to libraries and museums, then a steamboat ride on "the beautiful Delaware" to Philadelphia for some final shopping, then on by railroad to Harrisburg, then on farther by canal boat.

To cross the Allegheny Mountains, they traveled by a contrivance that hauled the canal boat up and over the mountains, something such as they never had experienced and that fascinated Hildreth.

Here we were drawn up an inclined plane by a stationary engine and a huge cable of hemp. This operation of drawing up is repeated five times by as many engines before reaching the summit. . . . The mountain scenery at this season of the year is fine. The chestnut is in full bloom and very abundant. . . .

At the summit there was a stop at a tavern for dinner. Then the descent down the western slope of the range required the same number of inclined planes as the eastern side. They then boarded a train and for five hours traveled thirty-eight miles to the village of Johnstown, where travel on the canal boat resumed to Pittsburgh. From there on as usual, the journey would continue on the Ohio.

Pittsburgh, for all its commercial and manufacturing importance, did not much appeal. "Pittsburgh is a very dirty, smoky town, especially on a rainy day. . . . The streets are filthy and badly paved." (Pittsburgh and New York, it would appear, were the only stops on the entire journey that Hildreth found not to his liking.)

Traveling on down the river on a steamboat called *Excell* was another matter. The trip on the Ohio that so charmed so many newly arrived visitors from abroad, or Americans on their first time west, had much the same effect on the Hildreths on their return to home.

They had been away for nearly three months, longer than they ever had or ever would again, and their joy in being back could not have been greater.

"We found the family all well, and rejoiced to see us again after so long an absence. Our hearts [were] rejoicing in the goodness of God, who has safely guided and protected us through the perils of the journey, suffering no accident or evil to befall us, from the day of our departure to the day of our return."

It would seem clear, too, that for all they had seen back east, all those they had met who were of such remarkable ability and accomplishment, nothing could compare to the time in New Haven. Months later Hildreth would write to Benjamin Silliman, "We often think and speak of our delightful visit at New Haven and especially of the kindness of yourself and family which has made a deep impression on our hearts."

By remarkable coincidence, while the Hildreths were on their eastern pilgrimage, a traveler from Boston stopped for the first time at Marietta and, much taken by what he saw, wrote one of the most enthusiastic descriptions ever of the town in a letter that appeared first in the Boston *Mercantile Journal* and later in the *Marietta Intelligencer.* He was Amasa Walker, a Boston businessman, economist, and future congressman.

"Let no New England man ever visit the valley of the Ohio, without stopping at least one day in Marietta. It will do his heart good. He will find it a charming town, so like the beautiful valleys of his own native land, that he will feel perfectly happy and at home.

We had no business at this place, and should not have stopped, but that Saturday night found us opposite the town, and as we do not travel on the Sabbath, we went on shore and took lodgings. This is the spot where the settlement of Ohio commenced in 1788. Here, fifty one years ago, General Rufus Putnam with his followers, landed, and began to clear and build, and now Ohio contains almost a million and a half of inhabitants!

He explained how the town, located on the rich bottomland at the junction of the Ohio and the Muskingum, was laid out with "great regularity." He said, "The buildings, a large proportion of which are brick, are handsome, and in finer order than any I have seen on the river," and that there were several churches, a courthouse, and other public buildings, as were a newly erected college, the president of which was "a truly excellent man," the Reverend Joel Harvey Linsley, lately of the Park Street Church in Boston.

Few places offer more instructive lessons than Marietta. Here we can see what half a century will effect in the West. The Ohio and Muskingum flow on as they did when Putnam landed, but all else how changed! . . . The maturity of this place is the most striking feature. Here are found all that we witness in the old settlements on the Atlantic, the same institutions, the same architecture, and the same general habits. The order and quiet of the place are worthy of note. The Sabbath has passed as silently as in the most rural hamlet in the land of the Pilgrims. In passing around the town I have noticed none of those low grog-shops which are the curse of almost all the western towns, and I have neither seen nor heard anything like intemperance and riot.

If the speculator on the abstract doctrine of political economy and the progress of population, wishes for a practicle illustration of what has been done, and is now doing at the west, let him visit this spot, and he will be astonished, perhaps confounded.

He will see that already accomplished which in Europe would require centuries; society in a high state of perfection, institutions established on a firm basis, and everything moving on in harmony and prosperity. Marietta cannot, it is true, vie with Cincinnati and some other towns in population, but there is a quiet elegance and beauty in the place, that no other which I have seen in this region, can boast.

1   Judge Ephraim Cutler, the oldest son of Manasseh Cutler, devoted much
of his life to making the ideals of the Northwest Ordinance established by
his father remain a reality—in continuing to exclude slavery and in keeping
higher education a main objective. Oil portrait by Sala Bosworth, circa 1840s.

2

Joseph Barker, talented carpenter, boat builder, and gifted, self-taught architect who designed and built many of the principal buildings of Marietta. This oil portrait, painted in his elder years by neighbor and portraitist, Lilly Martin Spencer, was intended also to show his great love of books.

3

Elizabeth Dana Barker, long remembered as a "loving gentle woman" whose word was "law," with her ten children. She encouraged them to get all the knowledge they could, make use of it, and "everywhere be useful." Portrait by Sala Bosworth, circa 1840s.

4

5

Harman Blennerhassett,
a wealthy Irish aristocrat.

Margaret Blennerhassett, his wife,
who was also his niece.

6

Blennerhassett Mansion, the palatial home built for the couple by Joseph
Barker on what became known as Blennerhassett Island, twelve miles
downstream from Marietta on the Ohio and within Virginia. Everything
was done to perfection and at a cost such as never known on the river.

On frequent excursions to Marietta on her white horse, Margaret sported a bright scarlet dress with brass buttons, a beaver hat with white ostrich feathers, and went accompanied by a slave on horseback.

In the spring of 1805, former vice president Aaron Burr arrived at Blennerhassett Island, having shot and killed Alexander Hamilton only the year before and now reputedly plotting some new mysterious pursuits in the west in which he was soon to involve Harman Blennerhassett.

Of all the gigantic trees that filled the forests of Ohio none was held in such regard as the buckeye, a favorite wood for making bowls, chairs, and cribs. It was the source for the buckeye nut, which in addition to its medicinal value was considered a reliable provider of good luck. It became Ohio's much loved state tree.

9

The Great Seal of the State of Ohio, depicting sunrise over the Scioto River, was first conceived in 1802, then made official the year following.

10

Chillicothe, about 100 miles west of Marietta on the Scioto River, became the first capital of Ohio. It was there at the first Ohio State House (above), that Ephraim Cutler, who was so ill he could barely get out of bed, cast what proved to be the deciding vote that kept Ohio from becoming a slave state, thus saving the cause of freedom so cherished by his father and others of the founding pioneers.

Locally built boats offshore at Marietta. Painting by Charles Sullivan, circa 1840.

Commodore Abraham Whipple, famous American Revolutionary War naval officer, based on a portrait by Edward Savage. In April 1801, a 110-ton oceangoing square-rigger, *St. Clair*, built at Marietta by Charles Greene, set sail down the Ohio. Under the skillful command of Whipple, the ship made history, sailing all the way to New Orleans and out to sea.

14

The steamboat *New Orleans*, built at Pittsburgh, set sail in October 1811 with its builder Nicholas Roosevelt in command. The voyage to New Orleans marked the start of the steamboat era on western waters.

15

The explosion of the steamboat *Washington* at Marietta the morning of June 5, 1816, was the first steamboat disaster on the western rivers.

Dr. Samuel Hildreth first arrived alone on horseback at Marietta in 1806 when still in his twenties, knowing no one, and soon established himself not only as an indispensable physician but as a man of many interests and remarkable abilities. He was to distinguish himself also as a naturalist of national reputation and the first chronicler of the Marietta story. Oil portrait by Aaron Houghton Corwine, painted in 1823.

16

Rhoda Cook Hildreth with her sixth child, Harriet Eliza. Oil portrait by Sala Bosworth, 1826.

17

Watercolor of the life cycle of a butterfly,
one of the many painted by Samuel Hildreth.

ABOVE: The town of Marietta in a landscape painted about 1840 by Charles Sullivan. The Congregational Church with its twin towers stands out clearly on the left, on Front Street overlooking the Muskingum River.

RIGHT: The Congregational Church in a photograph taken in the 1880s.

21

The Cutler family homestead, the Old Stone House,
and its abundant gardens, overlooking the Ohio River.
Painted by Sala Bosworth, about 1840.

Judge Ephraim Cutler, who in old age began his autobiography with classic understatement: "I have had rather an eventful life."

22

Julia Cutler, who looked after her father, kept house, worked with him on his autobiography, and corrected his spelling right to the end.

23

Wholehearted commitment to higher education, ever a main objective among the founding pioneers of Ohio, was notably achieved with the establishment of both Ohio University, in 1804, and Marietta College, in 1832.

ABOVE: Cutler Hall, the first building at Ohio University and still the centerpiece of the campus. Drawing by Henry Howe, 1846.

BELOW: Marietta College, also drawn by Henry Howe in 1846. The structure on the right, built in 1832 and only known as the College Building, no longer stands; that on the left, Erwin Hall with its tower, remains the proud symbol of the college.

CHAPTER TEN

Journey's End

I am glad to have Pa enjoy himself in his old age.

—JULIA CUTLER

I.

Life for Ephraim Cutler, now in his seventies, had eased off only somewhat. He was serving still as a judge and a trustee of Ohio University, as well as in one effort or another intended to benefit the Ohio way of life. Further, with the help of daughter Julia, he was under way writing his own story. "I have had rather an eventful life," it began with characteristic understatement.

Beyond all that, he was taking part with the political activists calling themselves Whigs, those in opposition to the anti-intellectual attitude of the Andrew Jackson administration, including many ministers, lawyers, doctors, and other well-educated Americans.

Nor had the social life at the Cutler homestead diminished. If anything it seemed busier than ever. Virtually all who gathered were known to be "admirable talkers," including most conspicuously attorney Caleb Emerson, who frequently stayed on as a guest a week or more, discussing "the old and the new" and in a way Ephraim's daughter Julia described as "most satisfactory to themselves, and instructive and delightful to those whose privilege it was to listen."

When in the summer of 1843, it became known that former president John Quincy Adams was to make an unprecedented expedition to Cincinnati in November to lay the cornerstone for what may have been the first public observatory in the western hemisphere it was felt that a small committee of Marietta leaders should take part in the occasion. Those chosen for the honor were Ephraim, Joseph Barker, and Caleb Emerson. Excitement in Marietta over the approaching event was like nothing since the visit of Lafayette.

Following his defeat by Andrew Jackson in the presidential election of 1828, Adams, as had no president before, returned to Washington as a member of Congress, and there he served still, steadily, relentlessly. He was known as "Old Man Eloquent." Short and plump, he had a voice that carried like no other and he spoke with marked fervor.

On receiving the invitation to take part in the occasion at Cincinnati that fall, Adams had accepted without hesitation.

Family and friends were gravely concerned that it was too late in the season, not to say too late in life—he was seventy-six—for such a long, difficult, possibly perilous journey. Adams saw it as a heaven-sent opportunity to take advantage of growing popular interest in astronomy and to build backing in Congress for the new Smithsonian Institution, one of his favorite causes. As he wrote in his diary, it was a duty he must fulfill in the cause of learning:

> My task is to turn this transit gust of enthusiasm for the science of astronomy at Cincinnati into a permanent and persevering national pursuit, which may extend the bounds of human knowledge and make my country instrumental in elevating the character and improving the condition of man on earth. The hand of God Himself has furnished me this opportunity to do good.

His plan was to leave his home in Quincy, Massachusetts, on the 12th of October, accompanied by a servant, Benjamin Andrews, and traveling by railroad, lake steamer, and canals, by way of Buffalo and

Cleveland, he hoped to reach Cincinnati on November 6. As it was—despite what for him was the acute monotony of rail travel ("There is no uniformity in human life more monotonous," he noted privately), despite snow and howling winds on Lake Erie and seemingly endless days on overcrowded Ohio canal barges, during which he caught a cold—enthusiastic crowds greeted him at every stop, and on November 8 he reached Cincinnati in bright sunshine.

A stop at Marietta was planned for his return trip by steamboat on the Ohio, and from there the Marietta dignitaries would accompany him as far as Pittsburgh, from which he would travel on to Washington by rail.

A tremendous crowd had gathered at the Cincinnati hotel, the Henry House, where Adams was staying, on the front of which was a large balcony overlooking the street. From there, as he would record in his diary, Mayor Henry Evans Spencer delivered "a complimentary address, welcomed me to the city, and introduced me to the assembled multitude, who answered by deafening shouts of applause."

Adams's answer, he was sorry to have to record, was "flat, stale, and unprofitable, without a spark of eloquence or a flash of oratory, confused, incoherent, muddy," and yet to his amazement it was "received with new shouts of welcome."

The crowd then dispersed, but a continual succession of visitors beset his hotel chamber until late into the evening.

The laying of the observatory cornerstone was to take place the next day, and though he had been working hard for some time on what was expected to be a long and important speech, he had still not finished.

> Worn down with fatigue, anxiety, and shame, as I was . . . I sat up till one in the morning, writing the address, which, from utter exhaustion, I left unfinished, and retired to a sleepless bed.

At four o'clock, he woke again and finished what he wanted to say.

The speech he had written was a long (nearly two hours, he figured), learned, and reverential dissertation on the history and importance of astronomy. A printed version would run to no less than sixty-three pages, but because of unexpected, adverse circumstances he delivered only about half of it.

On departure from the hotel by carriage, followed by a parade of other carriages, military companies, and a marching band, all headed for the hilltop where the cornerstone was to be laid, rain began to fall, increasing rapidly to torrents by the time they reached the hilltop.

A stage had been erected, from which Adams was to deliver his address, but now, he saw a whole plain "covered with an auditory of umbrellas, instead of faces." His manuscript became so blurred by the rain it was scarcely legible.

Cutting his talk short, he finished by saying, here would arise one day "Light House of the Skies!" Here they were gathered to lay the foundation of what they could hope would aid in the cause of science and improvement in after ages.

The "venerable patriot," as he was referred to in the Cincinnati press, had done his duty and on departure he left no doubt among the citizens of the city of his admiration for them, indeed of so many he had met in Ohio who were so naturally "frank, easy and unpretending in their manners, which commend them rapidly and highly to the stranger's estimation."

He departed the afternoon of November 12, heading for Marietta on board a steamboat that, after all the talk and celebration over the subject of science, bore the appropriate name of *Benjamin Franklin*.

———•·•———

Plans and preparations for the Adams visit had been going on at Marietta for months and with increasing enthusiasm. But then, on September 21, word had come that another of the outstanding much beloved early pioneers, Joseph Barker, had died at his home at Wiseman's Bottom, at age seventy-eight.

He had been actively involved in the life of and growth of Marietta from the time he first arrived more than half a century before, designing and constructing many of the finest buildings, building boats, and serving in numerous ways in times of crisis.

Samuel Hildreth, one of Joseph's numerous friends, as well as the Barker family doctor, was to write, "In hospitality, he was unsurpassed, fond of social intercourse, gifted with a ready flow of language, and a mind well-stored with historical facts, his conversation was both instructive and interesting."

Not the least of his achievements was the lively, colorful account of his life he had written to help Hildreth with the collection of pioneer memoirs Hildreth was at work on—an account that would later be published as a book unto itself.

He himself, it would seem, was proudest of all of his large devoted family. He was the father of ten children, all of whom were still alive but the one boy who had drowned in the Ohio River years past, and, in addition, there was a grand total of sixty-three grandchildren.

His wife, Elizabeth Dana Barker, had died in 1835, at the age of sixty-five.

The day following Joseph's death, a long line of carriages carrying family and friends, plus many more on horseback or on foot, comprised the funeral procession to Joseph Barker's final resting place beside his wife in the Putnam Cemetery, not far from the Barker homestead.

———

It was yet another rainy day, Wednesday, November 15, when at two in the afternoon, the *Benjamin Franklin* came into view downstream on the Ohio. Guns fired, bells rang. Former president John Quincy Adams had arrived.

A great crowd greeted him at the Marietta wharf, notwithstanding the rain, then followed him to the already crowded Congregational Church where he was to speak.

Deacon William Putnam, the son of Rufus Putnam, delivered a warm welcome, and Adams, without notes, stepped to the pulpit and to no one in the audience did what he said mean more than to Ephraim Cutler.

He spoke at the very start of the long connection he and his father, John Adams, had had with the pioneers who first settled at Marietta.

He recounted how his father had known and worked with the Reverend Manasseh Cutler. He told how he himself, when studying law in the town of Newburyport, Massachusetts, had visited the Reverend at his home the summer of 1788, just after his return from his own visit to Marietta. And how ever since that conversation he himself had "taken a deep interest in the whole west, and watched its progress, step by step, to its present great and flourishing condition."

He talked also of Rufus Putnam and others besides the Cutlers and credited much that he knew to accounts that had appeared in the Massachusetts papers at the time. "From this source," reported a later account of his talk, "Mr. Adams drew the materials of that admirable half hour's address, and the minuteness of his details, and the correctness of his names, dates, and other statements, proved the amazing accuracy and discipline of his memory."

His remarks concluded, Adams left the pulpit and, one by one, the congregation was presented to him. It would have been gratifying to him, he told those clustered about, had the elements allowed them to express their welcome without exposure to such an inclement day, but that so much of "the light of human kindness" was shown him that the name of Marietta would "ever dwell upon my heart."

At his request, he was then taken to the Mound Cemetery, which he had first learned about from Manasseh Cutler and desired to inspect. From there he went directly to the boat, where Ephraim Cutler, Caleb Emerson, and Joseph Barker, Jr., substituting for his father, also went on board to accompany Adams to Pittsburgh.

Ephraim could not have been more pleased. He had greatly admired Adams for a long time. As his daughter Julia recorded, he had even bought a new overcoat for the occasion.

———

Ephraim and Adams had much in common. They were the same age, seventy-six, and each the son of a famous and gifted father. Both cared intensely about education and equal opportunity. Both were unequivocally against slavery. And both loved to talk, as did famously Caleb Emerson.

The conversation among them on the boat went on well into the night and commanded the attention of all who were so fortunate as to be present, and particularly when Ephraim expressed to Adams the gratitude felt by so many in Ohio for the "wisdom and firmness" his father, John Adams, had shown in the negotiations at the Treaty of Paris in 1783 that secured the Northwest Territory for the United States.

As Ephraim wrote later, "I saw the tears gather in his eyes," and Caleb Emerson noted that Adams's voice faltered in saying that "he rejoiced to find that there were some who still remembered the services of his beloved father."

Ephraim further noted, "I also gave Mr. Adams a concise history of the convention that formed our state constitution . . . and the consequent exclusion of slavery. He said with emphasis, 'Slavery must and will soon have an end.' "

As was well known, Representative Adams had for years been battling against the so-called Gag Rule used by members of Congress to suppress debate on slavery, and though the struggle had taken its toll on his strength he had not given up.

All along the Ohio River, slavery was a growing cause of contention and particularly in and about Marietta, which had become one of the main escape routes for runaway slaves in what had become known as the Underground Railroad.

Notices appeared constantly in the Marietta paper offering rewards for black runaways from Virginia for as much as $300 to $500 or as little as $12.50. The $300 reward was for the return to Parkersburg of three slaves named Jack, Rose, and John:

Jack is a very handsome Negro, about 5 feet 10 inches high, a black complexion, erect in his appearance, and about 26 years of age—had on, when he absconded, a deep blue bearskin coat, etc.

Rose, the wife of Jack, is a likely woman of her age, about 5 feet 6 inches high, black complexion, hair tolerably long and tied at

the top, has holes in her ears but seldom wears [ear] rings, and
about 36 years of age—had on, when she absconded, a blue riding dress with white glass buttons.

John is about 5 feet, 7 inches high, very black complexion,
thick and well-set—had on linen pantaloons, etc.

For two others named Martin and Sam a full $500 was the offer for
their return to Clarksburg. Martin, at age twenty, was the youngest,
about five feet, eight inches and "very handsome." Sam, "very black,"
and "free and easy" to talk to.

For the return of a black man named Joseph, who claimed to be a
doctor and was fond of playing the fiddle, the reward was all of $20, and
there were more and more steadily crossing the river to escape.

Many in Marietta were helping the fugitives escape, but to make
known their part would have been putting themselves and their families at considerable risk. One notable exception was David Putnam, Jr.,
the great-grandson of General Israel Putnam and a leading merchant
whose large frame house at the head of Maple Street, across the Muskingum in Harmar, became a famous first stop for fleeing slaves. One
cold November night a mob of anti-abolitionists gathered outside the
house shouting that an escaped slave was hiding inside. Several leading
citizens appeared on the scene, including Caleb Emerson, and urged
everyone to calm down and go home, which was what happened.

Others, too, perhaps as many as fifty in Washington County, served
as "conductors" along the line of escape. The rest of the escape route
ran north to Oberlin, Ohio, then across Lake Erie to Canada. To what
degree Ephraim Cutler took part is difficult to know, but one particular
incident suggests he may have been quite involved.

Years later one of his grandsons, Rufus Dawes, the son of Cutler's
daughter Sarah, would tell how, as a boy visiting his grandfather's Old
Stone House by the Ohio, he was awakened in the night by what he took
to be the hoot of an owl, this followed by a similar, more distant answering cry from the Virginia shore. Then came the splash of a boat leaving
the Cutler riverbank.

The boy climbed out of bed and went to the window. In the heavy darkness he could make out the silhouettes of two boats filled with silent people approaching shore in front of the house. When he went to his mother's room, he found her down on her knees before her window praying.

———•·•———

After a "magnificent reception" on arrival at Pittsburgh, Adams bid farewell to his Marietta escorts and started for Washington while they headed back down the river.

Few there were who had traveled more of the world than John Quincy Adams, from the time when, as a ten-year-old boy, he had sailed for France with his father in the midst of the Revolutionary War. This, his journey to Ohio, was the last of his courageous travels.

On reaching his home on F Street, Adams collapsed. "My strength is prostrated beyond anything that I ever experienced before." But he was to keep on serving in Congress, battling slavery for five more years, until the late winter of 1848, when he collapsed at his desk. He was carried to the speaker's office just off the hall and there, two days later, he died.

In Marietta a town eulogy for John Quincy Adams was given at the Methodist Church on Putnam Street.

II.

It would be said of Ephraim Cutler that along with so many of his strengths, virtues, and worthy accomplishments, his place as the most notable of Ohio's surviving pioneers, he was also blessed in his family. "We have never seen a family that were united by stronger bonds of affection," it was said, and while he took great pleasure and pride in all his children, William, the youngest son, still in his thirties, had stepped in to carry on with his father's public roles and in admirable fashion.

William had little of his father's physical vitality and was of "retiring disposition." But in 1842 he had begun making speeches in an effort to be elected as a Whig in the state legislature, and though defeated, he ran again in 1844 and won by a handsome majority. Before the close of the session he was recognized as a leader on the floor.

Such achievement pleased his father no end and helped provide Ephraim a much needed lift of spirit when in June of that year, his ever loving brother Jervis died in Evansville, Indiana, at age seventy-five.

Writing to William early in the new year of 1846, sister Julia could report that "Pa's health has been better this winter, than it was last. He has fewer cares and appears to enjoy life better." It was their mother she worried about.

"Her limbs are very painfully affected with rheumatism. She cannot dress herself without assistance, and is unable to do anything, even reading seems to fatigue her. She sits up most of the day, and certainly bears her afflictions with a great deal of patience."

That fall, William was again nominated and again elected to the state legislature, and the difficulties of his return to Columbus in December, at least as far as Zanesville, appear to have been no less than in his father's day, and that his response to adversity had been no less than that of his father.

As he wrote in a letter to Ephraim, "The stage left Marietta at 11 o'clock Wednesday night, and we had a perilous time getting to Zanesville.

> We found the water over the bridge this side of Lowell so deep that the driver refused to cross. I prevailed upon him to let me have a horse and ride over and back, after which he ventured with the coach. We drove over Big Run bridge with the plank all afloat some eight or ten inches above the sleepers, the forewheels in some places pushing the planks up in heaps, and the hind wheels running on the sleepers. At another place we tried to swim, but the horses refused, and turned directly for the river at the mouth of the creek; we were barely saved by striking a high bank, which projected into the stream. At the bridge across Olive Green we found the plank afloat, and the driver and myself waded in and spent half an hour in the water loading the plank down with stones. But we were graciously preserved, and arrived

safely at Zanesville Thursday evening, and at Columbus [travel-
ing by rail] Friday night.

He then added to his father, knowing how it would please him,
"The Whigs, with great cordiality and unanimity, have placed me in the
speaker's chair."

Later, at the close of the session, a letter appeared in the *Cincinnati
Signal* by another member of the legislature named F. G. Squier that
seemed to speak for many and that, to Ephraim, could only have seemed
pure gold.

"Let us glance around the hall of the lower house," it began, "not to
admire its architectural wonders—and see if we can detect the 'men of
mark.'

Our attention first rests upon the speaker's chair. Its occupant is a
tall . . . perhaps we should say sallow man, dressed with the utmost
plainness. . . . He stoops slightly—is it from a sense of being tall
and without elegance? No. Although modest and retiring to a fault,
he never bestows a thought on outward appearance, nor calculates
outward impressions. . . . When . . . Mr. Cutler was called to the
capital, he came there with a healthy, well-balanced intellect and
nothing but a modesty almost painful in its excess prevented him
from at once assuming the lead of his party. Yet, without effort, he
soon became invested with an influence second to no other man's
on the floor, and his voice carried with it a predominating weight.

In Marietta, too, Ephraim, as he reported to William, was hearing
in "a lively manner, joy respecting your success." But he cautioned his
son with a fatherly reminder, "You must not let flattery spoil you, but do
your best to deserve approbation."

On June 30, 1846, Sally Parker Cutler, the wife of Ephraim Cutler for
thirty-eight years, and mother of their five children, died amid the fam-

ily circle at their home on the banks of the Ohio. As William would later write to Julia, "How little did we anticipate . . . that the <u>center</u> of that circle would be taken, leaving to us, but the bright recollection of virtues, unsurpassed and love unequalled."

In the early spring of 1849, Ephraim's oldest son, Charles, announced he was joining the rush to California for gold. "A year ago we had not <u>heard</u> of the gold of California, and even after the papers were filled with descriptions of the immense regions where it is found, and of the multitudes who went to seek it—It never occurred to me that any one dear to us would go there," wrote Julia. Again, as in her father's earlier days, the west was the future.

Two months later came word from California that Charles had died of cholera. The news shook the whole family in a way nothing had—"to think of his dying away from home and friends, buried upon those vast plains where no one knows even the place of his last rest," Julia wrote. And the blow fell hardest on Ephraim. "He is very much bowed down under the stroke—still he murmurs not, the language of his heart seems to be, 'I was dumb. I opened not my mouth, because thou God dids't it.' Occasionally we hear a suppressed groan as he walks his room with clasped hands."

III.

For all the changes taking place, Marietta remained a small town, its population by 1850 still less than 4,000. But for a considerable majority this remained part of the appeal and for many of those longtime residents who had played major roles in the local ways their commitment to the community, their pride in its appearance and way of life, was no less than ever.

To the citizenry of Marietta, and particularly the older element, there was considerable pride, too, in the fact that a community established on the precept of freedom of religion had kept faith with that pledge.

The first efforts to establish a Catholic place of worship in Marietta were made in 1830, in a two-story brick building with a grocery store on the first floor, and what served as a chapel on the second. The first actual Catholic church was built in the 1850s, under the direction of Father Peter Perry, and with the ever-increasing arrival of Irish and German Catholic immigrants, the number of Catholic citizenry kept growing steadily.

Among the earliest Jewish immigrants to arrive were two German brothers, Charles and Samuel Coblenz, who established a dry goods store on Greene Street in the 1840s. But the Jewish presence was to remain small in Marietta throughout the rest of the nineteenth century.

Considerable pride was taken in the town's tree-lined streets. Ironically, here where once not so very long past giant trees had been the enemy, now stood what was acclaimed as "the best shaded town in the state."

Samuel Hildreth, despite keen competition from seventeen physicians in Washington County, continued to "monopolize" the medical profession. Further, with the help of Ephraim Cutler and others of the "old timers," Hildreth, in 1848, published his long-awaited *Pioneer History*, on the early settlement of the Ohio Valley, a work like no other until then and one of great lasting value. Praise for the book was plentiful, but that which had greatest meaning to Hildreth came from Benjamin Silliman, who wrote to tell him his name would "be ever honorably associated with the early history of the West." In 1852 Hildreth followed with a second book, *Memoirs of the Early Pioneer Settlers of Ohio*, taking into account a cast of thirty-nine characters of note.

Ephraim lived on for seven years after Sally's death, during which Julia remained a devoted companion and, greatly to her pleasure and her credit, he remained much as he had been in health and outlook. "Pa spent a great deal of his time in his favorite occupation," she would write, "reading his chosen books and the newspapers, never losing interest in what was happening in the world." One of the young teachers at Muskingum Academy had observed much the same thing. "If he takes hold of a newspaper or an interesting book, everything else is sure to be neglected."

He also enjoyed accompanying Julia on occasional days in Marietta, making calls and "attending" to some shopping. One such day they found time to visit Samuel Hildreth's fine garden and cabinet of geological specimens. "The doctor's very excellent and highly cultivated taste is manifested in every part," Julia recorded.

Thanksgiving, Ephraim's favorite day, remained no less a grand family festival. "We did not intend to have any guests but our own family connections and those in the house," Julia recorded in her diary on Thursday, November 23, 1848. But the number who gathered was considerable all the same.

> Twenty-one sat down to dinner. Pa expressed himself much pleased with the cooking of the turkey, chicken, pie, etc., and praised all the accompaniments—which was sufficient reward for all this labor of preparation, as we always consider this, "Pa's Festival"—which his Yankee origin has made him prize above all others.

On his eighty-third birthday, April 13, 1850, he rode by horseback twenty-eight miles through snow and wind from Amesville back home. The farm, too, occupied his interest no less than ever. "My health and strength has thus far sustained me in seeing everyday to the hard work that is going on," he was glad to report to William in May.

Be a farmer, his own father had strongly advised, when Ephraim first started for the Ohio country.

———◆———

In the early spring of 1850, a shabby woman no more than five feet tall boarded a steamer at Cincinnati, where she had been living for seventeen years, and departed upstream on the Ohio. She was happily heading "home" to New England, to Brunswick, Maine, where her husband had recently joined the faculty of Bowdoin College, and where, in the year ahead, she was to write her first book, titled *Uncle Tom's Cabin*, which would have more far-reaching effects than any American novel ever written. She herself, Harriet Beecher Stowe, would also achieve an overnight fame such as no American woman had yet known.

The book, based largely on stories she had heard from black servants during her years in Cincinnati, was written from the heart and put slavery in terms of human beings and human suffering. Published in 1852, it was an immediate literary and political sensation, selling more than 300,000 copies in America within a year, and in England no less than 1.5 million. It would be said Mrs. Stowe made more converts to antislavery with her book than all the preachers and lecturers combined. For those like Ephraim Cutler, who had labored so long and hard to keep slavery out of Ohio, she was a hero.

———◆———

Except for trouble hearing and the loss of some teeth, Ephraim remained remarkably his old self, still making the ride on horseback to his farm in Amesville.

In the early spring of 1853, however, on a ride to Marietta, his horse stumbled and threw him to the ground. It had been a fall from a horse that long before took the life of his uncle Ephraim and so greatly changed the whole course of his boyhood. Now, still another fall from a horse would mark his own end.

He died of internal injuries that summer at the Old Stone House, on July 8, 1853. He was eighty-six.

In an eloquent "funeral discourse," the Reverend E. B. Andrews, a professor at Marietta College, who also ministered in Ephraim's church in Warren, declared flatly Ohio had never been blessed with "a truer statesman or more devoted servant," and gave praise particularly for his part in preventing the admission of slavery.

We can hardly predict what the consequences would have been, had there not been a few men such as Judge Cutler to resist the insidious aggressions of the monstrous evil of slavery. . . . We owe it to the heroic Puritan firmness of Judge Cutler . . . and to him must ever belong the high honor of drafting that article in the first constitution and fundamental law of the great state of Ohio which makes it the home of the free while the state shall last.

In a long tribute in the *Marietta Intelligencer*, he was credited as "the first man in the state to propose anything like a system of common school instruction" and for never in all his years as a trustee of Ohio University missing a meeting of the board.

"In every sphere and every relation of life, Judge Cutler was A USE-FUL MAN."

An editorial tribute in the *Ohio State Journal* would no doubt have pleased him most of all: "Judge Cutler belonged to that class of strictly upright, honest and true men, of whom the pioneers of this state afford so many noble examples."

He was put to rest beside his wife, Sally, in the Gravel Bank Cemetery on a hill not far from the family home overlooking the Ohio River.

———•+•———

By the time Samuel Hildreth lay dying ten years later, the pioneer era he had taken part in and chronicled was long past. The population of Ohio had reached an unimaginable 2,000,000 people and was still growing. Railroads and the telegraph had come of age. And overshadowing everything, the country was engulfed in a horrific civil war.

In 1860, William Cutler was elected to Congress. In 1862, on April 23, he made a long and powerful speech on the floor of the House denouncing slavery in no uncertain terms as a "public enemy" and so must be destroyed. With notable vigor and courage William had become the third generation of Cutlers to battle slavery.

In the summer of 1863 when the war's biggest battle had only just been fought at Gettysburg, Pennsylvania, on July 1–3, Ohio was suddenly in a state of alarm. A Confederate cavalry unit of more than 2,000 men commanded by Brigadier General John Morgan had crossed the Ohio River into Indiana, then crossed the line into Ohio close to Cincinnati and was advancing eastward, "plundering everybody without fear or favor."

The governor of Ohio had called out the militia. At Marietta 10,000 or more were encamped, in the event Morgan might strike there in an attempt to escape back over the river. Another militia encampment had been established downriver at Warren, using the Cutler homestead as its command center. Militiamen were busy digging rifle pits across the field above the house.

"We are getting accustomed to warlike sights and sounds," wrote Julia Cutler, "the glittering bayonets of the infantry, the bugle call of the artillery, the clanking of saber and carbine of the cavalry. . . .

> They [the soldiers] come to us for food, medicines, tools, cook-ing utensils, tubs, washboard, soap, books, newspapers . . . every shade tree has its group of loungers, reading, writing. . . . Some walk about the garden—some spend hours in the river—while others sleep their time away. All say they like this place better than any they have camped in.

General Morgan and his men kept rapidly on the move, until stopped at Buffington Island ford on the Ohio River, nearly sixty miles down-stream from Marietta in a sharp skirmish with Ohio militia. More than 700 of his men were taken prisoner. Still he moved on, turning north, crossing the Muskingum near McConnelsville, until finally stopped at Salineville, where he surrendered.

At Camp Marietta, meantime, Dr. George Hildreth, who was serv-ing with the militia there, had on July 20 suddenly requested a leave of absence to return to the family home on Putnam Street, such was the declining condition of his father. The request was granted by his com-mander, Colonel William Rufus Putnam, Jr.

———•—•———

Dr. Samuel Hildreth, now nearly eighty, remained one of Marietta's most accomplished, highly respected citizens. He had been honored with numerous awards for worthy achievement well beyond Marietta, yet remained ever devoted to the town and the town to him.

He had also remained in good health—a well-preserved and happy old gentleman, as said—until Sunday, July 5. That morning he had attended church as usual, but in the afternoon he suffered a stroke that paralyzed him.

Samuel Hildreth died on July 24, 1863, in the grand, red-brick home built by Joseph Barker. His wife, Rhoda, his physician son, George, and others of the family were at his side.

His funeral was held two days later at the Congregational Church. He was buried beside his father at the old Mound Cemetery. Rhoda Cook Hildreth, who died in 1868, would also be buried beside her husband.

Published in the *American Journal of Science and Arts*, a few months after Hildreth's death, Benjamin Silliman wrote, "In his private life he illustrated every virtue of a Christian gentleman. Bright and cheerful by nature, he loved nature with the simple enthusiasm of a child. Industrious and systematic in a high degree, no moment of his life was wasted."

A long obituary in the *Marietta Register* recounted Hildreth's many scientific and historic publications, that he had been president of the Medical Society of Ohio, that he had recently donated his collection of fossils, insects, and shells, some 4,000 specimens in natural history, arranged in cases and drawers, labeled, numbered, and entered in a catalogue—to Marietta College.

"Besides his laborious medical practice," the obituary continued, "he accomplished very much, as he himself expressed it, by *saving* the 'odds and ends of time.' . . . He was exact in all his dealings—an honest man, a Christian. His was a *complete* life, he 'finished his work.' "

But then it can be said, too, that those others of the foremost pioneers of Marietta had finished their work, each in his or her way, and no matter the adversities to be faced, propelled as they were by high, worthy purpose. They accomplished what they had set out to do not for money, not for possessions or fame, but to advance the quality and opportunities of life—to propel as best they could the American ideals.

ACKNOWLEDGMENTS

It was large-scale good luck that led me to writing this book, beginning back in 2004, when the president of Ohio University, Dr. Robert Glidden, invited me to deliver the commencement address in tribute to the university's 200th anniversary. The invitation was one for which I will ever be grateful.

I already had good feelings about pioneer times in Ohio, mainly because of the monumental trilogy by Conrad Richter, *The Trees*, *The Fields*, and *The Town*, among the finest ever works of American historical fiction. But I knew relatively little about the university and in my early efforts to understand its beginnings I learned that the oldest building on campus was called Cutler Hall. This led me to the story of the amazing Reverend Manasseh Cutler, a figure I had never heard of, and that eventually would lead me to Marietta, Ohio, and the Legacy Library at Marietta College.

Because I had other projects underway at the time, including a book on the Wright brothers set in another part of Ohio, it was not for several years before I got started on *The Pioneers* and came to grasp the full reach and importance of the story.

What was for me particularly exciting was the realization that I now had the opportunity to write about a cast of real-life characters of historic accomplishment who were entirely unknown to most Americans— to bring them to life, bring them center stage and tell their amazing and, I felt, important story.

It would also be a book such as I had long hoped I might one day attempt, ever since I first saw Thornton Wilder's play *Our Town*. But where or when, if ever, would I find a collection of primary source material—original letters, diaries, memoirs and the like—sufficient to make that possible?

Now there it was, and not in some long-forgotten attic, but in one fine, superbly staffed library at the center of a beautiful college campus in the very town at the center of the story.

The papers of General Rufus Putnam and those of the Ohio Company of Associates were all there, no fewer than forty-five hundred items. There, too, was the Ephraim Cutler Family Collection, numbering some five thousand items; and the Samuel Hildreth Collections, which include not only his letters, journals, and daily notes on the weather, but his voluminous natural history notes, articles, speeches, in addition to his notes and papers related to the history of the Ohio Valley.

The main body of Manasseh Cutler's journals and correspondence, beginning as early as 1765, was published in two volumes in 1888, but the Marietta College Library collection also includes some 350 original manuscript sermons, three original diaries from the 1820s, and fifty items of original correspondence.

Included also in the Marietta collection is an extensive collection of books and newspaper articles, maps, drawings, landscape paintings, and superb oil portraits of the principal characters done from life, a treasure in themselves.

In the diary I kept during my first visit to the Marietta College Library in September 2016, I wrote:

These were two of the very best research days ever—the material beyond anything expected and the librarians and Marietta history specialists among the best and most good-spirited I've ever worked with. The time spent has expanded my feeling for the subject in a way nothing else could have.

And then there is the remarkable keeper of the treasures, Linda Showalter, whose help, guidance, and immense knowledge of the subject were of such great importance from the start. Hardly a day went by when she did not turn up some surprise items from the collection. Most memorable was the point during that first visit when she came over to the work table where I was seated in the archives reading room and said simply with a smile, "I think this might be of interest to you."

She set before me what looked like it might be an old account book. I opened it and there, to my utter surprise, I found page after page of exquisite watercolor renderings of caterpillars morphing into a variety of bright-colored butterflies, all the work of the highly gifted Samuel Hildreth.

What a wonderful moment! To think that a young physician struggling with all he had to contend with there in the wilderness was also capable of doing works of art so superb.

I must include as well the legendary highway west, the Ohio River, which played such an important role in our history, the presence of which so nearby evokes at different times of day, different seasons and light so very much of the setting in times past. To get up early in the morning and step out of a hotel by the river, close by the very spot where the pioneers first landed, and watch the sun rise and the gray mist on the water, the geese and ducks, has also been for me an important and most pleasurable part of the work.

I wish to thank Douglas Anderson, director of the Legacy Library, Georgene Johnson and Ann Anderson, who helped with numerous requests and particularly with the Hildreth papers; Sally Norton, who transcribed the Lucy Backus Woodbridge letters; Barbara Binegar, Jeanne Catalano, Angela Burdiss, Joe Straw, Jeffrey Cottrell, and Peter Thayer, whose help was greatly appreciated.

Student interns Carly Matheny, Madison McCormick, and Maria Stickrath were also most helpful, and especially with the historic Marietta newspaper collection. So, too, was Professor Matt Young of the Marietta College history department, who generously volunteered his time and skills creating a map of Marietta, its surroundings and landmarks.

To William Ruud, president of the college, I am particularly grateful for the warm welcome to the campus he gave me at the very start.

And I am highly indebted to two leading specialists in the Marietta story. Bill Reynolds of the Campus Martius and Ohio River Museum, knows so much about the realities of pioneer life it is as if he had taken part himself. His walking tours of the museum exhibits and particularly of the Rufus Putnam house were outstanding; and Dr. Ray Swick, who knows more than anyone about the Blennerhassetts and led a private tour of Blennerhassett Island not once but twice, enlivening every hour with both insight and wit. My thanks, too, to Miles Evenson, superintendent of Blennerhassett Island Historical State Park, who made the visits possible.

Scott Britton and archaeologist Wes Clarke of the Castle Historical Museum in Marietta took time to give a most interesting tour of the Mound Cemetery, and Scott further provided a tour of the First Congregational Church in Marietta, along with the Reverend Linda N. Steelman, minister of the church.

Then there is my old friend Andy Masich, president of the Senator John Heinz History Center in Pittsburgh, who gave my manuscript a close reading and contributed valuable observations on Ohio River history and the native tribes of the area, and in addition provided a copy of the original Ebenezer Denny journal.

My thanks to William Kimok, archivist for special collections at Ohio University; to Marc Kibbey, associate curator of fishes, Museum of Biological Diversity, Ohio State University; to the ever helpful Peter Drummey of the Massachusetts Historical Society; to Deirdre Anderson and the staff at the Hingham Historical Society.

Thanks also to Louise C. Pempek, who provided a guided tour of the Cutler family neighborhood at Killingly, Connecticut, and Meredith and Al Konesni, owners of the old Cutler homestead, who opened the door of their house for my visit there.

And to Chris and Marcia Warrington of Rutland, Massachusetts, owners of the Rufus Putnam house there; and Cece Gough, Dr. David Horn, and Linda Coonrod, who welcomed me and my wife, Rosalee, on a first visit to Manasseh Cutler's First Congregational Church and rectory in Hamilton, Massachusetts, where so much of the story began; and Hampton Carey, who provided copies of the original Benjamin Silliman–Samuel Hildreth letters at Yale's Sterling Library.

Most helpful all the way has been the incomparable Mike Hill, whom

I have had the good fortune to work with for more than thirty-five years. Ever resourceful, energetic, ever cheerful and tireless, he has been indispensable. We made the expeditions to Marietta together many times over, always enjoying the work.

Linda Gudgel Konkel has typed and retyped my many drafts of every chapter, made valuable suggestions as to content, and worked closely with Mike on source notes. And thank you also to David Konkel for his help with the illustrations.

To my daughter Dorie McCullough Lawson I am again immensely indebted. She has read the manuscript in all its stages, offering important suggestions, and kept me on my toes the whole way. My daughter Melissa McCullough McDonald, too, read and commented on the manuscript, as did sons Geoffrey, who also contributed to some of the research, and David Jr., a teacher of English, who tactfully offered some further suggestions. Son Bill accompanied me on trips to Marietta and the Cutler home at Killingly, and lent a hand with the research at both.

I salute, too, my dear friend and literary agent, Morton Janklow, who loved the idea for the book from the start and on his first reading responded with such fervent praise and for all the reasons I could have hoped for.

And still again there have been the highly gifted, longtime friends at Simon & Schuster with whom it is a joy to work—Carolyn Reidy, Jonathan Karp, Julia Prosser, Johanna Li, and above all, Bob Bender, who came up with the title for the book the day I first explained what it was to be about and has since read with a keen editorial eye every line twice over and made a number of apt and much appreciated suggestions.

My sincere thanks as well to copy editor Fred Chase for his part and to Joy O'Meara for her design of the book.

Most important by far, most helpful, wise, and inspiriting, has, once again, been my editor-in-chief, my dearest friend of all, my beloved wife, Rosalee, to whom the book is dedicated.

NOTES

1. The Ohio Country

PAGE

3 "The Ohio is the grand artery": Crèvecoeur, "Letters from an American Farmer," *Ohio Archaeological and Historical Quarterly*, Vol. 3, 1900, 96–98.

3 *Manasseh Cutler:* For biographical information on Reverend Cutler, see Cutler and Cutler, *Life, Journals, and Correspondence of Rev. Manasseh Cutler, LL.D*, Vol. 1, 1–37; *Dictionary of American Biography*, Vol. 3, Allen Johnson and Dumas Malone, eds., New York: Charles Scribner's Sons, 1946, 12–14.

4 *"diligence and proficiency":* Cutler and Cutler, *Life, Journals*, Vol. 1, 6.

4 *"Prosecuted my study":* Manasseh Cutler Journal, November 1768, ibid., 19.

4 *"exceedingly":* Manasseh Cutler Journal, September 11, 1771, ibid., 35.

4 *"the old style, country type":* Ibid., Vol. 2, 358.

5 *"of great and varied excellence":* Wadsworth, "Discourse at Manasseh Cutler's Interment," *The Hesperian*, No. 1, Vol. 2, 1838, 431.

5 *third floor to the rectory:* Author tour of the First Congregational Church and the rectory, Hamilton, Massachusetts.

5 *"prepared for usefulness in the world":* Cutler, *Life and Times of Ephraim Cutler: Prepared from His Journals and Correspondence*, 5.

6 *"Engaged in the study of botany":* Manasseh Cutler Journal, March 10, 1780, Cutler and Cutler, *Life, Journals*, Vol. 1, 77.

6 *"This morning endeavored":* Manasseh Cutler Journal, May 18, 1780, ibid.

6 *"Studied":* For numerous references to Cutler's study regimen, see Manasseh Cutler Journal, August 31, 1770, December 21–23, 1773, July 25, 1772, ibid., 25, 44, 39.

6 "Felix, qui potuit rerum cognoscere causas": Ibid., 7.

6   *meeting at Bunch of Grapes tavern:* Ibid., 180.

7   *"No! Rather than relinquish our claim":* Cone, "The First Settlement in Ohio," *Magazine of American History*, Vol. 6, No. 4, April 1881, 244; Cone, *Life of Rufus Putnam, With Extracts from His Journal and an Account of the First Settlement in Ohio*, 92.

7   *265,878 square miles:* Hinsdale, *The Old Northwest: The Beginnings of Our Colonial System*, 280.

7   *La Belle Rivière:* Hulbert, *Waterways of Westward Expansion: The Ohio River and Its Tributaries, Historic Highways of America series*, Vol. 9, Arthur Clark Company, Cleveland, OH, 1903.

7   *"the back country":* Cutler and Cutler, *Life, Journals*, Vol. 1, 145.

7   *"the howling wilderness":* Cutler, *Life and Times of Ephraim Cutler*, 42.

7   *"the fair domain beyond the Ohio":* Cone, *Life of Rufus Putnam*, 85.

7   *"the Ohio country":* Cutler and Cutler, *Life, Journals*, Vol. 1, 179.

8   *"squatters":* Banta, *The Ohio*, 273.

8   *"Indian menace":* Shetrone, "The Indian in Ohio," *Ohio Archaeological and Historical Quarterly*, Vol. 27, 1919, 417.

8   *The story of Crawford's Fate:* See Butterfield, *An Historical Account of the Expedition Against Sandusky Under Colonel William Crawford in 1782*, 379–92; Heard, *Handbook of the American Frontier: Four Centuries of Indian-White Relationships*, Vol. 1, 118; James H. O'Donnell III, "William Crawford," *American National Biography*, Vol. 5, John A. Garraty and Mark C. Carnes, eds., 1999, 710–11.

9   *"no end to the beauty and plenty":* See Josiah Butler Journal in Taylor, *History of the State of Ohio, 1650–1787*, 447.

9   *"As time progressed":* Ichabod Nye quoted in Williams, *History of Washington County, Ohio*, 29–30.

9   *"The spirit of immigration":* Manasseh Cutler to Nathan Dane, March 16, 1787, Cutler and Cutler, *Life, Journals*, Vol. 1, 195.

10 *Rufus Putnam:* See Hildreth, *Biographical and Historical Memoirs of the Early Pioneer Settlers of Ohio: With Narratives of Incidents and Occurrences in 1775*, 13–119; *Dictionary of American Biography*, Vol. 8, Dumas Malone, ed., New York: Charles Scribner's Sons, 1963, 284.

10 *"gave it an outward, oblique cast":* Hildreth, *Biographical and Historical Memoirs*, 118.

10 *"He was not brilliant":* Cone, *Life of Rufus Putnam*, 72.

10 *"I am, sir":* Rufus Putnam to George Washington, June 16, 1783, ibid., 89.

11 *"not the least doubt":* Cutler and Cutler, *Life, Journals*, Vol. 1, 172.

11 *"Matters, as far as they have come to my knowledge":* George Washington to Rufus Putnam, June 2, 1784, Cone, *Life of Rufus Putnam*, 95.

11 *"engrosses many of my thoughts"*: Rufus Putnam to George Washington, April 5, 1784, ibid., 93.

11 *"Ohio Fever"*: Poole, *The Ordinance of 1787 and Dr. Manasseh Cutler as an Agent in Its Formation*, 30.

11 *"the Ohio cause"*: Putnam, *The Memoirs of Rufus Putnam and Certain Official Papers and Correspondence*, 225.

11 *"That after the year 1800"*: Poole, *The Ordinance of 1787*, 12.

11 *"usefulness"*: Meacham, *Thomas Jefferson: The Art of Power*, 174.

11 *"very pleasing description"*: Hildreth, *Pioneer History: Being an Account of the First Examinations of the Ohio Valley, and the Early Settlement of the Northwest Territory*, 195.

11 *"It is without doubt the most fertile country"*: Crèvecoeur, "A Voyage Down the Ohio River from Pittsburgh to Louisville in 1787," in Crammer, *History of the Upper Ohio Valley*, 303.

12 *"the most beautiful river on earth"*: Jefferson, *Notes on the State of Virginia*, 1832, 8.

12 *"What would homes be worth to New England"*: Hulbert, *The Ohio River: A Course of Empire*, 168.

13 *"lobbyist"*: Banta, *The Ohio*, 175.

13 *"agent"*: Cutler, *Life and Times of Ephraim Cutler*, 6.

13 *"The more I contemplate the prospect"*: Mannasseh Cutler to Winthrop Sargent, April 20, 1786, Cutler and Cutler, *Life, Journals*, Vol. 1, 190.

13 *"Lord's Day"*: Manasseh Cutler Journal, March 3, 1876, ibid., 54.

14 *Cutler visits Ezra Stiles:* Ibid., 217.

14 *"I sent for my trunk"*: Manasseh Cutler Journal, July 3, 1787, ibid., 220.

14 *"very bad"* and *"excessively bad"*: Manasseh Cutler Journal, July 5, 1787, ibid., 223–25.

14 *"miserable, dirty"*: Manasseh Cutler Journal, July 4, 1787, ibid., 223.

14 *"small, very narrow, and badly built"*: Manasseh Cutler Journal, July 5, 1787, ibid., 227.

14 *Plow and Harrow:* Ibid., 228.

15 *"a duty"*: Poole, *The Ordinance of 1787*, 24.

15 *"petition"*: Manasseh Cutler Journal, July 6, 1787, Cutler and Cutler, *Life, Journals*, Vol. 1, 230.

15 *"gross"*: Manasseh Cutler Journal, July 7, 1787, ibid., 231.

16 *"the greatest beauty"*: Manasseh Cutler Journal, July 8, 1787, ibid., 234.

16 *"debated on terms"*: Manasseh Cutler Journal, July 9, 1787, ibid., 237.

16 *"infinitely exceeds anything of the kind"*: Ibid., 238.

16 *Thomas Hutchins:* Knepper, *Ohio and Its People*, 59–60.

17 *"He gave me the fullest information"*: Manasseh Cutler Journal, July 9, 1787, Cutler and Cutler, *Life, Journals*, Vol. 1, 236.

17 *"For we must consider"*: Winthrop, *Winthrop Papers*, Vol. 2, 295.

17 *"I presume he had not less"*: Manasseh Cutler Journal, July 10, 1787, Cutler and Cutler, *Life, Journals*, Vol. 1, 241.

18 *"a little fatigued"*: Manasseh Cutler Journal, July 13, 1787, ibid., 253.

19 Manasseh Cutler's activities in Philadelphia, July 14–15, 1787, are detailed in Cutler and Cutler, *Life, Journals*, Vol. 1, 253–85.

19 *"This had the desired effect"*: Ibid.

19 *"very large and fine"*: Manasseh Cutler Journal, July 13, 1787, ibid., 257.

19 Cutler's visit with Charles Willson Peale: Ibid., July 13, 1787, 259–62.

19 Cutler's visit to the State House: Ibid., 262.

20 *"its unsavory contents"*: Ibid., 263.

20 Cutler's visit with Benjamin Franklin: Ibid., 267–70.

22 *"of every rank and condition of life"*: Ibid., 272.

22 Cutler's visit with William Bartram: Ibid., 272–74.

22 *"At every end"*: Ibid., 275.

23 *"This would have been a melancholy scene"*: Ibid., 281.

24 *"the most marked attentions"*: Ibid., footnote, 203.

24 *"Called on members of Congress"*: Manasseh Cutler Journal, July 19, 1787, ibid., 293.

25 *"decidedly opposed"*: Ibid.

25 *"Dane must be carefully watched"*: Ibid., 294.

25 *"If they can be brought over, I shall succeed"*: Ibid.

25 *"I told them I saw no prospect of a contract"*: Manasseh Cutler Journal, July 20, 1787, ibid., 294–95.

25 *"extend our contract"*: Ibid., 295.

25 *"He is a gentleman of the most sprightly abilities"*: Manasseh Cutler Journal, July 27, 1787, ibid., 306.

25 *"mortified"*: Manasseh Cutler Journal, July 20, 1787, ibid., 295.

26 *"discovered a much more"*: Manasseh Cutler Journal, July 21, 1787, ibid., 296.

26 *"made every exertion"*: Manasseh Cutler Journal, July 23, 1787, ibid., 297.

26 *"men who were so much used to solicit"*: Ibid., 298.

26 *"such is the intrigue"*: Manasseh Cutler Journal, July 25, 1787, ibid., 300.

26 *"highly approved"*: Ibid.

27 *"To suffer a wide-extended country"*: George Washington to James Duane, September 7, 1783, ibid., 132.

27 *"If we were able to establish"*: Manasseh Cutler Journal, July 25, 1787, ibid., 300.

27 *"so warmly engaged"*: Manasseh Cutler Journal, July 26, 1787, ibid., 302.

27 *"Friday, July 27"*: Ibid., 303.

27 *"without the least variation"*: Ibid., 305.

28 *"We are beholden to the Scioto Company"*: Manasseh Cutler to John May, December 15, 1788, "Sidelights on the Ohio Company of Associates from the John May Papers," *The Western Reserve Historical Society*, Tract No. 97, 1917, 137.

28 *"An Ordinance for the Government"*: Hildreth, *Pioneer History*, 216.

28 *"created a machinery"*: Hinsdale, *The Ordinance of 1787*, 10.

28 *"Religion, morality, and knowledge"*: Cutler and Cutler, *Life, Journals*, Vol. 2, 424.

29 *"given perpetually to the use of an university"*: Cutler, *Life and Times of Ephraim Cutler*, 176.

29 *"a first object"*: Manasseh Cutler to Ephraim Cutler, August 7, 1818, Poole, *The Ordinance of 1787*, 37.

29 *"utmost good faith shall always be observed"*: Cutler and Cutler, *Life, Journals*, Vol. 2, 425.

29 *"There shall be neither slavery nor involuntary servitude"*: Ibid., 426.

29 *"no graces of style, either native or borrowed"*: "Dr. Manasseh Cutler and the Ordinance of 1787," *The North American Review*, Vol. 123, No. 251, 1876, 255; Parsons, *Ancestry of Nathan Dane Dodge and of His Wife, Sarah (Shepherd) Dodge*, 61.

30 *"acting for associates, friends, and neighbors"*: Cutler and Cutler, *Life, Journals*, Vol. 1, 344.

30 *"Never was there a more ingenious"*: Hart, "The Westernization of New England," *Ohio Archaeological and Historical Publications*, Vol. 17, 1908, 271.

30 *"attention and generous treatment"*: Manasseh Cutler Journal, July 27, 1787, Cutler and Cutler, *Life, Journals*, Vol. 1, 305.

30 *"Thus I completed one of the most interesting and agreeable"*: Manasseh Cutler Journal, August 4, 1787, ibid., 318.

30 *"Determined to send men this fall"*: Manasseh Cutler Journal, August 31, 1787, ibid., 322.

31 *"may be greatly enlarged"*: Cutler and Cutler, *Life, Journals*, Vol. 2, 404.

32 *"a season of the most arduous labor"*: Cutler, *Life and Times of Ephraim Cutler*, 7.

32 *"General Putnam"*: Ibid.

32 *"superintendent"*: Rufus Putnam Journal, November 23, 1787, Cone, *Life of Rufus Putnam*, 64.

33 *"full of good advice and hearty wishes"*: Cutler and Cutler, *Life, Journals*, Vol. 1, 329.

33 *"For the Ohio"*: Ibid., 330.

2. Forth to the Wilderness

35 "December 31, 1787—Monday": Swayne, "The Ordinance of 1787 and The War of 1861," footnote, 19.

35 *"very useful"*: Cone, *Life of Rufus Putnam*, 13.

35 *"pursued the occupation"*: Hildreth, *Biographical and Historical Memoirs*, 14.

35 *"After I was nine years old"*: Cone, *Life of Rufus Putnam*, 14.

36 *"Had I been as much engaged in learning"*: Ibid., 14–15.

36 *"hardships of his early life were schoolmasters to fit him"*: Ibid., 15.

36 *"those singular circumstances"*: Rufus Putnam Journal, 1776, ibid., 45.

37 *Rufus Putnam house:* The author is grateful to Chris and Marcia Warrington for a tour of the Rufus Putnam house in Rutland, Massachusetts.

38 *"So great a quantity"*: Rufus Putnam Journal, January 24, 1788, Cone, *Life of Rufus Putnam*, 64.

38 *"Among that body of sterling men"*: Cutler, *The Founders of Ohio: Brief Sketches of the Forty-Eight Pioneers*, 23.

39 *"boats of a beautiful model"*: Hildreth, *Biographical and Historical Memoirs*, 242.

39 *"Traveling both these days very bad"*: Rufus Putnam Journal, February 4, 1788, MCSC.

39 *"[The] cold last night and this day"*: Rufus Putnam Journal, February 5, 1788, MCSC.

40 *"No boats built"*: Rufus Putnam to Manasseh Cutler, May 16, 1788, Cutler and Cutler, *Life, Journals*, Vol. 1, 379.

40 *"new spirit was infused"*: Hildreth, *Pioneer History*, 204.

40 *"fleet"*: Rufus Putnam Journal, March 30, 1788, MCSC; Leeper, "American Union Lodge, No. 1, F. & A. Masons, Marietta, Ohio," *The Masonic Review*, Vol. 73, No. 1, February 1, 1890, 354.

40 *"strongly timbered"*: Hildreth, *Pioneer History*, 205.

40 *"Adventure Galley"*: Ibid., 204–5.

40 *"Mayflower"*: Ibid., 205.

40 *"an irregular poor built place"*: John May Journal, May 7, 1788, May, *The Western Journals of John May: Ohio Company Agent and Business Adventurer*, Dwight L. Smith, ed., 37.

40 *"a lazy set of beings"*: Ibid.

41 *"money affairs"*: John May Journal, May 26, 1789, ibid., 19.

41 *"completely serpentine"*: Ashe, *Travels in America, Performed in 1806*, 68.

41 *"sawyers"*: Knepper, *Ohio and Its People*, 141.

41 *"Beautiful River"*: John May Journal, May 24, 1788, May, *The Western Journals of John May*, 46.

41 *"A very disagreeable time"*: John Mathews Journal, April 3, 1788, Hildreth, *Pioneer History*, 191.

41 *"tarried"*: John Mathews Journal, April 5, 1788, ibid.

42 *"delightsome"*: Williams, *History of Washington County, Ohio*, 463.

42 *"At half past nine got under way"*: John Mathews Journal, April 6, 1788, Hildreth, *Pioneer History*, 191.

42 *"I think it is time to take an observation"*: Cone, *Life of Rufus Putnam*, 106.

42 *"We arrived . . . most heartily congratulating each other"*: Extracts of a letter, May 18, 1788, in *Independent Chronicle*, Boston, Massachusetts, June 12, 1788; *The Salem Mercury*, June 17, 1788, MCSC.

43 *"As long as the sun and moon endured"*: Rufus Putnam to Isaiah Thomas, printer of the *Massachusetts Spy*, May 16, 1788, MCSC; *Gazette*, New Haven, Connecticut, June 26, 1788.

43 *"marquee"*: Cone, *Life of Rufus Putnam*, 107.

43 *"They commenced with great spirit"*: Joseph Buell Journal, April 7, 1788, Hildreth, *Pioneer History*, 160.

43 *"quite a different set of people"*: Josiah Harmar to Henry Knox, April 26, 1788, Denny, *The Record of the Court at Upland in Pennsylvania, and a Military Journal Kept by Major E. Denny, 1778–1795*, 430.

43 *"in-lot"* and *"out-lot"*: Knepper, *Ohio and Its People*, 79.

43 *"Old Hetuck"*: Barker, *Recollections of the First Settlement of Ohio*, 32.

44 *"girdled"*: Cone, *Life of Rufus Putnum*, 107.

44 *"The axe, in stalwart hands"*: Piatt, "The School Master's Story," from *The Lost Farm and Other Poems*, 12.

45 *"not strongly attached to government"*: Knepper, *Ohio and Its People*, 56.

45 *"O-Y-O"*: Hulbert, *The Ohio River*, 2.

45 *"elk's eye"*: Williams, *History of Washington County, Ohio*, 48.

45 *"Their monstrous growth"*: Cramer, *The Navigator*, 1821, 26.

46 *"persevering industry"*: Ibid., 54.

46 *"I was fully persuaded that the Indians"*: Rufus Putnam Journal, April 1, 1788, Cone, *Life of Rufus Putnam*, 64.

46 *"Drunkenness and desertion"*: Joseph Buell Journal, Hildreth, *Pioneer History*, 141.

47 *"Field of Mars"*: Campus Martius Secured, *Ohio Archaeological and History Quarterly*, Vol. 26. No. 1, January 1917, 297.

48 *"a plentiful repast"*: Cutler, *The Founders of Ohio*, 11.

48 *"doubtless preferring to encounter"*: Ibid., 12.

49 *"Ancient Works"*: Manasseh Cutler Journal, September 6, 1788, Cutler and Cutler, *Life, Journals*, Vol. 1, 418.

49 *"Great Mound"*: Hildreth, *Pioneer History*, 242.

49 *speculations of Ezra Stiles, Benjamin Franklin of the earthworks:* Silverberg, ". . . And the Mound-Builders Vanished from the Earth," *American Heritage*, Vol. 20, No. 4, June 1969.

49 *"It is too early to form theories"*: Jefferson, *The Writings of Thomas Jefferson 1784–1787*, Paul Leicester Ford, ed., Vol. 4, 1894, 447; Silverberg, ". . . And the Mound-Builders Vanished from the Earth," *American Heritage*, Vol. 20, No. 4, June 1969.

49 *"those works so perfect as to put it beyond all doubt"*: Rufus Putnam to Isaiah Thomas, printer of the *Massachusetts Spy*, May 16, 1788, MCSC.

49 *"Quadranaou"* and *"Capitolium"*: O'Donnell, *Ohio's First Peoples*, 14–15.

49 *"the covered way"*: Ibid.

50 *"It has . . . been currently reported here"*: Manasseh Cutler to Rufus Putnam, April 21, 1788, MCSC.

50 *"Have not received a line from you"*: Manasseh Cutler to Rufus Putnam, May 15, 1788, MCSC.

50 *"That part of the purchase I have been over"*: Extracts of a letter, Rufus Putnam to Isaiah Thomas, printer of the *Massachusetts Spy*, May 16, 1788, MCSC.

51 *It was a decision:* The author is grateful to Scott Britton and Wes Clarke of the Castle Historical Museum in Marietta, Ohio, for a tour of the Mound Cemetery. Both Mr. Britton and Mr. Clarke have done considerable research and investigation into the history and significance of the site.

51 *"At present, we do not think"*: Rufus Putnam to Manasseh Cutler, May 16, 1788, Cutler and Cutler, *Life, Journals*, Vol. 1, 377.

51 *"This country, for fertility of soil"*: Letter to Worcester, Massachusetts, from a settler, May 18, 1788, Hildreth, *Pioneer History*, 208.

51 *"mania for Ohio immigration"*: *Massachusetts Gazette*, Boston, June 20, 1788, MCSC.

52 *"No colony in America"*: Cutler, *Life and Times of Ephraim Cutler*, 24.

52 *"A spirit of immigration to the western country"*: George Washington to Marquis de Lafayette, February 7, 1788, *The Writings of George Wash-*

ington: From the Original Manuscript Sources, 1745–1799, Vol. 29, 412.

52 *"into the woods"*: Backus, Backus, and Backus, *A Genealogical Memoir of the Backus Family: With the Private Journal of James Backus*, 104.

53 *"pretty close crowded"*: John May Journal, May 24, 1788, May, *The Western Journals of John May*, 45.

53 *"Every prospect as to the goodness of our lands"*: Samuel Parsons to his wife, Hall, *Life and Letters of Samuel Holden Parsons*, 521.

53 *"All hands clearing land"*: John May Journal, June 2, 1788, May, *The Western Journals of John May*, 50.

53 *"answers the best description"*: John May Journal, May 27, 1788, ibid., 48.

54 *"I dare say not a market in the world"*: John May Journal, July 24, 1788, ibid., 67.

54 *"These men from New England"*: Ebenezer Denny Journal, May 28, 1788, *Military Journal of Major Ebenezer Denny: An Officer in the Revolutionary War and Indian Wars*, 119–20.

54 *"Those people appear"*: Ebenezer Denny Journal, July 15, 1788, ibid., 121.

54 *"Myriads of gnats"*: John May Journal, May 29, 1788, May, *The Western Journals of John May*, 49.

54 *"inflamed"*: John May Journal, June 10, 1788, ibid., 52.

54 *"Thunder and lightning all night"*: John May Journal, June 13, 1788, ibid.

55 *"I tried to catch the fellow"*: John May Journal, June 23, 1788, ibid., 57.

55 *"hellish Pow-wows"*: John May Journal, August 1–2, 1788, ibid., 69.

55 *"At Boston . . . we are alarmed"*: John May Journal, July 23, 1788, ibid., 67.

55 *"A number of poor devils—5 in all"*: John May Journal, June 15, 1788, ibid., 53.

55 *"sluggishly"*: John May Journal, July 26, 1788, ibid., 67.

55 *"It looked so tempting I could not refrain"*: John May Journal, July 27, 1788, ibid.

55 *"Putnam's Paradise"*: Summers, *History of Marietta*, 46.

55 *"Adelphia"*: Manasseh Cutler to Rufus Putnam, December 3, 1787, Cutler and Cutler, *Life, Journals*, Vol. 1, 376.

56 *"a natural gush of feeling"*: Hildreth, *Pioneer History*, 214.

56 *"to explore . . . the Paradise of America"*: Joseph Varnum, July 4, 1788, ibid., 507.

56 *"Pleased with our entertainment"*: John May Journal, July 4, 1788, May, *The Western Journals of John May*, 61.

57 *"a change came over him"*: Cone, *Life of Rufus Putnam*, 110.

57 *"excessively"*: Manasseh Cutler Journal, August 1, 1788, Cutler and Cutler, *Life, Journals*, Vol. 1, 399.

57 *"anxious"*: Manasseh Cutler Journal, August 7, 1788, ibid., 404.

57 *"very romantic"*: Manasseh Cutler Journal, August 17, 1788, ibid., 409.

57 *"a second education in the Army of the Revolution"*: Barker, *Recollections of the First Settlement of Ohio*, George Jordan Blazier, ed., 51.

58 *"Our buildings are decent and comfortable"*: Rowena Tupper to Mrs. Stone, November 18, 1788, Belcher and Nye, *The Nye Family of America Association, Proceedings of the First Reunion*, August 1905, 64.

58 *"Cabin Raisings"*: Fry, "Women on the Ohio Frontier: The Marietta Area," *Ohio History Journal Archive*, Vol. 90, No. 1, Winter 1981, 62.

58 *"city lots"*: Manasseh Cutler Journal, August 21, 1788, Cutler and Cutler, *Life, Journals*, Vol. 1, 412.

58 *"astonished"*: Ibid.

58 *"the great tree"*: Manasseh Cutler Journal, August 24, 1788, ibid., 413.

59 *"Took off his head"*: Manasseh Cutler Journal, August 28, 1788, ibid., 415.

59 *"almost drowned"*: Manasseh Cutler Journal, August 23, 1788, ibid., 413.

59 *"very well accomplished"*: Manasseh Cutler Journal, August 27, 1788, ibid., 415.

59 *"fine woman"*: Manasseh Cutler Journal, September 2, 1788, ibid., 417.

59 *"very agreeable"*: Manasseh Cutler Journal, September 7, 1788, ibid., 419.

59 *"We have had Indians to dine"*: Manasseh Cutler Journal, August 28, 1788, ibid., 416.

59 *"the squaws mostly drunk"*: Manasseh Cutler Journal, August 23, 1788, ibid., 413.

60 *"It may be emphatically said"*: Manasseh Cutler, August 24, 1788, Cutler and Cutler, *Life, Journals*, Vol. 2, 444.

61 *"New England Settlement"*: Mathews, *The Expansion of New England*, 175.

61 *"a mixture of log-cabin"*: Dunbar, *A History of Travel in America*, Vol. 1, 272.

61 *"The roof or deck of the boat"*: Audubon, *Audubon and His Journals*, Vol. 2, 458.

61 *"heralded a new era"*: Hulbert, *Waterways of Westward Expansion*, 108.

61 *"bushwhacking"*: Ibid., 110.

61 *"a distinct class"*: Ibid., 161.

62   *"If a town had a really malodorous repute"*: Banta, *The Ohio*, 255.

62   *"fine, large"*: Manasseh Cutler Journal, September 9, 1788, Cutler and Cutler, *Life, Journals*, Vol. 1, 420.

62   *"surprised to see a man of that age"*: Manasseh Cutler to Rev. Dr. Belknap, March 19, 1789, Cutler and Cutler, *Life, Journals*, Vol. 2, 253.

63   *"spirituous liquors"*: Hildreth, *Biographical and Historical Memoirs*, 110.

63   *"Destroy and starve out every white face"*: Joseph Barker, *Recollections of the First Settlement of Ohio*, George Jordan Blazier, ed., 61.

64   *"No one in particular can justly claim this [land]"*: Knepper, *Ohio and Its People*, 20.

64   *"insincere and hollow affair"*: Cone, *Life of Rufus Putnam*, 115.

64   *"This treaty under all circumstances"*: Putnam, *The Memoirs of Rufus Putnam*, 108.

64   *"very unhappy"*: Manasseh Cutler Journal, January 23, 1789, Cutler and Cutler, *Life, Journals*, Vol. 1, 441.

64   *"much uneasiness"*: Cayton, *The Frontier Republic: Ideology and Politics in the Ohio Country, 1780–1825*, 43.

64   *first general store*: Store inventories from Backus-Woodbridge Collection at the Ohio History Connection, Columbus, Ohio.

65   *"saw fit"*: Joseph Barker, *Recollections of the First Settlement of Ohio*, 61.

3. Difficult Times

67   "Spit on your hands and take a fresh holt": Richter, *The Town*, 45.

67   *"The little provisions which the settlers had"*: Ichabod Nye Journal, MCSC, 50.

67   *"for the long and unknown adventure"*: Ibid., 85.

67   *"I never made one word of complaint"*: Ibid., 96.

68   *"exclusively confined to handling books"*: Barker, *Recollections of the First Settlement of Ohio*, George Jordan Blazier, ed., 52.

68   *"We were all starving for bread"*: Ichabod Nye Journal, MCSC, 92.

68   *"without funds"*: Ibid., 96.

68   *Winthrop Sargent*: For background information on Sargent, see Pershing, "Winthrop Sargent: A Builder in the Old Northwest"; *Dictionary of American Biography*, Vol. 8, Dumas Malone, ed., New York: Charles Scribner's Sons, 1963, 369–70.

69   *"in such circumstances as indicate a strong presumption"*: Sibley's Harvard Graduates, 1768–1771, 614.

69   *"in such a manner as to endanger the lives and property"*: Ibid.

69   *"the fickleness of privateering"*: Ibid., 616.

69   *"a consummate tyrant and raskale"*: Ichabod Nye Journal, MCSC, 94.

69   *"amiable and agreeable"*: Manasseh Cutler to Winthrop Sargent, September 28, 1789, Cutler and Cutler, *Life, Journals*, Vol. 1, 448.

70   *"imperious and haughty"*: Ichabod Nye Journal, MCSC, 97.

70   *"most mortifying and trying"*: Ibid.

70   *"slave to whiskey"*: Winthrop Sargent to Manasseh Cutler, December 4, 1789, MCSC.

70   *"Spring opened with much activity"*: Ichabod Nye Journal, MCSC, 93.

71   *"The blacksmith was gunsmith, farrier"*: Buley, *The Old Northwest: Pioneer Period, 1815–1840*, 227.

71   *"Tis I can delve and plough, love"*: Hodgson, *Letters from North America*, Vol. 2, 84.

71   *"The women put up with all these inconveniences"*: Ichabod Nye Journal, MCSC, 49.

72   *"Working butter with wooden paddles"*: Buley, *The Old Northwest*, 217.

72   *heavy iron pots*: Author's tour of Rufus Putnam house with historian Bill Reynolds of the Campus Martius Museum was helpful in identifying the many tasks a woman on the frontier would have to contend with on a daily basis.

73   *"I never so severely felt the pain of being separated from you"*: Lucy Backus Woodbridge to parents, February 25, 1790, Backus-Woodbridge Collection, Microfilm Reel 1, Ohio History Connection, Columbus, Ohio.

73   *"I am happy to feel my attachment for this place"*: Lucy Backus Woodbridge to James Backus, February 1, 1792, Rau, "Lucy Backus Woodbridge, Pioneer Mother," *Ohio Archaeological and Historical Quarterly*, Vol. 44, No. 4, 1935, 422.

74   *"On ascending the bank"*: Hildreth, *Biographical and Historical Memoirs*, 438.

74   *"reconnoitering" the settlement*: John May Journal, July 18, 1789, May, *The Western Journals of John May*, 123.

74   *"a very good performance"*: John May Journal, July 19, 1789, ibid.

74   *"the howling wilderness"*: John May Journal, July 26, 1789, ibid., 125.

74   *"all the resources which I could bring into action"*: Ichabod Nye Journal, MCSC, 99.

75   *"in danger pretty considerable"*: Boorstin, *The Americans: The National Experience*, 290.

76 *"Oh God, I am killed!":* 1789, Hildreth, *Pioneer History*, 254.

76 *"He found them lying near where they fell":* John Mathews, July 13, 1789, ibid., 256.

77 *"quite a relish for hunting":* Hildreth, *Biographical and Historical Memoirs*, 415.

77 *"a little half-starved opossum":* Cutler, *Life and Times of Ephraim Cutler*, 275.

77 *"the milk":* Hildreth, *Pioneer History*, 265.

78 *Joseph Barker:* Hildreth, *Biographical and Historical Memoirs*, 433–63.

78 *"housewright":* Barker, *Recollections of the First Settlement of Ohio*, George Jordan Blazier, ed., ii.

78 *"canoo," "learge," "exelent," "sildom":* Ibid., 4, 9, 11, 13.

79 *"Starving Year":* Cone, *Life of Rufus Putnam*, 113.

79 *"strewed all their money":* Barker, *Recollections of the First Settlement of Ohio*, 63.

79 *"the hungry year":* Alan Taylor, "'The Hungry Year': 1789 on the Northern Border of Revolutionary America," in *Dreadful Visitations: Confronting Natural Catastrophe in the Age of Enlightment*, Alessa Johns, ed., 145–81.

80 *"Where poverty, improvidence, and scarcity meet":* Barker, *Recollections of the First Settlement of Ohio*, 63.

80 *"In this great scarcity it was wonderful":* Hildreth, *Pioneer History*, 265.

80 *One family in particular:* See biographical sketch of Isaac and Rebecca Williams in Hildreth, *Biographical and Historical Memoirs*, 475–91.

80 *"How many is there of you?":* Isaac Williams to Captain Devol and Isaac Barker, 1790, Barker, *Recollections of the First Settlement of Ohio*, 65.

80 *"Those who had cows":* Hildreth, *Pioneer History*, 265–66.

81 *"I am living in a little, clean log-cabin":* Joseph Barker to his wife, Elizabeth Barker, Hildreth, *Biographical and Historical Memoirs*, 439.

81 *"good, smooth poplar floors":* Barker, *Recollections of the First Settlement of Ohio*, 67.

82 *In June he headed back to Rutland:* Stone, "From Rutland to Marietta," *New England Magazine*, Vol. 16, New Series, April 1897; Crawford, "Rufus Putnam, and His Pioneer Life in the North West," *American Antiquarian Society*, New Series, Vol. 12, 1899.

82 *"Your company is much wished for":* Rufus Putnam to Manasseh Cutler, August 12, 1790, Cutler and Cutler, *Life, Journals*, Vol. 1, 464.

82 *"At length we arrived at Marietta":* Crawford, "Rufus Putnam, and His Pioneer Life in the North West," *American Antiquarian Society*, New Series, Vol. 12, 1899, 445.

83 *"Big Buckeye"*: Hildreth, *Biographical and Historical Memoirs*, 237.

83 *"Call every man's name"*: Barker, *Recollections of the First Settlement of Ohio*, 6.

83 *Serious trouble of a different kind:* For an excellent account and examination of the Scioto Company speculation, see Belote, *The Scioto Speculation and the French Settlement at Gallipolis.* New York: Burt Franklin, 1907.

83 *"an Englishman"*: Cutler and Cutler, *Life, Journals*, Vol. 1, 499.

84 *"I view my character"*: Manasseh Cutler to Rufus Putnam, November 18, 1788, MCSC.

84 *"prospectus"*: Cutler and Cutler, *Life, Journals*, Vol. 1, 499.

84 *"wholesome and delightful"*: Howe, *Historical Collections of Ohio*, Vol. 1, 669.

84 *"Nothing was talked of in every social circle, but the paradise"*: E. O. Randall, "Editorialana," Vol. 25, No. 1, January 1916, *Ohio Archaeological and Historical Quarterly*, 541.

85 *"strangers in a strange land"*: Cutler, *Life and Times of Ephraim Cutler*, 264.

85 *"There might have been more"*: Barker, *Recollections of the First Settlement of Ohio*, 60.

85 *"I have seen half a dozen at work in taking down a tree"*: Barber and Howe, *Our Whole Country*, Vol. 2, 954.

86 *"To some the surrounding woods might appear frightful deserts"*: Hurt, *The Ohio Frontier: Crucible of the Old Northwest, 1720–1830*, 193.

86 *"town located opposite"*: Cuming, *Cuming's Tour to the Western Country, 1807–1809*, 256.

86 *"It was as late as the 5th of November"*: Rufus Putnam to George Washington, December 20, 1790, *The Papers of George Washington*, Vol. 7, 100.

87 *"indulge . . . to excess"*: Henry Knox to Josiah Harmar, September 3, 1790, *Papers of George Washington; Presidential Series*, Vol. 6, Mark A. Mastromarino, ed., 168–69.

87 *"scandalous"*: Knepper, *Ohio and Its People*, 72.

88 *"When or where"*: Rufus Putnam to George Washington, December 20, 1790, *The Papers of George Washington*, Vol. 7, 101.

88 *Big Bottom Massacre:* Van Every, *Ark of Empire: The American Frontier, 1784–1803*, 226; Roosevelt, *The Winning of the West*, Vol. 3, 137–38; Sugden, *Blue Jacket: Warrior of the Shawnees*, 110.

89 *"From the ridge"*: Hildreth, *Pioneer History*, 431.

90 *"to prepare for the worst"*: Rufus Putnam Journal, January 2, 1791, Cone, *Life of Rufus Putnam*, 67.

4. Havoc

PAGE

91   "Beware of surprise!": Lodge, *George Washington, American States-man* series, Vol. 2, 95; Freeman, *George Washington: A Biography*, Vol. 6, 329; Flexner, *George Washington and the New Nation*, 299.

91   *"The sad and dreadful havoc"*: Abigail Adams to Cotton Tufts, December 18, 1791, *Adams Family Correspondence*, Vol. 9, 247.

91   *"A horrid savage war"*: Putnam, *The Memoirs of Rufus Putnam*, 247; *Salem Gazette*, February 15, 1791, MCSC.

92   *"spunk to the backbone"*: Catherine Barker Memoirs, October 21, 1880, 4, MCSC.

92   *"spies"*: Hildreth, *Biographical and Historical Memoirs*, 464.

92   *"the prudence of our people"*: Rufus Putnam to Caleb Strong, January 6, 1791, MCSC.

93   *"truly critical"*: Rufus Putnam to George Washington, January 8, 1791, Hildreth, *Pioneer History*, 279; *The Papers of George Washington*, Vol. 7, 208.

94   *"better that [the] government disband"*: Rufus Putnam to Henry Knox, January 8, 1791, Hildreth, *Pioneer History*, 281.

94   *"a dead man"*: Joseph Rogers, ibid., 283.

95   *"Well, boys"*: Ibid., 285.

95   *"All was consternation"*: Barker, *Recollections of the First Settlement of Ohio*, George Jordan Blazier, ed., 72–74.

96   *"Some whites are more savage"*: Essay of Horace Nye, "Recollections of the Settlement of Marietta and Campus Martius," Samuel Hildreth Papers, Vol. 1, MCSC.

96   *Arthur St. Clair: Dictionary of American Biography*, Vol. 8, Dumas Malone, ed., New York: Charles Scribner's Sons, 293–95; Chernow, *Washington: A Life*, 666.

97   *"filled the public mind"*: *Illinois Biographical Dictionary*, 2008–2009 edition, Vol. 1 (Hamburg, MI: State Historical Publications, 2008), 638.

97   *"as much appearance"*: Guthman, *March to Massacre: A History of the First Seven Years of the United States Army, 1784–1791*, 215.

97   *"The President of the United States"*: Henry Knox to Arthur St. Clair, August 4, 1791, ibid., 211.

97   *"totally unacquainted"*: Ebenezer Denny Journal, November 7, 1791, Denny, *Military Journal of Major Ebenezer Denny*, 170.

97   *"a matter of astonishment"*: Guthman, *March to Massacre*, 210.

98   *Until then the worst defeat*: Van Every, *Ark of Empire*, 235; Sugden, *Blue Jacket*, 127; and Sugden, *Tecumseh: A Life*, 63.

98   *Denny took St. Clair for a visit:* Denny, *Military Journal of Major Eb-enezer Denny*, May 23, 1788, 118.

98   *"Beware of surprise!":* Lodge, *George Washington*, Vol. 2, 95; Freeman, *George Washington*, Vol. 6, 329; Flexner, *George Washington and the New Nation*, 299.

99   *"stamina of soldiers":* Guthman, *March to Massacre*, 221.

99   *"deficiencies":* Ibid., 223.

100   *"We had no guides":* Ibid., 227–28.

100   *"compact":* Ibid., 223.

100   *"Cold and wet":* Ebenezer Denny Journal, October 15, 1791, Denny, *Military Journal of Major Ebenezer Denny*, 156.

100   *"Weather very bad," "very severe" frost, "ice upon the waters":* Ibid., October 17, 21, 1791, 157.

101   *"unpardonable mismanagement":* Ibid., October 19, 1791, 157.

101   *St. Clair gout:* Van Every, *Ark of Empire*, 232.

101   *"good effect":* Ebenezer Denny Journal, October 28, 1791, Denny, *Military Journal of Major Ebenezer Denny*, 160.

101   *"Our prospects are gloomy":* Guthman, *March to Massacre*, 229.

102   *"may be afraid to return":* Ibid., 230.

102   *As they were soon to learn:* Sugden, *Blue Jacket*, 117–27.

102   *"turncoat":* Banta, *The Ohio*, 233.

102   *"The Indians were never in greater heart":* Butts, *Simon Girty: Wilderness Warrior*, 204.

103   *"The few Indians that have been seen":* Calloway, *The Victory with No Name: The Native American Defeat of the First American Army*, 91.

103   *"all men unable to march":* Guthman, *March to Massacre*, 226.

103   *"small flight of snow":* Sargent, *Diary of Col. Winthrop Sargent*, 24.

103   *"principally by our own sentinels":* Guthman, *March to Massacre*, 237.

103   *"unclouded":* Sargent, *Diary of Col. Winthrop Sargent*, 25.

103   *"Not terrible, as has been represented":* Ibid.

104   *"Close upon the heels of the flying militia":* Ibid.

104   *"smart fire":* Ebenezer Denny Journal, November 4, 1791, Denny, *Military Journal of Ebenezer Denny*, 165.

104   *"The enemy from the front":* Ibid.

105   *"Indeed, they seemed not to fear anything":* Ibid., 166.

105   *"The Indians fought like hellhounds":* Sword, *President Washington's Indian War*, 183.

105   *"I wish I could describe that battle":* Ibid., 183.

105   *"As our lines were deserted":* Ebenezer Denny Journal, November 4, 1791, Denny, *Military Journal of Ebenezer Denny*, 166–67.

106 *"Delay was death"*: Ibid., 167.

106 *General Richard Butler*: Chernow, *Washington*, 667; *The Papers of George Washington*, Vol. 9, 250; Murray, "The Butlers of Cumberland Valley," *Historical Register: Notes and Queries, Biographical and Genealogical*, Vol. 1, No. 1, January 1883. Hogeland, *Autumn of the Black Snake: The Creation of the United States Army and the Invasion that Opened the West*, 11–18, 297–99.

106 *"weary with the work"*: Hill, *History of Knox County, Ohio*, 180.

107 *"Accordingly, . . . we set out a little after ten"*: Ebenezer Denny Journal, November 4, 1791, Denny, *Military Journal of Ebenezer Denny*, 169.

108 *"Every house in this town"*: Sargent, *Diary of Col. Winthrop Sargent*, November 9, 1791, 27.

108 *St. Clair's defeat*: Van Every, *Ark of Empire*, 235; Sugden, *Blue Jacket*, 127; Freeman, *George Washington*, Vol. 6, 339.

108 *"with what material the bulk of the army"*: St. Clair, *The St. Clair Papers: The Life and Public Services of Arthur St. Clair*, Vol. 2, William Henry Smith, ed., 262.

109 *"constantly on the alert"*: Ebenezer Denny Journal, November 7, 1791, Denny, *Military Journal of Ebenezer Denny*, 170–71.

109 *"This was a knowledge of the collected force"*: Ibid., 171.

110 *"these evil forebodings began to subside"*: Hildreth, *Pioneer History*, 297.

110 *"When I consider the multiplicity"*: Rufus Putnam to George Washington, December 26, 1791, MCSC.

111 *Tobias Lear and Washington*: Lodge, *George Washington*, Vol. 2, 95; Lossing, *Recollections and Private Memoirs of Washington*, 416–20; Decatur, *Private Affairs of George Washington*, 248; *The Papers of George Washington*, Vol. 9, 275.

112 *"unpleasant task"*: Ebenezer Denny Journal, December 19, 1791, Denny, *Military Journal of Ebenezer Denny*, 175.

113 *"The sad and dreadful havoc of our army"*: Abigail Adams to Cotton Tufts, December 18, 1791, *Adams Family Correspondence*, Vol. 9, 247.

113 *"attention and kindness"*: Ebenezer Denny Journal, December 19, 1791, Denny, *Military Journal of Ebenezer Denny*, 176.

113 *first congressional investigation in American history*: Calloway, *The Victory with No Name*, 5.

114 *"melancholy theater"*: Sargent, *Diary of Col. Winthrop Sargent*, appendix, 55.

114 *"Every twig and bush seems to be cut down"*: Ibid.

115 *"When I came to his house"*: Manasseh Cutler to Mary Balch Cutler,

March 5, 1792, Manasseh Cutler Journal, Cutler and Cutler, *Life, Journals*, Vol. 1, 484.

115 *"closeted"*: Ibid., 485.

116 *"not the remotest wish"*: Rufus Putnam to Henry Knox, Philadelphia, May 7, 1792, *The Memoirs of Rufus Putnam and Certain Official Papers and Correspondence*, 118.

116 General *"Mad Anthony" Wayne*: Chernow, *Washington*, 717; Howard, *Shawnee!: The Ceremonialism of a Native Indian Tribe and Its Cultural Background*, 17; Hogeland, *Autumn of the Black Snake*, 230.

116 *"debarred"*: Barker, *Recollections of the First Settlement of Ohio*, 18–19.

117 *"They were united in bonds of friendship"*: Hildreth, *Pioneer History*, 470.

117 *"Uncle Sam"*: Ibid., 471.

118 *battle of Fallen Timbers*: Sugden, *Blue Jacket*, 172–87; Chernow, *Washington*, 717.

118 *"scarcely be over-estimated"*: Cone, *Life of Rufus Putnam*, 126.

118 *"Compared to any previous effort"*: Knepper, *Ohio and Its People*, 79.

5. A New Era Commences

PAGE

121 *"Thus we left the scene of my early life"*: Ephraim Cutler Journal, June 15, 1795, Cutler, *Life and Times of Ephraim Cutler*, 17.

121 *"earnestly entreated"*: June 1770, ibid., 8.

122 *"impracticable"*: Ibid., 12.

122 *"a strong propensity to read"*: Ibid.

122 *"It has always been to me a source of regret"*: Ibid.

122 *"before I had attained my twentieth year"*: Ibid., 14.

123 *"I should esteem it one of the greatest pleasures"*: Ibid., 277.

123 *"suffer herself to be disheartened"*: June 15, 1795, ibid., 17.

123 *"conveyance"*: Ibid., 19.

124 *"Again we moved on in the usual slow way"*: Ibid., 21.

124 *"To add to our distress"*: Ibid.

124 *"much weakened"*: Ibid.

124 *"We had landed sick among strangers"*: September 18, 1795, ibid., 22.

125 *"There is probably no more beautiful and pleasant location"*: Ibid., 24–25.

125 *"principal inhabitants"*: Ibid., 23.

125 *"broken up former fixed habits of industry"*: Ibid.

126 *"found employment"*: Ibid., 29.

126 *"a great relief to me in my then needy circumstances"*: Ibid., 30.

126 *"overwhelming"*: Ibid., 31.

126 *"I have earnestly wished you to have a good farm"*: Manasseh Cutler to Ephraim Cutler, ibid., 35–36.

127 various *"circumstances"*: Ibid., 38.

127 *"The timber was large, principally beech and sugar-tree"*: Ibid., 40.

127 *"They sometimes visited us"*: Ibid., 41.

127 *"abundant"*: Ibid., 42.

128 *"In those early times"*: History of Hocking Valley, Ohio, 46–47.

129 *"to hold his scalp on"*: Joseph Barker, *Recollections of the First Settlement of the Ohio*, iv.

129 *"The fortitude and perseverance requisite"*: Hildreth, *Biographical and Historical Memoirs*, 455.

130 *"refinement"*: Ibid., 456.

130 *"to be useful, to be pleasant"*: Catherine Barker Memoir, October 26, 1880, 10, MCSC.

130 *"Count the day lost"*: Catherine Barker Memoir, October 29, 1880, ibid., 12.

130 *"I sometimes thought it terrible"*: Catherine Barker Memoir, October 21, 1880, ibid., 4.

131 *"ninety-one dwelling houses"*: Fry, "Women on the Ohio Frontier: The Marietta Area," *Ohio History Journal Archive*, Vol. 90, No. 1, Winter 1981, 63.

131 *Harman and Margaret Blennerhassett*: Hildreth, *Biographical and Historical Memoirs*, 491–528. The author is grateful to historian Dr. Ray Swick; Bill Reynolds, of the Campus Martius Museum; and Miles Evenson, Superintendent of the Blennerhassett Island Historical State Park for two separate detailed tours of the island and mansion.

132 *"the accidental effects of the electric fluid"*: Safford, *The Life of Harman Blennerhassett: An Authentic Narrative of the Burr Expedition*, 44.

133 *"Blanny"*: Ibid., 219.

133 *"the most perfect proportions"*: Hildreth, *Biographical and Historical Memoirs*, 501.

134 *The total outlay*: See, generally, Swick, *An Island Called Eden: The Story of Harman and Margaret Blennerhassett*, 15.

134 *"a scene of enchantment"*: Hildreth, *Biographical and Historical Memoirs*, 505.

134 *"the Enchanted Island"*: Swick, *An Island Called Eden*, 23.

134 *"Earthly Paradise"*: Hildreth, *Biographical and Historical Memoirs*, 506.

135 *"more sedate"*: Ibid., 505.

135 *"under the spotlight of history"*: Hood, "A Genealogy and Biography of Colonel Barker," in Barker, *Recollections of the First Settlement of Ohio*, George Jordan Blazier, ed., v.

135 *"Tis well"*: Irving, *Life of George Washington*, Vol. 5, 373.

135 *"her most esteemed, beloved and admired citizen"*: John Adams address to Senate, December 23, 1799, in Richardson, *A Compilation of the Messages and Papers of the Presidents*, Vol. 1, 299.

136 *"Falls"*: Gruenwald, *River of Enterprise: The Commercial Origins of Regional Identity in the Ohio Valley, 1790–1850*, 64.

137 *Jonathan Devol*: Hildreth, *Biographical and Historical Memoirs*, 254.

137 *"I am . . . fully convinced"*: Ephraim Cutler to Manasseh Cutler, March 18, 1802, Ephraim Cutler Papers, MCSC.

137 *"highly respected for their moral worth and standing"*: Catherine Barker Memoir, March 12, 1881, Vol. 2, 22, MCSC.

137 *"cherished"*: Ibid., 21.

138 *"distinguished seat of hospitality"*: Catherine Barker Memoir, March 14, 1881, Vol. 2, 27, MCSC.

138 *"It was so sudden"*: Manasseh Cutler to Ephraim Cutler, Boston, February 5, 1801, Ephraim Cutler Papers, MCSC.

139 *"I cannot close this letter"*: Manasseh Cutler to Ephraim Cutler, Boston, February 5, 1801, ibid.

139 *"I thank you for your advice"*: Ephraim Cutler to Manasseh Cutler, April 25, 1801, ibid.

140 *"remarkably pleasant"*: Manasseh Cutler to Betsy Poole, December 21, 1801, Cutler and Cutler, *Life, Journals*, Vol. 2, 51.

140 *"The block in which I live"*: Ibid., 50.

141 *"very little done"*: Manasseh Cutler Journal, January 5, 15, 22, 1802, ibid., 59–60.

141 *"conversed with great ease and familiarity"*: Manasseh Cutler Journal, January 2, 1802, ibid., 56.

141 *"social"*: Manasseh Cutler Journal, February 6, 1802, ibid., 72.

141 *"Rice soup, round of beef, turkey, mutton"*: Ibid., 71.

142 *"Before I came"*: Manasseh Cutler to Ephraim Cutler, March 14, 1802, ibid., 96.

142 *"rambled"*: Manasseh Cutler Journal, April 24, 1802, ibid., 106.

142 *"At five o'clock took leave"*: Manasseh Cutler Journal, May 4, 1802, ibid., 107.

143 *"I rejoice to hear you are well"*: Manasseh Cutler to Mary Balch Cutler, January 25, 1804, MCSC.

143 *"Your very affectionate letter of the 6th"*: Manasseh Cutler to Mary Balch Cutler, January 22, 1805, MCSC.

144 *"dirty, drunken"*: Ephraim Cutler to Manasseh Cutler, August 31, 1802, Ephraim Cutler Papers, MCSC.

144 *"No person shall be held in slavery"*: Cutler, *Life and Times of Ephraim Cutler*, 74.

145 *"The handwriting, I had no doubt"*: Ibid.

145 *"very desirous"* and *"warmth of feeling"*: Ibid.

145 *"the Jeffersonian version"*: Ibid., 76.

145 *"Cutler, you must get well"*: Ibid.

145 *"I went to the convention and moved to strike out"*: Ibid.

146 *"It cost me every effort"*: Ibid., 77.

146 *"To Ephraim Cutler, more than any other man"*: Ibid., 266.

146 *"considerable"*: Ibid., 89.

146 *"There was no other means"*: Ferris, *Dawes and Allied Families*, 227.

146 *"These trips over the mountains"*: Julia Perkins Cutler Journal, 1809, MCSC.

146 *"droves"*: Ephraim Cutler Journal, August 14, 1809, Cutler, *Life and Times of Ephraim Cutler*, 94.

147 *"This was a strange introduction"*: Cutler and Cutler, *Life, Journals*, Vol. 2, 33.

147 Marietta a *"city"*: Putnam, *The Memoirs of Rufus Putnam*, 216.

147 *"American University"*: Manasseh Cutler to General Rufus Putnam, June 30, 1800, Cutler and Cutler, *Life, Journals*, Vol. 2, 28.

147 *"the intellectual wants of the neighborhood"*: Ephraim Cutler, 1802, Cutler, *Life and Times of Ephraim Cutler*, 50.

147 *"Coonskin Library"*: Knepper, *Ohio and Its People*, 189.

148 *"choice books"*: Cutler, *Life and Times of Ephraim Cutler*, 51.

148 *"It is painful indeed to reflect"*: Manasseh Cutler to Ephraim Cutler, January 29, 1806, Ephraim Cutler Papers, MCSC.

148 *"He is in great spirits"*: Ephraim Cutler to Manasseh Cutler, March 18, 1802, MCSC.

149 *"no man in the territory more entirely deserved and enjoyed"*: Ephraim Cutler Journal, Cutler, *Life and Times of Ephraim Cutler*, 81.

149 *Ohio became the seventeenth state*: Knepper, *Ohio and Its People*, 92.

149 *On the evening of September 13*: *The Papers of Thomas Jefferson*, Vol. 41, 380–81; *Journals of the Lewis and Clark Expedition, August 30, 1803– August 24, 1804*, 81–82; *Letters of the Lewis and Clark Expedition, With Related Documents, 1783–1854*, 124.

150 *"He was quick and restless"*: Howe, *Historical Collections of Ohio*,

Vol. 2, 1904, 484–86. See, generally, Williams, *Johnny Appleseed in the Duck Creek Valley.*

6. The Burr Conspiracy

151 "Your talents and acquirements": Aaron Burr to Harman Blennerhassett, April 15, 1806, Safford, *The Life of Harman Blennerhassett,* 65–66.

151 *"floating house":* Isenberg, *Fallen Founder: The Life of Aaron Burr,* 293; Lomask, *Aaron Burr: The Conspiracy and Years of Exile, 1805–1836,* 58.

152 *"bold enough to think":* Hamilton, *The Intimate Life of Alexander Hamilton,* 388.

152 *five feet, six inches:* Parton, *The Life and Times of Aaron Burr,* 395.

152 *"He succeeded best with young men":* Ibid., 163.

152 *His lineage was highly distinguished: Dictionary of American Biography,* Vol. 2, Allen Johnson and Dumas Malone, eds., New York: Charles Scribner's Sons, 1958, 314–21; Lomask, *Aaron Burr,* 4, 3, 24–30.

153 *"Tho' small his stature":* Isenberg, *Fallen Founder,* 129.

153 *"with such animation":* Stewart, *American Emperor: Aaron Burr's Challenge to Jefferson's America,* 15.

153 *"Burr conspiracy":* Isenberg, *Fallen Founder,* 272.

153 *"How long will it be":* Stewart, *American Emperor,* 107.

154 *"an evil hour":* Hildreth, *Biographical and Historical Memoirs,* 506.

154 *"the usual hospitality of the island":* Lomask, *Aaron Burr,* 63.

154 *"That's an ill-omen!":* Melton, *Aaron Burr: Conspiracy to Treason,* 76.

155 *"I hope, sir":* Harman Blennerhassett to Aaron Burr, December 21, 1805, Safford, *The Blennerhassett Papers,* 118.

155 *"utmost pleasure":* Aaron Burr to Harman Blennerhassett, April 15, 1806, ibid., 119.

156 *"I immediately made a contract":* Dudley Woodbridge, Jr., in Robertson, *Trial of Aaron Burr for Treason,* Vol. 1, 583.

156 *"Letters from Marietta in Ohio":* See letters published in Massachusetts *Republican Spy,* MCSC.

156 *"a laudable undertaking":* Robertson, *Trial of Aaron Burr for Treason,* Vol. 1, 309.

156 *"under the auspice": The Debates and Proceedings in the Congress of*

the United States, 10th Congress, 1st Session, October 26, 1807— April 25, 1808, 480.

157 *"quite the most attractive figure"*: Hildreth, *Genealogical and Biographical Sketches of the Hildreth Family: From the Year 1652 Down to the Year 1840*, 184.

157 *"Not one of all that number"*: Hildreth, *Biographical and Historical Memoirs*, 509.

157 *"The Querist"*: Swick, *An Island Called Eden*, 40; Stewart, *American Emperor*, 154.

157 *"That he [Burr] has formed, and that he is now employed in executing"*: *Richmond Inquirer*, MCSC.

157 *"From information recently received, we have been induced to believe"*: *New York Commercial Advertiser*, MCSC.

158 *"Sir, Personal friendship for you"*: Anonymous to Thomas Jefferson, December 1, 1805, Thomas Jefferson Papers, Library of Congress; Meacham, *Thomas Jefferson*, 662.

158 *"Colonel Burr who was here"*: Cabinet Memoranda, October 22, 1806, McCaleb, *The Aaron Burr Conspiracy*, 101.

158 *"Burr is unquestionably"*: President Thomas Jefferson, note, November 3, 1806, *The Writings of Thomas Jefferson*, Vols. 17–18, Bergh, ed., 250.

158 *"a propensity for intrigue"*: Burr, *Memoirs of Aaron Burr*, Matthew L. Davis, ed., Vol. 1, 89.

159 *"This is indeed a deep, dark"*: James Wilkinson to Thomas Jefferson, November 12, 1806, McCaleb, *The Aaron Burr Conspiracy*, 162–63.

159 *"We trust that public rumor"*: Lomask, *Aaron Burr*, 187.

160 *"When the act of the Ohio legislature was passed"*: Hildreth, *Biographical and Historical Memoirs*, 509.

160 *"take forcible possession"*: Safford, *The Blennerhassett Papers*, 157.

160 *"hubbub and confusion"*: Stewart, *American Emperor*, 179.

161 *"There appeared to us"*: Hulbert, *The Ohio River*, 304.

162 *"sparkled like diamonds"*: Parton, *The Life and Times of Aaron Burr*, 444.

163 *"bare," "dingy"*: Lomask, *Aaron Burr*, 228.

163 *"Is he esteemed a man of vigorous talents?"*: Robertson, *Trial of Aaron Burr for Treason*, Vol. 1, 587.

163 *"could not be levied without"*: Marshall, *The Writings of John Marshall*, 1890, 63.

163 *"It is not proved by a single witness"*: Ibid., 108.

164 *"Misfortune having marked him for her own"*: Safford, *The Blennerhassett Papers*, 585.

7. Adversities Aplenty

PAGE

165 "Town property, as well as farms, sunk in value": Hildreth, *Genealogical and Biographical Sketches*, 198.

165 *"resembling very nearly the yellow fever"*: Waller, "Dr. Samuel P. Hildreth, 1783–1863," *Ohio Archaeological and Historical Quarterly*, Vol. 53, 1944, 327.

165 *"pain in the head"*: Hildreth, "Remarks on the Weather and Diseases in Some Parts of the State of Ohio," *The Medical Repository*, Vol. 5, 1808, 347.

166 *"Maj. Lincoln is dead"*: William Woodbridge to Dudley Woodbridge, September 5, 1807, Backus-Woodbridge Collection, item #380, Ohio History Connection, Columbus, Ohio.

166 *"paid considerable attention"*: Hildreth, *Genealogical and Biographical Sketches*, 138.

166 *"extravagantly fond"*: Ibid., 83.

166 *"passionately fond" of amusement*: Ibid., 144.

167 *"very fine music"*: Ibid., 144.

167 *"a perfect model in dress and manners"*: Ibid., 150.

167 *"I generally read"*: Ibid., 153.

167 *"The last year of the pupilage we were allowed to ride"*: Ibid., 153.

167 *"a severe task"*: Ibid.

167 *"cast my lot"*: Ibid., 155.

168 *"the beds most wretched"*: September 25, 1806, ibid., 173.

168 *"the beautiful Ohio"*: October 1, 1806, ibid., 177.

168 *Dr. Jabez True*: See biographical sketch of Dr. True in Hildreth, *Biographical and Historical Memoirs*, 329–37.

169 *"New England lady"*: Hildreth, *Genealogical and Biographical Sketches*, 184.

170 *"Marietta may be considered"*: Schultz, *Travels on an Inland Voyage*, Vol. 1, 143.

170 *"Shipbuilding will be a capital branch"*: Cutler and Cutler, *Life, Journals*, Vol. 2, 401.

170 Commodore Whipple: For background on Abraham Whipple, see biographical information in Hildreth, *Biographical and Historical Memoirs*, 120–64; and Cohen, *Commodore Abraham Whipple of the Continental Navy: Privateer, Patriot, Pioneer*.

170 *"This part of the country"*: Hulbert, *The Ohio River*, 247.

171 *"the workmanship and timber"*: Cutler, *A Topographical Description of the State of Ohio, Indiana Territory, and Louisiana*, 21.

171 *"Shipbuilding was carried on with considerable spirit"*: Cramer, *The Navigator*, 54.

171 *"bear testimony against the cruel policy of Jefferson"*: Bible of Abner Lord in Archives of Campus Martius Museum, Marietta, Ohio. Many thanks to Bill Reynolds of the museum for bringing Lord's notation to the attention of the author.

172 *"retrograded"*: Hildreth, *Genealogical and Biographical Sketches*, 198.

172 *"in the full vigor of health"*: Hildreth, *Biographical and Historical Memoirs*, 240.

172 *"Physician and Surgeon"*: *Ohio Gazette*, April 20, 1808, MCSC.

172 *"new responsibilities"*: Hildreth, *Genealogical and Biographical Sketches*, 187.

173 *"Marietta, at present"*: Hildreth, "A Concise Description of Marietta, Ohio," *The Medical Repository*, Vol. 6, January 17, 1809, 359.

173 *Congregational church*: The author is grateful to the Reverend Linda N. Steelman, pastor of the First Congregational Church in Marietta, and Scott Britton of the Castle Historical Museum for a tour of the church.

174 *"Whoever pursues the healing art"*: Hildreth, "The Pleasures and Privations of Physicians," originally printed in *The Medical Counselor*, Vol. 2, No. 10, March 8, 1856, 219. Copied from a bound volume from the Hildreth Cabinet Library, held by Marietta College Special Collections, entitled "Contributions to Magazines," 36.

174 *"notching stick"*: Hildreth, "Manners and Domestic Habits of the Frontier Inhabitants in the First Settlement of Ohio," originally printed in *The Medical Counselor*, Vol. 2, February 16, 1856, 36. Copied from a bound volume from the Hildreth Cabinet Library, held by Marietta College Special Collections, entitled "Contributions to Magazines," 36.

174 *"The roads were deep and muddy"*: Ibid., 33.

176 *"the blessed means of rescuing"*: Allen, Dudley P., "History of Early Legislation and Medical Societies in the State of Ohio," *Cleveland Medical Gazette*, Vol. 8, Albert R. Baker and Samuel W. Kelley, eds., 1893, 603, Hildreth, May, 1839, Cleveland Medical Convention Speech, in Cleveland: Buell & Hubbell.

176 *"During the spring, as he traverses the woodlands"*: Hildreth, "The Pleasures and Privations of Physicians," 220–21.

177 *"He observed and noticed"*: Howe, *Historical Collections of Ohio*, Vol. 2, 814.

177 *"terminated"*: Hildreth, *Genealogical and Biographical Sketches*, 197.

177 *"I have not language to express"*: Ibid., 95.

177 *"a never failing source of enjoyment amidst the perplexities of life"*: Ibid., 99.

178 *"decided symptoms"*: Cutler, *Life and Times of Ephraim Cutler*, 85.

178 *"We feel extremely anxious about her"*: Manasseh Cutler to Ephraim Cutler, April 20, 1807, MCSC.

179 *"It is with great diffidence"*: Ephraim Cutler to Sally Parker, March 11, 1808, MCSC.

179 *"awkward predicament"*: Sally Parker to Ephraim Cutler, March 15, 1808, MCSC.

180 *"She is a person of excellent character"*: Ephraim Cutler to Manasseh Cutler, April 4, 1808, MCSC.

180 *"The heart when full to overflowing seeks a vent"*: Ephraim Cutler to Sally Parker, April 4, 1808, MCSC.

180 *"I have no hesitation in advising you to do it"*: Manasseh Cutler to Ephraim Cutler, May 6, 1808, MCSC.

181 *"a perfect stranger"*: Manasseh Cutler to Ephraim Cutler, May 6, 1808, MCSC.

181 *"She is tall and of a very agreeable figure"*: Ephraim Cutler to Manasseh Cutler, June 7, 1808, MCSC.

182 *"She not only superintended and participated"*: Cutler, *Life and Times of Ephraim Cutler*, 263.

182 *"absorbed all my means"*: Ibid., 88.

182 *"A free hospitality characterized the early settlers"*: Ibid., 263.

182 *"Travelers, or persons visiting Marietta"*: Cutler, "Annals of the Homestead," Ephraim Cutler Collection, MCSC.

183 *"There is now on foot a new mode"*: Hulbert, *Waterways of Westward Expansion*, 137–38.

185 *"The first shock was at half-past two"*: Ephraim Cutler to Manasseh Cutler, February 19, 1812, Cutler, *Life and Times of Ephraim Cutler*, 108.

185 *"On the 3rd of February"*: Ephraim Cutler to Manasseh Cutler, February 19, 1812, ibid., 109.

186 *"unprovoked, unnecessary"*: Manasseh Cutler to Ephraim Cutler, March 23, 1813, ibid., 105.

186 *"Our Manifesto"*: *Western Spectator*, July 6, 1812, MCSC.

186 *"No sir, nothing that is generous"*: Rufus Putnam to Caleb Strong, September 15, 1814, MCSC.

186 *"Indian menace"*: Knepper, *Ohio and Its People*, 108.

186 *"The savages may now be expected"*: *Western Spectator*, August 29, 1812, MCSC.

187 *"a fine, gentle river"*: Cutler, *Life and Times of Ephraim Cutler*, 110.

187 *"In twenty-four hours"*: Hildreth, "A Brief History of the Floods in the Ohio River from 1772–1832," *Journal of the Historical and Philosophical Society of Ohio*, 1838, 55–56.

188 *"The rise was rapid beyond any before known"*: Ephraim Cutler Journal, January 24, 1840, Cutler, *Life and Times of Ephraim Cutler*, 111.

188 *"We have met the enemy, and they are ours"*: Knepper, *Ohio and Its People*, 107.

188 *"GLORIOUS NEWS!"*: *Western Spectator*, September 18, 1813, MCSC.

189 *"Shall we repose in apathy"*: Ibid., September 3, 1814, MCSC.

189 *"PEACE"*: Ibid., February 14, 1815, MCSC.

189 *"The house was brilliantly illuminated"*: Cutler, *Life and Times of Ephraim Cutler*, 107.

190 *"I reached my father's house"*: Hildreth, *Genealogical and Biographical Sketches*, 204.

191 *"We reached Marietta"*: Ibid., 207.

8. The Cause of Learning

PAGE

195 "If ignorance could be banished from our land": Ephraim Cutler Speech, October 20, 1829, *American Friend and Marietta Gazette*, December 5, 1829, MCSC.

195 *"one of the especially great thoroughfares"*: United States War Department Engineers Office, *Ohio River: Report on Examination of the Ohio River*, Doc. 492, January 13, 1908, 72.

195 *By 1815 Ohio's population:* The approximation of 500,000 in 1815, a noncensus year, was estimated from the rise in population for Ohio in 1810, which was some 230,000, to about 581,000 in 1820. Source: U.S. Census. See also Knepper, *Ohio and Its People*, 109.

196 *steamboat* Washington: See newspaper coverage in *American Friend*, Marietta, Ohio, June 7, 1816, June 14, *Commercial Advertiser*, New York, New York, June 13, 1816, *New-Bedford Mercury*, June 21, 1816, MCSC.

196 *"commodious"*: Kotar and Gessler, *The Steamboat Era: A History of Fulton's Folly on American Rivers, 1807–1860*, 59.

196 *"It was terrible beyond conception"*: Hunter, *Steamboats on the Western Rivers: An Economic and Technological History*, 283.

197 *"Several friends called on me"*: Ephraim Cutler to Sally Parker Cutler, December 7, 1819, Ephraim Cutler Papers, MSCS.

197 *"every feeling of your heart"*: Ephraim Cutler to Sally Parker Cutler, December 7, 1819, Ephraim Cutler Papers, MCSC.

197 *"on the whole there is an unaccountable procrastination"*: Ephraim Cutler to Sally Parker Cutler, December 22, 1819, MCSC.

198 *"I am appointed on a very important committee"*: Ephraim Cutler to Sally Parker Cutler, December 24, 1819, Cutler, *Life and Times of Ephraim Cutler*, 120.

198 *"thick-headed mortals"*: Ephraim Cutler to Sally Parker Cutler, December 29, 1819, ibid.

198 *"I am not without hopes"*: Ephraim Cutler to Sally Parker Cutler, January 9, 1820, ibid., 121.

198 *Among those who spoke:* Catherine Barker Memoir, October 25, 1880, Vol. 1, 11, MCSC.

199 *"I am oppressed with the responsible situation"*: Ephraim Cutler to Sally Parker Cutler, January 21, 1820, Ephraim Cutler Papers, MCSC.

199 *"As to the frequent use"*: Sally Parker Cutler to Ephraim Cutler, January 23, 1820, Ephraim Cutler Papers, MCSC.

199 *"I can truly say I am tired of it"*: Sally Parker Cutler to Ephraim Cutler, January 26, 1820, MCSC.

200 *"The act for regulating schools, which I originated"*: Ephraim Cutler, January 28, 1820, Cutler, *Life and Times of Ephraim Cutler*, 123.

200 *"We seek no further proof in favor of schools"*: Cincinnati Inquisitor, February 1, 1820.

200 *"total neglect"*: Manasseh Cutler to Ephraim Cutler, August 27, 1818, Cutler and Cutler, *Life, Journals*, Vol. 2, 321.

200 *"Her death was as surprising to me"*: Manasseh Cutler to Ephraim Cutler, December 6, 1815, MCSC.

200 *"I am just going off the stage"*: Manasseh Cutler to Ephraim Cutler, August 27, 1818, Cutler and Cutler, *Life, Journals*, Vol. 2, 323.

201 *"This day it is fifty years"*: Manasseh Cutler Journals, September 11, 1821, ibid., 369.

201 *"a pioneer in a new country"*: Humphrey, "Manasseh Cutler," *The American Naturalist*, Vol. 32, 1898, 80.

202 *"Drowned on Thursday the 30th"*: Item contained in Marietta, Ohio, newspaper extracts 1808–1827 compiled in MCSC.

202 *"Whereas my wife Eliza"*: Marietta Gazette, August 31, 1833, MCSC.

202 *"Reader!!! I WILL STATE"*: Marietta Gazette, September 21, 1833, MCSC.

203 *"abscounder"*: Item contained in Marietta, Ohio, newspaper extracts 1808–1827 compiled in MCSC.

203 *"Run so long, and run so fast"*: Ibid.

203 *"noxious"*: Hildreth, "Epidemic Fever," *The Philadelphia Journal of the Medical and Physical Sciences*, Vol. 9, 1824, 106.

203 *"No obstacles obstructed their course"*: Ibid., 108.

204 *"a terrible visitation of burning fever, wild delirium"*: Julia Perkins Cutler, "The Annals of the Homestead," Ephraim Cutler Papers, MCSC.

204 *"our dear departed son"*: Sally Parker Cutler to Ephraim Cutler, January 20, 1823, ibid.

204 *"My father concluded to make a visit to Ohio"*: Hildreth, *Genealogical and Biographical Sketches*, 58.

205 *"His health was generally firm"*: Ibid., 59.

205 *"the fast friend of Washington"*: *Massachusetts Spy*, May 26, 1824, quoted in the *Proceedings of the American Antiquarian Society*, Vol. 11, April 1896–April 1897, 233.

205 *"He did honor to human nature"*: *Vermont Gazette*, June 8, 1824, MCSC.

206 *"such goods as she shall choose"*: Andrews and Hathaway, *History of Marietta and Washington County, Ohio and Representative Citizens*, 95.

206 *"surrounded his modest, but commodious dwelling"*: Flint, *Recollections of the Last Ten Years*, 33–34.

206 *"possessing a rich fund of anecdote"*: Hildreth, *Biographical and Historical Memoirs*, 118–19.

207 *"And are you Ephraim Cutler's daughter!"*: Crawford, "Rufus Putnam and His Pioneer Life in the Northwest," *Proceedings of the American Antiquarian Society*, New Series, Vol. 12, 1899, 453.

207 *"My sun is far past its meridian"*: Rufus Putnam to the Grand Lodge of Masons, *Masonic Eclectic*, Vol. 3, 1867, 276.

207 *"Dr. Cutler and General Putnam"*: Williams, *History of Washington County, Ohio*, 34.

208 *Rufus Putnam's last will and testament*: A copy of Putnam's will and estate inventory were kindly provided to the author by Bill Reynolds of the Campus Martius Museum in Marietta, Ohio.

209 *"General Lafayette"*: Andrews and Hathaway, *History of Marietta and Washington County, Ohio*, 228–29.

209 *"I knew them well"*: Cutler, *Life and Times of Ephraim Cutler*, 203.

210 *"practically the whole population"*: Galbreath, "Lafayette's Visit to the Ohio Valley States," *Ohio History Journal*, Vol. 29, No. 1, January 1920, 245.

210 *And so to Barker he turned to design*: Southwick, "S. P. Hildreth and His Home," *Ohio Historical Quarterly*, Vol. 64, No. 1, January 1955.

211 *"We passed nearly an hour"*: Waters, *The History of St. Luke's Church, Marietta, Ohio*, 33.

211 *"So far as I am able to form a judgment"*: Ephraim Cutler to Sally Parker Cutler, December 21, 1823, Cutler, *Life and Times of Ephraim Cutler*, 139.

212 *"put constantly on the defensive"*: Ephraim Cutler to Sally Parker Cutler, January 15, 1824, ibid., 140.

212 *"a fine man"*: Ephraim Cutler to Sally Parker Cutler, December 28, 1824, ibid., 154.

212 *"schools and education shall be forever encouraged"*: Poole, *The Ordinance of 1787 and Dr. Manasseh Cutler as an Agent in Its Formation*, 34.

212 *"enterprising"*: Andrews and Hathaway, *History of Marietta and Washington County, Ohio*, Vol. 1, 312.

212 *David Putnam*: Ibid., 208.

213 *"keep school"*: Knight, "History of Educational Progress in Ohio," in Howe, *Historical Collections of Ohio, An Encyclopedia of the State*, Vol. 1, 1889, 141.

213 *"discretion"*: Cutler, *Life and Times of Ephraim Cutler*, 44.

214 *"as to pour out our thoughts to one we love"*: Ephraim Cutler to Sally Parker Cutler, April 4, 1808, Ephraim Cutler Papers, MCSC.

214 *"incessantly"*: Ephraim Cutler to Sally Parker Cutler, January 15, 1824, Cutler, *Life and Times of Ephraim Cutler*, 141.

214 *"You know when my mind is intensely engaged"*: Ephraim Cutler to Sally Parker Cutler, January 17, 1824, ibid., 141.

214 *"entirely insufficient"*: Ephraim Cutler to Sally Parker Cutler, January 19, 1824, ibid.

215 *"To say that I am concerned"*: Sally Parker Cutler to Ephraim Cutler, December 26, 1824, Ephraim Cutler Papers, MCSC.

216 *"dashed to the ground"*: Ephraim Cutler to Sally Parker Cutler, February 12, 1824, Cutler, *Life and Times of Ephraim Cutler*, 143.

216 *"These matters"*: Ibid., 142.

216 *"favorite wish of my heart"*: Ephraim Cutler to Sally Parker Cutler, December 28, 1824, ibid., 154.

216 *"Dear Sir—You are doing nobly"*: Caleb Atwater to Ephraim Cutler, January 22, 1825, ibid., 165–66.

217 *"I have little doubt the revenue law"*: Ephraim Cutler to Sally Parker Cutler, January 23, 1825, ibid., 166–67.

217 *"Lord, now lettest thou thy servant"*: Ephraim Cutler, ibid., 168.

217 *"the blessings of an enlightened education"*: Ephraim Cutler speech, August 11, 1824, ibid., 178.

218 *"a considerable number of strangers"*: Meeting of the Agricultural

Show Committee, October 20, 1829, as reported in *American Friend and Marietta Gazette*, November 28, 1829, MCSC.

218 *"the snowy whiteness and handsomely ornamented corners"*: Ibid.

219 *"It is said that certain epochs in the history of nations"*: Ephraim Cutler, October 20, 1829, Cutler, *Life and Times of Ephraim Cutler*, 198. Only portions of Ephraim Cutler's speech were included in *Life and Times*. For a full rendition of Cutler's speech, see the *American Friend and Marietta Gazette*, November 28, 1829, MCSC.

220 *"a natural outgrowth"*: Williams, *History of Washington County, Ohio: With Illustrations and Biographical Sketches*, 397.

220 *"genuine college of the New England type"*: Ibid., 400.

9. The Travelers

PAGE

221 "The use of traveling is to regulate imagination by reality": Curley, *Samuel Johnson and the Age of Travel*, 49.

221 *"The autumns of every part of our country are beautiful"*: Flint, *Recollections of the Last Ten Years*, 19.

222 *"There is something, too, in the gentle"*: Ibid., 27–28.

222 *"Our passage down the river"*: Buckingham, *The Eastern and Western States of America*, Vol. 2, 237–38.

222 *"and when we had put out into the middle of the river"*: Martineau, *Retrospect of Western Travel*, Vol. 2, 35–36.

223 *"truly does 'La Belle Rivière' "*: Trollope, *Domestic Manners of the Americans*, 47.

223 *"Trollope's folly"*: Foster, *Ohio Frontier: An Anthology of Early Writings*, 188.

223 *"reality"*: Trollope, *Domestic Manners of the Americans*, 106.

223 *"spoken openly by all"*: Ibid., 73.

223 *"All men are born free and equal"*: Ibid.

223 *"mischievous sophistry"*: Ibid.

224 *"every trace"*: Ibid., 106.

224 *"the detestable mosquitoes"*: Ibid., 90.

224 *"There is no charm, no grace"*: Ibid., 56.

224 *"all work and no play"*: Ibid., 244.

224 *"I am quite serious"*: Forster, *The Life of Charles Dickens*, Vol. 1, 1812–1842, 376.

224 *"All the passengers are very dismal"*: Dickens, *A Thousand Gems from Charles Dickens*, F. G. De Fontane, ed., 490.

224　"*the general absence of neatness and cleanliness*": Buckingham, *The Eastern and Western States of America*, Vol. 2, 446.

225　"*Where slavery sits brooding*": Tambling, *Lost in the American City*, 43.

225　"*They will owe their origin*": Tocqueville, *Democracy in America*, trans., Henry Reeve, Vol. 2, 315.

225　"*You call upon a gentleman*": Dickens, *A Thousand Gems from Charles Dickens*, 197.

226　"*ardent spirits*": Trollope, *Domestic Manners of the Americans*, 105.

226　"*the free and unrestrained use of ardent spirits*": Clark, *Gleanings by the Way, 1801–1843*, 1842, 84.

226　"*necessity of life*": Howe, *Historical Collections of Ohio*, Vol. 3, 524.

226　"*their red noses, blotched cheeks*": Hildreth, *Genealogical and Biographical Sketches*, 48.

227　"*Here I found a number of neighbors*": Journal of John Mathews, November 11, 1786, Hildreth, *Pioneer History*, 177.

227　"*graphically described*": Ibid., 177–78.

228　"*At dinner, there is nothing to drink upon the table*": Dickens, *A Thousand Gems from Charles Dickens*, 490.

228　"*propriety and necessity*": Cutler, *Life and Times of Ephraim Cutler*, 269.

228　"*beautiful . . . cheerful, thriving*": Dickens, *Pictures from Italy* and *American Notes*, 347.

228　"*intelligent, courteous, and agreeable*": Ibid., 349.

228　"*particularly pleased*": Ibid., 347–48.

229　"*Nor did I ever once, on any occasion*": Dickens, *Pictures from Italy* and *American Notes*, 331.

229　"*as to the gentlemen in traveling*": Martineau, *Society in America*, Vol. 2, 129.

229　"*scraped away without mercy*": Cuming, *Cuming's Tour to the Western Country, 1807–1809*, 208.

229　"*found a dozen stout young fellows*": Ibid., 210.

230　"*If the American character may be judged*": Trollope, *Domestic Manners of the Americans*, 180.

230　"*a moving account of their strong attachment*": Dickens, *Pictures from Italy and American Notes*, 381.

231　Hildreth journey to Cleveland: Hildreth, *Genealogical and Biographical Sketches*, 211–93.

232　"*In the short space of 55 years*": Ibid., 217.

232　"*To a person unacquainted with the grandeur*": Ibid.

232　"*angry billows*": Ibid., 218.

232　"*rested from our labors*": Ibid.

232 *"one dense, continuous forest"*: Hildreth, *Pioneer History*, 484.

232 *"On the bottoms, or alluviums"*: Ibid., 485–86.

233 *"Arrived at the harbor"*: Hildreth, *Genealogical and Biographical Sketches*, 220.

233 *"As we approached the falls"*: Ibid., 221.

233 *"or a mile in two minutes"*: Ibid., 225.

233 *"very grand"*: Ibid., 227.

233 *"very striking and annoying"*: Ibid., 229.

234 *"The Path Finder"*: Fulton and Thomson, *Benjamin Silliman: Path-finder in American Science, 1779–1864*, 1949.

234 Hildreth report to Benjamin Silliman on shells and grapes: See letters of Samuel Hildreth to Benjamin Silliman, October 14, 1833, July 21, 1835, and June 9, 1835, Silliman Family Papers, Sterling Library, Yale University.

234 *"vast period of time to hollow"*: Hildreth, *Observations on the Bituminous Coal and Deposits of the Valley of the Ohio, and the Accompanying Rock Strata*, 4.

234 *"recognize the enormous amount"*: Annual Report: *United States National Museum*, 330.

235 *"classic neatness"*: Hildreth, *Genealogical and Biographical Sketches*, 230.

235 *"imposing"*: Ibid.

235 *"richly endowed by nature physically as he was mentally"*: See sketch of Silliman in *Dictionary of American Biography*, Vol. 17, 162.

235 *"Death loses half its terrors"*: Hildreth, *Genealogical and Biographical Sketches*, 230.

235 *"without ready means of support"*: Trumbull, *Autobiography of John Trumbull*, 10.

235 *"very interesting"*: Hildreth, *Genealogical and Biographical Sketches*, 231.

236 *"very large"*: Ibid.

236 *"All the avails of the exhibitions of this gallery"*: Ibid., 232.

236 *"superior to that of any other in America"*: Ibid.

236 *"exceedingly rare and beautiful"*: Ibid.

237 *"He is now 84 years old"*: Ibid., 232–33.

237 *"very extensive"*: Ibid., 236.

237 *"My wife is highly gratified with the visit"*: Ibid., 265.

237 *"Examined with much interest"*: Ibid., 246.

237 *"the beautiful Delaware"*: Ibid., 280.

238 *"Here we were drawn up"*: Ibid., 285–86.

238 *"Pittsburgh is a very dirty"*: Hildreth, *Pioneer History*, 289.

238 *"We found the family all well"*: Hildreth, *Genealogical and Biographical Sketches*, 293.

238 *"We often think and speak"*: Samuel Hildreth to Benjamin Silliman, January 20, 1840, Silliman Family Papers, Sterling Library, Yale University.

239 *"Let no New England man ever visit"*: Marietta Intelligencer, September 5, 1839, MCSC.

10. Journey's End

PAGE

241 "I am glad to have Pa": Julia Perkins Cutler to William Parker Cutler, November 14, 1843, MCSC.

241 *"I have had rather an eventful life"*: Cutler, *Life and Times of Ephraim Cutler*, 1.

241 *"admirable talkers"*: Ibid., 264.

242 *"most satisfactory to themselves"*: Ibid.

242 *When in the summer of 1843*: Boston Emancipator and Free Press, August 24, 1843; Ohio State Journal, October 17, 1843.

242 *"Old Man Eloquent"*: Levy, *John Quincy Adams*, 95.

242 *"My task is to turn this transit gust"*: Adams, *Memoirs of John Quincy Adams: Comprising Portions of His Diary, 1795–1848*, Vol. 11, 1876, Charles Francis Adams, ed., 409.

242 *His plan was to leave his home*: For Adams's diary account of his journey to Cincinnati, Marietta, and Pittsburgh, see the Diaries of John Quincy Adams, Adams Family Papers, October 25, 1843–November 16, 1843, Massachusetts Historical Society, Boston, Massachusetts. See also *Ohio State Journal*, September 20, 1843, November 2, 1843; *Scioto Gazette*, October 27, 1843.

243 *"There is no uniformity in human life"*: Adams, *Memoirs of John Quincy Adams*, Vol. 11, 413.

243 *"a complimentary address"*: Ibid., 425. For additional accounts of Adams's visit to Cincinnati, see *Cincinnati Daily Commercial*, November 7, 1843, and *Ohio State Journal*, November 7, 1843.

243 *"Worn down with fatigue, anxiety, and shame"*: Ibid., 425.

244 *"covered with an auditory of umbrellas"*: Ibid., 426.

244 *"Light House of the Skies!"*: Traub, *John Quincy Adams: Militant Spirit*, 503.

245 *"In hospitality, he was unsurpassed"*: Hildreth, *Memoirs of the Early Pioneer Settlers of Ohio*, 462; Catherine Barker Memoirs, Vol. 11, 1880, 27, MCSC.

245 *It was yet another rainy day:* For weather, see account book of Samuel Hildreth, Hildreth Papers, MCSC.

246 *"taken a deep interest in the whole west":* Adams, *Memoirs of John Quincy Adams*, Vol. 11, 432.

246 *"From this source":* Williams, *History of Washington County, Ohio*, 433.

247 *"wisdom and firmness":* Cutler, *Life and Times of Ephraim Cutler*, 195.

247 *"I saw the tears gather in his eyes":* Ibid., 196.

247 *"Jack is a very handsome Negro":* Items from Marietta, Ohio, newspapers 1825–1853 compiled in the MCSC.

248 *"very handsome":* Ibid.

248 *Sam "very black" and "free and easy" to talk to:* Ibid.

248 *"conductors":* Banta, *The Ohio*, 462.

248 *"magnificent reception":* Adams, *Memoirs of John Quincy Adams*, Vol. 11, 433.

249 *"My strength is prostrated":* Parsons, *John Quincy Adams*, 259.

249 *"We have never seen a family that were united by stronger":* Cutler, *Life and Times of Ephraim Cutler*, 270–71.

249 *"retiring disposition":* Ibid., 280.

250 *"Pa's health has been better this winter":* Julia Perkins Cutler to William Parker Cutler, January 13, 1846, Ephraim Cutler Papers, MCSC.

250 *"The stage left Marietta at 11 o'clock":* Cutler, *Life and Times of Ephraim Cutler*, 281–82.

251 *"Let us glance around the hall of the lower house":* Ibid., 282.

251 *"a lively manner, joy respecting your success":* Ephraim Cutler to William Cutler, December 29, 1946, Ephraim Cutler Papers, MCSC.

252 *"How little did we anticipate":* William Parker Cutler to Julia Perkins Cutler, January 1, 1847, MCSC.

252 *"A year ago we had not _heard_ of the gold":* Julia Perkins Cutler Journals, March 26, 1849, MCSC.

252 *"to think of his dying away from home and friends":* Julia Perkins Cutler Journals, June 16, 1849, MCSC.

252 *Marietta population 1850:* Baldwin and Thomas, *Gazetteer of the United States*, 658.

253 *first established Catholic church:* Andrews and Hathaway, *History of Marietta and Washington County, Ohio*, 366–67.

253 *"the best shaded town in the state":* Howe, *Historical Collections of Ohio*, Vol. 2, 787.

253 *"monopolize":* Hildreth, *Genealogical and Biographical Sketches*, 200.

253 *"be ever honorably associated with the early history":* Benjamin Silliman to Samuel Hildreth, February 13, 1851, 223, MCSC.

254 *"The doctor's excellent and highly cultivated taste":* Julia Perkins Cutler Journals, July 24, 1838, MCSC.

254 *"We did not intend to have any guests":* Julia Perkins Cutler Journals, November 23, 1848, MCSC.

254 *"My health and strength have thus far sustained me":* Ephraim Cutler to William Parker Cutler, May 22, 1850, Ephraim Cutler Papers, MCSC.

255 *Harriet Beecher Stowe:* McCullough, *Brave Companions*, 37–51.

256 *"public enemy":* Cutler, *Life and Times of Ephraim Cutler*, 341.

257 *"plundering everybody without fear or favor":* Andrews and Hathaway, *History of Marietta and Washington County, Ohio*, 593.

257 *"We are getting accustomed to warlike sights and sounds":* Julia Perkins Cutler Journals, July 23, 1863, Ephraim Cutler Papers, MCSC.

258 *"In his private life":* Silliman, "Obituary," *American Journal of Science and Arts*, Vol. 36, November 1863, 313.

BIBLIOGRAPHY

Manuscript and Archival Sources

Special Collections and Archives, Legacy Library, Marietta College, Marietta, Ohio (hereinafter abbreviated MCSC)
    Joseph Barker Papers
    Ephraim Cutler Family Papers
    Samuel Hildreth Papers
    Ichabod Nye Papers
    Ohio Company Papers
    Rufus Putnam Papers
    William Rufus Putnam Papers

The following newspapers held by the Marietta College Library were also used:
    American Friend and Marietta Gazette
    Marietta Intelligencer
    Marietta Register
    The Ohio Gazette, and Virginia Herald
    Ohio Herald
    Ohio Statesman
    Western Spectator

Special Collections and Archives, Ohio University, Athens, Ohio
    Manasseh Cutler Papers

Ohio History Connection, State Historical Society, Columbus, Ohio
    Campus Martius Collection
    Putnam Family Papers
    Backus-Woodbridge Collection

Special Collections and Archives, Northwestern University, Evanston, Illinois
Manasseh Cutler Papers (microfilm edition)

Senator John Heinz Pennsylvania History Center, Pittsburgh, Pennsylvania
Ebenezer Denny Papers

Special Collections, Brown University Library, Providence, Rhode Island
Drowne Family Papers

Massachusetts Historical Society, Boston, Massachusetts
Winthrop Sargent Papers

Sterling Library, Special Collections and Archives, Yale University, New Haven,
Connecticut
Silliman Family Papers

American Antiquarian Society, Worcester, Massachusetts
Early American Newspaper Collection

Books

Abernethy, Thomas Perkins. *The Burr Conspiracy.* New York: Oxford University Press, 1954.
Adams Family Correspondence. Vol. 9, Margaret A. Hogan, C. James Taylor, et al., eds. Cambridge: Belknap Press of Harvard University Press, 2009.
Adams, John Quincy. *Memoirs of John Quincy Adams: Comprising Portions of His Diary, 1795–1848.* Vol. 11. Charles Francis Adams, ed. Philadelphia: J. B. Lippincott, 1876.
Allman, C. B. *The Life and Times of Lewis Wetzel.* New York: Devin-Adair, 1961.
Ambler, Charles Henry. *History of Transportation in the Ohio Valley.* Westport, CT: Greenwood Press, 1970.
American National Biography. Vol. 5. John A. Garraty and Mark C. Carnes, eds., New York: Oxford University Press, 1999.
Andrews, Martin R., and Seymour J. Hathaway. *History of Marietta and Washington County, Ohio and Representative Citizens.* La Crosse, WI: Brookhaven Press, 2003.
Annual Report: United States National Museum. Washington, D.C.: U.S. Government Printing Office, 1906.
Ashe, Thomas. *Travels in America, Performed in 1806.* London: Edmund M. Blunt, 1808.

Audubon, Maria R. *Audubon and His Journals.* Vol. 2. New York: Charles Scribner's Sons, 1897.

Backus, William, James Backus, and Sarah Backus. *A Genealogical Memoir of the Backus Family: With the Private Journal of James Backus.* Salem, MA: Higginson Book Company, 2000.

Baldwin, Thomas, and Joseph Thomas. *Gazetteer of the United States.* Philadelphia: J. B. Lippincott & Co., 1854.

Banta, Richard Elwell. *The Ohio.* New York: Rinehart, 1949.

Barber, John Warner, and Henry Howe. *Our Whole Country.* Vols. 1 and 2. Cincinnati: Charles Tuttle, 1863.

Barker, Joseph. *Recollections of the First Settlement of Ohio.* George Jordan Blazier, ed. Marietta, Ohio: Richardson Printing Corporation, 1958.

Belcher, Mrs. Henry Alden, and William Nye. *The Nye Family of America Association, Proceedings of the First Reunion.* N.p., August 1905.

Belote, Theodore Thomas. *The Scioto Speculation and the French Settlement at Gallipolis.* New York: Burt Franklin, 1907.

———. *Selections from the Gallipolis Papers.* Cincinnati: Press of Jennings & Graham, 1907.

Bigelow, Robert Payne. *American Naturalist: An Illustrated Magazine of Natural History.* Vol. 32. London, England: Forgotten Books, 2017.

Blennerhassett, Harman. *Breaking with Burr: The Harman Blennerhassett Journal, 1807.* Raymond E. Fitch, ed. Athens: Ohio University Press, 1988.

Boorstin, Daniel J. *The Americans: The National Experience.* New York: Vintage, 2010.

Buckingham, James Silk. *The Eastern and Western States of America.* Vols. 2 and 3. London: Fisher, Sons & Co., 1842.

Buell, Rowena, ed. *Memoirs of Rufus Putnam.* Boston: Houghton Mifflin & Co., 1903.

Buley, R. Carlyle. *The Old Northwest: Pioneer Period, 1815–1840.* Bloomington: Indiana University Press, 1951.

Burr, Aaron. *Memoirs of Aaron Burr.* Vol. 1. Matthew L. Davis, ed. New York: Harper's Brothers, 1855.

Butterfield, C. W. *An Historical Account of the Expedition Against Sandusky Under Colonel William Crawford in 1782.* Cincinnati: Robert Clarke & Co., 1873.

Butts, Edward. *Simon Girty: Wilderness Warrior.* Toronto: Dundurn, 2011.

Callahan, North. *Henry Knox: General Washington's General.* New York: Rinehart, 1958.

Calloway, Colin G. *The American Revolution in Indian Country: Crisis and Diversity in Native America.* New York: Cambridge University Press, 1995.

———. *The Shawnees and the War for America.* New York: Penguin, 2007.

———. *The Victory with No Name: The Native American Defeat of the First American Army.* New York: Oxford University Press, 2005.

Cayton, Andrew R. L. *The Frontier Republic: Ideology and Politics in the Ohio Country, 1780–1825.* Kent, OH: Kent State University Press, 1986.

———. *Ohio: The History of a People.* Columbus: Ohio State University Press, 2002.

———, and Stuart D. Hobbs, eds. *The Center of the Great Empire: The Ohio Country in the Early Republic.* Athens: Ohio University Press, 2005.

———, and Paula R. Riggs. eds., *City into Town: The City of Marietta, Ohio, 1788–1988.* Marietta, OH: Marietta College, 1991.

Chernow, Ron. *Alexander Hamilton.* New York: Penguin, 2004.

———. *Washington: A Life.* New York: Penguin, 2010.

Clark, John A. *Gleanings by the Way, 1801–1843.* New York: Robert Carter, 1842.

Cohen, Sheldon S. *Commodore Abraham Whipple of the Continental Navy: Privateer, Patriot, Pioneer.* Gainesville: University of Florida Press, 2010.

Cone, Mary. *Life of Rufus Putnam, With Extracts from His Journal and an Account of the First Settlement in Ohio.* Cleveland: William W. Williams, 1886.

Cramer, Zadok. *The Navigator.* 11th ed. Pittsburgh: Cramer, Spear, 1821.

Crammer, G. I. *History of the Upper Ohio Valley.* Madison, WI: Brant & Fuller, 1891.

Cresswell, Nicholas. *Journal of Nicholas Cresswell.* Port Washington, NY: Kennikat Press, 1968.

Crèvecoeur, J. Hector St. John de. *Letters from an American Farmer.* Vol. 3, 2nd. ed. New York: Doubleday, 1961.

Cuming, Fortescue. *Cuming's Tour to the Western Country, 1807–1809.* Pittsburgh: Cramer, Spear, 1810.

Curley, Thomas M. *Samuel Johnson and the Age of Travel.* Athens: University of Georgia Press, 1976.

Cutler, Jervis. *A Topographical Description of the State of Ohio, Indiana Territory, and Louisiana.* Boston: Charles Williams, 1812.

Cutler, Julia Perkins. *The Founders of Ohio: Brief Sketches of the Forty-Eight Pioneers.* Cincinnati: Robert Clarke & Co., 1888.

Cutler, Julia Perkins, ed. *Life and Times of Ephraim Cutler: Prepared from His Journals and Correspondence.* Cincinnati: Robert Clarke & Co., 1890.

Cutler, William Parker, and Julia Perkins Cutler, eds. *Life, Journals, and Correspondence of Rev. Manasseh Cutler, LL.D.* 2 Vols. Cincinnati: Robert Clarke & Co., 1888.

Daniel, Robert L. *Athens, Ohio: The Village Years.* Athens: Ohio University Press, 1997.

Decatur, Stephen. *Private Affairs of George Washington: From the Records and Accounts of Tobias Lear, Esquire, His Secretary.* New York: Da Capo, 1969.

DeWolfe, Barbara, ed. *Discoveries of America: Personal Accounts of British Emigrants to North America During the Revolutionary War.* Cambridge: Cambridge University Press, 1997.

Denny, Ebenezer. *Military Journal of Major Ebenezer Denny: An Officer in the Revolutionary War and Indian Wars.* Philadelphia: J. B. Lippincott, 1859.

———. *The Record of the Court at Upland in Pennsylvania, and a Military Journal Kept by Major E. Denny, 1778–1795.* Philadelphia: J. B. Lippincott, 1860.

Dickens, Charles. *Charles Dickens: Complete Works.* Boston: Estes & Lauriat, 1881.

———. *Pictures from Italy* and *American Notes.* Boston: Houghton, Osgood & Co., 1879.

———. *A Thousand Gems from Charles Dickens.* F. G. De Fontane, ed. New York: G. W. Dillingham, 1889.

Dictionary of American Biography. Vol. 3. Allen Johnson and Dumas Malone, eds. New York: Charles Scribner's Sons, 1946.

Doddridge, Joseph. *Notes on the Settlement and Indian Wars of the Western Parts of Virginia and Pennsylvania from 1763–1783.* New York: Garland, 1977.

Dunbar, Seymour. *A History of Travel in America.* Vol. 1. Indianapolis: Bobbs-Merrill Co., 1915.

Faux, William. *Faux's Memorable Days in America, 1819–1820.* New York: AMS Press, 1969.

Ferris, Mary Walton. *Dawes and Allied Families.* Privately printed: Wisconsin Cuneo Press, 1931.

Fitch, Raymond E., ed. *Breaking with Burr: Harman Blennerhassett's Journal, 1807.* Athens: Ohio University Press, 1988.

Flexner, James Thomas. *George Washington and the New Nation.* Boston: Little, Brown, 1970.

Flint, Timothy. *Recollections of the Last Ten Years.* Boston: Cummings, Hilliard & Co., 1826.

Foreman, Grant. *The Last Trek of the Indians.* Chicago: University of Chicago Press, 1946.

Forster, John. *The Life of Charles Dickens, 1812–1842,* Vol. 1. London: Cecil Palmer, 1872.

Foster, Emily, ed. *Ohio Frontier: An Anthology of Early Writings.* Lexington: University of Kentucky Press, 1996.

Freeman, Douglas Southall. *George Washington: A Biography*. Vol. 6. New York: Charles Scribner's Sons, 1954.

Fulton, John Farquhar, and Elizabeth Harriet Thomson. *Benjamin Silliman: Pathfinder in American Science, 1779–1864*. New York: H. Schuman, 1949.

Greene, Graham. *The Records of the Original Proceedings of the Ohio Company*. Vol. 2. BiblioLife, 2008.

Gruenwald, Kim M. *River of Enterprise: The Commercial Origins of Regional Identity in the Ohio Valley, 1790–1850*. Bloomington: Indiana University Press, 2002.

Guthman, William H. *March to Massacre: A History of the First Seven Years of the United States Army, 1784–1791*. New York: McGraw-Hill, 1975.

Hall, Charles S. *Life and Letters of Samuel Holden Parsons*. Forgotten Books: London, England, 2016.

Hamilton, Allan McLane. *The Intimate Life of Alexander Hamilton: Based Chiefly upon Family Letters and Other Documents*. New York: Charles Scribner's Sons, 1911.

Harris, Thaddeus Mason. *The Journal of a Tour into the Territory Northwest of the Allegheny Mountains*. Boston: Manning & Loring, 1805.

Hathaway, Seymour. *History of Marietta and Washington County, Ohio*. Chicago: Biographical Publications Co., 1902.

Havighurst, Walter. *Ohio: A Bicentennial History*. New York: W. W. Norton, 1976.

———. *Wilderness for Sale: The Story of the First Western Land Rush*. New York: Hastings House, 1956.

Heard, J. Norman. *Handbook of the American Frontier: Four Centuries of Indian-White Relationships*. Vol. 1. Metuchen, NJ: Scarecrow Press, 1987.

Heckewelder, John. *History, Manners and Customs of the Indian Nations Who Once Inhabited Pennsylvania and the Neighboring States*. New York: Arno Press, 1971.

Hildreth, Samuel P. *Biographical and Historical Memoirs of the Early Pioneer Settlers of Ohio: With Narratives of Incidents and Occurrences in 1775*. Cincinnati: H. W. Derby & Co., 1852.

———. *Contributions to the Early History of the Northwest Including the Moravian Mission in Ohio*. Cincinnati: Hitchcock & Walden, 1864.

———. *Genealogical and Biographical Sketches of the Hildreth Family: From the Year 1652 Down to the Year 1840*. Marietta, Ohio, 1840.

———. *Memoirs of the Early Pioneer Settlers of Ohio*. Clearfield Publishers, n.d.

———. *Observations on the Bituminous Coal Deposits of the Valley of the Ohio and the Accompanying Rock Strata.* Digitized book from University of Chicago, 2011.

———. *Pioneer History: Being an Account of the First Examinations of the Ohio Valley, and the Early Settlement of the Northwest Territory.* Cincinnati: H. W. Derby & Co., 1848.

Hill, Norman Newell. *History of Knox County, Ohio.* Mount Vernon, Ohio: A. A. Graham Co., 1881.

Hinsdale, B. A. *The Old Northwest: The Beginnings of Our Colonial System.* New York: Townsend MacCoun, 1888.

———. *The Ordinance of 1787: Origin, Features, and Results. An Address Delivered Before the Ohio State Teachers Association, Akron, Ohio, June 29, 1887.* Akron, OH: Educational Monthly, 1887.

History of Hocking Valley, Ohio. Chicago: Inter-State Publishing Co., 1883.

Hodgson, Adam. *Letters from North America.* Vol. 2. London: Hurst, Robinson & Co., 1824.

Hogeland, William. *Autumn of the Black Snake: The Creation of the United States Army and the Invasion That Opened the West.* New York: Farrar, Straus & Giroux, 2018.

Hoover, Thomas N. *The History of Ohio University.* Athens: Ohio University Press, 1954.

Horn, David. *A Story of God's Faithfulness: The History of the First Congregational Church of Hamilton.* Hamilton, MA: First Congregational Church, 2014.

Howard, James H. *Shawnee!: The Ceremonialism of a Native Indian Tribe and Its Cultural Background.* Athens: Ohio University Press, 1981.

Howe, Henry. *Historical Collections of Ohio: An Encyclopedia of the State.* Vols. 1 and 2. Cincinnati: C. J. Krehbiel Printers, 1900.

Howells, William Dean. *Stories of Ohio.* New York: American Book Co., 1897.

Hulbert, Archer Butler. *The Ohio River: A Course of Empire.* New York: G. P. Putnam's Sons, 1906.

———. *The Records of the Original Proceedings of the Ohio Company.* Marietta, OH: Marietta Historical Commission, 1917.

———. *Waterways of Westward Expansion: The Ohio River and Its Tributaries, Historic Highways of America Series.* Cleveland: Arthur Clark, 1903.

Hunter, Louis C. *Steamboats on the Western Rivers: An Economic and Technological History.* New York: Dover, 1993.

Hurt, Douglas R. *The Ohio Frontier: Crucible of the Old Northwest, 1720–1830.* Bloomington: University of Indiana Press, 1998.

Hutchins, Thomas. *Courses of the Ohio River.* Cincinnati: Historical and Philosophical Society of Ohio, 1942.

Imlay, Gilbert. *Topographical Description of the Western Territory of North America*. London: J. Debrett, 1793.

Irving, Washington. *Life of George Washington*, Vol. 5. New York: G. P. Putnam's Sons, 1882.

Isenberg, Nancy. *Fallen Founder: The Life of Aaron Burr*. New York: Viking, 2008.

Jakle, John P. *Images of the Ohio Valley: A Historical Geography of Travel, 1740–1860*. New York: Oxford University Press, 1977.

James, Alfred P. *The Ohio Company: Its Inner History*. Pittsburgh: University of Pittsburgh Press, 1959.

Jefferson, Thomas. *Notes on the State of Virginia*. Boston: Lilly & Wait, 1832.

———. *The Papers of Thomas Jefferson*. Vol. 41. Barbara B. Oberg, ed. Princeton: Princeton University Press, 2014.

———. *The Writings of Thomas Jefferson*, Vols. 17–18. Albert Ellery Bergh, ed. Washington, D.C.: Thomas Jefferson Memorial Association, 1907.

———. *The Writings of Thomas Jefferson 1784–1787*, Vol. 4. Paul Leicester Ford, ed. New York: G. P. Putnam Sons, 1894.

Johns, Alessa, ed. *Dreadful Visitations: Confronting Natural Catastrophe in the Age of Enlightenment*. New York: Rutledge, 1999.

Jones, Landon Y. *William Clark and the Shaping of the West*. New York: Hill & Wang, 2005.

Journals of the Lewis and Clark Expedition, August 30, 1803–August 24, 1804. Lincoln: University of Nebraska Press, 1986.

Knepper, George W. *Ohio and Its People*. Kent, OH: Kent State University Press, 1989.

Kotar, S. L. and J. E. Gessler. *The Steamboat Era: A History of Fulton's Folly on American Rivers, 1807–1860*. Jefferson, NC: McFarland, 2009.

Latrobe, John. *The First Steamboat Voyage on the Western Waters*. Ann Arbor: Making of America, 2000.

Letters of the Lewis and Clark Expedition, With Related Documents, 1783–1854. Donald Jackson, ed. Urbana: University of Illinois Press, 1978.

Levy, Debbie. *John Quincy Adams*. Minneapolis: Lerner Publishing, 2005.

Lewis, James. *The Burr Conspiracy: Uncovering the Story of an Early American Crisis*. Princeton: Princeton University Press, 2017.

Lodge, Henry Cabot. *George Washington*. American Statesman series. Vol. 2. Boston: Houghton Mifflin and Co., 1889.

Lomask, Milton. *Aaron Burr: The Conspiracy and Years of Exile, 1805–1836*. New York: Farrar, Straus & Giroux, 1982.

Lossing, Benson J. *Recollections and Private Memories of Washington by His Adopted Son George Washington Parke Custis with a Memoir of the Author*. Philadelphia: William Flint, 1859.

Marshall, John. *The Writings of John Marshall.* Washington, D.C.: William H. Morrison, 1890.

Martineau, Harriet. *Retrospect of Western Travel.* Vol. 2. London: Saunders & Otley, 1838.

———. *Society in America.* Vol. 2. London: Saunders & Otley, 1837.

Mathews, Lois Kimball. *The Expansion of New England: The Spread of New England Settlement and Institutions to the Mississippi River, 1620–1865.* Boston: Houghton Mifflin, 1909.

May, John. *The Western Journals of John May: Ohio Company Agent and Business Adventurer.* Dwight L. Smith, ed. Cincinnati: Historical and Philosophical Society of Ohio, 1961.

McCaleb, Walter Flavius. *The Aaron Burr Conspiracy.* New York: Dodd, Mead & Co., 1903.

McCullough, David. *Brave Companions.* New York: Prentice-Hall, 1991.

Meacham, Jon. *Thomas Jefferson: The Art of Power.* New York: Random House, 2012.

Melish, John. *Travels in the United States of America in the Years 1806, 1807, 1809, and 1811.* Philadelphia: T. & G. Palmer Printers, 1812.

Melton, Buckner F. *Aaron Burr: Conspiracy to Treason.* New York: Wiley, 2001.

O'Donnell III, James H. *Ohio's First Peoples.* Athens: Ohio University Press, 2004.

———. "William Crawford," in John A. Garraty and Mark C. Carnes, eds., *American National Biography*, Vol. 5, 1999.

Ogg, Frederic Austin. *The Old Northwest: A Chronicle of the Ohio Valley and Beyond.* New Haven: Yale University Press, 1919.

Ohio River: Report on the Examination of the Ohio River. United States War Department, Engineers Office, Doc. 492, January 13, 1908. Washington, D.C.: U.S. Government Printing Office, 1908.

Parsons, Lynn Hudson. *John Quincy Adams.* Lanham, MD: Rowman and Littlefield, 2001.

Parsons, Mary Alvina Dodge. *Ancestry of Nathan Dane Dodge and of His Wife Sarah (Shepard) Dodge with Notes.* Salem, MA: Salem Press, 1896.

Parton, James. *The Life and Times of Aaron Burr.* New York: Mason Brothers, 1858.

Perkins, Elizabeth. *Border Life: Experience and Memory in the Revolutionary Ohio Valley.* Chapel Hill: University of North Carolina Press, 1998.

Phillips, Josephine. *Wagons Away!* Parsons, WV: McClain Print Co., 1969.

Piatt, John James. *The Lost Farm and Other Poems.* Boston: James R. Osgood and Co., 1877.

Poole, William Frederick. *The Ordinance of 1787 and Dr. Manasseh Cutler as an Agent in Its Formation.* Cambridge, MA: Welch, Bigelow & Co., 1876.

Putnam, Rufus. *The Memoirs of Rufus Putnam and Certain Official Papers and Correspondence.* Boston: Houghton Mifflin & Co., 1903.

Rhodehamel, John. *George Washington: The Wonder of the Age.* New Haven: Yale University Press, 2018.

Richardson, James D. *A Compilation of the Messages and Papers of the Presidents.* Vol. 2. Tennessee: Bureau of National Literature and Art, 1908.

Richter, Conrad. *The Trees.* New York: Alfred A. Knopf, 1940.

———. *The Fields.* New York: Alfred Knopf, 1946.

———. *The Town.* New York: Alfred Knopf, 1950.

Robertson, David. *Trial of Aaron Burr for Treason.* Vol. 1. New York: James Cockcroft and Company, 1875.

Roosevelt, Theodore. *The Winning of the West.* Vol. 3. New York: G. P. Putnam's Sons, 1896.

Rorison, Arda Bates. *Major General Arthur St. Clair: A Brief Sketch.* Classic Reprint, London, England: Forgotten Books, 2015.

Safford, William H. *The Blennerhassett Papers: Embodying the Private Journal of Harman Blennerhassett and the Hitherto Unpublished Correspondence of Burr.* London, England: Forgotten Books, 2015.

———. *The Life of Harman Blennerhassett: An Authentic Narrative of the Burr Expedition.* Chillicothe, OH: Ely, Allen & Looker, 1850.

———. *The Life of Harman Blennerhassett.* BiblioLife, 1853.

Sargent, Winthrop. *Diary of Col. Winthrop Sargent.* Wormsloe, Georgia, 1851.

Schultz, Christian. *Travels on an Inland Voyage Through the States of New York, Pennsylvania, Virginia, Ohio, Kentucky and Tennessee: Performed in the Years 1807 and 1808.* Vol. 1. New York: Isaac Riley, 1810.

Sedgwick, John. *War of Two: Alexander Hamilton, Aaron Burr and the Duel That Stunned a Nation.* New York: Berkley, 2015.

Shevitz, Amy Hill. *Jewish Communities on the Ohio River.* Lexington: University of Kentucky Press, 2007.

Sibley, William Giddings. *The French Five-Hundred and Other Papers.* Westminster, MD: Heritage Books, 2010.

Sibley's Harvard Graduates: Biographical Sketches of Those Who Attended Harvard College, 1768–1771. Boston: Massachusetts Historical Society, 1975.

St. Clair, Arthur. *A Narrative of the Manner in Which the Campaign Against the Indians in the Year 1796 Was Conducted.* Philadelphia: Jane Aiken, 1819.

———, and William Henry Smith, ed. *The St. Clair Papers: The Life and Public Services of Arthur St. Clair.* Vol. 2. Cincinnati: Robert Clarke & Co., 1882.

St. George, Judith. *The Duel: The Parallel Lives of Alexander Hamilton and Aaron Burr.* St. Louis, MO: Turtleback Books, 2016.

Stewart, David O. *American Emperor: Aaron Burr's Challenge to Jefferson's America.* New York: Simon & Schuster, 2012.

Stuart, James. *Three Years in North America.* Vols. 1 and 2. Edinburgh, 1833.

Sugden, John. *Blue Jacket: Warrior of the Shawnees.* Lincoln: University of Nebraska Press, 2000.

———. *Tecumseh: A Life.* New York: Henry Holt, 1997.

Summers, Thomas Jefferson. *History of Marietta.* Marietta, OH: Leader Publishing Co., 1903.

Swayne, Wager. *The Ordinance of 1787 and The War of 1861.* New York: Printed by C. G. Burgoyne, 1892.

Swick, Ray. *An Island Called Eden: The Story of Harman and Margaret Blennerhassett.* Parkersburg, WV: Parkersburg Printing Co., 2008.

———, and Christina Little. *Blennerhassett Island.* Charleston, SC: Arcadia Publishing, 2005.

Sword, Wiley. *President Washington's Indian War.* Norman: University of Oklahoma Press, 1993.

Tambling, Jeremy. *Lost in the American City.* New York: Palgrave, 2001.

Taylor, James W. *History of the State of Ohio, 1650–1787.* Cincinnati: H. W. Derby & Co., 1854.

Thompson, Eben Francis. *A Brief Chronicle of Rufus Putnam and His Rutland Home.* Privately Printed, 1930.

Tocqueville, Alexis de. *Democracy in America.* Vol. 2., 2nd ed. Henry Reeve, trans. Cambridge: Sever Francis, 1863.

Traub, James. *John Quincy Adams: Militant Spirit.* New York: Basic Books, 2016.

Trollope, Frances. *Domestic Manners of the Americans.* London: Whittaker, Treacher & Co., 1832.

Trumbull, John. *Autobiography of Colonel John Trumbull, Patriot-Artist, 1759–1843.* Theodore Sizer, ed. New Haven: Yale University Press, 1953.

Van Every, Dale. *Ark of Empire: The American Frontier, 1784–1803.* New York: William Morrow, 1963.

Venable, W. H. *Beginnings of Literary Culture in the Ohio Valley.* Cincinnati: Robert Clarke & Co., 1891.

Vidal, Gore. *Burr.* New York: Random House, 1973.

Walker, Charles Manning. *History of Athens County, Ohio and Incidentally of the Ohio Land Company and the First Settlement of the State at Marietta.* Cincinnati: Robert Clarke & Co., 1869.

Washington, George. *The Papers of George Washington, Presidential Series.* Vols. 6, 7, and 9. Dorothy Twohig, Philander Chase, and Jack D. Warren, Jr., eds. Charlottesville: University of Virginia Press, 1996, 1998.

——. *The Writings of George Washington: From the Original Manuscript Sources, 1745–1799.* Vol. 29. John C. Fitzpatrick, ed. Washington: U.S. Government Printing Office, 1939.

Waters, Wilson. *The History of St. Luke's Church, Marietta, Ohio.* Marietta, OH: J. Mueller & Son, 1884.

Williams, Gary. *Johnny Appleseed in the Duck Creek Valley.* Johnny Appleseed Center for Creative Learning, Dexter City, OH: 1989.

Williams, H. Z. *History of Washington County, Ohio.* Cleveland: H. Z. Williams & Bro., 1881.

Winthrop, John. *Winthrop Papers.* Vol. 2, 1623–1630. Boston: Massachusetts Historical Society, 1931.

Zimmer, Louise. *True Stories of Pioneer Times: Northwest Territory, 1787–1812.* Marietta, OH: Broughton Foods Company, 1992.

——. *More True Stories from Pioneer Valley.* Marietta, Ohio: Sugden Book Store, 1993.

Articles

Allen, Dudley P. "History of Early Legislation and Medical Societies in the State of Ohio." *Cleveland Medical Gazette*, Vol. 8. Albert R. Baker and Samuel W. Kelley, eds., 1893.

Cone, Mary. "The First Settlement in Ohio." *Magazine of American History*, Vol. 6, No. 4, April 1881.

Cutler, Sarah J. "The Coonskin Library." *Ohio State Archaeological and Historical Quarterly*, Vol. 26, 1917.

Crawford, Sydney. "Rufus Putnam and His Pioneer Life in the Northwest." *Proceedings of the American Antiquarian Society*, New Series, Vol. 12, 1899.

Crèvecoeur, J. Hector St. John de. "Letters from an American Farmer." *Ohio Archaeological and Historical Quarterly*, Vol. 3, 1900.

"Dr. Manasseh Cutler and the Ordinance of 1787." *North American Review*, Vol. 123, No. 251, 1876.

Fry, Mildred Covey. "Women on the Ohio Frontier: The Marietta Area." *Ohio History Journal*, Vol. 90, No. 1, Winter 1981.

Galbreath, C. B. "Lafayette's Visit to the Ohio Valley States." *Ohio Archaeological and Historical Publications*, Vol. 29, No. 1, January 1920.

Hart, Albert Bushnell. "The Westernization of New England." *Ohio Archaeological and Historical Publications*, Vol. 17, 1908.

Hildreth, Samuel. "A Brief History of the Floods in the Ohio River from 1772–1832." *Journal of the Historical and Philosophical Society of Ohio*, 1838.

———. "A Concise Description of Marietta, Ohio." *The Medical Repository*, Vol. 6, January 17, 1809.

———. "Epidemic Fever." *The Philadelphia Journal of the Medical and Physical Sciences*, Vol. 9, 1824.

———. "Remarks on the Weather and Diseases in Ohio." *The Medical Repository*, Vol. 5, March 3, 1808.

———. "Manners and Domestic Habits of the Frontier Inhabitants, in the First Settlement of Ohio." *The Medical Counselor*, Vol. 2, No. 7, February 16, 1856.

———. "The Pleasures and Privations of Physicians." *The Medical Counselor*, Vol. 2, March 8, 1856.

Humphrey, James Ellis. "Manasseh Cutler." *The American Naturalist*, Vol. 32, 1898.

Jordan, Wayne. "The People of Ohio's First Company." *Ohio Archaeological and Historical Quarterly*, Vol. 49, No. 1, January 1940.

Leeper, W. H. "American Union Lodge, No. 1, F & A Masons, Marietta, Ohio." *The Masonic Review*, Vol. 73, No. 1, February 1, 1890.

Mayer, Vinnie J. "The Coonskin Library." *Wilson Library Bulletin*, Vol. 26, No. 1, September 1951.

Murray, Rev. J. A. "The Butlers of the Cumberland Valley." *Historical Register: Notes and Queries, Biographical and Genealogical*, Vol. 1, No. 1, January 1883.

Pallante, Martha. "The Trek West: Early Travel Narratives and Perceptions of the Frontier." *Michigan Historical Review*, Vol. 21, No. 1, Spring 1995.

Phillips, Josephine E. "Fine Timber." *Ohio Archaeological and Historical Quarterly*, Vol. 46, No. 1, January 1937.

Poole, W. F. "Dr. Manasseh Cutler and the Ordinance of 1787." *North American Review*, Vol. 123, No. 251, 1876.

Randall, E. O. "Editorialana," *Ohio Archaeological and Historical Quarterly*, Vol. 25, No. 1, January 1916.

———. "Rutland: 'The Cradle of Ohio,' A Little Journey to the Home of Rufus Putnam." *Ohio State Archaeological and Historical Quarterly*, Vol. 18, 1909.

Rau, Louise. "Lucy Backus Woodbridge: Pioneer Mother, January 31, 1757–October 6, 1817." *Ohio Archaeological and Historical Society*, Vol. 44, No. 4, 1935.

"Rufus Putnam to the Grand Lodge of Masons." *Masonic Eclectic*, Vol. 3, 1867.

Shetrone, H. C. "The Indian in Ohio." *Ohio Archaeological and Historical Quarterly*, Vol. 27, 1919.

"Side Lights on the Ohio Company of Associates from the John May Papers." *The Western Reserve Historical Society*, Tract No. 97, 1917.

Silliman, Benjamin. "Obituary—Dr. Samuel Prescott Hildreth." *The American Journal of Science and Arts*, Vol. 36, November 1863.

Silverberg, Robert. ". . . And the Mound-Builders Vanished from the Earth." *American Heritage*, Vol. 20, No. 4, June 1969.

Southwick, Erman Dean. "S. P. Hildreth and His Home." *Ohio Historical Quarterly*, Vol. 64, No. 1, January 1955.

Stone, Benjamin Franklin. "From Rutland to Marietta." *New England Magazine*, Vol. 16, New Series, April 1897.

Vance, John L. "The French Settlement and Settlers of Gallipolis." *Ohio Archaeological and Historical Quarterly*, Vol. 3, 1890–1891.

Wadsworth, Benjamin. "Discourse at Manasseh Cutler's Interment." *The Hesperian*, Vol. 2, No. 1, 1838.

Waller, A. E. "Dr. Samuel P. Hildreth 1783–1863." *Ohio Archaeological and Historical Quarterly*, Vol. 53, 1944.

Dissertations

Cayton, Andrew R. L. "The Best of All Possible Worlds: From Independence to Interdependence in the Settlement of the Ohio Country, 1780–1825." PhD diss., Brown University, 1981.

Pershing, Benjamin Harrison. "Winthrop Sargent in the Old Northwest." PhD diss., University of Chicago, December 1927.

Swick, Ray. "Harman Blennerhassett: An Irish Aristocrat on the American Frontier." PhD diss., Miami University, 1978.

Ulrich, Dennis Nicholas. "Samuel P. Hildreth: Physician and Scientist on the American Frontier, 1783–1863." PhD diss., Miami University, 1983.

INDEX

Adams, Abigail, 91, 113, 115–16
Adams, John, 6–7, 28–29, 115–16, 135, 138,
    144, 153, 245–46, 247
Adams, John Quincy, 242–44, 245–47, 249
alcohol. *See* whiskey/alcohol
Allegheny Mountains, 39, 55, 57, 96, 168, 238
Allegheny River, 17, 40
American Friend (Marietta newspaper),
    202, 204, 218
Ames/Amesville, 138–39, 147–48, 178, 255
"Ancient Works." *See* earthworks; Great
    Mound
animals, 45, 51, 55, 63-64, 79, 127, 203-4
apple trees, 82, 150, 211
Arbella (ship), 17
army, frontier
    and Battle of Fallen Timbers, 118
    behavior of, 87–88
    casualties in, 118
    and Indian attack at Big Bottom, 87–90
    Little Turtle defeats, 87–88
    organizing of, 87–88
    Putnam considered for commander of, 116
    recruitment and training of, 117
    size of, 117
    Wayne as commander of, 116, 117
army, St. Clair's
    burial of soldiers from, 114–15
    camp followers of, 99
    casualties in, 108, 113
    concerns about, 99, 101–2
    congressional investigation of, 113, 114
    defeat of, 106–15
    desertions in, 99, 101, 103
    food/provisions for, 101, 107–8
    hanging of members of, 101
    and Harmar, 97–98, 108–9, 114

and ignorance about Indians, 109
Indian attack on/defeat of, 102–15
and Indians as threat to settlers, 92–94
morale among, 99
public reactions to defeat of, 112–14
quality of troops in, 97, 99, 108–9
raising of, 96–99
retreat of, 106–11
and search for Indians, 99–102
size of, 99
St. Clair as commander of, 96–115
strategy for, 102
supplies for, 97
wages for, 99
and weather, 100–101, 103
astronomy, 242, 243–44
Atwater, Caleb, 212, 216–17
Atwood, Leah. *See* Cutler, Leah Atwood

Backus, Elijah, 73, 132, 157
Backus, James, 52–53, 64, 72
Backus, Lucy. *See* Woodbridge, Lucy Backus
Balch, Mary. *See* Cutler, Mary Balch
Barker, Catherine, 130, 137, 210
Barker, Elizabeth Dana, 78–79, 81, 82–83,
    129, 130, 245
Barker, Joseph
    achievements/honors of, 245
    and Adams (John Quincy) Ohio
        expedition, 242
    as architect/builder, 131, 133–35,
        137–38, 210–11, 244, 258
    Belpre move of, 129
    and Blennerhassett house, 133–35, 137
    as boat builder, 137, 156, 160
    and Burr, 156, 160
    as carpenter, 78, 79, 81

Barker, Joseph (*cont.*)
  comments about veterans by, 57–58
  Cutler family and, 137
  death/funeral of, 244–45
  as early Marietta settler, 79, 82–83, 129
  education of, 213
  as education proponent, 198–99
  family of, 129, 130, 137, 245
  and French emigrants in Marietta, 85
  and Hildreth, 210–11, 245, 258
  home of, 129, 130, 137–38, 244
  hospitality of, 138, 245
  and Indian attack on Rogers and
    Henderson, 95
  jobs of, 83
  land grant for, 129
  and life in Ohio Country, 82–83
  as militia member, 83
  personal/professional background of,
    78–79
  role in Marietta of, 83
  scientific interests of, 210
  as ship builder, 170
  and smallpox outbreak, 81
  and "Starving Year," 80
  as teacher, 129
Barker, Joseph Jr., 82–83, 218, 246
Barlow, Joel, 83, 84
Bartram, William, 22–23, 86
Battle of Fallen Timbers, 118
Beaver River, 41, 78, 94–95
Belpre
  Barker and Dana families at, 79, 81,
    82–83, 129
  Cutler (Ephraim) move to, 178
  fortifications at, 92
  Hildreth as doctor in, 165–66, 169
  Indians as threat to, 92, 93, 95
  influenza epidemic at, 169
  school in, 129
Benjamin Franklin (steamboat), 244, 245
Big Bottom attack, 87–90, 93, 110, 117
Blennerhassett, Harman
  appearance/personality of, 132
  arrest and trial of, 160, 162, 163
  articles by, 157–58
  on Blennerhassett Island, 132–35
  boat for, 137
  and Burr conspiracy, 151, 154–63
  Cutler (Ephraim) and, 135
  death of, 164

  escape of, 160–61
  financial affairs of, 164
  and Hildreth, 157
  library of, 169
  in Mississippi Territory, 162, 164
  as Ohio emigrant, 131–32
  post-trial life of, 164
  pseudonym of, 157
  reputation of, 163
Blennerhassett, Margaret, 131–32, 133,
    134, 135, 157, 161–62, 163, 164
Blennerhassett Island
  Blennerhasset buying of, 32
  Blennerhassett family departure from,
    160–62
  and Burr conspiracy, 160, 162
  Burr on, 154–55, 156
  house on, 133–35, 137, 161, 162, 164
  Pittsburgh men on, 161
  and slavery, 133
Blue Jacket (Shawnee chief), 102, 118
Board of Treasury, 18, 25, 26, 28–29, 83
boats. *See* ships/boats; *type of boat*
Boston
  Bunch of Grapes meeting in, 6, 8, 9,
    11–12, 205
  and Dorchester Heights attack, 36–37
  and Hildreth visit to East Coast, 237
  Hollis Street Congregational Church in,
    173
Braddock's (Edward) Defeat, 98, 108, 113
Brough, John, 156–57, 168
Buckingham, J.S., 222, 223, 224–25
Buell, Joseph, 43, 46–47
Bullard, Asa, 89, 90
Bullard, Eleazer, 89, 90
Bunch of Grapes meeting (Boston), 6, 8, 9,
    11–12, 205
Burr, Aaron
  appearance of, 152, 153, 162
  arrest and trial of, 162–63
  and Blennerhassett, 151, 154–55, 156,
    157–58
  and boat building, 155–56, 160
  boat of, 151–52
  conspiracy of, 153–54, 156–62
  death of, 164
  elections of 1800 and, 153
  financial affairs of, 154
  and Hamilton duel, 152, 154
  as Ohio Company stockholder, 154

personal/professional background of, 152–53

personality of, 152, 153

post-trial life of, 164

western expedition of, 151–52, 153–55

Cajoe (aka Micajah Phillips), 133, 135, 160, 162

Campus Martius

    Court of Common Pleas at, 128–29

    Cutler (Manasseh) sermon at, 59–60, 219

    descriptions of, 54, 117–18

    and early settlements in Ohio Country, 54

    and Indian attacks/threats, 92, 95

    initial impressions of, 58

    Putnam home at, 206, 207

    school at, 64

    Tupper home at, 68

    See also stockade

Captain Pipe, 43, 46, 51, 55, 56, 63–64, 106

Carrington, Edward, 15, 25

Catholics, 252–53

Chapman, John "Johnny Appleseed," 150

Cherokee Indians, 51

children

    as army camp followers, 99

    and Cutler (Manasseh) visit to Marietta, 59

    death of, 59, 124, 130, 166, 204

    food/provisions for, 80

    health of, 78, 81, 110

    and Indian-St. Clair army battle, 106, 108

    and life in Marietta, 73

    See also specific person

Chillicothe, 143, 144–45, 147–48, 159, 185, 229, 230

Chippewa Indians, 55, 59, 102

Choate, Francis, 89, 90

Choate, Isaac, 89, 90

Cincinnati

    Adams (John Quincy) expedition to, 242–44

    Dickens description of, 228

    economy of, 170

    growth of, 195, 228

    industry in, 196, 228

    Marietta compared with, 240

    as "Queen City" of west, 172

    Sargent move to, 86

    schools in, 212, 228

    St. Clair move to, 86

    and St. Clair's army retreat, 108

    territorial governor's office in, 86

    Trollope in, 223

    See also Fort Washington

Civil War, 256–57

Clarkson, Gerardus, 19, 22

Cleveland, 212, 231–32

climate. See weather

Columbus

    as state capital, 197, 211

    See also Ohio legislature

communication: with early settlers, 50–52

Congregational Church

    in Ipswich Hamlet/Hamilton, 3, 179

    in Marietta, 173, 208, 218–19, 245, 258

Congress, U.S.

    and Burr conspiracy, 158

    Cutler (Manasseh) as representative to, 138–43

    and Embargo Act, 171

    Gag Rule in, 247

    and Indians as threat, 96

    and Northwest Ordinance, 83

    and Ohio constitution, 149

    and Putnam as commander of frontier army, 116

    St. Clair Defeat investigation by, 113, 114

    toasts to, 56

    War of 1812 and, 189

    and Washington's death, 135

    See also Continental Congress

Constitution, U.S., 56, 60

Constitutional Convention, 13, 18, 19–24

Continental Congress, 9–11, 12–14, 15–18, 24, 25–30

Cook, Rhoda. See Hildreth, Rhoda Cook

Cornplanter (Seneca chief), 62

Court of Common Pleas, 126, 128–29, 204, 241

Crawford, William, 8, 43

Creek Indians, 102

Crèvecoeur, J. Hector St. John de, 3, 11–12

Cutler, Charles, 148–49, 228, 252

Cutler, Ephraim

    accomplishments/honors of, 255–56

    and Adams (John Quincy) Ohio expedition, 242, 245, 246–47

    appearance of, 121

    Atwater appreciation for efforts of, 216–17

    autobiography of, 241

Cutler, Ephraim (*cont.*)
Barker family and, 137
birth of, 4
and Blennerhassett, 135
and Board of Treasury-Ohio Company
contract, 30
and Charles's (brother) death, 148
and Charles's (son) death, 252
childhood/youth of, 121–22
commissions for, 126
as Court of Common Pleas judge, 126,
128–29, 241
death of, 255
deaths of children of, 124
"droving business" of, 146–47
and earthquake, 185
education of, 122, 213–14
as education proponent, 29, 147–48, 183,
195, 197–200, 211, 212, 213–16, 217,
219–20, 256
and Erie Canal, 217
family of, 127, 182, 197, 199, 249
as farmer, 121–22, 126–27, 148, 254, 255
financial affairs of, 129, 146, 182
and first expedition to Ohio Country, 32
and flooding in Marietta, 188
health/illness of, 124, 145–46, 204,
215–16, 250, 254
and Hildreth, 253, 254
hospitality of, 182–83, 189–90, 228,
241–42, 254
and Indians as threat, 127
and Jervis, 149, 250
journey to Ohio Country of, 123–24
as justice of the peace, 126
late years of, 241–42, 253–54, 255
and Leah's health/death, 177–78, 179
as librarian, 148
and Manasseh as congressman, 138
Manasseh compared with, 121
Manasseh criticisms of, 139
Manasseh relationship with, 121–22,
126–27, 137, 138, 142–43, 144, 149,
178, 179–82, 185–86, 200–201
marriages of, 122–23, 178-82
militia commission of, 126
as new emigrant, 121, 123–24
and Ohio constitution, 144, 145–47
as Ohio legislator, 138–39, 143, 178, 183,
185, 197–200, 204, 211–12, 214–15,
216–17, 255–56

and Ohio University, 200–201, 211, 212,
215–16, 217, 241, 256
as orator, 199, 218–20
Parker marriage to, 178–82
and Putnam (Rufus), 143
road building by, 143
Sally letters to/from, 178–82, 197, 198,
199–200, 204, 211, 214–15, 216, 217
slavery views of, 144, 145–47, 197, 206,
213, 247, 248–49, 255–56
as surveyor, 126
and taxation, 198, 216, 217
and temperance movement, 228
views about politicians of, 198
War of 1812 and, 185–86, 189–90
Washington County Agricultural Fair
speech of, 218–20
Washington, D.C. visit of, 142–43
Waterford move of, 125–26, 127
William's relationship with, 249–51, 254
Cutler, Jervis
birth of, 4
book by, 171
businesses of, 149, 170–71
communications from, 50
and Cutler (Manasseh) visit to Marietta,
58
death of, 250
and expeditions/settlements in Ohio
Country, 32, 33, 39, 43, 47–48, 77,
122, 148
as lost in woods, 77
marriage of, 123
in Ohio militia, 170
reputation of, 149
return from Ohio Country of, 123
Cutler, Julia Perkins, 30, 146, 182–83, 228,
241–42, 246, 250, 252, 253, 254, 257
Cutler, Leah Atwood (Ephraim's wife),
122–23, 124, 127, 177–78, 179
Cutler, Manasseh
Adams (John Quincy) visit with, 246
as "agent" for Ohio Company, 3, 6, 12,
13–24, 25–31, 115–16
appearance/personality of, 4, 5, 6, 15,
16, 24
and Board of Treasury-Ohio Company
contract, 29
and Bunch of Grapes meeting, 6, 11
character of, 32, 60, 84, 126
and Charles's death, 148–49

communication between first settlers
    and, 50
as congressman, 138–43, 179
and Cutler's emigration to Ohio
    Country, 32
death of, 201, 204
and descriptions of Ohio Country, 12,
    31–32
and earthworks, 49, 62
education of, 4, 5–6
as education proponent, 29, 30, 31–32,
    147, 181, 200–201, 213, 219
Ephraim compared with, 121
Ephraim relationship with, 121–22,
    126–27, 137, 138, 139, 142–43, 144,
    149, 178, 179–82, 185–86, 200–201
and Ephraim-Sally marriage, 179–82
family of, 139–40
financial affairs of, 5
and first expedition to Ohio Country,
    31–33, 40
health of, 200, 201
and Hildreth as Ohio emigrant, 168
honors/accomplishments of, 201, 207–8
and Indian-settler relations, 59, 62
intellectual/scientific interests of, 5–6, 14,
    20, 21–23, 31–32, 58–59, 60, 62, 201
Jefferson dinner with, 141–42
letters of introduction for, 3, 14, 24
and library, 148
Marietta visit of, 57–60, 62
and naming of first settlement, 55–56
and Northwest Ordinance, 30, 122, 201
and Northwest Territory as land of
    opportunity, 9
and Ohio University, 200–201
pamphlet about Ohio Country by,
    31–32, 84
as pastor, 3–4, 122, 179
personal/professional background of,
    3–6
Philadelphia visit of, 18–24
and politics in Marietta, 144
Putnam relationship with, 45, 50, 51, 82,
    84, 207–8
Revolutionary War service of, 6
and Sargent-Tupper relationship, 69, 70
and Scioto Company, 84
and shares of Ohio Company, 12
and shipbuilding in Marietta, 170
and slavery, 30, 146, 201

St. Clair and, 116
and Story as Marietta pastor, 74
and Varnum death, 64
War of 1812 and, 185–86
Cutler, Manasseh (Ephraim's son), 205
Cutler, Mary Balch (wife), 4, 5, 16, 115, 116,
    124, 143, 200
Cutler, Sally Parker
    death/burial of, 251–52, 256
    Ephraim letters to/from, 178–82, 183,
        197, 198, 199–200, 204, 211, 214–15,
        216, 217
    Ephraim's courtship and marriage to,
        178–82, 183
    health of, 204, 250
    and son's death, 204
Cutler, Sarah. See Dawes, Sarah Cutler
Cutler, William Parker, 30, 217, 249–51,
    252, 254, 256

Dana, Elizabeth. See Barker, Elizabeth Dana
Dana, Mary Bancroft, 78–79
Dana, William, 78–79, 82
Dane, Nathan, 9, 25, 30
Dawes, Rufus, 248–49
Dawes, Sarah Cutler, 137, 207, 248
Declaration of Independence, 19, 30
Delaware Indians
    and Big Bottom attack, 89
    and Crawford murder, 8
    and Cutler (Manasseh) visit to Marietta,
        59
    and first expedition/settlements in Ohio
        Country, 43, 55
    and Hutchins survey of Ohio River, 17
    and Indian-settler relations, 51, 63
    massacre (1782) by, 8
    "Pow-wows" of, 55
    Putnam concerns about, 88
    removal of, 230
    and St. Clair's defeat, 102, 106
    as threat to settlers, 87, 88, 92
    treaties with, 63
Denny, Ebenezer, 54, 98–102, 104–13
Devol, Jonathan, 38–39, 40, 42, 47, 110,
    130–31, 137, 170, 171, 219
Devol, Stephen, 136
Dickens, Charles, 224–25, 227–29,
    230
Dorchester Heights: British attack (1776)
    on, 36–37

drought, 203
"droving business," 146–47
Duer, William, 17–18, 25–26, 27, 83,
    84–85, 86

earthquake: in Marietta, 184–85
earthworks, 48–50, 51, 53–54, 59, 62, 69,
    86. *See also* Great Mound
economy: and shipbuilding, 170–72
education
    Cutler (Ephraim) as proponent of,
        147–48, 183, 195, 197–200, 211, 212,
        213–16, 217, 219–20, 246, 256
    Cutler (Manasseh) views about, 29, 30,
        31–32, 60, 147, 181, 200–201, 213,
        219
    and German immigrants, 213
    importance of, 12, 29, 219–20
    and Northwest Ordinance, 12, 29, 30,
        31–32, 212
    and Ohio Company, 147
    See also schools; *specific person or
        institution*
elections of 1800, 138, 141, 144, 153
elections of 1828, 242
Embargo Act, 171, 183
Emerson, Caleb, 186, 220, 241–42, 246,
    247, 248
emigrants/emigration
    arrival of new Ohio, 70–75
    enthusiasm for, 50, 51, 53–54
    foreign, 195–96
    French, 84–86, 87
    German, 228, 253
    increase in number of, 50–52, 60–62,
        118, 173, 195–96
    Irish, 228, 253
    Jewish, 253
    as leaving Ohio Country, 110–11
    and Northwest Territory as land of
        opportunity, 9, 11
    Putnam comments about, 110–11
    reactions to Marietta by, 73–75
    regrets of, 67
    types of transportation for, 60–62
    views about, 50–52
    women as, 71–73
    See also specific person
Erie Canal, 199, 216, 217, 233
Erie (steamboat), 233
Excell (steamboat), 238

Fearing, Paul, 52, 125, 131, 166, 204
Federal Creek, 138, 148
fiddling-wolves story, 65
financial panic, 8–9
first expedition to Ohio Country
    and boat building, 39, 40
    departure from Sumerill's Ferry of, 40
    departure from Massachusetts of, 33, 35
    food/provisions for, 33, 40, 41
    and health conditions, 40
    and Indians, 43
    members of, 32, 33, 38–39
    morale on, 42–43
    plans/preparations for, 31–33, 37
    Putnam as leader of, 32, 33, 35, 37, 39,
        40, 42, 43–44
    travel conditions for, 33, 38, 39–43
    wages on, 33
    wagon for, 33
    See also settlers/settlements, first;
        specific person
flatboats, 61
Flint, Thomas, 221–22
food/provisions
    for children, 80
    and early expeditions/settlers in Ohio
        Country, 33, 40, 41, 54, 65, 67–68, 70
    generosity concerning, 80–81
    for Marietta, 67–68, 77, 79–82
    for Mathews surveying party, 75
    for St. Clair's army, 101, 107–8
    and "Starving Year," 79–81
    and weather, 77
forests/trees, 44, 45–46, 49, 58, 100, 171,
    232–33
Fort Duquesne, 98
Fort Frye, 126
Fort Hamilton, 99, 100, 107
Fort Harmar, 17, 42, 43, 45, 46–47, 54,
    56–57, 62, 63–64, 92, 93
Fort Jefferson, 103, 107
Fort Pitt, 17, 40–41, 62
Fort Ticonderoga, 96–97, 102, 114
Fort Washington, 86, 97, 99, 100, 101, 107,
    108, 109–10, 117
France, 79, 84–86, 87. *See also* French and
    Indian War
Franklin, Benjamin, 4, 18, 20–22, 49, 56
free blacks: voting by, 144
French and Indian War, 17, 36, 38, 98. *See
    also* Braddock's (Edward) Defeat

Gag Rule, 247
Gallipolis: French in, 85–86
Gardner, John, 47–48
German immigrants, 213, 228, 253
Gerry, Elbridge, 19, 20, 21
Girty, Simon, 102
Great Mound, 48–49, 50, 59, 62, 64, 69,
    154. *See also* earthworks
Greene & Company, 170
Greene, Charles, 136
Guilford, Nathan, 212, 217

Hamilton, Alexander, 19, 22, 152, 154
Hamilton, Massachusetts: Ipswich Hamlet
    renamed, 138
Harmar, Josiah, 43, 45, 53, 87–88, 92,
    97–98, 102, 108–9, 114
Harmar, Mrs. Josiah, 59
Harrison, William Henry, 59, 189
Harvard College/University, 4, 5, 30, 69,
    140, 167, 201, 220
health conditions
    and Cutler (Manasseh) visit to Marietta,
        59
    and drought conditions, 203–4
    and early expeditions/settlers to Ohio
        Country, 40, 51, 54–55
    fever outbreaks and, 165–66, 205
    in Marietta, 77, 78, 81, 110
    See also specific person or disease
Heath, William, 36–37
Henderson, Edward, 94, 95
Herald (steamboat), 209–10
Hildreth, Charles, 191, 231
Hildreth, George, 231, 257, 258
Hildreth, Rhoda Cook (wife), 169, 172,
    231–32, 237, 239, 258
Hildreth, Samuel P.
    and alcohol, 226–27
    appearance of, 167
    and Barker (Joseph), 210, 245
    and Big Bottom Indian attack, 89
    and Blennerhasset, 157, 169
    and Burr conspiracy, 157, 160
    character/personality of, 166–67, 258
    and Cutler (Ephraim), 253, 254
    death/funeral of, 256, 258
    and descriptions of Marietta, 165, 172–73
    drought comments of, 203–4
    and earthquake, 185
    East Coast visit by, 231–39

education of, 166, 167
    as educator, 169
    family of, 172, 190–91, 210
    and family visit to Ohio, 204–5
    and father's death, 205
    and fever outbreak, 165–66
    financial affairs of, 166, 168, 191
    and flooding in Marietta, 187
    health of, 257, 258
    honors/tributes for, 156, 172, 177, 257–58
    house for, 210–11, 258
    initial journey/arrival in Marietta of, 156,
        168–69
    library of, 169
    and Marietta College, 220, 258
    marriage of, 169
    Massachusetts visit of, 190–91
    medical practice of, 165–66, 172,
        173–76, 177, 204, 210, 253
    medical speeches of, 231, 232
    Methuen as birthplace of, 237
    personal/professional background of, 166
    and Putnam memories, 206
    as representative to Ohio legislature, 177
    scar on top of head of, 190–91
    scientific interests of, 172, 176–77, 187,
        210, 232, 234–35, 258
    and Silliman, 234, 235, 236, 237, 239,
        253, 258
    "Starving Year" comments of, 80
    and True, 204
    writings/publications by, 169, 206, 211,
        226–27, 234, 245, 253, 258
    Yale visit by, 234–37, 239
historic preservation, 51
Hocking River (Hockhocking River), 77, 147
Hutchins, Thomas, 16–17, 18, 38, 187

Indians
    attacks on first settlers by, 55
    and communications from first settlers,
        50
    concerns about settlers of, 63–64
    and Cutler (Manasseh) visit to Marietta,
        59
    drunkeness among, 59
    and earthworks, 49
    and first expedition to Ohio Country, 43
    foreign travelers views about, 230
    Fort Washington as base of operations
        against, 86

Indians (cont.)
    and Harmar's frontier army, 87–90
    and hostility toward surveyors, 75–76
    killing of animals by, 63–64, 79
    and names in Ohio, 230
    and Northwest Ordinance, 29
    Northwest Territory as rightful domain
        of, 8
    and Ohio Company-Board of Treasury
        contract, 29
    at the Point, 43
    Putnam's views about, 43, 46–47, 51, 64,
        87–88, 90, 206
    removal of, 230
    settlers relationship with, 46–47, 58,
        63–64, 86–88, 91–94, 206
    squatters dislike for, 45
    and St. Clair's army, 99–115
    as threat to settlers, 8, 55, 75–77, 87–88,
        91–94, 95–99, 110, 117, 125, 127, 186
    treaties with, 14, 38, 62, 63–64
    women, 59
    See also specific person, tribe, attack/
        battle, or treaty
influenza epidemic, 169, 183, 204
Ipswich Hamlet (Massachusetts), 3–4, 33, 138
Irish immigrants, 228–29, 253

Jackson, Andrew, 189, 241, 242
Jefferson, Thomas
    and Burr conspiracy, 157, 158–59, 162
    Burr relationship with, 152, 159
    Cutler (Manasseh) dinner with, 141–42
    description of Ohio River by, 12
    as designer of Virginia Hall of Delegates,
        163
    elections of 1800 and, 138, 141, 144, 153
    and Embargo Act, 171, 183
    and Louisiana purchase, 149
    mound interests of, 49
    and Northwest Ordinance, 11
    Ohio appointments by, 149
    and Ohio constitution, 145, 149
    and slavery, 145, 223
    and St. Clair as governor, 149
    Washington (Martha) views about, 141
    Washington's relationship with, 141
Jewish immigrants, 253
"Johnny Appleseed." See Chapman, John
    "Johnny Appleseed"
July 4 celebrations, 56, 57, 228

keelboats, 61–62, 170, 197
Kerr's Island, 42, 62
Kickapoo Indians, 102
Knox, Henry
    appearance of, 16
    Cutler (Manasseh) discussion with,
        15–16
    and Harmar's frontier army, 87, 114
    and Indians as threat to settlers, 87, 94,
        97, 98
    as Ohio Company stockholder, 16, 19
    and Putnam as commander of frontier
        army, 116
    and St. Clair's army, 102–3, 109, 110,
        111, 113, 114

Lafayette, Marquis de, 52, 209–10, 219, 242
Lake Erie, 232, 243, 248. See also Erie Canal
Lear, Tobias, 111, 112
learning. See education; scientific interests
Lewis and Clark expedition, 149–50
Lewis, Meriwether, 142, 149–50
libraries, establishment of, 148
Linnaeus, Carolus, 22
Little Turtle (Miami chief), 87, 102
Lord, Abner, 170, 171
Louisiana Territory
    and Burr conspiracy, 153–54, 157,
        158–59
    Jefferson's purchase of, 149

Madison, James, 19, 22, 185–86, 189
Malbone, Christopher (aka Kit Putnam),
    144
manners, American, 229
Marie Antoinette (Queen of France), 56
Marietta
    and Adams (John Quincy) death, 249
    and Adams (John Quincy) Ohio
        expedition, 242, 243, 244, 245–46
    and Burr conspiracy, 159–61
    Burr visit to, 151–52, 154–55
    Catholics in, 252–53
    Cincinnati compared with, 240
    as "City upon the Hill," 17, 205–6
    Congregational Church in, 173, 208,
        218–19, 245, 258
    construction of, 58
    crime in, 202–3
    Cutler (Manesseh) visit to, 57–60, 62
    deaths among early settlers of, 59, 78

descriptions of, 74, 110–11, 125, 131, 165, 170, 172–73, 202–5, 239–40, 252–53
earthquake in, 184–85
economy of, 170, 171–72
emigrants as leaving, 110–11
emigrants' reactions to, 73–75
first general store in, 72
flooding in, 187–88
food/provisions for, 67–68, 77, 79–82
fortifications at, 92, 111
French emigrants in, 85
generousity toward settlers in, 80–81
growth of, 173
health conditions in, 77, 78, 81, 110, 165–66
increase of emigrants to, 60–61, 68, 70–75, 130–31
Indians as threat to settlers in, 75–77, 91–94, 96, 110, 117, 118, 125
Jewish immigrants in, 253
July 4 celebration in, 56
Lafayette visit to, 209–10, 219, 242
naming of, 55–56
as New England in miniature, 170
Ohio Company directors meeting in, 147
politics in, 144–45
population of, 64–65, 173, 252
revival of, 130–31
and runaway slaves, 247–49
schools in, 64, 131, 206, 212–13, 253
and Scioto Company, 84
selection of site/plans for, 17, 37, 44–45, 187, 205–6
ship/boat building in, 135–36, 137, 170–72
and St. Clair Defeat, 110
steamboats in, 184
veterans as early settlers in, 57–58
War of 1812 and, 186, 188–89
Washington County Agricultural Fair in, 218–20
way of life in, 125
weather in, 77, 203
See also specific person
Marietta College, 220, 239, 255, 258
Marietta Gazette (newspaper), 218
Marietta Intelligencer (newspaper), 239, 256
Marietta Register (newspaper), 258
Marshall, John, 162–63, 164
Martineau, Harriet, 222, 229
Mary Avery (ship), 137

Mason, George, 19, 22
Massachusetts
    Constitution of, 28–29
    financial panic in, 8–9
    Hildreth visit to, 190–91
    and Shays rebellion, 9
    See also specific town
Massachusetts Medical Society, 5, 167
Massachusetts Spy (newspaper), 50–51, 112, 123
Mathews, John, 41, 42, 43, 75–76, 226–27
May, John, 53–55, 56, 74
Mayflower (boat), 40, 41, 42, 47
McCurdy, William, 59
measles, 78, 81
medical schools, 234
Medical Society of Ohio, 258
Memoirs of the Early Pioneer Settlers of Ohio (Hildreth), 253
men, attire of, 73, 175
Messenger (steamboat), 224, 227–28
Mexico: and Burr conspiracy, 153–54, 155, 159
Miami Indians, 63, 87, 102
military
    wages for, 115
    Washington's expansion of, 115
    See also army, frontier; army, St. Clair's; militia, Marietta; militia, Ohio; veterans, Revolutionary War
militia, Marietta, 83, 160
militia, Ohio, 159, 160–61, 170, 257
Mingo Indians, 51, 59
Mississippi River, 7, 17, 136, 149, 153, 156, 162, 170, 183, 184, 196
Mohawk Indians, 102
Monongahela River, 17, 40, 124, 168
Morgan, John, 256–57
Morse, Moses, 71
Moulton, William, 39, 70–71, 95
Mound Cemetery, 205, 208, 245, 258
Muller's The Field Engineer: influence on Putnam of, 36–37
music, 117–18, 229
Muskingum Academy (Marietta), 131, 253
Muskingum River
    bottomlands of, 43–44
    confluence of Ohio River and, 17, 37, 42, 43–44, 45
    descriptions of, 45, 187, 240
    and earthworks, 49–50

Muskingum River (*cont.*)
  and first expedition/settlement in Ohio
    Country, 35, 42, 43–45, 47, 52
  Hutchins recommendation about, 17
  May swimming in, 55
  shipbuilding along, 170–72
  and stockade, 47
  wharf on, 47

The Navigator (guidebook), 183–84
New England settlement system, 7
New Haven, Connecticut: Hildreth visit to,
  233–37, 239
New Orleans (steamboat), 184
New York City
  Continental Congress in, 15–17, 25–30
  Cutler (Manasseh) as "agent" for Ohio
    Company in, 15–17, 25–31
  Cutler (Manasseh) views about, 30–31
  Hildreth views about, 238
Newburgh Petition, 10–11, 13, 205
Niagara Falls: Hildreth visit to, 233
Northwest Ordinance
  and American way of life, 13
  and Congress, U.S., 83
  and Cutler (Manasseh), 30, 122, 201
  and education, 12, 29, 30, 31–32, 212
  importance of, 28, 30
  and Indians, 29
  Massachusetts Constitution compared
    with, 28–29
  and Ohio Company-Board of Treasury
    contract, 28
  passage of, 28–30, 56
  and religion, 12, 28, 29, 30
  and slavery, 11, 13, 29–30, 144–45, 146,
    201
Northwest Territory
  boundaries of, 6–7
  Chillicothe named capital of, 143
  description of, 7–8
  government for, 18, 25–30
  governor's office for, 86
  lack of settlements in, 7–8
  as land of opportunity, 9
  Ohio as first state in, 149
  and Paris Peace Treaty, 6–7, 247
  remoteness of, 7–8
  and slavery, 11, 13, 29–30
  St. Clair as governor of, 57, 114
  states formed in, 7, 12

  See also Northwest Ordinance; Ohio
    Company of Associates; Ohio
    Country; *specific person or settlement*
Nye, Ichabod, 67–68, 69, 70, 71, 74–75, 96,
  126, 218

Ohio Company of Associates
  additional land grants for, 115
  apple trees stipulation by, 82
  Board of Treasury contract with, 28–29,
    83
  and Bunch of Grapes meeting, 6, 8, 9,
    11–12, 205
  Continental Congress deal with, 25–30,
    83
  Cutler (Manasseh) as "agent" for, 3, 6, 12,
    13–24, 25–31, 115–16
  directors of, 14, 53, 55–56, 147
  economic problems of, 115
  as education proponent, 147
  formation of, 11–12, 219
  and French emigrants, 85
  funding for, 12, 68
  Hildreth comments about, 232
  and Indians at Big Bottom, 88
  and Indian treaties, 38
  investors in, 16
  and Mathews surveying party, 75, 76
  and Northwest Ordinance, 83
  purpose of, 11
  Putnam as chairman of, 12
  and Revolutionary War veterans, 6, 219
  Sargent as secretary of, 69
  and Scioto Company, 83–85
  and selection/naming of Marietta
    settlement, 55–56, 187
  and "Starving Year," 80
  stockholders in, 19, 29, 54, 154, 178–79,
    182
  Tyler trip for, 68
  See also first expedition to Ohio
    Country; *specific person*
Ohio Country
  Cutler pamphlet about, 31–32, 84
  descriptions of, 11–12, 31–32, 84
  education in, 31–32
  emigrants as leaving, 110–11
  first expedition to, 35–57
  importance of, 3
  Indians as threat to, 75–77, 87–88
  and Newburgh Petition, 10–11

plans for first town in, 37
preparations for first expedition to,
    31–33
surveys of, 38
travelers descriptions of, 221–30, 232–33
university for, 29, 32
Washington as land owner in, 10, 42, 132
and Washington letter to Congress,
    10–11
See also specific person or topic
Ohio Gazette, and Virginia Herald
    (Marietta newspaper), 157–58, 172
Ohio legislature
    and Burr conspiracy, 159, 160
    in Columbus, 197–200
    housing for, 143
    See also specific person or topic
Ohio River
    bottomlands of, 43–44
    and boundary of Northwest Territory, 7
    confluence of Muskingum River and, 17,
        37, 42, 43–44, 45
    Cutler tragedy on, 124
    descriptions of, 45, 222–23, 224–25,
        240
    and drought, 203
    and escape route for runaway slaves,
        247–49
    "Falls" on, 136
    and first expedition to Ohio Country, 33,
        40, 41, 42, 43–44
    flooding of, 187–88
    freezing of, 68
    importance of, 3, 68, 195
    as Indian name, 230
    scientific interest in, 234
    and selection of site for first settlement,
        44–45
    ships/boats along, 137, 170–72, 183–84,
        196–97
    surveys along, 17, 43–44
    traffic/trade on, 170
    travelers stories about, 222–25
    weather on, 65
    See also Erie Canal; specific ship/boat
Ohio (state)
    Adams (John Quincy) expedition to,
        242–44, 245–47, 249
    constitution for, 143–47, 149, 247,
        255–56
    economy of, 195

establishment of state university for,
    147–48
Indian names in, 230
as part of Northwest Territory, 7
population of, 173, 195, 256
and removal of Indians, 230
and slavery, 144–47, 247, 255–56
St. Clair as first governor of, 149
statehood for, 149
See also Ohio legislature
Ohio University, 29, 32, 147–48, 200–201,
    206, 211, 212, 215–16, 217, 241, 256
Osgood, Samuel, 18, 26–27
Ottawa Indians, 59, 63, 102, 230
Owen, James, 53
Owen, Mary, 53, 81

Paris Peace Treaty (1783), 6–7, 247
Parker, Sally. *See* Cutler, Sally Parker
Parker, William, 178–79, 180
Parsons, Samuel Holden
    and Cutler (Manasseh), 14, 58
    death of, 78, 94–95
    and earthworks, 49
    as emigrant to first settlement, 53
    and enthusiasm for emigration, 52
    importance of, 78
    and Indian attack on Mathews surveying
        party, 75
    and Indian treaty in Northwest Territory,
        14
    and Ohio Company–Board of Treasury
        contract, 28
    as Ohio Company director/shareholder,
        14, 28
    and Putnam appointment as territorial
        judge, 82
    welcoming of migrants by, 58
Peale, Charles Willson, 19–20
Philadelphia
    Constitutional Convention in, 13, 19–24
    and Cutler (Manasseh) as "agent" for
        Ohio Company, 18–24, 115–16
    Denny-Washington meeting in, 111–12,
        113
    St. Clair-Washington meeting in,
        113
    Washington-Knox-St. Clair meeting in,
        98
Philadelphia Hospital, Cutler-Rush tour of,
    23–24

Phillips, Micajah. *See* Cajoe
Physicians Society of Ohio, 231, 232
Pioneer History (Hildreth), 253
Pittsburgh
  and Adams (John Quincy) Ohio
    expedition, 243, 246, 249
  Denny career in, 113
  and first expedition to Ohio Country,
    40–41, 42
  as Gateway to the West, 41
  Hildreth views about, 238
  and steamboats, 184, 196
  Tyler in, 68
Playfair, William, 83, 84
poem, Ohio Valley, 44
Point, 42–43, 58, 64, 92, 95, 169
Pottawatomie Indians, 102
Putnam, Elizabeth Ayres, 36, 207
Putnam, Israel, 123, 144
Putnam, Persis Rice, 36, 37, 82, 207
Putnam, Rufus
  and accomplishments/tributes, 205–9,
    219
  Adams (John Quincy) comments about,
    246
  appearance of, 9–10
  and apple trees, 150
  barge for, 47
  and Barker, 83
  and Battle of Fallen Timbers, 118
  and Big Bottom attack, 88, 90
  and Bunch of Grapes meeting, 9, 11, 12
  Burr and, 154
  and Campus Martius, 206
  Captain Pipe and, 43
  character/personality of, 10, 92, 149,
    206
  as commander of frontier army, 116
  and communications from first settlers,
    50–51
  and Cutler (Ephraim), 123, 125, 126, 143,
    145, 219
  Cutler (Manasseh) relationship with, 45,
    50, 51, 82, 84, 123, 207–8
  and Cutler (Manasseh) visit to Marietta,
    58
  death/funeral of, 205–6, 209
  and descriptions of Marietta, 239
  and earthworks, 48–50
  education of, 35–36, 78, 213
  as education proponent, 147, 206

  emigrant comments of, 52, 110–11
  and family move to Ohio Country,
    82
  and first expedition/settlement in Ohio
    Country, 32, 33, 35, 37, 38, 39, 40, 42,
    43–44, 46–47
  and French emigrants, 85
  and growth of Marietta, 131
  headquarters for, 43
  health of, 116–17, 207
  Hildreth comments about, 206
  home of, 82, 207
  and Indian-settler relations, 43, 46–47,
    51, 64, 87–88, 90, 91–94, 96, 116, 206
  and Lafayette visit to Marietta, 209
  land distribution policies of, 64
  library of, 208–9
  and management of Marietta, 68
  and Marietta as "City upon the Hill,"
    205–6
  and Marietta College, 220
  and Marietta Congregational Church, 173
  and Marietta militia, 83
  marriages of, 36
  military background of, 36–37
  and naming of first settlement, 55–56
  and Newburgh Petition, 10–11, 13, 205
  and Nye in Marietta, 68
  as Ohio Company "agent," 115
  and Ohio Company-Board of Treasury
    contract, 28
  as Ohio Company chairman/share-
    holder, 12, 28
  and Ohio constitution, 144
  as Ohio legislator, 206
  and Ohio University, 206
  personal/professional background of,
    35–37
  and plan for Marietta, 170
  Rutland as home for, 35, 37, 82
  and Sargent-Tupper wedding, 70
  and Scioto Company, 84
  and shipbuilding in Marietta, 170
  and slavery, 144, 145, 206
  and St. Clair Defeat, 110
  and stockade, 46, 47
  as surveyor general of U.S., 149
  as territorial judge, 82
  and Thomas letter, 50–51
  Trumbull portrait of, 236
  Varnum relations with, 64

War of 1812 and, 186
Washington's relationship with, 10–11, 36, 37, 86–88, 93–94, 110–11
welcoming of migrants/visitors by, 58
will of, 208–9
Putnam, William, 245
Putnam, William Rufus Jr., 257

rangers: and Indians as threat, 92, 94
religion
    Cutler's (Manasseh) views about, 30, 60
    and Northwest Ordinance, 12, 28, 29, 30
Removal Bill (1830), 230
Revolutionary War
    Adams in France during, 249
    battles during, 96–97
    debt from, 26
    and Dorchester Heights attack, 36–37
    French support during, 56
    Indian attacks on militia during, 8
    and praise for Marie Antoinette, 56
    See also veterans, Revolutionary War; specific person or battle
Rice, Persis. See Putnam, Persis Rice
Richmond, Virginia: Burr trial in, 162–63
Rogers, Joseph, 78, 94–95
Roosevelt, Nicholas, 184
Round Bottom, 42
Rush, Benjamin, 18, 19, 23–24

Sargent, Rowena Tupper, 69–70
Sargent, Winthrop
    appearance of, 68–69
    and Bunch of Grapes meeting, 12
    character/personality of, 68–69, 70
    Cincinnati move of, 86
    and Continental Congress-Ohio Company deal, 18, 25, 26, 27
    Cutler (Mannaseh) letter to, 13
    Denny praise for, 109
    education of, 69
    as emigrant to first settlement, 53
    family of, 70
    financial affairs of, 69
    marriage of, 69–70
    Nye relationship with, 68, 69, 70
    and Ohio Company-Board of Treasury contract, 28
    as Ohio Company secretary/shareholder, 12, 28, 69
    personal/professional background of, 69

and return of emigrants, 111
scientific/botanical interests of, 69, 86, 100
as secretary of Northwest Territory, 69, 86
and St. Clair's army, 98–99, 100, 101, 102, 103–4, 106–7, 108, 109, 114–15
and Tupper family, 68, 69–70
welcoming of migrants/visitors by, 58
scarlet fever, 110
schools, 64, 169, 183, 206, 212–13, 228, 253. See also education
Schuylkill River, 22, 23, 115
scientific interests, 219, 234. See also specific person
Scioto Company, 28, 83–85, 86
Scioto River, 26, 51
Seneca Indians, 41, 59, 230
settlers/settlements, first
    accomplishments of, 54
    arrival of new, 52–54, 70–75
    building the, 44–48
    characteristics of, 125
    as City upon the Hill, 17
    clearing land for, 45–46, 47–48, 53, 55
    communications from, 50–52, 75
    descriptions of, 45–46, 50–51, 54
    discouragement of, 55
    food/provisions for, 54, 65, 67–68, 70
    and health conditions, 51, 54–55
    and historic preservation, 51
    Indian relations with, 46–47, 55, 58, 63–64, 86–88, 91–94, 95–99
    morale of, 51, 126
    naming of, 55–56
    as "new New England," 44
    population of, 53
    reactions of new, 70–75
    return East of early, 55
    selection of site/plans for, 17, 18, 37, 43–45
    socializing of, 53
    surveying for, 43–44
    systems of, 7
    and veterans, 54
    Washington's views about, 52
    and weather, 44, 55, 65
    and wharf on Muskingum River, 47
    women as, 53, 54, 71–73
    See also Campus Martius; earthworks; Marietta; stockade; specific person or settlement

Shawnee Indians, 17, 48, 51, 59, 63, 76–77, 87, 102, 230
Shays (Daniel) rebellion, 9
ships/boats
    and Burr, 151–52, 155–56, 160
    and Devol, 39, 40, 47
    and economy, 170–72
    and Embargo Act, 171–72
    and first expedition to Ohio Country, 39, 40
    in Marietta, 135–36, 137, 170–72
    along Muskingum River, 170–72
    along Ohio River, 137, 170–72, 183–84, 196–97
    at Wiseman's Bottom, 137
    See also flatboats; keelboats; steamboats; specific ship or boat
Shreve, Henry M., 196
Silliman, Benjamin, 234, 235, 236, 237, 239, 253, 258
slavery
    Adams (John Quincy) views about, 247, 249
    and Blennerhassett Island, 133
    Cutler (Ephraim) views about, 197, 206, 213, 247, 248–49, 255–56
    and Cutler (Manasseh), 30, 146, 201
    Cutler (William) views about, 256
    and escape route along Ohio River, 247–49
    foreign traveler comments about, 223, 225
    and Gag Rule, 247
    and Jefferson, 223
    and Newburgh Resolution, 13
    Northwest Ordinance and, 11, 13, 29–30, 144–45, 146, 201
    and Northwest Territory, 11, 13, 29–30
    and Ohio Company-Board of Treasury contract, 29–30
    and Ohio constitution, 144–47, 247, 255–56
    and Putnam, 206
    and runaway slaves, 247–49
    Stowe book about, 254–55
smallpox, 40, 81, 110, 129
soldiers, 46–47. See also army, frontier; army, St. Clair's; Marietta militia; militia, Ohio; veterans, Revolutionary War

Splendid (steamboat), 233, 235
Sproat, Ebenezer, 38, 40, 43, 52, 83, 95, 125, 154, 172, 219
squatters, 45
St. Clair, Arthur
    Braddock's Field visit by, 98
    Cincinnati move of, 86
    as commander of army, 96–101, 102–15, 118
    and Cutler (Ephraim) commissions, 126
    Cutler views about, 116
    death of, 149
    financial affairs of, 149
    at Fort Harmar, 56–57
    Fort Ticonderoga abandoned by, 96–97, 102, 114
    as governor of Northwest Territory, 57, 86, 96, 114
    as governor of Ohio (state), 149
    and Indians as threat to settlers, 92, 96–99
    personal/professional background of, 96–97
    personality of, 97
    physical disabilities of, 97, 101, 103, 104, 107, 108, 112, 149
    resignation of commission by, 113
    and return of emigrants, 111
    stockade home of, 81
    Washington's relationship with, 98, 112, 113
    See also army, St. Clair's
St. Clair, Phoebe Bayard, 96
St. Clair (ship), 136, 170
St. Clair's Defeat, 106–15
"Starving Year," 79–81
steamboats, 183–84, 196–97, 226, 227–28, 232. See also specific boat
Stiles, Ezra, 6, 14, 49
stockade, 46–47, 70, 81, 83. See also Campus Martius
Story, Daniel, 74, 131
Stowe, Harriet Beecher, 254–55
Strong, Caleb, 92, 186
Sumerill's Ferry, 39–40, 42, 67
Supreme Court, U.S., 163
surveyors: Indian hostility toward, 75–76
Systema Vegetabilium (Linnaeus), 21–22

taxation, 198, 216, 217
Taylor, Peter, 133, 162

teachers, 212–13
Tecumseh (Shawnee Indian), 102, 186, 189
temperance movement, 228–29
Temple, Sir John, 16, 27, 28
Thomas, Eliud, 202–3
Thomas, Isaiah, 50–51
Tiffin, Edward, 144, 159
Treaty of Greenville (1795), 118
trees. *See* forests/trees
Trinity College, 131
Trollope, Frances, 223, 224, 226, 230
Troop, Zebulon, 89–90
True, Jabez, 52, 125, 167, 168–69, 204
True, John, 167
Trumbull, John, 235–36
Tupper, Benjamin
    and Bunch of Grapes meeting, 11
    drinking by, 70
    and enthusiasm for emigration, 52
    and Indian attack on Mathews surveying party, 75
    and Indians as threat, 8
    and management of Marietta, 68
    Marietta home for, 68
    and Marietta militia, 83
    as migrant to Marietta, 57, 58
    regrets about emigration of, 67
    Sargent relationship with, 69–70
    and Shays rebellion, 9
Tupper, Minerva (wife), 57, 67
Tupper, Rowena. *See* Sargent, Rowena Tupper
Turk (Wyandot Indian), 64
Tyler, Dean, 68, 74, 126
typhoid fever, 204

"Uncle Sam" (musician), 117–18
university, plans for, 29, 32. *See also* Ohio University
Upper Sandusky, 8, 230

Varnum, James, 52, 53, 58, 64, 78, 84
Vesuvius (steamboat), 184
veterans, Revolutionary War
    and Bunch of Grapes meeting, 6
    and Burr, 154
    and Cutler (Ephraim) hospitality, 183
    as early Marietta settlers, 54, 57–58
    elections of 1800 and, 144
    and financial panic, 8

and Lafayette visit to Marietta, 209
Newburgh Petition and, 10–11
and Northwest Territory as land of opportunity, 9
and Ohio Company, 6, 219
and Trumbull paintings, 236
and Washington's death, 135
vocabulary/local expressions, 225–26

Wabash Indians, 116
Wabash River: St. Clair–Indian battle near, 103–4
wages, 33, 47, 115
Walker, Amasa, 239–40
War of 1812, 185–87, 188–90, 195
Warren (town), 182, 189–90, 257
Washington County
    Cutler (Ephraim) as territorial delegate from, 138–39
    and escape routes for fugitive slaves, 248
    founding of, 56
    Hildreth as representative of, 177
    medical doctors in, 253
Washington County Agricultural Fair, 218–20
Washington, D.C.
    Cutler (Manasseh) as congressman in, 139–43
    War of 1812 and, 189
Washington, George
    and conditions in Marietta, 110–11
    and Continental Congress-Ohio Company deal, 27
    death of, 135
    and French and Indian War, 98
    and French emigrants, 85
    and Indians as threat, 87, 91, 93–94, 96, 97, 98
    Jefferson's relationship with, 141
    letter to Congress from, 10–11
    and military expansion, 115
    and Newburgh Petition, 10
    as Ohio Country land owner, 10, 42, 132
    and "Ohio Fever," 52
    portrait of, 16
    Putnam and, 10–11, 36, 37, 82, 86–88, 93–94, 110–11, 149
    and Revolutionary War battles, 36–37, 96–97
    and St. Clair Defeat, 109–10, 111–12, 113, 114

Washington, George (*cont.*)
  streets named after, 44
  sworn in as president, 75
  and Wayne as commander of frontier
    army, 116
Washington, Martha, 141
Washington (steamboat), 196
Waterford (town), 125–26, 127
Wayne, Anthony "Mad Anthony," 116, 117,
  118, 123
weather
  and Cutler (Manasseh) visit, 59
  and first expedition/settlement in Ohio
    Country, 38, 39, 40, 41, 42, 44, 55, 65
  and food/provisions, 77
  and Indians as threat, 94
  in Marietta, 59, 77, 203
  and St. Clair's army, 100–101, 103
  and travelers' descriptions of Ohio
    Country, 222
Western Spectator (Federalist newspaper),
  186, 189
Wheeling (Virginia territory), 41–42, 196
Whigs, 241, 251
Whipple, Abraham, 136, 170
whiskey/alcohol, 39, 41, 58, 64, 99, 101,
  168, 226–29
White, Haffield, 33, 39
Wilkinson, James, 158–59
Williams, H. Z., 207–8
Wiseman's Bottom, 129–30, 137–38, 244
Wolf Creek, 93, 162
wolves-fiddling story, 65
women
  as army camp followers, 99, 105, 106,
    108
  attire of, 73, 175

  and Cutler (Manasseh) visit to Marietta,
    59
  as emigrants, 71–73
  first-person accounts of, 72
  and first settlement in Ohio Country,
    54
  Indian, 59
  and Indian attacks, 90, 105, 106, 108
  respect for, 229
  role of, 71–72
  and "Starving Year," 80–81
  Trollope comments about, 224
  See also specific person
Woodbridge, Dudley Jr., 137, 155–56, 161,
  163, 166
Woodbridge, Dudley Sr., 64, 72, 137
Woodbridge, Lucy Backus, 72–73, 132,
  137, 166
Wyandot Indians, 43, 51, 59, 63, 88, 89,
  102, 230

Yale College/University
  congressmen as graduates of,
    140
  and Cutler (Ephraim), 122
  Cutler (Manasseh) and, 4, 14, 201
  Hildreth visit to, 234–37, 239
  and Marietta College, 220
  Medical Institution at, 234, 236
  Putnam (David) at, 212
  and Silliman, 234, 235, 236, 237,
    239
  and Trumbull, 235–36
yellow fever, 165
Youghiogheny River, 39–40

Zanesville, as Ohio state capital, 185

IMAGE CREDITS

Insert 1

1, 3, 5, 7–10, 15, 17, 19–21: Courtesy of Marietta College Library Special Collections
2: The Miriam and Ira D. Wallach Division of Art, Prints and Photographs: Print
Collection, the New York Public Library 4: Courtesy of Ohio University Archives
6: "Landing of the Pioneers," courtesy of the Benjamin H. Putnam Family Planning
Trust 11: Courtesy of the Rare Books & Manuscripts Library of the Ohio State
University Libraries 12: Courtesy of the Ohio History Connection 14: University
of Michigan Digital Collections 16: Originally published in black and white in *The
Century* Magazine (volume 92, May to October, 1916). Wood engraving by Alfred
Waud/Granger, New York 18: National Portrait Gallery, Smithsonian Institute / John
Trumbull, Dec. 3, 1790, pencil on paper

Insert 2

1–4, 6, 8–10, 11, 13–15, 18–20, 22–25: Courtesy of Marietta College Library Special
Collections 5: Courtesy of the Missouri Historical Society, St. Louis, Accession
#1948-059-0001 7: *Harper's New Monthly Magazine,* 1877, courtesy of Blennerhassett
Island Historical State Park 12: "The Ohio at Marietta," courtesy of the Ohio History
Connection 16: Ohio History Connection / Campus Martius Museum, Marietta, Ohio
/ Photograph by Bruce Wunderlich 17: Courtesy of the Huntington Museum of Art,
Huntington, West Virginia / Oil, Sala Bosworth (American, 1805–1890) ca. 1826–1827,
Bequest of Janet Seaton Humphrey, 1.1.1999 21: "Home of Ephraim Cutler," courtesy of
The Dawes Arboretum, Newark, Ohio

Endpaper

"Marietta from Harmar Hill," courtesy of the Ohio History Connection / Oil, Charles
Sullivan / Painting Hanging in Campus Martius Museum, Marietta, Ohio

Maps

Maps by David Atkinson, handmademaps.com
"Southeastern Ohio Around Marietta" and "Town of Marietta" maps: Research and
layout by Matthew Young

Also by
DAVID McCULLOUGH

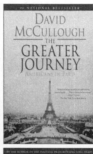
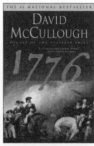
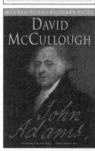
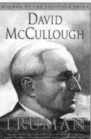

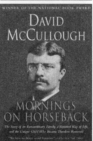
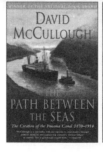
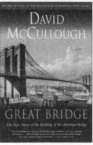
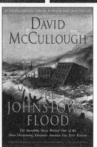

Pick up or download your copies today!

66557